Lecture Notes in Computer Scie

Commenced Publication in 1973
Founding and Former Series Editors:
Gerhard Goos, Juris Hartmanis, and Jan van Leeuwe

T0237984

Editorial Board

Marco Bernardo   Alessandro Bogliolo (Eds.)

Formal Methods
for Mobile Computing

5th International School on Formal Methods for the Design
of Computer, Communication, and Software Systems
SFM-Moby 2005
Bertinoro, Italy, April 26-30, 2005
Advanced Lectures

Volume Editors

Marco Bernardo
Alessandro Bogliolo
Università degli Studi di Urbino "Carlo Bo"
Istituto di Scienze e Tecnologie dell'Informazione
Piazza della Repubblica 13, 61029 Urbino, Italy
E-mail: {bernardo, bogliolo}@sti.uniurb.it

Library of Congress Control Number: 2005924063

CR Subject Classification (1998): D.2, D.3, F.3, C.3, C.2.4

ISSN   0302-9743
ISBN-10   3-540-25697-0 Springer Berlin Heidelberg New York
ISBN-13   978-3-540-25697-7 Springer Berlin Heidelberg New York

Springer is a part of Springer Science+Business Media

springeronline.com

© Springer-Verlag Berlin Heidelberg 2005
Printed in Germany

Typesetting: Camera-ready by author, data conversion by Scientific Publishing Services, Chennai, India
Printed on acid-free paper   SPIN: 11419822   06/3142   5 4 3 2 1 0

Preface

This volume collects a set of papers accompanying the lectures of the fifth edition of the International School on Formal Methods for the Design of Computer, Communication and Software Systems (SFM).

This series of schools addresses the use of formal methods in computer science as a prominent approach to the rigorous design of computer, communication and software systems. The main aim of the SFM series is to offer a good spectrum of current research in foundations as well as applications of formal methods, which can be of help for graduate students and young researchers who intend to approach the field.

SFM 2005 (Moby) was devoted to formal methods and tools for the design of mobile systems and mobile communication infrastructures. This volume is organized into four parts related to mobile computing, which cover models and languages, scalability and performance, dynamic power management, and middleware support. Each part is composed of two papers.

The opening paper by Montanari and Pistore gives an overview of history-dependent automata, an extension of ordinary automata that overcomes their limitations in dealing with named calculi. In particular, the authors show that history-dependent automata allow for a compact representation of π-calculus processes, which is suitable both for theoretical investigations and for the verification of models of agents and code mobility. Bettini and De Nicola's paper presents X-KLAIM, an experimental programming language specifically designed to develop distributed systems composed of several components interacting through multiple distributed tuple spaces and mobile code. Through a series of examples, the authors show that many mobile code programming paradigms can be naturally implemented by means of the considered language, which combines explicit localities as first-class data with coordination primitives.

Gerla, Chen, Lee, Zhou, Chen, Yang and Das provide an introduction to MANET, a mobile ad hoc wireless network established for a special, often extemporaneous service customized to applications. After emphasizing the self-configurability, mobility and scalability attributes of MANET, the authors concentrate on mobility and show its impact on protocols and operations. Grassi presents an overview of the performance issues raised by the high variability and heterogeneity of mobile systems, together with some approaches to the careful planning of the performance validation of such systems. The author then focuses on the definition of model-based transformations from design-oriented models to analysis-oriented models that comprise non-functional attributes.

Acquaviva, Aldini, Bernardo, Bogliolo, Bontà and Lattanzi illustrate in their paper a methodology for predicting the impact on the overall system functionality and efficiency of the introduction of a dynamic power management policy within a battery-powered mobile device. The predictive methodology relies on a combination of formal description techniques, noninterference analysis, and performance evaluation to properly tune the dynamic power manager operation rates. The methodology is then used by Acquaviva, Bontà and Lattanzi in the framework of the IEEE 802.11 standard, in order to provide a power-accurate model of a wireless network interface card that allows the energy/performance trade-off to be studied as a function of traffic patterns imposed by the applications.

Lattanzi, Acquaviva and Bogliolo address the limited storage memory of wireless mobile terminals through the concept of network virtual memory. The authors first compare the performance and energy of network swapping with those of local swapping on microdrives and flash memories, then present an infrastructure providing efficient remote memory access to mobile terminals. The closing paper, by Corradini and Merelli, reports on Hermes, a middleware system for the design and the execution of activity-based applications in distributed environments. While middleware for mobile computing has typically been developed to support physical and logical mobility, Hermes provides an integrated environment where application-domain experts can focus on designing the activity workflow.

We believe that this book offers a quite comprehensive view of what has been done and what is going on worldwide at present in the field of formal methods for mobile computing. We wish to thank all the lecturers and all the participants for a lively and fruitful school. We also wish to thank the whole staff of the University Residential Center of Bertinoro (Italy) for the organizational and administrative support, as well as the Regione Marche, which sponsored the school within the CIPE 36/2002 framework.

April 2005   Marco Bernardo and Alessandro Bogliolo
                                                      SFM 2005 (Moby) Directors

Table of Contents

History-Dependent Automata:
An Introduction

Ugo Montanari[1] and Marco Pistore[2]

[1] University of Trento, Italy
marco.pistore@unitn.it
[2] University of Pisa, Italy
ugo@di.unipi.it

Abstract. In this paper we give an overview of History Dependent Automata, an extension of ordinary automata that overcomes their limitations in dealing with named calculi. In a named calculus, the observations labelling the transitions of a system may contain names which represent features such as communication channels, node identifiers, or the locations of the system. An example of named calculus is π-calculus, which has the ability of sending channel names as messages and thus of dynamically reconfiguring process acquaintances and of modeling agents and code mobility. We show that History-Dependent Automata allow for a compact representation of π-calculus processes which is suitable both for theoretical investigations and for practical purposes such as verification.

1 Introduction

In the context of process calculi (e.g., Milner's CCS [Mil89]), *automata* (or *labelled transition systems*) are often used as operational models. They allow for a simple representation of process behavior, and many concepts and theoretical results for these process calculi are independent from the particular syntax of the languages and can be formulated directly on automata. In particular, this is true for the *behavioral equivalences* and preorders which have been defined for these languages, like bisimulation equivalence [Mil89, Par80]: in fact they take into account only the labelled actions a process can perform. Automata are also important from an algorithmic point of view: efficient and practical techniques and tools for verification [IP96, Mad92] have been developed for *finite-state* automata. Finite state verification is successful here, differently than in ordinary programming, since the control part and the data part of protocols and hardware components can be often cleanly separated, and the control part is usually both quite complex and finite state. Particularly interesting is also the possibility to associate to each automaton — and, consequently, to each process — a *minimal realization*, i.e., a minimal automaton which is equivalent to the original one. This is important both from a theoretical point of view — equivalent systems give rise to the same (up to isomorphism) minimal realization — and from a practical point of view — smaller state spaces can be obtained.

This ideal situation, however, does not apply to all process calculi. In the case of *named calculi*, in particular, infinite-state transition systems are generated instead, also

M. Bernardo and A. Bogliolo (Eds.): SFM-Moby 2005, LNCS 3465, pp. 1–28, 2005.

by very simple processes. In a *named calculus*, the observations labelling the transitions of a system may contain names which are used to identify different features of the modeled system, such as the communication channels, the agents participating to the system, or the locations describing the spatial structure of the system. A quite interesting example of named calculus is π-calculus [MPW92, Mil93]. It has the ability of sending channel names as messages and thus of dynamically reconfiguring process acquaintances. More importantly, π-calculus names can model objects (in the sense of object oriented programming [Wal95]) and name sending thus models higher order communication and mobile code [San93b].

The operational semantics of π-calculus is given via a labelled transition system. However labelled transition systems are not fully adequate to deal with the peculiar features of the calculus and complications occur in the creation of new channels. Consider process $p = (\nu y)\,\bar{x}y.y(z).0$. Channel y is initially a local channel for the process (prefix $(\nu y)\,$ _ is the operator for scope restriction) and no global communication can occur on it. Action $\bar{x}y$, however, which corresponds to the output of name y on the global channel x, makes name y known also outside the process; after the output has taken place, channel y can be used for further communications, and, in fact, y is used in $y(z).0$ as the channel for an input transition: so the communication of a restricted name creates a new public channel for the process. The creation of this new channel is represented in the ordinary semantics of the π-calculus by means of an infinite bunch of transitions of the form $p \xrightarrow{\bar{x}(w)} w(z).0$, where w is any name that is not already in use (i.e., $w \neq x$ in our example, since x is the only name in use by p; notice that $w = y$ is just a particular case). This way to represent the creation of new names has some disadvantages: first of all, also very simple π-calculus processes, like p, give rise to infinite-state and infinite-branching transition systems. Moreover, equivalent processes do not necessarily have the same sets of channel names; so, there are processes q equivalent to p which cannot use y as the name for the newly created channel. Special rules are needed in the definition of bisimulation to take care of this problem and, as a consequence, standard theories and algorithms do not apply to π-calculus.

The ideal situation of ordinary automata can (at least in part) be recovered also in the field of named calculi, by introducing a new operational model which is adequate to deal with these languages, and by extending to this new model (part of) the classical theory for ordinary automata. As model we propose the *history-dependent automata (HD-automata* in brief). As ordinary automata, they are composed of states and of transitions between states. To deal with the peculiar problems of named calculi, however, states and transitions are enriched with sets of local names: in particular, each transition can refer to the names associated to its source state but can also generate new names, which can then appear in the destination state. In this manner, the names are not global and static, as in ordinary labelled transition systems, but they are explicitly represented within states and transitions and can be dynamically created.

This explicit representation of names permits an adequate representation of the behavior of named processes. In particular, π-calculus processes can be translated into HD-automata and a first sign of the adequacy of HD-automata for dealing with π-calculus is that a large class of *finitary* π-calculus processes can be represented by finite-state HD-automata. We also give a general definition of bisimulation for HD-automata.

An important result is that this general bisimulation equates the HD-automata obtained from two π-calculus processes if and only if the processes are bisimilar according to the ordinary π-calculus bisimilarity relation. The most interesting result on HD-automata is that they can be minimized. It is possible to associate to each HD-automaton a minimal realization, namely a minimal HD-automaton that is bisimilar to the initial one. As in the case of ordinary automata, this possibility is important from a theoretical but also from a practical point of view.

In this paper we give an introduction to HD-automata. Some of the basic results on ordinary automata and an overview of the π-calculus are briefly presented in Section 2. Section 3 introduces HD-automata, defines bisimulation on HD-automata, and presents the translation of π-calculus processes to HD-automata. Section 4 describes how HD-automata can be minimized by taking into account symmetries on the names enriching states and transitions. Finally, in Section 5 we propose some concluding remarks. Further results on HD-automata (as well as the proofs of the results that we present in this paper) can be found in [MP98b, MP98a, MP99, MP00].

2 Background

2.1 Ordinary Automata

Automata have been defined in a large variety of manners. We choose the following definition since it is very natural and since, as we will see, it can be easily modified to define HD-automata.

Definition 1 (ordinary automata). *An* automaton $\mathcal{A}$ *is defined by:*

- *a set L of* labels;
- *a set Q of* states;
- *a set T of* transitions;
- *two functions $s, d : T \to Q$ that associate a* source *and a* destination *state to each transition;*
- *a function $o : T \to L$ which associates a label to each transition;*
- *an* initial state $q_0 \in Q$.

Given a transition $t \in T$, we write $t : q \xrightarrow{l} q'$ if $s(t) = q$, $d(t) = q'$ and $o(t) = l$.

Notation 2. *To represent the components of an automaton we will use the name of the automaton as subscript; so, for instance, $Q_{\mathcal{B}}$ are the states of automaton $\mathcal{B}$ and $d_{\mathcal{B}}$ is its destination function. In the case of automaton $\mathcal{A}_x$, we will simply write Q_x and d_x rather than $Q_{\mathcal{A}_x}$ and $d_{\mathcal{A}_x}$. Moreover, the subscripts are omitted whenever there is no ambiguity on the referred automaton.*
Similar notations are also used for the other structures we define in the paper.

Often *labelled transition systems* are used as operational models in concurrency. The difference with respect to automata is that in a labelled transition system no initial state is specified. An automaton describes the behavior of a single system, and hence the initial state of the automaton corresponds to the starting point of the system; a labelled transition system is used to represent the operational semantics of a whole concurrent formalism, and hence an initial state cannot be defined.

Various notions of behavioral preorders and equivalences have been defined on automata. The most important equivalence is *bisimulation equivalence* [Par80, Mil89].

Definition 3 (bisimulation on automata). *Let A_1 and A_2 be two automata on the same set L of labels. A relation $R \subseteq Q_1 \times Q_2$ is a* simulation *for A_1 and A_2 if $q_1 \, R \, q_2$ implies:*

for all transitions $t_1 : q_1 \xrightarrow{l} q_1'$ of A_1 there is some transition $t_2 : q_2 \xrightarrow{l} q_2'$ of A_2 such that $q_1' \, R \, q_2'$.

A relation $R \subseteq Q_1 \times Q_2$ is a bisimulation *for A_1 and A_2 if both R and R^{-1} are simulations.*
Two automata A_1 and A_2 on the same set of labels are bisimilar, *written $A_1 \sim A_2$, if there is some bisimulation R for A_1 and A_2 such that $q_{01} \, R \, q_{02}$.*

An important result in the theory of automata in concurrency is the existence of *minimal representatives* in the classes of bisimilar automata. Given an automaton, a reduced automaton is obtained by collapsing each class of equivalent states into a single state (and similarly for the transitions). This reduced automaton is bisimilar to the starting one, and any further collapse of states would lead to a non-bisimilar automaton. The reduced automaton is hence "minimal". Moreover, the same minimal automaton (up to isomorphisms) is obtained from bisimilar automata: thus it can be used as a canonical representative of the whole class of bisimilar automata.

In the definition below we denote with $[q]_{R_A}$ the class of equivalence of state q with respect to the largest bisimulation equivalence R_A on automaton A. With a light abuse of notation, we denote with $[t]_{R_A}$ the class of equivalent of transition t, where

$$t_1 \, R_A \, t_2 \quad \text{iff} \quad s(t_1) \, R_A \, s(t_2), \quad d(t_1) \, R_A \, d(t_2) \quad \text{and} \quad o(t_1) = o(t_2).$$

Definition 4 (minimal automata). *The* minimal automaton $A_{\min}$ *corresponding to automaton A is defined as follows:*

- $L_{\min} = L$;
- $Q_{\min} = \{[q]_{R_A} \mid q \in Q\}$ and $T_{\min} = \{[t]_{R_A} \mid t \in T\}$;
- $s_{\min}([t]_{R_A}) = [s(t)]_{R_A}$ and $d_{\min}([t]_{R_A}) = [d(t)]_{R_A}$;
- $o_{\min}([t]_{R_A}) = o(t)$;
- $q_{0\min} = [q_0]_{R_A}$.

2.2   The π-Calculus

In this section we describe the π-calculus [MPW92, Mil93], a process calculus in which channel names can be used as values in the communications, i.e., channels are first-order values. This possibility of communicating names gives to the π-calculus a rich expressive power: in fact it allows to generate dynamically new channels and to change the interconnection structure of the processes. The π-calculus has been successfully used to model object oriented languages [Wal95], and also higher-order communications can be easily encoded in the π-calculus [San93a], thus allowing for code migration.

Many versions of π-calculus have appeared in the literature. For simplicity, we consider only the *monadic* π-calculus, and we concentrate on the *ground* variant of its semantics.

Let $\mathcal{N}$ be an infinite, denumerable set of *names*, ranged over by $a, b, \ldots y, z \ldots$, and let *Var* be a finite set of *process identifiers*, denoted by $A, B, \ldots$; the π-calculus (monadic) *processes*, ranged over by $p, q, \ldots$, are defined by the syntax:

$$p ::= \mathbf{0} \mid \pi.p \mid p|p \mid p+p \mid (\nu x)\, p \mid A(x_1, \ldots, x_n)$$

where the *prefixes* π are defined by the syntax:

$$\pi ::= \tau \mid \bar{x}y \mid x(y).$$

The occurrences of y in $x(y).p$ and $(\nu y)\, p$ are bound; *free* and *bound names* of process p are defined as usual and we denote them with $\mathrm{fn}(p)$ and $\mathrm{bn}(p)$ respectively. For each identifier A there is a definition $A(y_1, \ldots, y_n) \stackrel{\mathrm{def}}{=} p_A$ (with y_i all distinct and $\mathrm{fn}(p_A) \subseteq \{y_1, \ldots, y_n\}$); we assume that, whenever A is used, its arity n is respected. Finally we require that each process identifier in p_A is in the scope of a prefix (guarded recursion).

Some comments on the syntax of π-calculus are now in order. As usual, $\mathbf{0}$ is the terminated process. In process $\pi.p$ the prefix π defines an action to execute before p is activated. The prefix $\tau.p$ describes an internal (invisible) action of the process. The *output* prefix $\bar{x}y.p$ specifies the channel x for the communication and the value y that is sent on x. In the *input* prefixes $x(y).p$, name x represents the channel, whereas y is a formal variable: its occurrences in p are instantiated with the received value. Process $p|q$ is the parallel composition with synchronization of p and q, whereas $p+q$ is the nondeterministic choice. Process $(\nu x)\, p$ restricts the possible interactions of process p, disabling communications on channel x.

We use σ, ρ to range over name substitutions, and we denote with $\{y_1/x_1 \cdots y_n/x_n\}$ the substitution that maps x_i into y_i for $i = 1, \ldots, n$ and that is the identity on the other names.

We now introduce a *structural congruence* of π-calculus processes. This structural congruence allows us to identify all the processes which represent essentially the same system and which differ just for syntactical details. The structural congruence $\equiv$ is the smallest congruence which respects the following equivalences

(alpha)	$(\nu x)\, p \equiv (\nu y)\, (p\{y/x\})$ if y does not appear in p
(sum)	$p+\mathbf{0} \equiv p \qquad p+q \equiv q+p \qquad p+(q+r) \equiv (p+q)+r$
(par)	$p|\mathbf{0} \equiv p \qquad p|q \equiv q|p \qquad p|(q|r) \equiv (p|q)|r$
(res)	$(\nu x)\, \mathbf{0} \equiv \mathbf{0} \qquad (\nu x)\,(\nu y)\, p \equiv (\nu y)\,(\nu x)\, p$
	$(\nu x)\,(p|q) \equiv p|(\nu x)\, q$ if x does not appear in p

The structural congruence is useful in practice to obtain finite state representations for classes of processes. It can be used to garbage-collect terminated component — by exploiting rule $p|0 \equiv p$ — and unused restrictions — by using the rules above, if α does not appear in p then $(\nu\alpha)\,p \equiv p$: in fact, $(\nu x)\,p \equiv (\nu x)\,(p|0) \equiv p|(\nu x)\,0 \equiv p|0 \equiv p$.

By exploiting the structural congruence $\equiv$, each π-calculus process can be seen as a set of *sequential processes* that act in parallel, sharing a set of channels, some of which are global (unrestricted) while some other are local (restricted). Each sequential process is represented by a term of the form

$$s \; ::= \; \pi.p \; \Big| \; p+p \; \Big| \; A(x_1, \ldots, x_n)$$

that can be considered as a "program" describing all the possible behaviors of the sequential process.

The *ground* semantics of the π-calculus is the simplest operational semantics that can be defined for this language. It differs from other semantics, such as the *early* and *late* semantics, in the management of input transitions [MPW93]. According to the early semantics, process $x(y).p$ can perform a whole bunch of input transitions

$$x(y).p \xrightarrow{\;xz\;} p\{z/y\}$$

corresponding to the different names z that the environment can send to the process to instantiate the formal input parameter y. In the ground semantics, instantiation of the input parameters are not taken into account, and process $x(y).p$ can perform only one input transition:

$$x(y).p \xrightarrow{\;x(y)\;} p.$$

Ground bisimilarity is easy to check[1]. However, it is less discriminating than early bisimilarity, and does not capture the possibility for the environment of communicating an already existing name during an input transition of a process. For instance,

$$x(y).(\bar{y}y.\mathbf{0}|z(w).\mathbf{0}) \text{ and } x(y).(\bar{y}y.z(w).\mathbf{0} + z(w).\bar{y}y.\mathbf{0})$$

are not equivalent according to the early semantics, since, performing input xz we obtain

$$\bar{z}z.\mathbf{0}|z(w).\mathbf{0} \text{ and } \bar{y}y.z(w).\mathbf{0} + z(w).\bar{y}y.\mathbf{0}$$

and a synchronization (i.e., a τ transition) is possible in the first process but not in the second. However,

$$x(y).(\bar{y}y.\mathbf{0}|z(w).\mathbf{0}) \text{ and } x(y).(\bar{y}y.z(w).\mathbf{0} + z(w).\bar{y}y.\mathbf{0})$$

are equivalent according to the ground semantics since the reception of the already existing name z is not allowed. For simplicity, in this paper we consider only the ground semantics. The presented results, however, can easily be extended to the other π-calculus semantics.

The *ground actions* that a process can perform are defined by the following syntax:

$$\mu \; ::= \; \tau \; \Big| \; x(y) \; \Big| \; \bar{x}y \; \Big| \; \bar{x}(y)$$

---

[1] . . . and, as we will see, easy to model with HD-automata.

Table 1. Free and bound names of π-calculus actions

μ	fn(μ)	bn(μ)	n(μ)
τ	$\emptyset$	$\emptyset$	$\emptyset$
$x(y)$	$\{x\}$	$\{y\}$	$\{x,y\}$
$\overline{x}y$	$\{x,y\}$	$\emptyset$	$\{x,y\}$
$\overline{x}(y)$	$\{x\}$	$\{y\}$	$\{x,y\}$

Table 2. Ground operational semantics of π-calculus

$$[\text{PREF}]\ \pi.p \xrightarrow{\pi} p \qquad\qquad [\text{SUM}]\ \frac{p_1 \xrightarrow{\mu} p'}{p_1+p_2 \xrightarrow{\mu} p'}$$

$$[\text{COMM}]\ \frac{p_1 \xrightarrow{\overline{x}y} p_1' \quad p_2 \xrightarrow{x(z)} p_2'}{p_1|p_2 \xrightarrow{\tau} p_1'|(p_2'\{y/z\})} \qquad [\text{PAR}]\ \frac{p_1 \xrightarrow{\mu} p_1'}{p_1|p_2 \xrightarrow{\mu} p_1'|p_2} \ \text{if bn}(\mu) \cap \text{fn}(p_2) = \emptyset$$

$$[\text{OPEN}]\ \frac{p \xrightarrow{\overline{x}y} p'}{(\nu y)\,p \xrightarrow{\overline{x}(y)} p'} \ \text{if } x \neq y \qquad [\text{CLOSE}]\ \frac{p_1 \xrightarrow{\overline{x}(y)} p_1' \quad p_2 \xrightarrow{x(y)} p_2'}{p_1|p_2 \xrightarrow{\tau} (\nu y)\,(p_1'|p_2')}$$

$$[\text{RES}]\ \frac{p \xrightarrow{\mu} p'}{(\nu x)\,p \xrightarrow{\mu} (\nu x)\,p'} \ \text{if } x \notin \text{n}(\mu)$$

$$[\text{IDE}]\ \frac{p_A\{y_1/x_1 \cdots y_n/x_n\} \xrightarrow{\mu} p'}{A(y_1,\ldots,y_n) \xrightarrow{\mu} p'} \ \text{if } A(x_1,\ldots,x_n) \stackrel{\text{def}}{=} p_A$$

and are called respectively *synchronization, input, free output* and *bound output* actions.

The *free names, bound names* and *names* of an action μ, respectively written fn(μ), bn(μ) and n(μ), are defined as in Table 1.

The transitions for the *ground operational semantics* are defined by the axiom schemata and the inference rules of Table 2. We remind that rule

$$\frac{p \equiv p' \quad p' \xrightarrow{\mu} p'' \quad p'' \equiv p''}{p \xrightarrow{\mu} p''}$$

is implicitly assumed.

Notice that the actions a π-calculus process can perform are different from the prefixes. This happens due to the bound output actions. These actions are specific of the π-calculus; they represent the communication of a name that was previously restricted, i.e., it corresponds to the generation of a new channel between the process and the environment: this phenomenon is called *name extrusion*.

Now we present the definition of the ground bisimulation for the π-calculus.

Definition 5 (ground bisimulation). *A relation* $\mathcal{R}$ *over processes is an ground simulation if whenever p* $\mathcal{R}$ *q then:*

for each p $\xrightarrow{\mu}$ *p' with* bn(μ) $\cap$ fn($p|q$) $= \emptyset$ *there is some q* $\xrightarrow{\mu}$ *q' such that p'* $\mathcal{R}$ *q'.*

A relation $\mathcal{R}$ *is an ground bisimulation if both* $\mathcal{R}$ *and* $\mathcal{R}^{-1}$ *are ground simulations.*

Two processes p and q are ground bisimilar, *written* $p \sim_g q$, *if* $p \, \mathcal{R} \, q$ *for some ground bisimulation* $\mathcal{R}$.

In the definition above, clause "$\mathrm{bn}(\mu) \cap \mathrm{fn}(p|q) = \emptyset$" is necessary to guarantee that the name, that is chosen to represent the newly created channel in a bound output transition, is fresh for both the processes. This clause is necessary since equivalent processes may have different sets of free names.

As for other process calculi, a labelled transition system is used to give an operational semantics to the π-calculus. However, this way to present the operational semantics has some disadvantages. Consider process $q = (\nu y) \, \bar{x}y.y(z).\mathbf{0}$. It is able to generate a new channel by communicating name y in a bound output. The creation of a new name is represented in the transition system by means of an infinite bunch of transitions $q \xrightarrow{\bar{x}(w)} w(z).\mathbf{0}$, where, in this case, w is any name different from x: the creation of a new channel is modeled by using all the names which are not already in use to represent it. As a consequence, the definition of bisimulation is not the ordinary one: in general two bisimilar process can have different sets free names, and the clause "$\mathrm{bn}(\mu) \cap \mathrm{fn}(p|q) = \emptyset$" has to be added in Definition 5 to deal with those bound output transitions which use a name that is used only in one of the two processes. The presence of this clause makes it difficult to reuse standard theory and algorithms for bisimulation on the π-calculus — see for instance [Dam97].

3 History-Dependent Automata

Ordinary automata are successful basic process calculi like CCS. For more sophisticated calculi, however, they are not: in fact, they are not able to capture the particular structures of these languages, that is represented in ordinary automata only in an implicit way. As a consequence, infinite-state automata are often obtained also for very simple programs. To model these languages, it is convenient to enrich states and labels with (part of) the information of the programs, so that the particular structures manipulated by the languages are represented explicitly. These enriched automata are hence more adherent to the languages than ordinary automata.

Different classes of enriched automata can be defined by changing the kind of additional information. Here we focus on a simple form of enriched automata. They are able to manipulate generic "resources": a resource can be allocated, used, and finally released. At this very abstract level, resources can be represented by names: the allocation of a resource is modeled by the generation of a fresh name, that is then used to refer to the resource; since we do not assume any specific operation on resources, the usage of a resource in a transition is modeled by observing the corresponding name in the label; finally, a resource is (implicitly) deallocated when the corresponding name is no more referenced.

We call this class of enriched automata *History-Dependent Automata,* or *HD-automata* in brief. In fact, the usage of names described above can be considered a way to express dependencies between the transitions of the automaton; a transition that uses a name depends on the past transition that generated that name.

In this section we introduce HD-automata and HD-bisimulation and we show that they are able to capture in a convenient way the ground semantics of π-calculus, where the names are use to represent the communication channels.

3.1   HD-Automata

HD-automata extend ordinary automata by allowing sets of names to appear explicitly in states and labels. We assume that the names that are associated to a state or a label are *local* names and do not have a global identity. This is very convenient, since a single state of the HD-automaton can be used to represent all the states of a system that differ just for a renaming (that is, HD-automata work up to bijective substitutions of names). In this way, however, each transition is required to represent explicitly the correspondences between the names of source, target and label. As the reader can see in Figure 1, to represent these correspondences we associate a set of names also to each transition, and we embed the names of the source and target states, and of the label into the names of the transition.

Technically, we represent states, transitions and labels of a HD-automaton by means of *named sets* and use *named functions* to associate a source state, a target state and a label to each transition.

In a named set E, each element e is enriched with a set of names that we denote with E[e]. A function from named set E to named set F maps each element e of the first in an element f of the second; moreover, it also fixes a correspondence between the names of e and the names of f. More precisely, this correspondence provides an embedding of the names of the target element f into the names of the source element e; that is, the names of f are seen, through the name correspondence, as a subset of the names of e.

Now we introduce some notation on functions that we will use extensively in the following. Then we define formally named sets and, based on them, the HD-automata.

Notation 6. *A relation $\mathcal{R}$ on sets A and B is a subset of $A \times B$. If $(a, b) \in \mathcal{R}$ then we also write $a \; \mathcal{R} \; b$. In this case, $\mathrm{dom}(\mathcal{R}) = \{a \mid (a, b) \in \mathcal{R}\}$ is the domain of $\mathcal{R}$ and $\mathrm{cod}(\mathcal{R}) = \{b \mid (a, b) \in \mathcal{R}\}$ is its codomain. We denote with $\mathcal{R}^{-1}$ the inverse relation of $\mathcal{R}$; that is, $\mathcal{R}^{-1} = \{(b, a) \mid (a, b) \in \mathcal{R}\} \subseteq B \times A$. If $\mathcal{R}$ is a relation on A and B and $\mathcal{S}$ is a relation on B and C, then we denote with $\mathcal{R}; \mathcal{S}$ the composition of $\mathcal{R}$ and $\mathcal{S}$; that is, $\mathcal{R}; \mathcal{S} = \{(a, c) \mid (a, b) \in \mathcal{R} \text{ and } (b, c) \in \mathcal{S}\} \subseteq A \times C$.*

Special notations are used for particular classes of relations.

We represent with $f : A \to B$ a function from set A to set B; that is, $f \subseteq A \times B$ such that for each $a \in A$ there is exists exactly one $a \in A$ such that $(a, b) \in f$.

We represent with $f : A \longleftrightarrow B$ a partial bijection from set A to set B; that is, $f \subseteq A \times B$ such that if $(a, b), (a', b') \in f$ then $a = a'$ iff $b = b'$.

We represent with $f : A \longleftrightarrow B$ an injection from set A to set B; that is, $f \subseteq A \times B$ such that for each $a \in A$ there exists exactly one $b \in B$ such that $(a, b) \in f$, and for each $b \in B$ there is at most one $a \in A$ such that $(a, b) \in f$.

We represent with $f : A \longleftrightarrow B$ an inverse injection from set A to set B; that is, $f \subseteq A \times B$ such that for each $b \in B$ there exists exactly one $a \in A$ such that $(a, b) \in f$, and for each $a \in A$ there is at most one $b \in B$ such that $(a, b) \in f$.

We represent with $f : A \longleftrightarrow B$ a total bijection from set A to set B; that is, $f \subseteq A \times B$ such that for each $a \in A$ there exists exactly one $b \in B$ such that $(a,b) \in f$ and, conversely, for each $b \in B$ there exists exactly one $a \in A$ such that $(a,b) \in f$.

We use also on these subclasses the notations that we have introduced on relations to denote domain, codomain, inverse and composition.

Definition 7 (named sets). *Let $\mathcal{N}$ be an infinite denumerable set of names and let $\mathcal{P}(\mathcal{N})$ be the power-set of $\mathcal{N}$.*
A named set E is a set, denoted by E, and a family of subset of names indexed by E, namely $\{E[e] \subseteq \mathcal{N}\}_{e \in E}$, or, equivalently $\mathsf{E}[\_]$ is a map from E to $\mathcal{P}(\mathcal{N})$.
Given two named sets E and F, a named function $\mathsf{m} : \mathsf{E} \to \mathsf{F}$ is a function on the sets $m : E \to F$ and a family of name embeddings indexed by m, namely $\{\mathsf{m}[e] : \mathsf{E}[e] \longleftrightarrow \mathsf{F}[f]\}_{(e,f) \in m}$:

$$
\begin{array}{ccccc}
\mathsf{E} & \ni & e & & \mathsf{E}[e] \\
\Big\downarrow{\scriptstyle m} & & \Big\downarrow{\scriptstyle m} & & \Big\uparrow{\scriptstyle m[e]} \\
\mathsf{F} & \ni & f & & \mathsf{F}[f]
\end{array}
$$

A named set E is finitely named if $\mathsf{E}[e]$ is finite for each $e \in E$. A named set E is finite if it is finitely named and set E is finite.

We remark that, in the definition of named function, we use an inverse injection from $\mathsf{E}[e]$ to $\mathsf{F}[f]$ to represent the correspondence between the names of e and the names of f: this inverse injection, in fact, can be seen as an embedding of the names of f into the names of e.

Now we define HD-automata: essentially, they have the same components of ordinary automata (Definition 1), but named sets and named functions are use rather than plain sets and functions.

Definition 8 (HD-automata). *A HD-automaton $\mathcal{A}$ is defined by:*

- *a named set L of labels;*
- *a named set Q of states;*
- *a named set T of transitions;*
- *a pair of named functions $\mathsf{s}, \mathsf{d} : \mathsf{T} \to \mathsf{Q}$, which associate to each transition the source and destination states respectively (and embed the names of the source and of the destination states into the names of the transition);*
- *a named function $\mathsf{o} : \mathsf{T} \to \mathsf{L}$, which associates a label to each transition (and embeds the names of the label into the names of the transition);*
- *an initial state $q_0 \in Q$ and an initial embedding $\sigma_0 : \mathsf{Q}[q_0] \longleftrightarrow \mathcal{N}$ of the local names of q_0 into the infinite, denumerable set $\mathcal{N}$ of global names.*

Let $\mathsf{T}[t]_{\mathrm{old}} \stackrel{\mathrm{def}}{=} \{n \in \mathsf{T}[t] \mid n \in \mathrm{dom}(\mathsf{s}[t])\}$ and $\mathsf{T}[t]_{\mathrm{new}} \stackrel{\mathrm{def}}{=} \{n \in \mathsf{T}[t] \mid n \notin \mathrm{dom}(\mathsf{s}[t])\}$ be respectively the old names and the new names of transition $t \in T$.
A HD-automaton is finitely named if L, Q and T are finitely named; it is finite if, in addition, Q and T are finite.

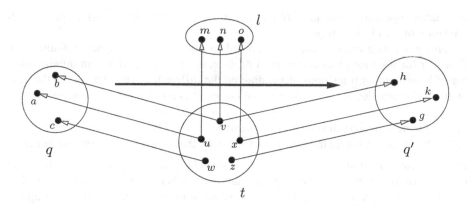

Fig. 1. A transition $t : q \xrightarrow{l} q'$ of a HD-automaton

Let t be a generic transition of a HD-automaton such that $s(t) = q$, $d(t) = q'$ and $o(t) = l$ (in brief $t : q \xrightarrow{l} q'$); one of such transition is represented in Figure 1. Then $s[t] : T[t] \hookleftarrow Q[q]$ embeds, by means of an inverse injection, the names of q into the names of t, whereas $d[t] : T[t] \hookleftarrow Q[q']$ embeds the names of q' into the names of t; in this way, a partial correspondence is defined between the names of the source state and those of the target; so, in the case of the transition in figure, name h of the target state corresponds to name b of the source. The names that appear in the source and not in the target (that is, names a and c in Figure 1) are discarded, or forgotten, during the transition, whereas the names that appear in the target but not in the source (that is, names g and k in figure) are created during the transition.

3.2   From Ground π-Calculus to Basic HD-Automata

We are interested in the representation of the ground π-calculus semantics as HD-automata. First we define the named set of labels L^{π_g} for this language: we have to distinguish between synchronizations, bound inputs, free outputs and bound outputs. Thus the set of labels is

$$L^{\pi_g} = \{\mathtt{tau}, \mathtt{bin}, \mathtt{out}, \mathtt{out}_2, \mathtt{bout}\}$$

where $\mathtt{out}_2$ is used when subject and object names of free outputs coincide (these special labels are necessary, since the function from the names associated to a label into the names associated to a transition must be injective). No name is associated to $\mathtt{tau}$, one name (n) is associated to $\mathtt{out}_2$, and two names (n_{sub} and n_{obj}) are associated to $\mathtt{bin}$, $\mathtt{out}$ and $\mathtt{bout}$.

In order to associate a HD-automaton to a π-calculus process, we have to represent the derivatives of the process as states of the automaton and their transitions as transitions in the HD-automaton; the names corresponding to a state are the free names of the corresponding process, the names corresponding to a transition are the free names of the source state plus, in the case of a bound input and bound output transition, the new name appearing in the label of the transition. A label of $L^{\pi g}$ is associated to each transition in the obvious way.

This naive construction can be improved to obtain more compact HD-automata. Consider for instance process $p = (\nu z)\,\bar{x}z.B(x, y, z)$; it can perform an infinite number of bound output transitions, depending on the different extruded name. In the case of HD-automata, due to the local nature of names, it is not necessary to consider all the different bound output (and bound input) transitions that differ only on the name used to denote the new created channel. The syntactic identity of that name, in fact, is inessential in the model. A single transition can be chosen from each of these infinite bunches. Here we use transition $p \xrightarrow{\bar{x}(z)} p'$ where $z = \min\left(\mathcal{N} \setminus \mathrm{fn}(p)\right)$. It is worth to stress out that, differently from the case of ordinary automata, where particular care is needed in the choice of this transition, in the case of HD-automata any policy for choosing the fresh name will work: in this case, in fact, we do not have to guarantee that equivalent states choose the same name.

Definition 9 (representative transitions). *A π-calculus transition $p \xrightarrow{\mu} q$ is a representative transition if*

$$\mathrm{n}(\mu) \subseteq \mathrm{fn}(p) \cup \left\{\, \min\left(\mathcal{N} \setminus \mathrm{fn}(p)\right)\,\right\}.$$

According to this definition, all the synchronization and free output transitions are representative (in this case $\mathrm{n}(\mu) \subseteq \mathrm{fn}(p)$). A bound input or a bound output is representative only if the communicated name is the smallest name not appearing free in the process.

The following lemma shows that the representative transitions express, up to α-conversion, all the behaviors of a process.

Lemma 1. *Let $p \xrightarrow{\mu} q$, with $\mu = ax$ (resp. $\mu = \bar{a}(x)$), be a non-representative π-calculus transition. Then there is some representative transition $p \xrightarrow{\mu'} q'$, with $\mu' = ay$ (resp. $\mu' = \bar{a}(y)$), such that $q' = q\{y/x\,{}^x\!/y\}$.*

If only representative transitions are used when building a HD-automaton from a π-calculus process, the obtained HD-automaton is *finite-branching*, i.e., it has a finite set of transitions from each state.

Another advantage of using local names is that two processes differing only for a bijective substitution can be collapsed in the same state in the HD-automaton: we assume to have a function norm that, given a process p, returns a pair $(q, \sigma) = \mathrm{norm}(p)$, where q is the representative of the class of processes differing from p for bijective substitutions and $\sigma : \mathrm{fn}(p) \longleftrightarrow \mathrm{fn}(q)$ is the bijective substitution such that $q = p\sigma$.

Definition 10 (from π-calculus to HD-automata). *The HD-automaton $\mathcal{A}_p^{\pi g}$ corresponding to the ground semantics of π-calculus process p is defined as follows:*

- *if $\mathrm{norm}(p) = (q_0, \sigma_0)$ then:*
  - *$q_0 \in Q$ is the initial state and $Q[q_0] = \mathrm{fn}(q_0)$;*
  - *$\sigma_0^{-1} : \mathrm{fn}(q_0) \longleftrightarrow \mathrm{fn}(p)$ is the initial embedding;*

Table 3. Relations between π-calculus labels and labels of HD-automata

μ		τ	$x(y)$		$\bar{x}y$		$\bar{x}x$	$\bar{x}(y)$	
l		tau	bin		out		out$_2$	bout	
$\square = \lambda(\Diamond) \in \mathrm{n}(\mu)$	/		x	y	x	y	x	x	y
$\Diamond = \kappa(\square) \in \mathsf{L}^{\pi\varepsilon}[l]$	/		n_{sub}	n_{obj}	n_{sub}	n_{obj}	n	n_{sub}	n_{obj}

- *if $q \in Q$, $t : q \xrightarrow{\mu} q'$ is a representative transition and $\mathrm{norm}(q') = (q'', \sigma)$, then:*
  - *$q'' \in Q$ and $\mathsf{Q}[q''] = \mathrm{fn}(q'')$;*
  - *$t \in T$ and $\mathsf{T}[t] = \mathrm{fn}(q) \cup \mathrm{bn}(\mu)$;*
  - *$s(t) = q$, $d(t) = q''$, $\mathsf{s}[t] = \mathrm{id}_{\mathrm{fn}(q)}$ and $\mathsf{d}[t] = \sigma$;*
  - *$o(t) = l$ and $\mathsf{o}[t] = \kappa$ are defined as in Table 3.*

Table 3 defines the correspondence between the labels of π-calculus transitions and the HD-automaton labels: so, for instance, an input action $x(y)$ of a π-calculus process is represented in the HD-automaton by means of label bin. Moreover, the table also fixes the correspondence between the names that appear in the π-calculus label and the names of the HD-automaton label. This correspondence is defined by means of two functions: function κ maps the names of a π-calculus label μ into the names of the corresponding label l of the HD-automaton, while λ maps the names of l into the names of μ. Both functions are total bijections, and clearly $\kappa = \lambda^{-1}$. In the case of the input action $x(y)$, we have $\mathrm{n}(x(y)) = \{x, y\}$ and $\mathsf{L}^{\pi\varepsilon}[\mathrm{bin}] = \{n_{\mathrm{sub}}, n_{\mathrm{obj}}\}$; in this case, according to Table 3, functions $\kappa : \{x, y\} \to \{n_{\mathrm{sub}}, n_{\mathrm{obj}}\}$ and $\lambda : \{n_{\mathrm{sub}}, n_{\mathrm{obj}}\} \to \{x, y\}$ are defined as follows: $\kappa(x) = n_{\mathrm{sub}}$ and $\lambda(n_{\mathrm{sub}}) = x$; $\kappa(y) = n_{\mathrm{obj}}$ and $\lambda(n_{\mathrm{obj}}) = y$. We have used function κ in Definition 10; function λ will become useful in the following.

For each π-calculus process p, the HD-automaton $\mathcal{A}_p^{\pi_g}$ is obviously finitely named. Now we identify a class of processes that generate finite HD-automata. This is the class of *finitary* π-calculus processes.

Definition 11 (finitary processes). *The* degree of parallelism $\deg(p)$ *of a π-calculus process p is defined as*

$$\deg(\mathbf{0}) = 0 \qquad\qquad \deg(\pi.p) = 1$$
$$\deg((\nu x)\, p) = \deg(p) \qquad\qquad \deg(p|q) = \deg(p) + \deg(q)$$
$$\deg(p{+}q) = \max\{\deg(p), \deg(q)\} \quad \deg(A(x_1, \ldots, x_n)) = 1$$

A π-calculus process p is finitary *if* $\max\{\deg(p') \mid p \xrightarrow{\mu_1} \cdots \xrightarrow{\mu_i} p'\} < \infty$.

Theorem 1. *Let p be a finitary π-calculus process. Then the HD-automaton $\mathcal{A}_p^{\pi_g}$ is finite.*

We remark that, it is only semidecidable whether a process is finitary. Also in this case, however, there is a syntactic conditions that guarantees that a π-calculus process is finitary: the *finite-control* condition. A process p has a finite control if no parallel composition appears in the recursive definitions used by p.

Corollary 1. *Let p be a finite-control π-calculus process. Then the HD-automaton $\mathcal{A}_p^{\pi_g}$ is finite.*

3.3 Bisimulation on HD-Automata

We introduce now bisimilarity on HD-automata and give some of its basic properties. We also show that ground bisimilarity of π-calculus processes is captured exactly by the bisimulation on HD-automata.

Due to the private nature of the names appearing in the states of HD-automata, bisimulations cannot simply be relations on the states; they must also deal with name correspondences: a HD-bisimulation is a set of triples of the form $\langle q_1, \delta, q_2 \rangle$ where q_1 and q_2 are states of the automata and δ is a partial bijection between the names of the states. The bijection is partial since we allow for equivalent states with different numbers of names.

Suppose that we want to check if states q_1 and q_2 are bisimilar via the partial bijection $\delta : Q[q_1] \rightharpoonup Q[q_2]$ and suppose that q_1 can perform a transition $t_1 : q_1 \xrightarrow{l} q_1'$: an instance of this situation is represented in Figure 2. Then we have to find a transition $t_2 : q_2 \xrightarrow{l} q_2'$ that matches t_1, i.e., not only the two transitions must have the same label, but also the names associated to the labels must be used consistently. This means that, given a name n of the label:

- either n is *old* in both transitions, i.e., it corresponds to some name n_1 of state q_1 and to some name n_2 of q_2 (via the suitable name embeddings), and these names n_1 and n_2 are in correspondence by δ; this is the case of name h of label l in Figure 2: it corresponds to names a_1 and a_2 in the source states, and these are related by δ;
- or n is *new* in both transitions, i.e., it does not correspond to any name n_1 of state q_1, nor to any name n_2 of q_2; this is the case of name k of label l in Figure 2: in fact, the corresponding names y_1 and y_2 in the transitions are new.

This behavior is obtained by requiring that a partial bijection $\zeta : T[t_1] \rightharpoonup T[t_2]$ exists such that: (i) ζ coincides with δ if restricted to the names of the source states (obviously, via the embeddings $s[t_1]$ and $s[t_2]$), and extends δ with a partial correspondence ξ between the new names of t_1 and t_2; (ii) the names associated to the labels are the same, via ζ, and (iii) the destination states q_1' and q_2' are bisimilar via a partial bijection δ' which is compatible with ζ (i.e., if two names are related by δ' in the destination states, then the corresponding names in the transitions are related by ζ). The reader can check that all these requirements are satisfied in Figure 2.

We remark that it is *not* required that two names of the destination states are related by δ' if the corresponding names of the transitions are related by ζ. That is, we allow some of the correspondences that hold in the transitions to be discarded in the destination states. In Figure 2, for instance, names f_1 and f_2 of the target states are not related by δ', even if the corresponding names of the transitions, namely z_1 and z_2, are related by ζ. We will comment further on this choice later in this section. We anticipate that the same equivalence on HD-automata is obtained also by requiring that no correspondence can be discarded in the target states.

Definition 12 (HD-bisimulation). *Let $\mathcal{A}_1$ and $\mathcal{A}_2$ be two HD-automata. A HD-simulation for $\mathcal{A}_1$ and $\mathcal{A}_2$ is a set of triples $\mathcal{R} \subseteq \{\langle q_1, \delta, q_2 \rangle \mid q_1 \in Q_1, q_2 \in Q_2, \delta : Q_1[q_1] \rightharpoonup Q_2[q_2]\}$ such that, whenever $\langle q_1, \delta, q_2 \rangle \in \mathcal{R}$ then:*

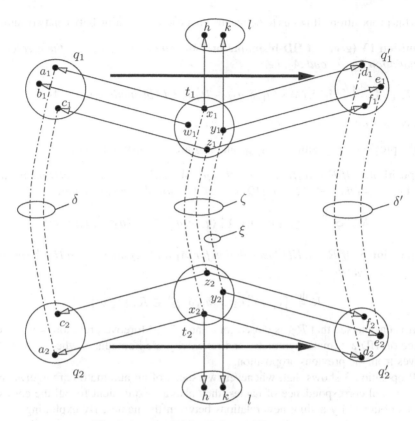

Fig. 2. A step of bisimulation on HD-automata

for each $t_1 : q_1 \xrightarrow{l} q_1'$ in $\mathcal{A}_1$ there exist some $t_2 : q_2 \xrightarrow{l} q_2'$ in $\mathcal{A}_2$, some
$\xi : T_1[t_1]_{new} \hookleftarrow\!\!\!\rightarrow T_2[t_2]_{new}$, *and some* $\zeta : T_1[t_1] \hookleftarrow\!\!\!\rightarrow T_2[t_2]$ *such that:*
- $\zeta = \big(s_1[t_2]; \delta; s_2[t_2]^{-1}\big) \cup \xi$,
- $o_1[t_1] = \zeta; o_2[t_2]$,
- $\langle q_1', \delta', q_2' \rangle \in \mathcal{R}$ *where* $\delta' \subseteq d_1[t_1]^{-1}; \zeta; d_2[t_2]$.

A HD-bisimulation *for $\mathcal{A}_1$ and $\mathcal{A}_2$ is a set of triples $\mathcal{R}$ such that $\mathcal{R}$ is a HD-simulation for $\mathcal{A}_1$ and $\mathcal{A}_2$ and $\mathcal{R}^{-1} = \{\langle q_2, \delta^{-1}, q_1 \rangle \mid \langle q_1, \delta, q_2 \rangle \in \mathcal{R}\}$ is a HD-simulations for $\mathcal{A}_2$ and $\mathcal{A}_1$.*

A HD-bisimulation *for $\mathcal{A}$ is a HD-bisimulation for $\mathcal{A}$ and $\mathcal{A}$.*

The HD-automata $\mathcal{A}_1$ and $\mathcal{A}_2$ are HD-bisimilar *(written $\mathcal{A}_1 \sim \mathcal{A}_2$) if there exists some HD-bisimulation for $\mathcal{A}_1$ and $\mathcal{A}_2$ such that $\langle q_{01}, \delta, q_{02} \rangle \in \mathcal{R}$ for some $\delta \subseteq \sigma_{01}; \sigma_{02}^{-1}$.*

Now we present some basic properties of HD-bisimulations.

Proposition 1. *Let $\{\mathcal{R}_i \mid i \in I\}$ be a (finite or infinite) set of HD-bisimulations for $\mathcal{A}_1$ and $\mathcal{A}_2$. Then $\bigcup_{i \in I} \mathcal{R}_i$ is a HD-bisimulation for $\mathcal{A}_1$ and $\mathcal{A}_2$.*

This proposition allows us to define the greatest bisimulation between two automata.

Definition 13 (greatest HD-bisimulation). *We denote with* $\mathcal{R}_{\mathcal{A}_1;\mathcal{A}_2}$ *the greatest HD-bisimulation for* $\mathcal{A}_1$ *and* $\mathcal{A}_2$, *i.e.:*

$$\mathcal{R}_{\mathcal{A}_1;\mathcal{A}_2} \stackrel{\text{def}}{=} \{\langle q_1, \delta, q_2\rangle \mid \langle q_1, \delta, q_2\rangle \in \mathcal{R}, \mathcal{R} \text{ HD-bisimulation for } \mathcal{A}_1 \text{ and } \mathcal{A}_2\}$$

We denote with $\mathcal{R}_{\mathcal{A}}$ *the greatest HD-bisimulation for* $\mathcal{A}$.

By the previous proposition, $\mathcal{R}_{\mathcal{A}_1;\mathcal{A}_2}$ and $\mathcal{R}_{\mathcal{A}}$ are HD-bisimulations.

Proposition 2. *If* $\mathcal{R}$ *is a HD-bisimulation for* $\mathcal{A}_1$ *and* $\mathcal{A}_2$ *and* $\mathcal{S}$ *is a HD-bisimulations for* $\mathcal{A}_2$ *and* $\mathcal{A}_3$ *then* $\mathcal{R} \frown \mathcal{S}$ *is a HD-bisimulation for* $\mathcal{A}_1$ *and* $\mathcal{A}_3$, *where:*

$$\mathcal{R} \frown \mathcal{S} \stackrel{\text{def}}{=} \{\langle q_1, (\delta; \delta'), q_3\rangle \mid \langle q_1, \delta, q_2\rangle \in \mathcal{R}, \langle q_2, \delta', q_3\rangle \in \mathcal{S}\}.$$

Proposition 3. *If* $\mathcal{R}$ *is a HD-bisimulation for* $\mathcal{A}_1$ *and* $\mathcal{A}_2$ *then* $\widehat{\mathcal{R}}$ *is a HD-bisimulation for* $\mathcal{A}_1$ *and* $\mathcal{A}_2$, *where:*

$$\widehat{\mathcal{R}} \stackrel{\text{def}}{=} \{\langle q_1, \delta', q_2\rangle \mid \langle q_1, \delta, q_2\rangle \in \mathcal{R}, \delta \subseteq \delta'\}.$$

It is easy to see that $\mathcal{R}_{\mathcal{A}}$ is closed for $\widehat{}$ and - $\frown$ -. Moreover, relation $\sim$ is an equivalence on HD-automata: symmetry and reflexivity are immediate, whereas transitivity derives from the previous proposition.

Proposition 3 shows that, whenever two states of an automaton are equivalent via some partial correspondence of names, they also are equivalent for all the correspondences obtained by adding new relations between the names. By exploiting this fact, we can define HD-bisimulation with a stronger condition on the correspondence δ' for the destination states: in fact, we can require $\delta' = \mathsf{d}_1[t_1]^{-1}; \zeta; \mathsf{d}_2[t_2]$. Also with this alternative definition the same equivalence on HD-automata is obtained, and also the greatest bisimulation $\mathcal{R}_{\mathcal{A}_1;\mathcal{A}_2}$ does not change.

The possibility of discarding correspondences in the definition of δ', though, is very convenient. First of all, it permits to exhibit smaller relations to prove HD-bisimilarity of two HD-automata. Furthermore, some important properties of HD-bisimulation do not hold if the discarding is not allowed. This is the case for instance of the concatenation property of Proposition 2: in fact, if we consider the HD-automaton of Figure 3, then relations

$$\mathcal{R} = \{\langle q_1, \delta_{12}, q_2\rangle, \langle q_1', \emptyset, q_2'\rangle\} \qquad \text{with } \delta_{12}(a) = b$$
$$\mathcal{S} = \{\langle q_2, \delta_{23}, q_3\rangle, \langle q_2', \emptyset, q_3'\rangle\} \qquad \text{with } \delta_{23}(b) = c$$

are HD-bisimulations; however, their concatenation

$$\mathcal{R} \frown \mathcal{S} = \{\langle q_1, \delta_{13}, q_3\rangle, \langle q_1', \emptyset, q_3'\rangle\} \qquad \text{with } \delta_{13}(a) = c$$

is *not* a HD-bisimulation if we do not permit to discard name correspondences, since names a' and c' of the target states are not related by $\mathcal{R} \frown \mathcal{S}$, even if the corresponding names a and c of the source states are related.

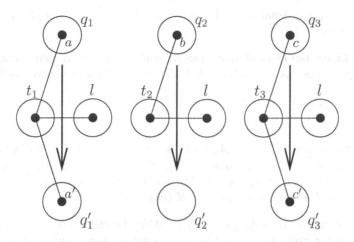

Fig. 3. A tricky example for concatenation of HD-bisimulations

3.4   Global States and Global Bisimulation

Now we give an alternative characterization of HD-bisimulation, which is based on global (rather than local) names. This alternative characterization is very useful to show that HD-bisimulation, when applied to HD-automata obtained from π-calculus processes, coincides with bisimilarity relation $\sim_g$.

We have seen that a state of a HD-automaton is obtained from a π-calculus process by normalizing its names, so that all the processes that differ for a renaming are represented by the same state. Conversely, a particular π-calculus process can be recovered from a state q of the HD-automaton by giving a global identity of the local names of q. Following this intuition, if q is a state of a HD-automaton and $\sigma : Q[q] \hookrightarrow \mathcal{N}$, then (q, σ) is a *global state*, i.e., a state where a global identity is assigned to the names. Global transitions are defined similarly.

Definition 14 (global state and global transition). *A global state of a HD-automaton $\mathcal{A}$ is a pair $g = (q, \sigma)$, where $q \in Q$ and $\sigma : Q[q] \hookrightarrow \mathcal{N}$. We denote with $G_{\mathcal{A}}$ the set of global states of $\mathcal{A}$. We denote with G_A the named set of global state of $\mathcal{A}$, obtained by defining $\mathsf{G}_A[(q, \sigma)] \stackrel{\text{def}}{=} \sigma(Q[q])$.*
A global transition is a pair $u = (t, \rho)$, where $t \in T$ and $\rho : T[t] \hookrightarrow \mathcal{N}$. We denote with $U_{\mathcal{A}}$ the set of global transitions of $\mathcal{A}$. We denote with U_A the named set of global transitions of $\mathcal{A}$, obtained by defining $\mathsf{U}_A[(t, \rho)] \stackrel{\text{def}}{=} \rho(U[t])$. Moreover we use the notations $\mathsf{U}_A[(t, \rho)]_{\text{old}} \stackrel{\text{def}}{=} \rho(\mathsf{T}[t]_{\text{old}})$ and $\mathsf{U}_A[(t, \rho)]_{\text{new}} \stackrel{\text{def}}{=} \rho(\mathsf{T}[t]_{\text{new}})$.
If $t : q \stackrel{l}{\longrightarrow} q'$ then we write $(t, \rho) : (q, \sigma) \stackrel{(l,\lambda)}{\longrightarrow} (q', \sigma')$, where $\sigma = \mathsf{s}[t]^{-1}; \rho$, $\lambda = \mathsf{o}[t]^{-1}; \rho$ and $\sigma' = \mathsf{d}[t]^{-1}; \rho$.

For the global states and global transitions of a HD-automaton we use notations similar to those for the components of the HD-automaton; so, the global transitions of HD-automaton $\mathcal{B}$ are denoted by $\mathsf{T}_{\mathcal{B}}$; also, if we consider two HD-automata $\mathcal{A}_1$ and $\mathcal{A}_2$, then their global states are denoted by G_1 and G_2 respectively.

Now we give the definition of bisimulation which is based on global states and global transitions.

Definition 15 (global bisimulation). *Let A_1 and A_2 be two HD-automata. A global simulation for A_1 and A_2 is a relation $R \subseteq G_1 \times G_2$ such that whenever $g_1 \, R \, g_2$ then:*

for all $u_1 : g_1 \xrightarrow{k} g_1'$ in U_1 with $U_1[u_1]_{\text{new}} \cap G_2[g_2] = \emptyset$ there exists some $u_2 : g_2 \xrightarrow{k} g_2'$ such that $g_1' \, R \, g_2'$.

A global bisimulation for A_1 and A_2 is a relation $R \subseteq G_1 \times G_2$ such that both R is a global simulation for A_1 and A_2 and R^{-1} is a global simulation for A_2 and A_1.
The HD-automata A_1 and A_2 are global-bisimilar *iff there exists some global bisimulation for A_1 and A_2 such that $(q_{01}, \sigma_{01}) \, R \, (q_{02}, \sigma_{02})$.*

Notice the clause "$U_1[u_1]_{\text{new}} \cap G_2[g_2] = \emptyset$" in the definition above, that discards all those global transitions of g_1 that use as new name a name which is old in g_2. This is necessary in the global bisimulation, since names have a global identity here; in fact, this clause plays the same role of clause "$\text{bn}(\mu) \cap \text{fn}(p|q) = \emptyset$" in the definitions of bisimulation in π-calculus (Definition 5).
Global bisimilarity coincides with HD-bisimilarity.

Proposition 4. *Two HD-automata are HD-bisimilar if and only if they are global bisimilar.*

We now show that two π-calculus processes are bisimilar if and only if the corresponding HD-automata are bisimilar. To obtain this result we exploit the global characterization of HD-bisimulation presented in the previous section. The following is the main lemma.

Lemma 2. *Let (q, σ) be a global state of the HD-automaton $A_p^{\pi_g}$ corresponding to a π-calculus process p. Then:*

- *if $q \xrightarrow{\mu} q''$ is a π-calculus transition with $\text{bn}(\mu) \cap \text{fn}(q\sigma) = \emptyset$, then there is some global transition $(t, \rho) : (q, \sigma) \xrightarrow{(l,\lambda)} (q', \sigma')$ of $A_p^{\pi_g}$; and*
- *if $(t, \rho) : (q, \sigma) \xrightarrow{(l,\lambda)} (q', \sigma')$ is a global transition of $A_p^{\pi_g}$, then there is some π-calculus transition $q\sigma \xrightarrow{\mu} q''$*

where in both cases $q'' = q'\sigma'$, and (l, λ) are related to μ as in Table 3.

Theorem 2. *Let p_1 and p_2 be π-calculus processes. Then $p_1 \sim_g p_2$ iff $A_{p_1}^{\pi_g} \sim A_{p_2}^{\pi_g}$.*

4   Minimization of HD-Automata

In this section we address the problem of defining minimal realizations for HD-automata. As we have already discussed for ordinary automata, having a minimal canonical representative for a class of bisimilar automata is important both from a theoretical point of view and from a practical point of view. Unfortunately enough, minimization is

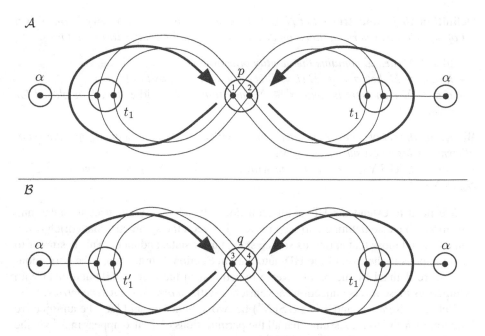

Fig. 4. Two non isomorphic minimal HD-automata

not possible on the HD-automata we introduced in Section 3. In Figure 4 we show two equivalent HD-automata: they are both "minimal", in the sense that it is not possible to reduce them further; however they are not isomorphic. In each of the HD-automata there is a single state with two names, and two transitions: each transition exhibits in the label one of the two names. The difference between the two HD-automata is that the names are switched along the transitions in HD-automaton $\mathcal{B}$, while they are not in $\mathcal{A}$. Still, the HD-automata are equivalent: their behavior is symmetric w.r.t. the two names; and in fact a bisimulation for these HD-automata is:

$$\mathcal{R} = \{\langle p, \delta, q\rangle, \langle p, \delta', q\rangle \mid \delta(1) = 3,\ \delta(2) = 4 \text{ and } \delta'(1) = 4,\ \delta'(2) = 3\}$$

The impossibility of representing explicitly the symmetry between names 1 and 2 (and 3 and 4) is precisely the cause of the impossibility of having a common minimal realization for the two HD-automata. In fact, there is no way to quotient HD-automaton $\mathcal{A}$ with respect to its greatest bisimulation $\mathcal{R}_{\mathcal{A}} = \{\langle p, \delta, p\rangle \mid \delta(1) = 2,\ \delta(2) = 1\}$.

In the following, we show how this problem can be solved by allowing symmetries on names to appear explicitly in the states of the HD-automata.

4.1   Symmetries and HD-Automata with Symmetries

In the following we define an extended version of HD-automata where each state, label, and transition of a HD-automaton is enriched by a set of names *and* by a symmetry on this set of names. We start defining *symmetries* on names and functions between them.

Definition 16 (symmetries). *Let $N \in \mathcal{N}$ be a set of names. A symmetry Σ on N is a set of bijections (or permutations) on N that is a group for composition; that is:*

- $\mathrm{id}_N \in \Sigma$ *(i.e., Σ contains the identity bijection);*
- *if $\sigma, \sigma' \in \Sigma$ then $\sigma; \sigma' \in \Sigma$ (i.e., Σ is closed for composition);*
- *if $\sigma \in \Sigma$ then there is some $\sigma' \in \Sigma$ such that $\sigma; \sigma' = \mathrm{id}_N$ (i.e., Σ is closed for inversion).*

We denote the set of all the symmetries on N with $\mathcal{S}ym(N)$ and with $\mathcal{S}ym_{\mathcal{N}}$ the set of all symmetries on all subsets $N \subseteq \mathcal{N}$.
For all $\Sigma \in GS\mathcal{N}ames$, we denote with $\mathrm{n}(\Sigma)$ the set N of names such that $\Sigma \in \mathcal{S}ym(N)$.

We need to extend the HD-automaton not only adding symmetries to states and transitions, but also defining correspondences between the symmetry that enrich every transition and those that enrich its source state, target state, and label. This is similar to what happens in the case of the HD-automata in Section 3: in that case the correspondences are defined by means of inverse injections; in the case of HD-automata with symmetries these inverse injections are enriches with *embeddings on symmetries*.

Let $\Sigma \in \mathcal{S}ym(N)$ and $\Sigma' \in GS(N')$ be two symmetries and let ρ be an injective function from N' to N. Assume that all the permutations of Σ also appear in Σ' via the function ρ, i.e., that $\rho; \Sigma; \rho^{-1} \subseteq \Sigma'$, where

$$\rho; \Sigma; \rho^{-1} \stackrel{\text{def}}{=} \{\rho; \sigma; \rho^{-1} \mid \sigma \in \Sigma\}.$$

Then ρ is an embedding of Σ into Σ'. We remark that $\rho; \Sigma; \rho^{-1} \subseteq \Sigma'$ can hold only if there is no permutations in Σ which exchange names in the image of ρ with names outside the image: otherwise, $\rho; \Sigma; \rho^{-1}$ would contain partial correspondences on N which are not bijections. Therefore, ρ splits N in two separated sets of names, those in the image and those outside the image. Permutations in Σ can only switch names within such sets, but cannot switch names within the image with names outside it. Notice also that the same embedding is defined, in general, by more than one bijection. In fact, we do not want to distinct between two bijections ρ and ρ' if there is some symmetry $\sigma \in \Sigma'$ such that $\rho' = \rho; \sigma$. Hence, we define an *embedding* from Σ to Σ' as a class of those equivalent bijections.

Definition 17 (embeddings on symmetries). *Let $\Sigma \in GS(N)$ and $\Sigma' \in GS(N')$ be two symmetries on $\mathcal{N}$. An embedding f of Σ into Σ' (written $f : \Sigma \rightarrow \Sigma'$) is a set of injections from N' to N such that:*

- *if $\rho \in f$, then $\rho; \Sigma; \rho^{-1} \subseteq \Sigma'$ (i.e., all the permutations of Σ also appear, via f, in Σ'); and*
- *if $\rho \in f$ then $f = \Sigma'; \rho$ (i.e., f contains all the variants of the same embedding).*

Now we define *named sets with symmetries*: they are similar to named sets (Definition 7), but in this case the elements are enriched with symmetries on names, rather than by sets of names. Based on named sets with symmetries, we then defined HD-automata with symmetries.

Definition 18 (named sets with symmetries). *A named set with symmetries* E *is a set denoted by* E, *and a family of symmetries on* $\mathcal{N}$, *indexed by* E, *namely* $\{E[e] \in Sym_{\mathcal{N}}\}_{e \in E}$, *or, equivalently* E[_] *is a map from* E *to* $Sym_{\mathcal{N}}$.

Given two named sets with symmetries E *and* F, *a* named function with symmetries m : E → F *is a function on the sets* m : E → F *and a family, indexed by* m, *of embeddings on symmetries, namely* $\{m[e] : E[e] \to F[f]\}_{(e,f) \in m}$:

Definition 19 (HD-automata with symmetries). *A* HD-automaton with symmetries $\mathcal{A}$ *is defined by:*

- *a named set with symmetries* L *of labels;*
- *a named set with symmetries* Q *of states;*
- *a named set with symmetries* T *of transitions;*
- *a pair of named functions with symmetries* s, d : T → Q, *which associate to each transition the* source *and* destination *states respectively (and embed the symmetry of the transition into the symmetries of the source and of the destination states);*
- *a named function with symmetries* o : T → L, *which associates a label to each transition (and embeds the symmetry of the transition into the symmetry of the label);*
- *an* initial state $q_0 \in Q$ *and an* initial embedding $f_0 : \{id_{\mathcal{N}}\} \to Q[q_0]$, *that gives a global identity to the local names of* q_0.

In the initial embedding, $\{id_{\mathcal{N}}\}$ is the symmetry on the full set on names that is composed only by the identity permutation. We remark that the initial embedding f_0 gives a global meaning to the names of the initial state q_0 only up to the symmetry $Q[q_0]$ that is defined on these names.

Each HD-automaton can be "promoted" to a HD-automaton with symmetries, by associating to each state, transition, and label the symmetry consisting only of the identity permutation. As a consequence, we can easily adapt Definition 10 to map π-calculus processes into HD-automata with symmetries.

4.2   Bisimulation on HD-Automata with Symmetries

Now we introduce bisimulation on HD-automata with symmetries and describe some of its basic properties. Similarly to what happens for HD-bisimulations on basic HD-automata (Section 3.3), also a HD-bisimulation on HD-automata with symmetries is a set of triples of the form $\langle q_1, \delta, q_2 \rangle$ where q_1 and q_2 are states of the automata and δ is a partial correspondence between the names of the states.

Let us consider the HD-automata with symmetries in Figure 5. We want to check if states q_1 and q_2 are bisimilar via the bijection δ. State q_1 can perform a transition $t_1 : q_1 \xrightarrow{l} q_1'$. We cannot requite that this transition is matched by a single transition of q_2: in fact, in state q_1 there is a symmetry between names 1 and 2, so, in transition t_1 the name in the label can correspond both to name 1 and to name 2 of the source state. In state q_2 there is no symmetry between names 1 and 2, but there are two transitions, that use name 1 and 2, respectively. We consider bisimilar these two HD-automata with symmetries, proviso the target states are bisimilar according to the correspondences

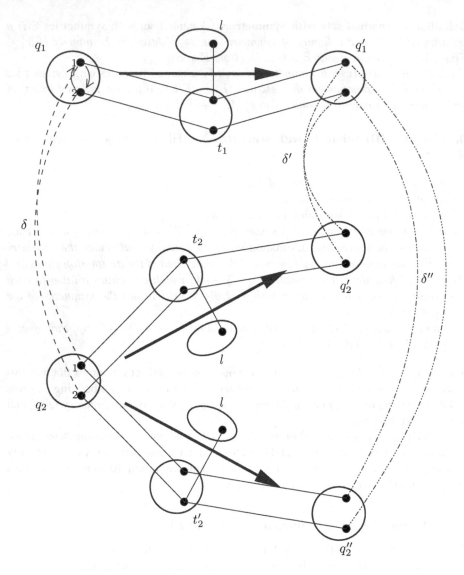

Fig. 5. A step of bisimulation on HD-automata with symmetries

δ' and δ'' represented in figure; in fact, we do not want to distinguish between the symmetries in the behaviors that are "declared" in the states and those that are implicit in the transitions of the HD-automaton with symmetries. So, transition t_1 to be matched by the pair of transitions t_2 and t_2', one for each of the symmetric behaviors of t_1. In the definition of bisimulation for HD-automata with symmetries, this is obtained by requiring that, given transition $t_1 : q_1 \xrightarrow{l} q_2$, for each injection $\alpha_1 \in s_1[t_1]$ there exist a transition t_2 from q_2 and an injection $\alpha_2 \in s_2[t_2]$ so that t_1 and t_2 match w.r.t. α_1 and α_2. In the general case, we have to take into account not only the symmetries of the source state, but also those of the label and of the target state of a transition. So, a matching has to be found for a transition $t_1 : q_1 \xrightarrow{l} q_1'$ and three bijections $\alpha_1 \in s_1[t_1]$, $\gamma_1 \in l_1[t_1]$ and $\beta_1 \in d_1[t_1]$.

Definition 20 (HDS-bisimulation). *Let A_1 and A_2 be two HD-automata with symmetries. A HDS-simulation for A_1 and A_2 is a set of triples $\mathcal{R} \subseteq \{\langle q_1, \delta, q_2 \rangle \mid q_1 \in Q_1, q_2 \in Q_2, \delta : \mathrm{n}(Q_1[q_1]) \longleftrightarrow \mathrm{n}(Q_2[q_2])\}$ such that, whenever $\langle q_1, \delta, q_2 \rangle \in \mathcal{R}$ then:*

for each $t_1 : q_1 \xrightarrow{l} q_1'$ in A_1 and for each $\alpha_1 \in s_1[t_1]$, $\gamma_1 \in o_1[t_1]$ and $\beta_1 \in d_1[t_1]$, there exist some $t_2 : q_2 \xrightarrow{l} q_2'$ in A_2, some injections $\alpha_2 \in s_2[t_2]$, $\gamma_2 \in o_2[t_2]$ and $\beta_2 \in d_2[t_2]$, some $\xi : \mathrm{n}(T_1[t_1])_{\mathrm{new}} \longleftrightarrow \mathrm{n}(T_2[t_2])_{\mathrm{new}}$, and some $\zeta : \mathrm{n}(T_1[t_1]) \longleftrightarrow \mathrm{n}(T_2[t_2])$ such that:
- $\zeta = (\alpha_1; \delta; \alpha_2^{-1}) \cup \xi$,
- $\gamma_1 = \zeta; \gamma_2$,
- $\langle q_1', \delta', q_2' \rangle \in \mathcal{R}$ where δ' is such that $\zeta = \beta_1; \delta'; \beta_2^{-1}$.

A HDS-bisimulation for A_1 and A_2 is a set of triples $\mathcal{R}$ such that $\mathcal{R}$ is a HDS-simulation for A_1 and A_2 and $\mathcal{R}^{-1} = \{\langle q_2, \delta^{-1}, q_1 \rangle \mid \langle q_1, \delta, q_2 \rangle \in \mathcal{R}\}$ is a HDS-simulations for A_2 and A_1.

A HDS-bisimulation for A is a HDS-bisimulation for A and A.

The HD-automata with symmetries A_1 and A_2 are HDS-bisimilar (written $A_1 \sim A_2$) if there exists some HDS-bisimulation for A_1 and A_2 such that $\langle q_{01}, \delta, q_{02} \rangle \in \mathcal{R}$ for $\delta = \sigma_{01}; \sigma_{02}^{-1}$.

If $\mathcal{R}$ is a HDS-bisimulation for A_1 and A_2, and a pair of transitions t_1 in A_1 and t_2 in A_2 satisfy the bisimulation condition in definition above holds, then we write, with a light abuse of notation, that $\langle t_1, \rho, t_2 \rangle \in \mathcal{R}$, where $\rho = \alpha_1; \delta; \alpha_2^{-1}$.

It is easy to see that, in the case of HD-automata with symmetries consisting only of identity permutations, this definition of HD-bisimulation coincides with the one of Definition 12.

We now investigate the basic properties of HD-bisimulation. Similarly to the HD-bisimulations defined in Section 3, also the HDS-bisimulations are closes w.r.t. union, concatenation, and operator $\widehat{-}$. As a consequence, greatest HDS-bisimulations exist: we denote with $\mathcal{R}_{A_1;A_2}$ the greatest HDS-bisimulation for A_1 and A_2, and with $\mathcal{R}_A$ the greatest HDS-bisimulation for A. Moreover, relation $\sim$ is an equivalence on HD-automata with symmetries.

In the case of HDS-bisimulations a new operator can be defined, that closes a bisimulation w.r.t. all the symmetries that are present in the states of the HD-automata.

Proposition 5. *If $\mathcal{R}$ is a HDS-bisimulation for A_1 and A_2 then $\widetilde{\mathcal{R}}$ is a HDS-bisimulation for A_1 and A_2, where:*

$$\widetilde{\mathcal{R}} \overset{\text{def}}{=} \{\langle q_1, \delta', q_2 \rangle \mid \langle q_1, \delta, q_2 \rangle \in \mathcal{R}, \delta' = \sigma_1; \delta; \sigma_2 \text{ and } \sigma_1 \in Q_1[q_1], \sigma_2 \in Q_2[q_2]\}.$$

4.3 Minimizing HD-Automata with Symmetries

In this section we show that, given a HD-automaton with symmetries A, it is possible to minimize it, i.e., to define a HD-automaton with symmetries $A_{\min}$ that is bisimilar to

$\mathcal{A}_{\min}$

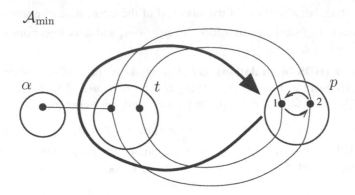

Fig. 6. A minimal realization for the HD-automata of Figure 4

$\mathcal{A}$ and that is "minimal" in the class of HD-automata bisimilar to $\mathcal{A}$ — we define below what is the meaning of "minimal".

We start by showing that the counter-example on the existence of minimal HD-automata presented at the beginning of this section (see Figure 4) does not apply to the case of HD-automata with symmetries. Indeed, the minimal HD-automaton corresponding to the two HD-automata in Figure 4 is represented in Figure 6. HD-automaton $\mathcal{A}_{\min}$ has a single state p, with one infinite repository and two distinct names 1 and 2. Moreover the symmetry associated to state p declares that names 1 and 2 can be switched without affecting the behavior. HD-automaton $\mathcal{A}_{\min}$ has one transition t, that exhibits one of the two names in the label α. Also the transition and the label have one infinite repository. In the figure, we have not represented explicitly that the infinite repositories of p, t and α are in correspondence along the transition. The possibility of declaring the symmetry on the two names 1 and 2 of state p is the key feature for obtaining a canonical minimal HD-automaton with symmetries. Indeed, this symmetry makes it possible to use a single transition t of $\mathcal{A}_{\min}$ to represent both transitions of $\mathcal{A}$ and $\mathcal{B}$ — the two transitions t_1 and t_2 in the HD-automata differ only for the choice of the name to exhibit in the action. Moreover, the symmetry between 1 and 2 makes ephemeral the fact that the two names are exchanged or not along transition t.

We start by describing the fine structure of $\mathcal{R}_{\mathcal{A}}$. This will be useful to guide the construction of the minimal automaton. First of all, relation $\mathcal{R}_{\mathcal{A}}$ is closed for concatenation, so it defines a partition on the states Q of $\mathcal{A}$; that is, relation $\equiv_{\mathcal{A}}$ is an equivalence, where

$$p \equiv_{\mathcal{A}} q \qquad \text{iff} \qquad \langle p, \delta, q \rangle \in \mathcal{R}_{\mathcal{A}} \text{ for some } \delta.$$

Consider two states $p, q \in Q$, and let $\Delta_{\mathcal{A}}(p, q)$ be the set of correspondences that exist, according to $\mathcal{R}_{\mathcal{A}}$, between the names of p and of q:

$$\Delta_{\mathcal{A}}(p, q) \overset{\text{def}}{=} \{\delta \mid \langle p, \delta, q \rangle \in \mathcal{R}_{\mathcal{A}}\}.$$

Let us now consider more in detail $\Delta_{\mathcal{A}}(q, q)$. It consists of a set of partial mappings on the names in $Q[q]$. The fact that these mappings are partial is an evidence that state q

can contain names which do not play any important role in the future behavior: indeed, according to the definition of $\Delta_\mathcal{A}$, state q exhibits the same behaviors also if the identity of the names outside the partial mappings is lost. More precisely, let $\mathrm{an}_\mathcal{A}(q)$ be the names that appear in the domain of every partial mapping in $\Delta_\mathcal{A}(q, q)$. Then these are the only *active names* in state q and all other names can be safely discarded from the state, since they are not relevant for the future behaviors. The following property formalized the notion of active names and investigates some of their properties.

Proposition 6. *Let $\mathcal{A}$ be a HD-automaton, and let*

$$\underset{\mathcal{A}}{\mathrm{an}}(q) \overset{\text{def}}{=} \bigcap_{\delta \in \Delta_\mathcal{A}(q,q)} \mathrm{dom}(\delta) \quad and \quad \Delta_{\mathrm{an}\,\mathcal{A}}(q) \overset{\text{def}}{=} \{\delta \cap (\underset{\mathcal{A}}{\mathrm{an}} \times \underset{\mathcal{A}}{\mathrm{an}}) \mid \delta \Delta_\mathcal{A}(q, q)\}$$

for all $q \in Q$. Then:

1. $\Delta_{\mathrm{an}\,\mathcal{A}}(q)$ *is a symmetry on* $\mathrm{an}_\mathcal{A}(q)$;
2. $Q[q] \cap (\mathrm{an}_\mathcal{A}(q) \times \mathrm{an}_\mathcal{A}(q)) \subseteq \Delta_{\mathrm{an}\,\mathcal{A}}(q, q)$;
3. $\Delta_\mathcal{A}(q) = \{\delta \in Q[q] \overset{}{\longmapsto} Q[q] \mid (\delta \cap (\mathrm{an}_\mathcal{A}(q) \times \mathrm{an}_\mathcal{A}(q))) \in \Delta_{\mathrm{an}\,\mathcal{A}}(q)\}$.

The results described above for the states of an HD-automaton with symmetries also hold for the transitions. More precisely, let us define

$$t \equiv_\mathcal{A} t' \qquad \text{iff} \qquad \langle t, \rho, t' \rangle \in \mathcal{R}_\mathcal{A} \text{ for some } \rho.$$

This relation turns out to be an equivalence. Moreover, by defining

$$\Delta_\mathcal{A}(t, t') = \{\rho \mid \langle t, \rho, t' \rangle \in \mathcal{R}_\mathcal{A}\},$$

the results of Proposition 6 also hold for transitions.

We are now ready to define the minimal HD-automaton corresponding to a given HD-automaton with symmetries $\mathcal{A}$. This minimal realization is obtained by replacing each class of equivalent states and transitions of $\mathcal{A}$ with a single state or transition. The names associated to states and transitions of the minimal HD-automaton are the active names and the associated symmetries are those defined by $\Delta_{\mathrm{an}\,\mathcal{A}}$: these, in fact, express all the symmetries that exist between the names, not only those "declared" in HD-automaton $\mathcal{A}$. We remark that it is the possibility of representing the symmetries defined by the HDS-bisimulations directly in the states of an automaton that allows for the definition of minimal HD-automata.

In the definition of the minimal HD-automaton, we denote with $[q]_{\equiv_\mathcal{A}}$ the equivalence classes of the states w.r.t. $\equiv_\mathcal{A}$; that is, $[q]_{\equiv_\mathcal{A}} = \{q' \mid q \equiv_\mathcal{A} q'\}$. We also assume that a canonical representative is defined for any such class, and we denote with $\lfloor q \rfloor_{\equiv_\mathcal{A}}$ the canonical representative of class $[q]_{\equiv_\mathcal{A}}$; that is, $\lfloor q \rfloor_{\equiv_\mathcal{A}} \in [q]_{\equiv_\mathcal{A}}$ and whenever $q \equiv_\mathcal{A} q'$ then $\lfloor q \rfloor_{\equiv_\mathcal{A}} = \lfloor q' \rfloor_{\equiv_\mathcal{A}}$. Similar notations are used for the transitions.

The definition of minimal HD-automaton follows.

Definition 21 (minimal HD-automaton with symmetries). *The minimal HD-automaton with symmetries $\mathcal{A}_{\min}$ for $\mathcal{A}$ is defined as follows:*

- $L_{min} = L$ and $L_{min}[l] = L[l]$ for each $l \in L_{min}$;
- $Q_{min} = \{\lfloor q \rfloor_{\equiv_A} \mid q \in Q,\ q$ reachable state$\}$ and $Q_{min}[q] = \Delta_{an_A}(q, q)$ for every $q \in Q_{min}$;
- $T_{min} = \{\lfloor t \rfloor_{\equiv_A} \mid t \in T,\ t$ reachable transition$\}$ and $T_{min}[t] = \Delta_{an_A}(t, t)$ for every $t \in T_{min}$;
- $o_{min}(t) = o(t)$ and $o_{min}[t] = o[t]$ for every $t \in T_{min}$;
- $s_{min}(t) = \lfloor s(t) \rfloor_{\equiv_A}$ and $s_{min}[t] = \{\sigma \mid \sigma = (\sigma'; \sigma'') \cap (an_A(\lfloor s(t) \rfloor_{\equiv_A}) \times an_A(t))$ for $\sigma' \in \Delta_A(s(t), \lfloor s(t) \rfloor_{\equiv_A})$ and $\sigma'' \in s(t)\}$ for every $t \in T_{min}$;
- $d_{min}(t) = \lfloor d(t) \rfloor_{\equiv_A}$ and $d_{min}[t] = \{\sigma \mid \sigma = (\sigma'; \sigma'') \cap (an_A(\lfloor d(t) \rfloor_{\equiv_A}) \times an_A(t))$ for $\sigma' \in \Delta_A(d(t), \lfloor d(t) \rfloor_{\equiv_A})$ and $\sigma'' \in d(t)\}$ for every $t \in T_{min}$;
- $q_{0\,min} = \lfloor q_0 \rfloor_{\equiv_A}$ and $f_{0\,min} = \{\sigma \mid \sigma = (\sigma'; \sigma'') \cap (an_A(\lfloor q_0 \rfloor_{\equiv_A}) \times \mathcal{N})$ for $\sigma' \in \Delta_A(q_0, q_{min\,0})$ and $\sigma'' \in f_0\}$.

In the definition above, by reachable states and reachable transitions we mean those states and transitions that can be reached from the initial state following the transitions in the automaton.

A first, important property of minimal HD-automata is that $\mathcal{A}_{min}$ is HDS-bisimilar to the original HD-automaton $\mathcal{A}$.

Proposition 7. *Let $\mathcal{A}$ be a HD-automaton with symmetries. Then $\mathcal{A} \sim \mathcal{A}_{min}$.*

Minimal HD-automata are unique, up to isomorphism, for each class of bisimilar HD-automata.

Theorem 3. *Let $\mathcal{A}$ and $\mathcal{B}$ be two HD-automata with symmetries. Then $\mathcal{A} \sim \mathcal{B}$ if and only if $\mathcal{A}_{min}$ and $\mathcal{B}_{min}$ are isomorphic.*

The obtained HD-automaton $\mathcal{A}_{min}$ is *minimal* since it has the minimum number of states and of transitions among the HD-automata that are bisimilar to $\mathcal{A}$; moreover, it has the maximum set of symmetries in these states and transitions. Notice that increasing the symmetries in states and transitions is considered a step toward minimization: in fact, if larger symmetries are present, then a smaller number of transitions is sufficient to represent the same behaviors. If we collapse further states and transitions of $\mathcal{A}_{min}$, or if we enlarge symmetries of its states and transitions, a non-equivalent HD-automaton is obtained.

5   Concluding Remarks

We have presented History-Dependent Automata and we have shown that they are an operational model particularly adequate for named calculi such as the π-calculus. An important property that holds only for HD-automata enriched with symmetries is the existence, in each class of equivalent HD-automata, of a minimal representative. As it happens for ordinary automata, this minimal HD-automaton can be considered the semantic object corresponding to the class of equivalent HD-automata.

Several results on HD-automata have not been covered in this paper. An extended version of HD-automata with symmetries has been defined in [Pis99], in order to capture the early and late semantics of the π-calculus. In [MP99] a particular variant of

HD-automata, namely HD-automata with *negative transitions*, is proposed in order to deal with the asynchronous π-calculus [HT91, ACS98]. In [MP00] a co-algebraic semantics for the π-calculus is defined. It is based on the idea of extending states and transitions with an algebra of names and symmetries. A variant of HD-automata is shown to come out naturally as a compact representation of the co-algebraic models. Finally, a categorical characterization of HD-automata and of HD-bisimulation is given in [MP98b, MP98a].

HD-automata also provide the core of HAL [FFG⁺97, GR97], a verification environment for concurrent systems described in the π-calculus and other named calculi: HD-automata allow for a compact representation of the behaviors of these concurrent systems, and can be used in the algorithms as a common format for named calculi.

References

[ACS98]   R. Amadio, I. Castellani, and D. Sangiorgi. On bisimulations for the asynchronous π-calculus. *Theoretical Computer Science*, 192(2):291–324, 1998.

[Dam97]   M. Dam. On the decidability of process equivalences for the π-calculus. *Theoretical Computer Science*, 183(2):215–228, 1997.

[FFG⁺97]   G. Ferrari, G. Ferro, S. Gnesi, U. Montanari, M. Pistore, and G. Ristori. An automata based verification environment for mobile processes. In *Proc. TACAS'97*, volume 1217 of *LNCS*. Springer Verlag, 1997.

[GR97]   S. Gnesi and G. Ristori. A model checking algorithm for π-calculus agents. In *Proc. ICTL'97*. Kluwer Academic Publishers, 1997.

[HT91]   K. Honda and M. Tokoro. On asynchronous communication semantics. In *Proc. ECOOP'91*, volume 612 of *LNCS*. Springer Verlag, 1991.

[IP96]   P. Inverardi and C. Priami. Automatic verification of distributed systems: The process algebras approach. *Formal Methods in System Design*, 8(1):1–37, 1996.

[Mad92]   E. Madelaine. Verification tools for the CONCUR project. *Bullettin of the EATCS*, 47:110–126, 1992.

[Mil89]   R. Milner. *Communication and Concurrency*. Prentice Hall, 1989.

[Mil93]   R. Milner. The polyadic π-calculus: a tutorial. In *Logic and Algebra of Specification*, volume 94 of *NATO ASI Series F*. Springer Verlag, 1993.

[MP98a]   U. Montanari and M. Pistore. History dependent automata. Technical Report TR-11-98, Università di Pisa, Dipartimento di Informatica, 1998.

[MP98b]   U. Montanari and M. Pistore. An introduction to history dependent automata. In *Proc. Second Workshop on Higher-Order Operational Techniques in Semantics (HOOTS II)*, volume 10 of *ENTCS*. Elsevier, 1998.

[MP99]   U. Montanari and M. Pistore. Finite state verification for the asynchronous π-calculus. In *Proc. TACAS'99*, LNCS. Springer Verlag, 1999.

[MP00]   U. Montanari and M. Pistore. π-calculus, structured coalgebras and minimal hd-automata. In *Proc. MFCS 2000*, volume 1893 of *LNCS*. Springer Verlag, 2000.

[MPW92]   R. Milner, J. Parrow, and D. Walker. A calculus of mobile processes (parts I and II). *Information and Computation*, 100(1):1–77, 1992.

[MPW93]   R. Milner, J. Parrow, and D. Walker. Modal logic for mobile processes. *Theoretical Computer Science*, 114(1):149–171, 1993.

[Par80]   D. Park. *Concurrency and Automata on Infinite Sequences*, volume 104 of *LNCS*. Springer Verlag, 1980.

[Pis99]   M. Pistore. *History Dependent Automata*. PhD thesis, Università di Pisa, Diparti-
            mento di Informatica, 1999.
[San93a]   D. Sangiorgi. *Expressing Mobility in Process Algebras: First-Order and Higher-
            Order Paradigms*. PhD thesis, University of Edinburgh, 1993.
[San93b]   D. Sangiorgi. From π-calculus to higher-order π-calculus – and back. In *Proc.
            TAPSOFT'93*, volume 668 of *LNCS*. Springer Verlag, 1993.
[Wal95]   D. Walker. Objects in the π-calculus. *Information and Computation*, 116(2):253–
            271, 1995.

Mobile Distributed Programming in X-KLAIM[*]

Lorenzo Bettini and Rocco De Nicola

Dipartimento di Sistemi e Informatica, Università di Firenze,
Viale Morgagni 65, 50134 Firenze, Italy
{bettini, denicola}@dsi.unifi.it

Abstract. Network-aware computing has called for new programming languages that exploit the mobility paradigm as a basic interaction mechanism. In this paper we present X-KLAIM, an experimental programming language specifically designed to program distributed systems composed of several components interacting through multiple distributed tuple spaces and mobile code. The language consists of a set of coordination primitives inspired by Linda, a set of operators for building processes borrowed from process algebras and a few classical constructs for sequential programming. X-KLAIM naturally supports programming with explicit localities; these are first-class data that can be manipulated like any other data, and coordination primitives that permit controlling interactions among located processes. Via a series of examples, we show that many mobile code programming paradigms can be naturally implemented by means of the considered language.

1 Introduction

Technological advances of both computers and telecommunication networks, and development of more efficient communication protocols are leading to an ever increasing integration of computing systems and to diffusion of so called Global Computers [Car96, Car97]. These are massive networked and dynamically reconfigurable infrastructure interconnecting heterogeneous, typically autonomous and mobile components, that can operate on the basis of incomplete information.

Important requirements on applications for Global Computers are [Car99]:

- *Scalability*: high numbers of users and nodes have to be envisaged;
- *Heterogeneity*: different operating systems and applications have to inter-operate;
- *Autonomy*: independent administration of domains has to be guaranteed;
- *Adaptability*: dynamic and unpredictable changes have to be taken into account;
- *Mobility*: migration of processes, code and data has to be considered.

Global Computers are thus fostering a new style of distributed programming that has to take into account variable guarantees for communication, cooperation and mobility, resource usage, security policies and mechanisms for dealing with failures. This

---

[*] This work has been funded by EU-FET on Global Computing, project MIKADO IST-2001-32222 and project AGILE IST-2001-32747. The funding body is not responsible for any use that might be made of the results presented here.

M. Bernardo and A. Bogliolo (Eds.): SFM-Moby 2005, LNCS 3465, pp. 29–68, 2005.

has stimulated the proposal of new theories, computational paradigms, linguistic mechanisms and implementation techniques. We have thus witnessed the birth of many calculi and kernel languages intended to support programming according to the new style and to provide tools for formal reasoning over the modeled systems.

In this paper we present X-KLAIM, an experimental programming language specifically designed to program distributed systems composed of several components interacting through multiple tuple spaces and mobile code (possibly object-oriented). X-KLAIM is based on KLAIM the *Kernel Language for Agents Interaction and Mobility* introduced in [DFP99]. The distinguishing features of the approach is the explicit use of localities for accessing data or computational resources. The choice of its primitives was heavily influenced by Process Algebras [Hoa85, Mil89] and Linda [Gel85, CG89b].

KLAIM can be seen as an asynchronous higher–order process calculus whose basic actions are the original Linda primitives enriched with explicit information about the location of the nodes where processes and tuples are allocated.

The *blackboard* approach, of which tuple space based models are variants, is one of the most appreciated model for dealing with mobile agents (see, e.g., [Deu01], that examines several messaging models for mobile agents) also because of its flexibility. The Linda *asynchronous* communication model permits

- *time uncoupling*: tuples' life time is independent of the producer process' life time,
- *destination uncoupling*: the creator of a tuple is not required to know the future use or the destination of that tuple,
- *space uncoupling*: communicating objects need to know a single interface, i.e., the operations over the tuple space. This approach is also called *flow-of-objects* [AFH99] as opposed to *method invocation*, which requires many interfaces for the operations supplied by remote objects.

When moving to open distributed systems and large-scale, multi-users applications, the Linda coordination model suffers from the lack of *modularity* and *scalability*: identification tags of tuples, which are conceptually part of different contexts, may collide. In other words, processes of different computations could interfere and a mechanism to structure communication and hide information, e.g., to create areas restricted to a subset of the processes, is needed. Explicit localities enable the programmer to distribute and retrieve data and processes to and from the sites of a net and to structure the tuple space as multiple, located spaces. Moreover, localities, considered as first–order data, can be dynamically created and communicated over the network. The overall outcome is a powerful programming formalism that, for example, can easily be used to model encapsulation. In fact, an encapsulated module can be implemented as a tuple space at a private locality, and this ensures controlled accesses to data.

The rest of this tutorial is organized as follows. In the next section we provide a short introduction to Linda, while Section 3 introduces KLAIM and Section 4 shows some simple programming examples. The syntax and the informal semantics of X-KLAIM are introduced in Section 5. Some examples are provided in Section 6 and 7. Section 8 explains the connectivity actions of X-KLAIM and Section 9 shows the implementation of a chat system. In the concluding section we sum up our contribution and briefly discuss related work.

2   A Brief Presentation of Linda

Linda [Gel85, CG89b] is a coordination language that relies on an asynchronous and associative communication mechanism based on a shared global environment called *tuple space*, a multiset of *tuples*. Tuples are ordered sequence of information items (called *fields*). There can be *actual fields* (i.e., expressions, processes, localities, constants, identifiers) and *formal fields* (i.e., variables). Syntactically, a formal field is denoted with !*ide*, where *ide* is an identifier. In various Linda dialects, the first field is required to be an actual field and is usually referred to as the *logical* name or the *tag*. Tuples are usually denoted by t (possibly indexed).

Tuples are anonymous and content-addressable. The basic interaction mechanism is *pattern–matching*; it is an indivisible action and it is used to select tuples in a tuple space (often abbreviated as TS). Two tuples match if they have the same number of fields and the corresponding fields match: a formal field matches any value of the same type, and two actual fields match only if they are identical (but two formals never match). For instance, tuple ("foo", "bar", $100 + 200$) matches with ("foo", "bar", !*Val*). After matching, the variables of the formal fields get the value of the matched field: in the previous example, after matching, *Val* (an integer variable) will contain the integer value 300.

Linda has four primitives for manipulating tuple spaces: two blocking operations that are used for accessing and removing tuples from TS and two non-blocking operations that are used for adding tuples to TS.

- **in**(t) triggers the evaluation of t and then searches for a tuple t' in TS that matches t. If and when t' is found, it is removed from TS; the corresponding values of t' are assigned to the variables of T and the process continues. If no matching tuple is found, the process is suspended until one is available.
- **read**(t) is similar to **in**(t), but it does not provoke removal of the matched tuple t' from TS.
- **out**(t) triggers the evaluation of t and adds the outcoming tuple to TS.
- **eval**(t) is similar to **out**(t), but the actual evaluation t is not performed by the process executing **eval**(t); a new process is spawned to evaluate t and eventually add the resulting tuple to TS.

Some versions of Linda [CG89a] also introduce predicative forms of the blocking operations that are useful when one wants to search for a matching tuple in a tuple space without running the risk of blocking. The non-blocking version of the retrieval operations, namely **readp** and **inp** act like **read** and **in**, but, if no matching tuple is found, they do not suspend the executing process but simply return `false`. These operations can be used where a boolean expression is expected. For instance, **readp** can be used to test whether a tuple is present in a tuple space.

It is worth noting that nondeterminism is inherent in the definition of Linda primitives. It arises both when different **in/read** operations are suspended waiting for the same tuple and such a tuple becomes available (only one of the suspended operations is nondeterministically selected to proceed) and when an **in/read** operation has more than one matching tuple(one is arbitrarily chosen).

The following example, borrowed from [CG89b], is a simple C-Linda [She90] solution of the dining philosophers problem. A classical problem of concurrent programming.

Five philosophers sit around a circular table. Each philosopher spends his life alternatively thinking and eating. In the center of the table is a large plate of noodles. A philosopher needs two chopsticks to eat a helping of noodles. Unfortunately, the philosophers can only afford five chopsticks. One chopstick is placed between each pair of philosophers and they agree that each will only use the chopstick to his immediate right and left. The problem is programming the philosophers so that they behave politely and possibly no deadlock arises.

The solution proposed below has an initialization phase that drops on the table 5 chopsticks and, to avoid deadlock, 4 tickets. For eating, a philosopher needs to acquire first a ticket and then the chopsticks close to him (positions are indicated by the indexes).

```
phil(i)
  int i;
{
  while(1) {
    think();
    in("room ticket");
    in("chopstick", i);
    in("chopstick", (i + 1)mod 5);
    eat();
    out("chopstick", i);
    out("chopstick", (i + 1)mod 5);
    out("room ticket");
  }
}
```

```
initialize()
{
  int i;
  for (i = 0; i < 5; i + +) {
    out("chopstick", i);
    eval(phil(i));
    if (i < 4) out("room ticket");
  }
}
```

The use of actual fields in the argument tuple of an **in/read** instruction is known as "structured naming". It makes TS content–addressable, in the sense that processes may select from a collection of tuples by matching the value of the component fields. Formal fields of tuples already in the tuple space are never updated, even when those tuples are used for matching **in/read** operations.

The Linda model is known as *Generative Communication* [Gel85]. Indeed, once a tuple is added to TS (generated), its life-time is independent from that of the producer process. This permits writing programs where complex data structures are distributed to allow different programs to work simultaneously on their elements.

Linda's communication mechanism, somewhat similarly to "explicit message passing", makes the interactions of a program with its environment explicit. Indeed, one can easily write Linda programs that essentially communicate via messages. Thus the simple basic Linda model can deal with parallelism of all grain sizes.

3   An Overview of KLAIM

Before describing the basic concepts of X-KLAIM we give a very brief introduction to KLAIM (we refer the interested reader to [BBD+03] and to the KLAIM web page, http://music.dsi.unifi.it, for more complete descriptions of the formal model).

KLAIM extends Linda by handling multiple distributed tuple spaces. Tuple spaces are placed on *nodes* (or *sites*), which are part of a *net*. Each node contains a tuple space and number of processes in execution, and can be accessed through its *locality*. There are two kinds of localities: *physical localities* are the identifiers through which nodes can be uniquely identified within a net; *logical localities* are symbolic names for nodes. A reserved logical locality, self, can be used by processes to refer to their execution node. Physical localities have an absolute meaning within the net, while logical localities have a relative meaning depending on the node where they are interpreted and can be thought as aliases for network resources. Logical localities are associated to physical localities through *allocation environments*, represented as partial functions. Each node has its own environment that, in particular, associates self to the physical locality of the node. A node is represented as $s::_\rho P$, where s is the physical locality, P are processes running on the node and ρ is the allocation environment (omitted if not relevant). A net is then the parallel composition of nodes: $s_1::_{\rho_1} P_1 \parallel \dots \parallel s_n::_{\rho_n} P_n$.

KLAIM processes may run concurrently, both at the same node or at different nodes, and can execute the following operations over tuple spaces and nodes:

- **in**$(t)@l$: evaluates tuple t and looks for a matching tuple t' in the tuple space located at l. Whenever a matching tuple t' is found, it is removed from the tuple space. The corresponding values of t' are then assigned to the formal fields of t and the operation terminates. If no matching tuple is found, the operation is suspended until one is available.
- **read**$(t)@l$: differs from **in**$(t)@l$ only because the tuple t' selected by pattern-matching is not removed from the tuple space located at l.
- **out**$(t)@l$: adds the tuple resulting from the evaluation of t to the tuple space located at l.
- **eval**$(P)@l$: spawns process P for execution at l. This primitive, although apparently more restrictive, is indeed more general because we can simulate **eval**$(t)@l$ by means of **eval**(**out**$(t))@l$
- **newloc**(l): creates a new node in the net and binds its physical locality to l. The node can be considered as a "private" node because it can be accessed by the other nodes only if the creator communicates the value of variable l, which is the only way to access the fresh node. This operator was not present in Linda and is needed to deal with node dynamism and node creation

During tuple evaluation, expressions are computed and logical localities are mapped into physical ones. Evaluating a process implies substituting it with its *closure*, namely the process along with the environment of the node where the evaluation is taking place. Hence, a remarkable difference between **out**$(P)@l$ and **eval**$(P)@l$ is that **out** adds the closure of P to the tuple space located at l, while **eval** sends P, not its closure, for execution at l. This affects the evaluation of logical localities: when a process needs to map a logical locality into a physical one, first its own allocation environment is used (if it has one) and then, if the translation fails, the environment of the node where the process runs is used. This means that a process delivered with an **out** will use a *static scoping* strategy for logical localities while a process remotely spawned with an **eval** will use a *dynamic scoping* strategy. Thus, for instance, in the case of **out**$(P)@l$, self in P will refer to the originating site, while, in the case of **eval**$(P)@l$, self in P will refer to the new execution site of P.

The original KLAIM model of [DFP98] has been extended in [BLP02] to deal more directly with *open nets*. The original formalism is enriched with explicit connectivity actions and with a new kind of processes, that we called *Node Coordinators*, which are the only ones allowed to perform privileged connectivity actions. This distinction provides a fine-grain separation between the coordination level and the standard action execution level. The new model of KLAIM, called *hierarchical* KLAIM, also permits the programmer to decide explicitly whether the evaluation of tuples and processes has to take place. Furthermore, in the hierarchical model, the allocation environment can be modified dynamically with the primitive **bind**.

In the hierarchical model, any node plays both the role of computational environment (for processes and tuples), and a *gateway*, (for managing subnets of other nodes). Nodes can act both as clients (belonging to a specific subnet) and as servers (taking charge of, possibly private, subnets). Logical localities represent the names that client nodes can specify when entering the subnet of a server node, and allocation environments, that can be dynamically updated with such information, actually represent dynamic tables mapping logical names (possibly not known in advance) into physical addresses; these mappings are allowed to change during the evolution. The client-server relation among nodes smoothly leads to a hierarchical model, also because of the way logical names are "resolved": in order to find the mapping for a locality, allocation environments of nodes in this hierarchy are now inspected from the bottom upwards. This resembles name resolution within DNS servers. We shall consider further this issue in Section 8, where we will describe how node connectivity is managed in X-KLAIM.

We conclude this section with a description of the dining philosophers problem in in KLAIM. We will have a node for each chopstick (c_i) and a node for each philosopher (p_i). To indicate that the i−th chopstick is *free* we put the tuple ("chopstick") at c_i. Philosophers at p_i are described by the recursive processes below.

$$P_i =$$

> \# *think...*
> **in**("chopstick")@c_i.
> **in**("chopstick")@$c_{(i+1)\mathbf{mod}\ n}$.
> \# *eat...*
> **out**("chopstick")@c_i.
> **out**("chopstick")@$c_{(i+1)\mathbf{mod}\ n}$.
> P_i

The full system is described by the following term, where the local tuple spaces of a node is rendered by placing the relevant tuples after the name of the node.

$$c_0::(\text{"chopstick"}) \parallel p_0::P_0 \parallel$$
$$c_1::(\text{"chopstick"}) \parallel p_1::P_1 \parallel$$
$$c_2::(\text{"chopstick"}) \parallel p_2::P_2 \parallel$$
$$c_3::(\text{"chopstick"}) \parallel p_3::P_3 \parallel$$
$$c_4::(\text{"chopstick"}) \parallel p_4::P_4 \parallel$$
$$c_5::(\text{"chopstick"}) \parallel p_5::P_5$$

Obviously the solution presented above is prone to deadlock and tickets should be used to limit the number of philosophers attempting to grab a chopstick. This could be modeled by adding a locality T (table) where tickets are placed and philosophers need to get a ticket from the table before attempting to get the forks and to put it back after eating.

4 Programming Examples

In this section we will show that a few programming paradigms can be naturally modeled by means of the KLAIM based approach. We shall also consider a simple programming example that make evident the expressive power of KLAIM. We will also use the process algebra operators | and + for parallel composition of processes and nondeterministic choice [Mil89].

Programming Paradigms

Mobile Applications are distributed applications whose distinctive feature is the exploitation of "code mobility" [Tho97]. According to the classification proposed in [CGPV97], we can single out three paradigms for mobile computing that are largely used in network programming:

- *Remote Evaluation.* Any component of a distributed application can invoke services from other components by transmitting both the data needed to perform the service and the code that describes how to perform the service.
- *Mobile Agent* [Kna96, HCK94, Whi96]. A process (i.e., a program and an associated state of execution) on a given node of a network can migrate to a different node where it continues its execution from the current state.
- *Code On–Demand.* A component of a distributed application running on a given node, can dynamically download from a different component and link the code to perform a given task.

Below, we shall show how these paradigms for code mobility can be rendered in KLAIM. In the next section we shall also consider the issue of process mobility and discuss the differences between *weak*, *strong* and *full* mobility.

Remote Evaluation. Suppose we want to require that server located at location l evaluates code P with values $v_1, \ldots, v_n$ assigned to variables $x_1, \ldots, x_n$. We can use the instruction

$$\mathbf{out}(\mathbf{in}(!y_1, \ldots, !y_n)@l.A\langle y_1, \ldots, y_n\rangle, v_1, \ldots, v_n)@l$$

if we assume that $A(x_1, \ldots, x_n) \stackrel{def}{=} P$ and that the server performs

$$\mathbf{in}(!X, !x_1, \ldots, !x_n)@\texttt{self}.\mathbf{out}(x_1, \ldots, x_n)@\texttt{self}.X$$

or a similar actions.

Mobile Agents. Execution of process P at a remote location l can be implemented as

- **eval**$(P)@l$, if a dynamic scoping discipline for resolving location names is adopted,
- **newloc**$(!u).\mathbf{out}(P)@u.\mathbf{in}(!X)@u.\mathbf{eval}(X)@l$, when it is needed to guarantee the closure of P before moving it.

Code On-demand. It is simply programmed by means of an instruction of the form, **read**($!X$)@l, that permits downloading a program code P stored in a tuple with one field only (which contains P) from a (perhaps remote) location l.

Remote Procedure Calls

Also **Remote Procedure Calls** can be naturally modeled in KLAIM. We consider the case of a caller process (*caller*) that sends a request to the callee (*callee*) and waits for a response. The request, together with the name of the procedure and its actual parameters, contains the *caller*'s private locality where the response has to be delivered.

$$caller = \textbf{newloc}(u).\ \textbf{out}(procid, e_1, \ldots, e_n, u)@\ell_{callee}.$$
$$\textbf{in}(!y_1, \ldots, !y_k)@u.\ \langle \text{next behavior} \rangle.$$

Process *callee* waits for an invocation, executes the related procedure and sends back the results using the locality, passed together with the service request.

$$callee = \textbf{in}(!pid, !x_1, \ldots, !x_n, !u)@\texttt{self}.(callee \mid$$
$$\langle\ pid(x_1, \ldots, x_n) \rangle).\textbf{out}(r_1, \ldots, r_k)@u.\textbf{nil}).$$

When processes are allocated in a net, the local environment of *caller* assigns to the locality ℓ_{callee} the site where *callee* is located. Hence, we have:

$$N = s_1 ::_{\{s_1/\texttt{self}, s_2/l_{callee}\}} caller \parallel s_2 ::_{\{s_2/\texttt{self}\}} callee$$

A crucial role in this example is played by **newloc**(u) which permits a private data space to be created and accessed only via the variable u.

A Dynamic Newsgatherer

Consider the following scenario. User P needs additional information on a piece of data represented by *item*. Part of the behavior of P depends on this information. However, there are some activities which are independent of it. P can look for the required information in a database distributed over the network. We assume that at each node of the database reachable from ℓ_{item} contains either a tuple of the form $(item, v)$, with the desired information, or a tuple of the form $(item, \ell_{next})$, with the information about the next node to search for the additional information.

  The user process P asks for the execution at ℓ_{item} (the starting point of the search, which can be chosen according to the search key *item*) of the agent *gatherer*, which dynamically travels between nodes looking for a tuple that contains information on *item*. This agent takes as its parameters the research key *item* and a fresh locality u, which provides the address of the user's private tuple space where the result of the search has to be placed. Once *gatherer* has been spawned, P splits its behavior into two parallel components: one waits for the additional information and the other proceeds. Thus, those activities that do not need the additional information are decoupled from the search activity, which might be complex and expensive.

$$P = \textbf{newloc}(u).\textbf{eval}(gatherer(item, u))@\ell_{item}.((\textbf{in}(!x)@u.P_1) \mid P_2)$$

Process *gatherer* can match two alternative tuples. The first one captures the additional information on *item* (e.g., the price). If this is found then it is placed at locality *u* and *gatherer* terminates. The second tuple is used to obtain the address of the node where the search has to be repeated.

$$gatherer(item, u) = \quad \textbf{read}(item, !x)\,@\,\texttt{self}.\textbf{out}(x)\,@\,u.\textbf{nil}$$
$$+ \textbf{read}(item, !u')\,@\,\texttt{self}.\textbf{eval}(gatherer(item, u))\,@\,u'.\textbf{nil}$$

Our assumption about the structure of the distributed database guarantees that *gatherer* never deadlocks (because either the associated information or a location where the search can be repeated certainly found), but it does not ensure that the search activity will terminate successfully: *gatherer* might loop indefinitely. This could happen if its second tuple, the one with location information, always finds a match in the tuple spaces.

5   The Programming Language X-KLAIM

X-KLAIM (*eXtended* KLAIM) is an experimental programming language specifically designed to program distributed systems composed of several components interacting through multiple tuple spaces and mobile code (possibly object-oriented). X-KLAIM extends KLAIM with a high level syntax for processes: it provides variable declarations, enriched operations, assignments, conditionals, sequential and iterative process composition and object-oriented features based on mixin inheritance.

In the rest of the paper we will describe the syntax of X-KLAIM and provide some programming examples. The language relies on the hierarchical model of KLAIM, hinted in Section 3. Thus, it also provides all the primitives for explicitly dealing with node connectivity. However, X-KLAIM still provides flat network functionalities; in the first examples we present, we rely on a flat network topology, while hierarchical features are introduced in Section 8. The flat model can be enabled by using passing to the xklaim compiler the command line option -T 1; otherwise, by default, the compiler will generate code with hierarchical model features.

Moreover, X-KLAIM provides object-oriented features, i.e., object-oriented code mobility, structured via mixin-based inheritance, according to the philosophy of MoMi [BBV02, BBV04]. The object-oriented features of X-KLAIM will not be described in this paper (we refer to [Bet03]).

Syntax

X-KLAIM has a syntax that is quite similar to *Pascal* syntax; blocks of code are delimited by **begin end** and the character ';' is used as a separator for instructions and not as a terminator. This implies that the code

begin instr1 ; instr2 **end**

is syntactically correct, while the following one is not:

begin instr1 ; instr2 ; **end**

RecProcDefs	::= **rec** id formalparams procbody | **rec** id formalparams **extern**
	| RecProcDefs ; RecProcDefs
formalParams	::= [ ] | [paramlist]
paramlist	::= id : type | **ref** id : type | paramlist , paramlist
procbody	::= declpart **begin** proc **end**
declpart	::= ε | **declare** decl
decl	::= **const** id := expression | **locname** id | **var** idlist : type | decl ; decl
idlist	::= id | idlist , idlist
proc	::= KAction | **nil** | id := expression | **var** id : type | proc ; proc
	| **if** boolexp **then** proc **else** proc **endif**
	| **while** boolexp **do** proc **enddo**
	| **forall** Retrieve **do** proc **enddo**
	| procCall | **call** id | (proc) | **print** exp
KAction	::= **out**(tuple)@id | **eval**(proc)@id | Retrieve | **go**@id | **newloc**(id)
Retrieve	::= Block | NonBlock
Block	::= **in**(tuple)@id | **read**(tuple)@id
NonBlock	::= **inp**(tuple)@id | **readp**(tuple)@id | Block **within** numexp
boolexp	::= NonBlock | *standard bool exp*
tuple	::= expression | proc | **!** id | tuple , tuple
procCall	::= id (actuallist)
actuallist	::= ε | expression | proc | id | actuallist , actuallist
expression	::= ∗ expression | *standard exp*
id	::= *string*
type	::= **int** | **str** | **loc** | **logloc** | **phyloc** | **process** | **ts** | **bool**

Table 1. X-KLAIM process syntax. Syntax for other standard expressions is omitted

X-KLAIM is case-insensitive for keywords, but not for variable and process names. Comments start with the symbol # and terminate at the end of the line. An X-KLAIM program is made of some global process definitions and some node definitions.

The main computational unit in KLAIM and thus also in X-KLAIM is a process. The syntax of X-KLAIM processes is shown in Table 1. A process is addressable in an X-KLAIM program through its name, and can receive arguments and declare some local variables. Arguments are passed to a process by value, unless **ref** is used for declaring a formal parameter.

Variables and Localities

Local variables of processes are declared in the **declare** section of the process definition. Standard base types are available (**str**, **int**, **bool**) as well as X-KLAIM typical types, such as **loc**, **logloc** and **phyloc** for locality variables, **process** for process variables and **ts**, i.e., tuple space, for implementing data structures by means of tuple spaces, e.g., lists, that can be accessed through standard tuple space operations.

A formal parameter has simply the form <name>:<type>. A variable (resp. a list of variables with the same type) can be declared as follows:

var <name> : <**type**>
var <name_1>, ..., <name_n> : <**type**>

The same style can be used to declare a variable in the process body. A variable declared in the **declare** section is visible in the whole process body, while a variable declared in the process body is visible only in the code block where it is declared.

Constant variables are declared without specifying the type, since this is automatically inferred from their values:

const s := "foo" ; # *a string constant*
const b := **true** ; # *a boolean constant*
const i := 1971 ; # *an integer constant*

Logical locality constants are declared by using the type **locname**; the value of such a constant is represented by the symbol name itself.

A locality variable can be initialized with a string that will correspond to its actual value. Logical localities are basically names, while physical localities must have the form <IP_address>:<port>, so a physical locality variable has to be initialized with a string corresponding to an Internet address. The type **loc** represents a generic locality, without specifying whether it is logical or physical, while **logloc** (resp. **phyloc**) represents a logical (resp. physical locality). A simple form of subtyping is supplied for locality variables in that

$$\textbf{logloc} <: \textbf{loc} \qquad \textbf{phyloc} <: \textbf{loc}$$

Here are some examples of locality variable manipulations:

var l : **loc**;
var output : **logloc**;
var server : **phyloc**;
output := "screen";
server := "192.168.1.10:9999";
l := output; # *OK: a logical locality can be assigned to a locality*
l := server; # *OK: a physical locality can be assigned to a locality*

Logical locality resolution depends on the network model used in the program: the resolution takes place automatically in the flat model while, in the hierarchical model, it has to be explicitly invoked by putting the operator ∗ in front of the locality that has to be evaluated:

l := ∗output; # *retrieve the physical locality associated to output*
out(∗output)@self; # *insert the physical locality associated to output*

However logical localities used as "destination" are still evaluated automatically in both network models, i.e., if the locality used after the @ is a logical one, it is first translated to a physical locality.

Operations

Apart from standard KLAIM operations, X-KLAIM provides a non-blocking version of the retrieval operations, namely **readp** and **inp**; these act like **read** and **in**, but, if no matching tuple is found, they do not block the running process and simply return false. Thus these operations can be used where a boolean expression is expected.

```
if readp(!i, !j)@l and (not in("foo", !k)@self within 3000) then
  out(i, j)@self
else
  out(k)@self
endif
```

Listing 1. A more complex retrieval operation

Furthermore, a timeout (expressed in milliseconds) can be specified for **in** and **read**, through the keyword **within**; the operation is then a boolean expression that can be tested to determine whether the operation succeeded:

```
if in(!x, !y)@l within 2000 then
  # ... success!
else
  # ... timeout occurred
endif
```

Time-outs can be used when retrieving information for avoiding that processes block due to network latency bandwidth or to absence of matching tuples.

These boolean expressions can be combined in order to execute more complex retrieval operations, as in the example in Listing 1: the **if** succeeds if a tuple matching $(!i, !j)$ is present at l and no tuple matching $("foo", !k)$ is found at self within 3 seconds.

The compiler also performs some static analysis in order to check whether an identifier is initialized within a specific scope. The retrieval operations in X-KLAIM are binders for the formal fields of their tuples in the sense that after such an operation succeeded, the identifiers used as formal fields can be considered initialized. Thus, in the example in Listing 1, the out(i, j)@self is correct, since in the **then** branch both i and j are initialized; on the contrary out(k)@self is rejected, since the test of the if statement may have failed because of the readp(!i, !j)@l; thus in the **else** branch k may not be initialized. If **or** had been used, instead of **and**, in Listing 1, then out(k)@self would have been correct in the else branch, while out(i, j)@self would have been rejected in the then branch. The evaluation of boolean expressions in X-KLAIM is *lazy*.

Iterations

It is often useful to iterate over all elements of a tuple space matching a specific template. However, due to the inherent nondeterministic selection mechanism of pattern matching a subsequent **read** (or **readp**) operation may repeatedly return the same tuple, even if several other tuples match. Thus the following piece of code that aims at copying to a different node all tuples matching $(\mathbf{int}, \mathbf{str})$ after incrementing the first element is destined to fail

```
while readp(!i, !s)@self do
  out(i + 1, s)@l
enddo
```

since it could end up in an infinite loop, always modifying the same tuple. Repeatedly withdrawing such a tuple with **inp** does not solve the problem, since, in order not to be destructive on the original site, it would force to reinsert the withdrawn tuple, thus incurring in the same problem as above.

For this reason X-KLAIM provides the construct **forall** that can be used for iterating actions through a tuple space by means of a specific template. Its syntax is:

forall Retrieve **do**
 proc
enddo

We refer the reader to Table 1 for the syntax of "Retrieve". The informal semantics of this operation is that the loop body "proc" is executed each time a matching tuple is available. Even duplicate tuples are repeatedly retrieved by the **forall** primitive; it is however guaranteed that each tuple is retrieved only once. In Particular,

> **forall** guarantees that, given a template, each matching tuple is retrieved only once.

Thus, instead of the while-based code above we write:

forall readp(!i, !s)@`self` **do**
 out($i + 1$, s)@l
enddo

Now, if the tuple space contains three matching tuples (of which two are identical): (10, `"foo"`), (10, `"foo"`), (20, `"bar"`), after the execution of the loop instruction the tuple space at l will contain the tuples (11, `"foo"`), (11, `"foo"`), (21, `"bar"`).

Notice however that the tuple space is not blocked when the execution of the **forall** is started, thus this operation is not atomic: the set of tuples matching the template can change before the command completes. A locked access to such tuples can be explicitly programmed. Our version of **forall** is different from the one proposed in [BWA94] since parallel processes are not created for each retrieved tuple (this would not be consistent with the "iterating" nature of **forall**; a similar functionality could be easily achieved by using **eval** in the loop body). Our **forall** is similar to the **all** variations of retrieval operations in *PLinda* [AS92].

The **forall** primitive has a different semantics depending on the nature of the retrieval operation: if a blocking action is used, then the process executing **forall** is blocked until another (never retrieved) tuple becomes available; instead, when a nonblocking action is used, the process exits from the **forall** loop and continues its execution.

Data structures can be implemented by means of the data type **ts**; a variable declared with such type can be considered as a tuple space and can be accessed through standard tuple space operations, apart from **eval** that would not make sense when applied to variables of type **ts**. Furthermore **newloc** (see Section 8) has a different semantics when applied to a variable of type **ts**: it empties the tuple space.

forall is then useful for iterating through such data structures; for instance the following piece of code transforms a list, stored in the variable `list` of type **ts**, containing data of the form (**str**, **int**) into a list containing data of the form (**int**, **str**):

```
declare
  var s : str;
  var i : int;
  var list : ts;
...
forall inp(!s, !i)@list do
  out(i, s)@list
enddo
```

Notice that we use the non-blocking version of **in**, otherwise the process would be blocked when it finished iterating through the list.

Process Mobility

The operation **eval**(*P*)@*l* starts the process *P* on the node at locality *l*; *P* can be either a process name (and its arguments):

eval(P("foo", 10))@l

or the code (i.e., the actions) of the process to be executed:

eval(**in**(!i)@self; **out**(i)@l2)@l

Processes can also be used as tuple fields, such as in the following code:

out(P("foo", 10), **in**(!i)@self; **out**(i)@l2)@l

However, in this case, these processes are not started automatically at *l*: they are simply inserted in its tuple space. They can be retrieved (e.g., by another process executing at *l*) and explicitly evaluated:

in(!P1, !P2)@self;
eval(P1)@self;
eval(P2)@self

Thus, basically, **eval** provides *remote evaluation* functionalities, while **out** can be used to implement the *code on-demand* paradigm.

As for logical locality resolution, the network model used to compile and execute X-KLAIM programs influences the evaluation of processes sent with **out**: if the flat model is used, then the *closure* of the process is sent (as explained in Section 3 this means that all the logical localities of the sent process are translated before the process is sent, using the allocation environment of the starting node), while in the hierarchical model the process is sent without the closure (i.e., without the allocation environment). In the hierarchical model, if one wants to send the closure, he must prefix the process with * just like for localities.

According to the requirements made on the run-time support, code mobility can be classified as follows [CGPV97, HY98]:

- *weak mobility*: code coming from a different site can be dynamically linked;
- *strong mobility*: a thread can move its code and execution state to a different site and resume its execution on arrival;

— *full mobility*: in addition to strong mobility, the whole state of the running program is moved, and this includes all threads' stacks, namespaces (e.g., I/O descriptors, file-system names) and other resources, so that migration is completely transparent.

Full mobility can be considered orthogonal to mobile agents and requires a strong support from the operating system layer. Strong mobility is the notion of mobility that fits best in with the classical concept of mobile agent: the execution state of a migrating agent is suspended, and its stack and program counter are sent to the destination site, together with the relevant data; at the destination site, the stack of the agent is reconstructed and the program counter is set appropriately, i.e., to the first instruction after the migration action. Instead, weak mobility does not meet the intuitive idea of mobile agent, because automatic resumption of execution thread is one of the main features of mobile agents (it exalts their autonomy). X-KLAIM provides *strong mobility* by means of the action **go**@*l* (this is obtained through a preprocessing transformation at compile time, described in [BD01]) that makes an agent migrate to *l* and resume its execution at *l* from the instruction following the migration action. Thus in the following piece of code an agent retrieves a tuple from the local tuple space, then it migrates to the locality 1 and inserts the retrieved tuple into the tuple space at locality 1:

in(!i, !j)@self;
go@l;
out(i, j)@self

Input/Output

Also I/O operations in X-KLAIM are implemented as tuple space operations. For instance the logical locality *screen* can be attached (mapped) to the output device. Hence, operation **out**("foo\n")@*screen* corresponds to printing the string "foo\n" on the screen. Similarly, the locality *keyb* can be attached to the input device, so that a process can read what the user typed with a **in**(!s)@*keyb*. Further I/O devices, such as files, printers, etc., can also be handled through the locality abstraction. An example of this usage is shown in Section 9.

However, in order to make programming in X-KLAIM slightly easier, we also supply the instruction **print** that, given a string, prints it to the standard output, followed by a carriage return. String concatenation can be used to compose complex strings. Symbols and constants that do not have type **str** are automatically converted by the compiler:

print "the value of i is " + i + ". Is it < 10? " + (i < 10)

Type casts are supplied by X-KLAIM but only in a safe way. Indeed they are only a means for solving possible ambiguities. For instance the following instruction

out(**inp**(10)@self)@l

inserts the process **inp**(10)@self in the tuple space corresponding to *l*: since X-KLAIM is a higher-order language, the action **inp**(10)@self is interpreted as a process made only by such action. If on the contrary the programmer wants to actually insert the boolean result of **inp**(10)@self, he can do that by performing an explicit cast to type **bool**:

out((**bool**) **inp**(10)@self)@l

This way the program assumes the following semantics:

var b : **bool**;
b := **inp**(10)@self;
out(b)@1

Notice that every cast is checked by the compiler to verify that its validity; for instance the instruction

out((**bool**) **in**(10)@self)@1

would be rejected by the compiler, because **in** does not return a boolean value.

Apart from the implicit cast to string used for expressions printed with **print**, the compiler also performs other implicit cast when passing arguments to a process; thus, if P is a process that receives a boolean and a process, the process call

P(**inp**(10)@self, **inp**(10)@self)

is automatically converted to

P((**bool**) **inp**(10)@self, **inp**(10)@self)

Nodes

A process can execute only on a node since in KLAIM nodes are the execution engines. The syntax for defining a node in X-KLAIM is in Table 2. A node is defined by specifying its name (*id*), its allocation environment, some options (described later) and a set of processes running on it. An allocation environment contains the mapping from logical localities to physical localities of the form

    logical_locality_variable $\sim$ physical_locality_constant

thus it also implicitly declares the logical locality variables for all the processes defined in the node. Processes defined in a node have the same syntax of Table 1 but they do not have a name, since these processes are visible and accessible only from within the node where they were defined and not in the whole program. Basically the processes defined in a node correspond to the main entry point in languages such as Java and C.

NodeDefs	::= ε | **nodes** nodedefs **endnodes**
ProcDefs	::= ε | RecProcDefs
nodedefs	::= id **::** { environment } nodeoptions nodeprocdefs
	| nodedefs **;** nodedefs
environment	::= ε | id $\sim$ id | environment **,** environment
nodeprocdefs	::= procbody | nodeprocdefs **||** nodeprocdefs
nodeoptions	::= **class** id | **port** num

Table 2. X-KLAIM node syntax

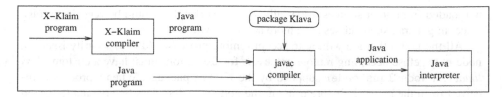

Fig. 1. The framework for X-KLAIM

With the option **class** it is possible to specify the actual Java class that has to be used for this node, and the option **port** can be used to specify the Internet port where the node is listening. Notice that, together with the IP address of the computer where the node will run, the port number defines the physical locality of the node.

Implementation

The implementation of X-KLAIM consists in the Java package KLAVA that provides the run-time system for X-KLAIM operations, and a compiler that translates X-KLAIM programs into Java programs that use KLAVA. The structure of such framework is depicted in Figure 1. Both X-KLAIM and KLAVA can be downloaded from `http://music.dsi.unifi.it`.

KLAVA [BDP02] can be seen both as a middleware for X-KLAIM programs and as a Java framework for programming according to the KLAIM paradigm. Thus, the programmer can use X-KLAIM to write the high level parts of a mobile application and can rely on KLAVA if he must write some customized low level parts in Java.

Java [AGH00] has been chosen as the implementation language because it supplies a natural support for programming distributed applications with mobile code. Indeed, Java supplies architectural independence, i.e., *on-line portability* [Car97], class libraries for network programming, tools for synchronization, dynamic class loading and customizable security mechanisms.

The code mobility issue is taken care by KLAVA in a transparent way. In KLAVA, processes can be sent as part of a message and executed at the destination site, where however their Java classes, i.e., their code, may be unknown. It is then necessary to make such code available for execution at remote hosts. Instead of an *on-demand* approach (where the code is requested to the server from which an agent is downloaded when it is needed), we prefer to collect all the code that a process needs, before dispatching it. This approach better complies with the mobile agents paradigm: during a migration, an agent will bring all the information that it may need for later executions. Moreover, our choice has the advantage of simplifying the handling of *disconnected operations* [PR98]: the agent owner does not have to stay connected after sending the agent and can connect later just to check whether his agent has terminated. This may not be possible with the on-demand approach: the server that sent the process must always be on-line in order to provide the classes needed by remote hosts.

Therefore, a process will be sent along with its class binary code, and with the class code of all the objects the process uses. Obviously, only the code of user defined classes has to be sent, as the other code (e.g. Java and KLAVA classes) is common to every KLAVA application. This guarantees that classes belonging to java sub-packages are not loaded from other sources (especially, the network); this would be very dangerous, since, in general, such classes have more access privileges.

All the nodes that are willing to accept remote processes (due to security issues, a node may refuse accepting remote processes for execution) must have a custom *class loader*: a NodeClassLoader supplied by the KLAVA package. When a process is received from the network, before using it, the node adds the class binary data (received along with the process) to its class loader's table. During process execution, whenever a class code is needed, if the class loader does not find the code in the local packages, then it can find it in its own local table of class binary data.

The names of user defined classes are retrieved by means of class introspection (*Java Reflection API*). Just before dispatching a process to a remote site, a recursive procedure is called for collecting all classes that are used by the process when declaring: data members, objects returned by or passed to a method/constructor, exceptions thrown by methods, inner classes, the interfaces implemented by its class, the base class of its class.

Due to security concerns Java does not allow dynamic inspection of byte code stack; this makes impossible to save the execution state for later use. For this reason, KLAVA can only permit *weak mobility* of agents that have to be restarted after the migration. On the contrary, as shown in Section 4, X-KLAIM, by relying on a source level transformation [BD01], also provides *strong mobility* by means of **go**@*l* operation (the mobile agent automatically resumes execution from the point after the migration).

Downloading code from the net exposes the executing machine to security risks, since this code could execute dangerous operations that could damage the system or the other executing processes. Klava provides a KlavaSecurityManager, which, if activated by the node, does not allow processes, downloaded from the net, or sent by remote nodes, to execute operations on system resources (such as files, and system properties).

6   Hello World in X-KLAIM

Usually the first program ever written in a language is the famous "Hello World". In this section we present several versions of the "Hello World" program in X-KLAIM. In particular, we shall present some local and some distributed variants.

Local Versions

This is the most direct way of writing "Hello World" in X-KLAIM:

```
# HelloWorld.xklaim
nodes
hello_world :: {}
 begin
  print "Hello World!"
 end
endnodes
```

After compiling the file HelloWorld.xklaim with the X-KLAIM compiler,

```
   xklaim HelloWorld.xklaim
```

and after compiling the resulting generated file `HelloWorld.java` with the Java compiler,

```
javac HelloWorld.java
```

the program can be started with the command

```
java HelloWorld
```

This will start the node `hello_world` listening on the standard port (9999) and the process printing `"Hello World"` is started on this node.

Notice: You must have the Java package KLAVA installed in order to compile the Java code generated by the compiler and then to run the Java programs.

An alternative way of writing the same program is to define a process for printing the string, and then run that process from within the node:

 # HelloWorld2.xklaim
rec HelloProc[]
  begin
   print "Hello World!"
  end

nodes
hello_world2 :: {}
  begin
   eval(HelloProc())@`self`
  end
endnodes

By compiling this program you will notice that the compiler generates a Java program with the same name of the original source (e.g., containing the class `HelloWorld2` with the `main` method), and a separate Java source for each process (e.g., `HelloProc.java`). Of course you have to compile all the Java sources generated by the compiler in order to run the program.

This way the code of the process `HelloProc` can be reused by other nodes in the same program. Indeed, it can also be used by other programs: they can import its implementation as follows

rec HelloProc[] **extern**

nodes
hello_world3::{}
  begin
   eval(HelloProc())@`self`
  end
endnodes

Of course, the `HelloProc.java` must have already been generated by the `xklaim` compiler. Notice, however, that in this case the `xklaim` compiler will not actually check that a process `HelloProc` is actually defined in some other source. If this is not the case, when you compile the corresponding generated Java sources, you may get an error by the Java compiler if such a process cannot be found anywhere. Thus, the **extern** keyword is exactly the same as in the language C.

Distributed Versions

A distributed version of the "Hello World" program can be easily built in X-KLAIM. We can write the sender and the receiver into two separate files:

```
# HelloSender.xklaim, compile it with option −T 1
rec HelloSenderProc[ dest : loc ]
 begin
  out("Hello World!")@dest
 end

nodes
hello_sender::{receiver ~ localhost:11000}
 port 10000
 begin
  eval(HelloSenderProc(receiver))@self
 end
endnodes
```

The sender node maps the logical locality *receiver* to the physical locality `localhost:11000`, and passes the logical locality to the sender process that simply puts a tuple containing the string `"Hello World"` in the tuple space of the remote node[1]. Notice that this node also specifies its physical locality, by declaring its port. Finally, in order to keep the example simple, we rely on the flat network model of KLAIM, where all nodes belong to the same net, and they are all at the same level. For this reason, we have to pass the option `-T 1` to the `xklaim` compiler when we compile this source:

```
xklaim HelloSender.xklaim -T 1
```

The receiver node, that is executing on `localhost` listening on port 11000, simply waits for a tuple made of a string and prints the received message (again use the option `-T 1`):

```
# HelloReceiver.xklaim, compile it with option −T 1
nodes
hello_receiver::{}
 port 11000
```

---

[1] In this simple example, we assume that all nodes run on the same machine — for this reason we use the `localhost` address. Of course, you can experiment by running the two nodes on different machines and in that case you have to substitute `localhost` with the correct IP of the receiver node

```
declare
 var msg : str
begin
 in(!msg)@self;
 print "received: " + msg
end
endnodes
```

Now, after compiling all the programs (and also the generated Java sources), you cannot simply run the two programs, since the two nodes expect to connect to a net server (we are using the flat model in these examples). Thus, you must first run the KLAVA net server (the port number is optional, by default it is 9999):

```
java Klava.Net 9999
```

and then run the receiver node, by specifying the address and the port number of the net server:

```
java HelloReceiver localhost 9999
```

and when the receiver node is connected to the net server, you can start the sender:

```
java HelloSender localhost 9999
```

Since the two nodes are connected to the same net server, they will be able to communicate.

Another possibility is to send the HelloSenderProc process directly to the receiver site so that it can out the tuple locally:

```
# HelloSender2.xklaim, compile it with option −T 1
rec HelloSenderProc[ dest : loc ] extern

nodes
hello_sender2::{receiver ˜ localhost:11000}
 port 10000
 begin
  eval(HelloSenderProc(self))@receiver
 end
endnodes
```

Notice that the process that outs the tuple is just the same as before (since it is parameterized over the destination locality), and the sender passes self as the destination locality to the process and spawns the process for execution at the receiver site. Further mobility examples are shown in Section 7.

7   Mobility Examples

In this section we show a few programming examples taking advantage of process mobility, implemented in X-KLAIM.

```
rec NewsGatherer[ item : str, itemVal : str, finish : bool, retLoc : loc ]
 declare
   var itemVal : str ;
   var nextLoc : loc
 begin
   if not finish then
     if read( item, !itemVal )@self within 10000 then
       eval( NewsGatherer( item, itemVal, true, retLoc ) )@retLoc
     else
       if readp( item, !nextLoc )@self then
         eval( NewsGatherer( item, "", false, retLoc ) )@nextLoc
       else
         eval( NewsGatherer( item, "", true, retLoc ) )@retLoc
       endif
     endif
   else
     if itemVal != "" then print "found " + itemVal
     else print "search failed" endif
   endif
 end
```

Listing 2. X-KLAIM implementation of a news gatherer using **eval**

News Gathering

The first example is a *news gatherer*, that relies on mobile agents for retrieving information on remote sites (it is the implementation in X-KLAIM of the KLAIM program shown in Section 4). We assume that some data are distributed over the nodes of an X-KLAIM net and that each node either contains the information we are searching for, or, possibly, the locality of the next node to visit in the net.

The agent *NewsGatherer* first tries to read a tuple containing the information we are looking for, if such a tuple is found, the agent returns the result back home; if no matching tuple is found within 10 seconds, the agent tests whether a link to the next node to visit is present at the current node; if such a link is found the agent migrates there and continues the search, otherwise it reports the failure back home.

The first implementation of such an agent is shown in Listing 2 and employs **eval** for spawning an instance of the agent to a remote site. Since **eval** implements weak mobility, it is necessary to explicitly spawn a new copy to the new site, passing all the parameters representing the execution state of the agent: the boolean finish says whether the agent has visited all the possible sites, and the search is considered successful if itemVal is not empty.

Notice that the source of the agent is a little bit complex, since it might not be clear, at first glance, what the agent is supposed to do. One can use strong mobility in order to make the source clearer. The implementation of the agent exploiting strong mobility (by means of the migration operation **go**) is reported in Listing 3.

Information Retrieval

The next example is still an autonomous information retrieval agent in the context of a virtual *market place*: suppose that someone wants to buy a specific product at a mar-

```
rec NewsGatherer[ item : str, retLoc : loc ]
 declare
   var itemVal : str ;
   var nextLoc : loc ;
   var again : bool
 begin
  again := true;
  while again do
   if read( item, !itemVal )@self within 10000 then
     go@retLoc;
     print "found  " + itemVal;
     again := false;
   else
    if readp( item, !nextLoc )@self then
     go@nextLoc
    else
     go@retLoc;
     print "search failed";
     again := false
    endif
   endif
  enddo
 end
```

Listing 3. X-KLAIM implementation of a news gatherer using strong mobility

ket made of geographically distributed shops. To decide at which shop to buy, she/he activates a migrating agent which is programmed to find and return the name of the closest shop (i.e., the shop within the chosen area, determined by a maximal distance parameter) with the lowest price. The implementation of the agent MarketPlaceAgent is shown in Listing 4.

The MarketPlaceAgent takes as parameters the product name, the maximal distance and the locality where the result of the search must be returned. The agent is sent (by means of an **eval** not shown here) for execution at the node containing the marketplace directory, where it asks for the list of the shops in the selected shopping area. Then, MarketPlaceAgent migrates to the first shop in the list. At each shop, MarketPlaceAgent checks the price of the wanted product, possibly updating the information about the lowest price and the shop that offers it, and migrates to the next shop in the list. If there are no more shops to visit, MarketPlaceAgent sends the result of the search back to the locality received as parameter. The list of nodes to visit is stored in a list (implemented through a **ts**) and **forall** is used for iterating over this list.

Screenshot 1 shows a client that performs some searches through the MarketPlaceAgent in two shops. In this example there are two shops affiliated to the market place: Shop1 at physical locality 127.0.0.1:11000 with a distance of 3, and Shop2 at physical locality 127.0.0.1:11005 with a distance of 5; this information is shown in the window of the market place directory (up left). The client sends the agent searching for a camera within a distance of 10, so the market place directory provides the agent with a list made of the localities of the two shops, and after visiting both, the agent reports home that the first shops sells the searched item at the lower cost.

```
rec MarketPlaceAgent[ ProductMake : str, retLoc : loc, distance : int ]
 declare
  var shopList : TS ;
  var nextShop, CurrentShop, thisShop : loc ;
  var CurrentPrice, newCost : int ;
  locname screen
 begin
  out( "cshop", distance )@self; # ask for a list of shops within a distance
  in( "cshop", !shopList )@self;
  out( "retrieved list: ", shopList )@screen;
  CurrentPrice := 0 ;
  CurrentShop := self ;
  forall inp( ! nextShop )@shopList do  # while there are shops to visit
   thisShop := nextShop ;
   go@nextShop ; # migrate to the next shop ;
   out( "AgentClient: searching for ", ProductMake )@screen ;
   if read( ProductMake, ! newCost )@self within 10000 then
    if ( CurrentPrice = 0 OR newCost < CurrentPrice ) then
     CurrentPrice := newCost; # update the best price
     CurrentShop := thisShop
    endif
   endif
  enddo ;
  out( ProductMake, CurrentShop, CurrentPrice )@retLoc # OK, let's send the results
 end
```

Listing 4. X-KLAIM implementation of an agent visiting shops of a virtual market place searching for an item with the lowest price

Screenshot 1. The market place directory (up left), the market client (down left) and two shops of the virtual market place

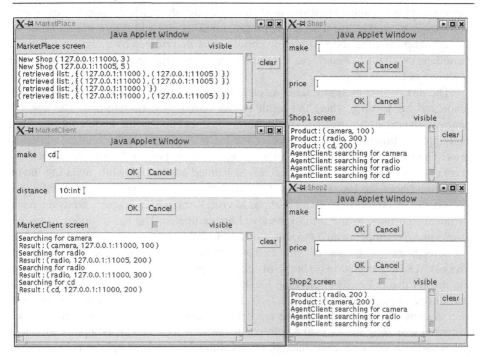

The second query has basically the same parameters but the agent has to search for a `radio` and this time the second shop sells it at the lower price. Then it still searches for a radio but within a closer distance (e.g., 4) and this time the second shop is not even visited (since its distance is 5, so the market place directory does not put it into the list communicated to the agent). Finally a `cd` is searched for (within a wider distance) and when visiting the second shop a timeout is raised, since that shop does not sell that item.

Load Balancing

We conclude this section by presenting an example that uses the remote evaluation paradigm, thus, the code does not to autonomously migrate: it is moved by another process. This example implements a *load balancing system* that dynamically redistributes mobile code among several processors: we suppose that remote clients send processes for execution to a server node that distributes the received processes among a group of processors by using, each time, the (estimated) idlest one. Each processor sends a number of "credits" to the server (this number corresponds to the processor availability to perform computations on behalf of the server); the server stores the number of credits in a database and, when needed, it chooses the processor with the highest number of credits and decreases this number.

When a processor receives a process, it immediately starts executing the process (in a parallel thread) and sends a credit back to the server. Indeed, the system is based on the heuristic that if a processor is busy, it cannot send a credit back, or at least it does not send a credit immediately (this is also known as *Leaky Bucket Of Credits* pattern [ACG+96]).

```
rec DeliverProcess[ ProcessorDB : ts ]
  declare
    var P : process ;
    var HighestCredit, Credits : int ;
    var Processor, HighestProcessor : loc
  begin
    while ( true ) do
      in( !P )@self ; # wait for a process
      HighestCredit := 0 ;
      forall readp( !Processor, !Credits )@ProcessorDB do
        if ( Credits > HighestCredit ) then
          HighestCredit := Credits ;
          HighestProcessor := Processor
        endif
      enddo ;
      out( P )@HighestProcessor ;
      # update its credits
      in( HighestProcessor, HighestCredit )@ProcessorDB ;
      out( HighestProcessor, HighestCredit − 1 )@ProcessorDB
    enddo
  end
```

```
rec ReceiveProcess[ server : loc ]
  declare
    var P : process ;
    locname screen
  begin
    while ( true ) do
      in( !P )@self ;
      eval( P )@self ;
      out( "SERVER", "CREDIT",
           self )@server
    enddo
  end
```

Listing 5. Load balancing: (left) the server receives a process and dispatches it to the idlest processor; (right) the processor node receives a process and executes it locally and sends a credit back to the server

This example is implemented by the code fragment in Listing 5 that shows the server that dispatches the received process to the idlest processor (left) and the processor that receives a process for execution from the server and sends a credit back to it. The code presented here is simplified in order to concentrate on the code mobility related parts (e.g., it does not handle cases such as all credits are exhausted for all processors). Notice that processes are exchanged by means of **out** and **in**. Since in the hierarchical mode processes are not automatically "closed" when sent with an **out**, then when a process is executed in a processor it will actually use the local resources.

The overall architecture of this load balancing system is based on a *push* model, in that the server delivers the processes to be executed to a chosen processor node. An alternative implementation could be based on a *pull* model: a processor node, when idle, asks the server for a process to be executed. This architecture can be employed to develop systems similar to *SETI@home* [KWA+01] that uses Internet-connected computers in the *Search for Extraterrestrial Intelligence* (*SETI*): users that want to help the project can install this software that downloads data to be analyzed from the server when the computer is idle (for instance when the screen saver starts).

8   Node Connectivity in X-KLAIM

X-KLAIM provides all the primitives for explicitly dealing with node connectivity (see Section 3). Consistently with the hierarchical model of KLAIM such actions can be performed only by *node coordinators*. The syntax of node coordinators is shown in Table 3, and is basically the same of standard X-KLAIM processes (Table 1) apart from the new privileged actions. We briefly comment these new actions:

- **login**(*loc*), where *loc* is an expression of type **loc**, logs the node where the node coordinator is executing at the node at locality *loc*; **logout**(*loc*) logs the node out from the net managed by the node at locality *loc*. **login** can be used as a boolean expression in that it returns **true** if the login succeeds and **false** otherwise.

```
NodeCoordinator ::= rec NodeCoordDef
NodeCoordDef    ::= nodecoord id formalparams declpart nodecoordbody
                  |  nodecoord id formalparams extern
nodecoordbody   ::= begin nodecoordactions end
nodecoordaction ::= standard process action | login( id ) | logout( id )
                  |  accept( id ) | disconnected( id ) | disconnected( id , id )
                  |  subscribe( id , id ) | unsubscribe( id , id )
                  |  register( id , id ) | unregister( id )
                  |  newloc( id ) | newloc( id , nodecoordactions )
                  |  newloc( id , nodecoordactions , num , classname )
                  |  bind( id , id ) | unbind( id )
                  |  dirconnect( id ) | acceptconn( id )
```

Table 3. X-KLAIM node coordinator syntax. This syntax relies on standard process syntax shown in Table 1

```
rec nodecoord SimpleLogin[ server : loc ]
  begin
    print "try to login to " +
      server + "...";
    if login( server ) then
      print "login successful";
      out("logged", true)@self
    else
      print "login failed!"
    endif
  end


rec nodecoord SimpleLogout[ server : loc ]
  begin
    in("logged", true)@self;
    print "logging off from " +
      server + "...";
    logout(server);
    print "logged off."
  end
```

```
rec nodecoord SimpleAccept[]
  declare
    var client : phyloc
  begin
    print "waiting for clients...";
    accept(client);
    print "client " + client + " logged in"
  end

rec nodecoord SimpleDisconnected[]
  declare
    var client : phyloc
  begin
    print "waiting for disconnections...";
    disconnected(client);
    print "client " + client +
      " disconnected."
  end
```

Listing 6. An example showing **login** and **logout** (left) and the corresponding **accept** and **dis-connected**

- **accept**(*l*) is the complementary action of **login** and indeed, the two actions have to synchronize in order to succeed; thus a node coordinator on the server node (the one at which other nodes want to log) has to execute **accept**. This action initializes the variable *l* to the physical locality of the node that is logging. **disconnected**(*l*) notifies that a node has disconnected from the current node; the physical locality of such node is stored in the variable *l*. **disconnected** also catches connection failures. Notice that both **accept** and **disconnected** are blocking in that they block the running process until the event takes place. Instead, **logout** does not have to synchronize with **disconnected**.

An example of these four operations is shown in Listing 6, where the node coordinators executing on the client are presented on the left, and the complementary ones executing on the server are presented on the right. Notice that the process that executes the **login** communicates with the one that has to execute the **logout** by using a tuple. **accept** and **disconnected** are initializers for the corresponding variables.

- **subscribe**(*loc*, *logloc*) is similar to **login**, but it also permits specifying the logical locality (*logloc* is an expression of type **logloc**) with which a node wants to become part of the net coordinated by the node at locality *loc*; this request can fail also because another node has already subscribed with the same logical locality at the same server. **unsubscribe**(*loc*, *logloc*) performs the opposite operation.
- **register**(*pl*, *ll*), where *pl* is a physical locality variable and *ll* is a logical locality variable, is the complementary action of **subscribe** that has to be performed on the server; if the subscription succeeds *pl* and *ll* will respectively contain the physical and the logical locality of the subscribed node. The association *pl* ∼ *ll* is automatically added to the allocation environment of the server. **unregister**(*pl*, *ll*) records

```
rec nodecoord SimpleSubscribe[ server : phyloc, name : logloc ]
  begin
    print "try to subscribe at " + server +
    " as " + name + "...";
    if subscribe( server, name ) then
      print "subscribe successful";
      out("subscribed", true)@self
    else
      print "subscribe failed!"
    endif
  end


rec nodecoord SimpleUnsubscribe[ server : phyloc, name : logloc ]
  begin
    in("subscribed", true)@self;
    print "now unsubscribing from " + server +
    " as " + name + "...";
    unsubscribe(server, name);
    print "unsubscribed."
  end


rec nodecoord SimpleRegister[]
  declare
    var clientloc : logloc;
    var client : phyloc
  begin
    print "waiting for clients to subscribe...";
    if register(client, clientloc) then
      print "client " + clientloc + "~" +
        client + " subscribed"
    else
      print "client failed to subscribe"
    endif
  end


rec nodecoord SimpleUnregister[]
  declare
    var client : logloc
  begin
    print "waiting for unsubscription...";
    unregister(client);
    print "client " + client + " unsubscribed."
  end
```

Listing 7. An example showing **subscribe** and **unsubscribe** (left) and the corresponding **register** and **unregister**

the unsubscriptions. Notice that an alternative version of **disconnected**, namely **disconnected**(*pl, ll*) is supplied, in order to detect lost connections with nodes, that also specifies the logical locality with which a node was subscribed. As the other **disconnected** explained above, this action is more powerful in that it is able to catch also connections brutally closed without an **unsubscribe**. Let us observe that **disconnected** catches also the events of **unregister** so if program uses both, it is up to the programmer to coordinate the two notification actions (an example of such a scenario is shown in Section 9).

An example using these actions is presented in Listing 7; the processes are basically similar to those presented in Listing 6, but they also deal with logical localities.

bind(*logloc, phyloc*) allows to dynamically modify the allocation environment of the current node: it adds the mapping *logloc* ~ *phyloc*. On the contrary, **unbind**(*logloc*) removes the mapping associated to the logical locality *logloc*. These two operations privileged and only node coordinators can execute them.

In this version of X-KLAIM **newloc** has become a privileged action and is supplied in three forms in order to make programming easier: apart from the standard form that only takes a locality variable, where the physical locality of the new created node is stored, also the form **newloc**(*l*, *nodecoordinator*) is provided. Since **newloc** does not automatically logs the new created node in the net of the creating node, this second form allows to install a node coordinator in the new node that can perform this action (or other privileged actions).

Notice that this is the only way of installing a node coordinator on another node: due to security reasons, node coordinators cannot migrate, and cannot be part of a tuple. In order to provide better programmability, this rule is slightly relaxed: a node coordinator can perform the **eval** of a node coordinator, provided that the destination is self.

Finally the third form of **newloc** takes two additional arguments: the port number where the new node is going to be listening (and this also determines its physical lo-

```
rec nodecoord SimpleDirConn[ peer : loc ]
  declare
    var test : str
  begin
    print "establishing direct connection to " +
    peer;
    if dirconnect(peer) then
      print "established";
      out("TEST")@peer;
      in(!test)@peer;
      print "sent and receive " + test
    else
      print "direct connection to " +
      peer + " failed."
    endif
  end
;

rec nodecoord SimpleAcceptConn[]
  declare
    var peer : phyloc
  begin
    print "waiting for direct connections...";
    acceptconn(peer);
    print "accepted direct connection from " + peer
  end

nodes
mandirconnpeer2 :: { }
  port 11000
  class "NetNode"
  start
  declare
    var peer : phyloc
  begin
    eval(SimpleAcceptConn())@self;
    peer := "127.0.0.1:9999";
    eval(SimpleDirConn(peer))@self
  end
endnodes
```

Listing 8. An example showing **dirconnect** and **acceptconn** for establishing a *peer to peer* direct communication

cality, since the IP address will be the same of the creator node), and the (Java) class of the new node. Since I/O devices can be abstracted into nodes, this form of **newloc** enables to construct, for instance, the graphical interface of a node, made up of several I/O sub-nodes. For an example, see Section 9, where some I/O logical localities are used as interfaces for text areas, and input text boxes and lists.

In this scenario communications among nodes belonging to the same subnet take place, through the gateway node. In case of firewalls or network restrictions the access to a remote node may be permitted only through a server. For instance, an applet can only open a network connection towards the computer it has been downloaded from. If on this computer there is a `NetNode` running that is willing to act as a gateway, the applet is still able to indirectly communicate with all the nodes and, possibly, with applets that are part of that net managed by that gateway. In this sense, a `NetNode` gateway allows nodes to communicate even if they belong to different restricted domains. However, when there are no network restrictions, direct connections can still be established in order to use a direct (probably faster) communication between nodes of the same, or different, subnet.

In X-KLAIM *direct connections* can be dealt with explicitly, so we provide the complementary privileged action **dirconnect**(*loc*) and **acceptconn**(*l*) that allow to create a unidirectional direct communication channel. Thus if a node n_1 establishes a direct connection with the node n_2 every time n_1 sends a message to n_2 it will do this directly, i.e., without passing through a possible common server. This situation is not symmetric since the direct connection is unidirectional. Should one want a bidirectional *peer to peer* communication, this has to be programmed explicitly so that upon accepting a direct connection from a node, also the other way direction is established.

```
rec nodecoord SimpleAcceptConnAndConnect[]
  declare
    var peer : phyloc
  begin
    print "waiting for direct connections...";
    acceptconn(peer);
    print "accepted direct connection from "
      + peer;
    print "now connecting to " + peer;
    if dirconnect(peer) then
      print "established"
    else
      print "direct connection to " +
        peer + " failed."
    endif
  end


nodes
mandirconnpeer1 :: { }
  class "NetNode"
  start
  begin
    eval(SimpleAcceptConnAndConnect())@self
  end
endnodes
```

Listing 9. An example showing **dirconnect** and **acceptconn** for establishing a *peer to peer* direct communication

An example is presented in Listing 8 and 9; here also the node definitions are shown in order to clarify the scenario: `mandirconnpeer2` (Listing 8) wants to engage a peer to peer communication with the node at locality `127.0.0.1:9999`, thus, it executes a node coordinator for establishing the direct connection, and also executes a node coordinator for accepting the corresponding direct connection request (from the other peer). The other peer `mandirconnpeer1` (Listing 9) executes the complementary protocol by running a node coordinator that first accepts a direct connection and then establishes a direct connection to the same node.

The node that first tries to establish the direct connection (`mandirconnpeer2` in this example) should execute the **dirconnect** and **acceptconn** in two parallel processes: if it executed the two actions in sequence, the **acceptconn** would not be guaranteed to start before the other peer started its request. This would probably lead to a deadlock. The other peer (`mandirconnpeer1` in this example), instead, can safely execute the complementary **acceptconn** and **dirconnect** in sequence.

9   A Chat System with Connectivity Actions

In this section we present the implementation in X-KLAIM of a chat system. The chat system we present in this section is simplified, but it implements the basic features that are present in several chat systems. The system consists of a `ChatServer` and many `ChatClients`.

The system is dynamic because new clients can enter the chat and existing clients may disconnect. The server represents the gateway through which the clients can communicate, and the clients logs in the chat server by specifying their "nickname", represented here by a logical locality. A client that wants to enter the chat must subscribe at the chat server. The server must keep track of all the registered clients and, when a client sends a message, the server has to deliver the message to every connected client. If the message is a private one, it will be delivered only to the clients in the list specified along with the message.

The Chat Server

When a new client issues a subscription request, the server accepts it only if there is no other client with the same nickname, and in case the access is granted, every client is notified about the new client; moreover the new client is also provided with the list of the clients currently in the chat (Listing 10). The server keeps a database of all connected clients in a variable `usersDB` of type **ts** where there is a tuple of the shape (`nickname`, `locality`) for each client, where `nickname` is a logical locality and `locality` is a physical one. Notice that all the processes running on the chat server share this database.

The server uses two (node coordinator) processes for intercepting clients' disconnections: `HandleUnregister` and `HandleDisconnected`. The second one would be useless if the network communications are reliable (i.e., no communication suddenly crashes without further notice); however, this assumption may be too strong in a realistic scenario. Thus `HandleDisconnected` intercepts also this kind of disconnections. As we said above the **disconnected** action returns even after an ordinary unsubscrip-

```
rec nodecoord HandleLogin[ usersDB : ts ]
 declare
   var nickname : logloc ;
   var client : phyloc ;
   locname users, screen, server
 begin
   while ( true ) do
    if register( client, nickname ) then
      out( nickname, client )@usersDB ;
      out( true )@client ;
      SendUserList( client, usersDB ) ;
      out( (str)nickname )@users ;
      out( "Entered Chat : " )@screen ;
      out( nickname, client )@screen ;
      BroadCast( "USER", "ENTER",
              nickname, server, usersDB )
    endif
   enddo
 end

rec SendUserList[ newEnter : phyloc, usersDB : ts ]
 declare
   var nickname : logloc ;
   var userLoc : phyloc ;
   var userList : ts
 begin
   newloc( userList ) ;
   forall readp( !nickname, !userLoc )@usersDB do
    if ( userLoc != newEnter ) then
      out( nickname )@userList
    endif
   enddo ;
   out( userList )@newEnter
 end
```

```
rec nodecoord HandleDisconnected[ usersDB : ts ]
 declare
   var nickname : logloc ;
   var client : phyloc ;
   locname screen
 begin
   while ( true ) do
    disconnected(client, nickname);
    out("disconnected: ", nickname, client)@screen;
    RemoveClient(nickname, usersDB)
   enddo
 end

rec nodecoord HandleUnregister[ usersDB : ts ]
 declare
   var nickname : logloc ;
   locname screen
 begin
   while ( true ) do
    unregister(nickname);
    out("unsubscription: ", nickname)@screen;
    RemoveClient(nickname, usersDB)
   enddo
 end

rec RemoveClient[ nickname : logloc, usersDB : ts ]
 declare
   var client : phyloc ;
   locname screen, users, server
 begin
   if inp( nickname, !client )@usersDB and
      inp( (str)nickname )@users then
      out( "Left Chat : " )@screen ;
      out( nickname, client )@screen ;
      BroadCast( "USER", "LEAVE",
              nickname, server, usersDB )
   endif
 end
```

Listing 10. Node coordinators of the chat server dealing with clients' subscriptions

tion, so the process RemoveClient has to further check whether a client has already been removed from the database.

The broadcasting of messages to clients is managed by two processes running on the ChatServer node: BroadCast and BroadCastTo (Listing 11): the former sends a message to all connected clients while the latter sends a message only to the clients specified in the list to. This second version is useful when delivering *personal* messages.

All messages have the following tuple shape:

$$(\texttt{communication\_type, message\_type, message, from})$$

where communication_type and message_type specify the type of message (e.g., the values "USER" together with "ENTER" indicate that a user entered the chat, while "MESSAGE" and "ALL" indicate a chat message that is destined to every client). message is the content of the message (e.g., the nickname of the user that entered the chat or the body of a chat message) and from is the nickname (logical locality) of the client that originated the message.

```
rec HandleMessage[ usersDB : ts ]
declare
  var message : str ;
  var sender : logloc ;
  var from : phyloc
begin
  while ( true ) do
    in( "MESSAGE", !message, !from )@self ;
    if readp( !sender, from )@usersDB then
      BroadCast( "MESSAGE", "ALL",
            message, sender, usersDB )
    endif # ignore errors
  enddo
end


rec HandlePersonal[ usersDB : ts ]
declare
  var message : str ;
  var sender : logloc ;
  var from : phyloc ;
  var to : ts
begin
  while ( true ) do
    in( "PERSONAL", !message, !to, !from )@self ;
    if readp( !sender, from )@usersDB then
      BroadCastTo( "MESSAGE", "PERSONAL",
            message, to, sender, usersDB )
    endif
  enddo
end
```

```
rec BroadCast[ communication_type : str, message_type : str,
            message : str, from : logloc, usersDB : ts ]
declare
  var nickname : logloc ;
  var user : phyloc
begin
  forall readp( !nickname, !user )@usersDB do
    out( communication_type, message_type,
            message, from )@user
  enddo
end


rec BroadCastTo[ communication_type : str, message_type : str,
            message : str, to : ts, from : logloc, usersDB : ts ]
declare
  var nickname : str ;
  var user : phyloc
begin
  forall inp( !nickname )@to do
    # recipients are specified as strings in the "to" list
    # so we have to convert them first
    if readp( (logloc) nickname, !user )@usersDB then
      out( communication_type, message_type,
            message, from )@user
    endif
  enddo
end
```

Listing 11. Processes on the server dealing with message dispatching

Messages are received by the chat server by means of two processes `HandleMessage` and `HandlePersonal` (respectively for standard chat messages and for personal messages) also shown in Listing 11. When a client wants to send a personal message it has to specify also a list (a **ts** tuple field) containing the nicknames of the clients it is destined to). These processes are responsible for delivering a message to all the recipient clients.

The Chat Client

A chat client executes two processes for handling messages dispatched by the server (Listing 12): `HandleMessages` takes care of processing chat messages and `HandleServerMessages` handles server messages informing of new clients joining the chat or existing clients leaving (the list of connected clients is updated accordingly). This information is printed on the screen of the client (attached to the locality `screen`).

The user can insert messages for the server (i.e., commands for entering and exiting from the chat) and standard chat messages in two text fields that are attached, respectively, to the localities `serverKeyb` and `messageKeyb`. For each of these localities there is a process, respectively `HandleServerKeyboard` and `HandleMessageKeyboard` (also in Listing 12) that read the input of the user and communicate with the server. When `HandleServerKeyboard` reads a tuple of the shape (`"ENTER"`, `nickname`) it tries to subscribe at the chat server with that specific nickname. On the contrary, if the tuple contains `"LEAVE"` it unsubscribes.

```
                                          rec nodecoord HandleServerKeyboard[]
                                            declare
                                              locname server, screen, serverKeyb, usersList;
                                              var command, nick : str ;
                                              var nickname : logloc ;
                                              var response : bool ;
                                              var chat_server : phyloc ;
                                              var userList : ts
                                            begin
                                              chat_server := *server;
  rec HandleMessages[]                        while ( true ) do
    declare                                     in( !command, !nick )@serverKeyb ;
      locname screen ;                          if ( command != "ENTER" and command != "LEAVE" ) then
      const standard_message := "MESSAGE";        out( "Unknown command: " )@screen ;
      var message, message_type : str ;           out( command )@screen ;
      var from : logloc                           out( "\n" )@screen
    begin                                       else
      while ( true ) do                           # nick was entered as a string
        in( standard_message, !message_type,      nickname := (logloc) nick;
          !message, !from )@self ;                if command = "ENTER" then
        if message_type = "PERSONAL" then           if subscribe( chat_server, nickname ) then
          out( "PERSONAL " )@screen                    out( "Succeeded command: " )@screen ;
        endif;                                         in( !userList )@self ;
        out( "(" )@screen ;                            UpdateUserList( userList )
        out( (str)from )@screen ;                    else
        out( ") " )@screen ;                            out( "Failed command: " )@screen
        out( message )@screen ; out( "\n" )@screen     endif
      enddo                                         else # it is a LEAVE
    end                                               unsubscribe( chat_server, nickname ) ;
                                                       out("command", "removeAll")@usersList
                                                     endif ;
  rec HandleServerMessages[]                         out( command, nickname )@screen
    declare                                        endif
      locname screen, usersList ;                enddo
      const user_message := "USER" ;           end
      var command, nickname : str;
      var from : logloc
    begin                                     rec HandleMessageKeyboard[]
      while ( true ) do                         declare
        in( user_message, !command,               const ID := "messageKeyboard" ;
          !nickname, !from )@self ;               var message : str ;
        if command = "ENTER" then                 var selected : str ;
          out( nickname )@screen ;                var selectedUsers : ts ;
          out( " entered chat\n" )@screen ;       locname messageKeyb, usersList, server
          if not readp(nickname)@usersList then begin
            out( nickname )@usersList              while ( true ) do
          endif                                      in( !message )@messageKeyb ;
        else                                         # is there someone selected?
          if command = "LEAVE" then                  out( "command", "getSelectedItem", ID )@usersList ;
            out( nickname )@screen ;                  in( "command", "getSelectedItem", ID, !selected )@usersList ;
            out( " left chat\n" )@screen ;            if ( selected != "" ) then
            inp( nickname )@usersList                   newloc( selectedUsers ) ;
            # ignore non existing names                 out( selected )@selectedUsers ;
          endif                                         # there's some one selected
        endif                                          out( "PERSONAL", message, selectedUsers, *self )@server
      enddo                                          else
    end                                                out( "command", "getSelectedItems", ID )@usersList ;
                                                       in( "command", "getSelectedItems",
                                                         ID, !selectedUsers )@usersList ;
                                                       if readp( !selected )@selectedUsers then
                                                         # there's some one selected
                                                         out( "PERSONAL", message, selectedUsers, *self )@server
                                                       else
                                                         # no one selected: broadcast
                                                         out( "MESSAGE", message, *self )@server
                                                       endif
                                                     endif
                                                   enddo
                                                 end
```

Listing 12. Node coordinators and processes running on a chat client

Screenshot 2. Three chat clients and the chat server

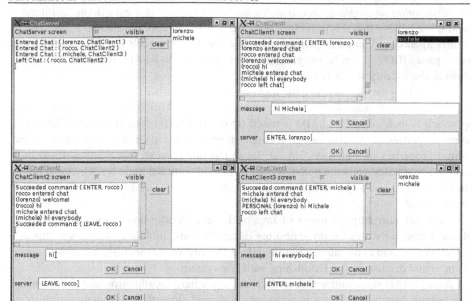

A user can specify that a chat message is destined only to a restricted number of clients by selecting them from the list of connected clients. Such list is indeed attached to the locality usersList that, in turn, is a special tuple space that provides a sort of interface for accessing the items of such list (in the KLAVA implementation this tuple space is an interface for a java.awt.List object). Thus a process can access the elements of such a list through tuples that start with the string "command" and consist of a specific command and its arguments. For each command the template of the tuple is different. If the result of a command has to be retrieved the request is issued with an **out** and the response retrieved with an **in**. An identifier has to be provided so that a process does not retrieve the result of the request of another process. For instance the following two lines retrieve multiple selected items in the list (the result is stored in the **ts** variable selected):

```
out( "command", "getSelectedItem", ID )@usersList ;
in( "command", "getSelectedItem", ID, !selected )@usersList ;
```

If there is some client selected in this list, the message is sent as "PERSONAL" and the list of recipients is sent along with the message; otherwise the message is considered destined to all connected clients.

Screenshot 2 shows three chat clients and the chat server.

10   Conclusions and Related Works

We have presented X-KLAIM, a programming language for implementing distributed applications that can exploit mobile code and run over a heterogeneous network environment. X-KLAIM extends the Linda coordination paradigm with multiple distributed tuple spaces. Thus, the underlying model enables *space uncoupling*, *time uncoupling* and *destination uncoupling*, and *asynchronous*, *associative* and *anonymous* communication. We believe that this programming model is suitable for distributed applications, mobile agents, and, more in general, mobile code. Other models [Deu01], such as the *home-proxy* [LO98], can be programmed on top of the X-KLAIM basic model by exploiting the locality abstractions.

X-KLAIM provides support for moving processes (with strong mobility) and all the code they will need for execution at remote sites. An interesting spin-off of our approach is that, since X-KLAIM is based upon the KLAIM formal model [BBD+03], some properties of systems can be formally proved (e.g., in [BDL04] we prove some formal properties of a chat system similar to the one presented in Section 9 and of a mobile agent based software update system). Indeed, a modal logic for KLAIM is being studied [DL04] and a system to automatically prove KLAIM system properties is under development.

There are currently a number of Java packages, libraries and frameworks that implement functionalities for programming distributed and mobile systems, and that are based on the Linda communication model. In the rest of this section, we review some of them and discuss their relationships with our system.

Jada [CR97] is a coordination toolkit for Java where coordination and communication among distributed objects is achieved via shared *ObjectSpaces* that are implementations of tuple spaces. Remote access to ObjectSpaces is achieved by specifying the complete IP address and port number, i.e., no locality abstraction is used. Private ObjectSpaces can be dynamically created. No code mobility is supplied by Jada that aims at providing a coordination kernel for implementing more complex Internet languages and architectures.

MARS [CLZ98] is a coordination tool for Java-based mobile agents that defines Linda-like tuple spaces programmable to react when accessed by agents. Such a mechanism can be used to control accesses to specific tuples. In X-KLAIM, this is obtained either by using dynamically created private tuple spaces or by adding to the language the capability-based type system presented in [DFP99, DFPV00].

Jini [AOS+99] is a connection technology that enables many devices to be plugged together to form a community on a network in a scalable way and without any planning, installation, or human intervention. Each device defines services that other devices in the community may use and drivers that can be downloaded when needed. Jini is developed on top of the *JavaSpaces* [AFH99] technologies, a framework for using Linda-like communication. JavaSpaces introduces some extensions of the Linda original paradigm, such as *event notification*, which allows a process to register its interest in future occurrences of some event and then to receive communication when the event occurs, and *blocking operations with timeouts* and *leasing*, which allows the presence of a tuple in a tuple space, or a notification request, to be granted only for a period of time. Leasing can be obtained also in our language by means of timeouts: a process can sleep for some time (using timeout), and then can take a tuple away from the tuple space (if it is still available). JavaSpaces *transactions* can be programmed in X-KLAIM, by means of dedicated tuples, which represent transaction life time.

IBM *T Spaces* [FLMW98] is a network middleware package that supplies tuple space-based network communication with database capabilities; it is implemented in Java by relying on its portability. T Spaces is basically a message processor, in fact a client's view of T Spaces is that of a message center and a message database. A DBMS could be implemented in X-KLAIM by means of a process listening for requests (e.g., SQL strings) passed via tuples, to obtain a similar behavior.

Lime [PMR99] exploits the multiple tuple spaces paradigm [Gel89] to coordinate mobile agents and adds mobility to tuple spaces: it allows processes to have private tuple spaces and to transiently share them. Although in X-KLAIM tuple spaces are bound to nodes and nodes cannot move, processes can have objects of the class `TupleSpace` as data members and, hence, when processes move, `TupleSpace` objects move as well. However, `TupleSpace` objects are never shared and merged automatically.

Systems such as [BH00, PS97, RASS97, ARS97], implement strong mobility in Java, by modifying the Java Virtual Machine, to access, save and restore the execution state of threads. However, this solution can jeopardize one of the most desirable advantages of Java: portability across platforms. Indeed, one needs to run the modified version of the JVM in order to use such agents. This is the reason why we preferred not to include strong mobility in KLAVA; however, this feature is available in X-KLAIM and it is implemented on top of KLAVA by means of an appropriate precompilation phase [BD01].

A feature that is present in systems such as *MARS*, *Lime*, *Sumatra* and *T Spaces*, but not in X-KLAIM, is the ability to react to events such as the insertion of a tuple. This could be programmed by means of a process waiting for a certain tuple, but this does not exactly implement reactions due to the non-determinism in the selection of the process waiting for a tuple.

Acknowledgments. We are greatly indebted to Gianluigi Ferrari and Rosario Pugliese with whom Klaim was conceived and designed. We wish to thank the friends that have worked on KLAIM and its extensions: Viviana Bono, Daniele Gorla, Michele Loreti, Eugenio Moggi, Emilio Tuosto and Betti Venneri. Many thanks are due also to Marco Bernardo and Alessandro Bogliolo for giving us the opportunity and the stimulus to write these notes.

References

[ACG⁺96] M. Adams, J. Coplien, R. Gamoke, R. Hanmer, F. Keeve, and K. Nicodemus. Fault-tolerant telecommunication system patterns. In J.M. Vlissides and J.O. Coplien, editors, *Pattern Languages of Program Design 2*, pages 549–562. Addison-Wesley, 1996.

[AFH99]   K. Arnold, E. Freeman, and S. Hupfer. *JavaSpaces Principles, Patterns and Practice*. Addison-Wesley, 1999.

[AGH00]   K. Arnold, J. Gosling, and D. Holmes. *The Java Programming Language*. Addison-Wesley, 3rd edition, 2000.

[AOS⁺99] K. Arnold, B. O'Sullivan, R.W. Scheifler, J. Waldo, and A. Wollrath. *The Jini Specification*. Addison-Wesley, 1999.

[ARS97]   A. Acharya, M. Ranganathan, and J. Saltz. Sumatra: A Language for Resource-aware Mobile Programs. In Vitek and Tschudin [VT97], pages 111–130.

[AS92]   B. G. Anderson and D. Shasha. Persistent Linda: Linda + Transactions + Query Processing. In J. P. Banatre and D. Le Metayer, editors, *Proc. of Research Directions in High–Level Parallel Programming Languages*, volume 574 of *LNCS*, pages 93–109. Springer, 1992.

[BBD⁺03]   L. Bettini, V. Bono, R. De Nicola, G. Ferrari, D. Gorla, M. Loreti, E. Moggi, R. Pugliese, E. Tuosto, and B. Venneri. The KLAIM Project: Theory and Practice. In C. Priami, editor, *Global Computing. Programming Environments, Languages, Security, and Analysis of Systems, IST/FET International Workshop, GC 2003, Revised Papers*, volume 2874 of *LNCS*, pages 88–150. Springer, 2003.

[BBV02]   L. Bettini, V. Bono, and B. Venneri. Coordinating Mobile Object-Oriented Code. In F. Arbarb and C. Talcott, editors, *Proc. of Coordination Models and Languages*, number 2315 in LNCS, pages 56–71. Springer, 2002.

[BBV04]   L. Bettini, V. Bono, and B. Venneri. O'KLAIM: a coordination language with mobile mixins. In *Proc. of Coordination 2004*, volume 2949 of *LNCS*, pages 20–37. Springer, 2004.

[BD01]   L. Bettini and R. De Nicola. Translating Strong Mobility into Weak Mobility. In G. P. Picco, editor, *Mobile Agents*, number 2240 in LNCS, pages 182–197. Springer, 2001.

[BDL04]   L. Bettini, R. De Nicola, and M. Loreti. Formulae Meet Programs Over the Net: A Framework for Correct Network Aware Programming. *Automated Software Engineering*, 11(3):245–288, June 2004. Special Issue on Distributed and Mobile Software Engineering.

[BDP02]   L. Bettini, R. De Nicola, and R. Pugliese. KLAVA: a Java package for distributed and mobile applications. *Software – Practice and Experience*, 32(14):1365–1394, 2002.

[Bet03]   L. Bettini. *Linguistic Constructs for Object-Oriented Mobile Code Programming & their Implementations*. PhD thesis, Dip. di Matematica, Università di Siena, 2003. Available at http://music.dsi.unifi.it.

[BH00]   S. Bouchenak and D. Hagimont. Pickling Threads State in the Java System. In *Proc. of the Technology of Object-Oriented Languages and Systems (TOOLS)*, 2000.

[BLP02]   L. Bettini, M. Loreti, and R. Pugliese. An Infrastructure Language for Open Nets. In *Proc. of ACM SAC 2002, Special Track on Coordination Models, Languages and Applications*, pages 373–377. ACM, 2002.

[BWA94]   P. Butcher, A. Wood, and M. Atkins. Global Synchronisation in Linda. *Concurrency: Practice and Experience*, 6(6):505–516, 1994.

[Car96]   L. Cardelli. Global computation. In *ACM Computing Surveys*. 1996. 28(4es), Article 163.

[Car97]   L. Cardelli. Mobile computation. In Vitek and Tschudin [VT97], pages 3–6.

[Car99]   L. Cardelli. Abstractions for Mobile Computation. In Vitek and Jensen [VJ99], pages 51–94.

[CG89a]   N. Carriero and D. Gelernter. How to Write Parallel Programs: A Guide to the Perplexed. *ACM Computing Surveys*, 21(3):323–357, 1989.

[CG89b]   N. Carriero and D. Gelernter. Linda in Context. *Communications of the ACM*, 32(4):444–458, 1989.

[CGPV97]   G. Cugola, C. Ghezzi, G.P. Picco, and G. Vigna. Analyzing Mobile Code Languages. In Vitek and Tschudin [VT97].

[CLZ98]   G. Cabri, L. Leonardi, and F. Zambonelli. Reactive Tuple Spaces for Mobile Agent
           Coordination. In K. Rothermel and F. Hohl, editors, *Proc. of the 2nd Int. Workshop
           on Mobile Agents*, volume 1477 of *LNCS*, pages 237–248. Springer, 1998.

[CR97]   P. Ciancarini and D. Rossi. Jada - Coordination and Communication for Java Agents.
           In Vitek and Tschudin [VT97], pages 213–228.

[Deu01]   D. Deugo. Choosing a Mobile Agent Messaging Model. In *Proc. of ISADS 2001*,
           pages 278–286. IEEE, 2001.

[DFP98]   R. De Nicola, G. Ferrari, and R. Pugliese. KLAIM: a Kernel Language for Agents
           Interaction and Mobility. *IEEE Transactions on Software Engineering*, 24(5):315–
           330, 1998.

[DFP99]   R. De Nicola, G. Ferrari, and R. Pugliese. Types as Specifications of Access Policies.
           In Vitek and Jensen [VJ99], pages 117–146.

[DFPV00]   R. De Nicola, G. Ferrari, R. Pugliese, and B. Venneri. Types for Access Control.
           Theoretical Computer Science, 240(1):215–254, 2000.

[DL04]   R. De Nicola and M. Loreti. A Modal Logic for Mobile Agents. *ACM Transactions
           on Computational Logic*, 5(1):79 – 128, 2004.

[FLMW98]   D. Ford, T. Lehman, S. McLaughry, and P. Wyckoff. T Spaces. *IBM Systems Jour-
           nal*, pages 454–474, August 1998.

[Gel85]   D. Gelernter. Generative Communication in Linda. *ACM Transactions on Program-
           ming Languages and Systems*, 7(1):80–112, 1985.

[Gel89]   D. Gelernter. Multiple Tuple Spaces in Linda. In E. Odijk, M. Rem, and J. Syre,
           editors, *Proc. Conf. on Parallel Architectures and Languages Europe (PARLE 89)*,
           volume 365 of *LNCS*, pages 20–27. Springer, 1989.

[HCK94]   C. Harrison, D. Chess, and A. Kershenbaum. Mobile agents: Are they a good idea?
           Research Report 19887, IBM Research Division, 1994.

[Hoa85]   C.A.R. Hoare. *Communicating Sequential Processes*. Prentice-Hall International,
           1985.

[HY98]   M. Hohlfeld and B.S. Yee. How to Migrate Agents. Available at
           http://www.cs.ucsd.edu/~bsy, 1998.

[Kna96]   F. Knabe. An overview of mobile agent programming. In *Proceedings of the Fifth
           LOMAPS workshop on Analysis and Verification of Multiple - Agent Languages*,
           number 1192 in LNCS. Springer, 1996.

[KWA+01]   E. Korpela, D. Werthimer, D. Anderson, J. Cobb, and M. Lebofsky. SETI@home:
           Massively Distributed Computing for SETI. *IEEE Computing in Science and Engi-
           neering*, January 2001.

[LO98]   D. Lange and M. Oshima. *Programming and Deploying Java Mobile Agents with
           Aglets*. Addison-Wesley, 1998.

[Mil89]   R. Milner. *Communication and Concurrency*. Prentice Hall, 1989.

[PMR99]   G.P. Picco, A.L. Murphy, and G.-C. Roman. LIME: Linda Meets Mobility. In D. Gar-
           lan, editor, *Proc. of the 21st Int. Conference on Software Engineering (ICSE'99)*,
           pages 368–377. ACM Press, 1999.

[PR98]   A.S. Park and P. Reichl. Personal Disconnected Operations with Mobile Agents. In
           Proc. of 3rd Workshop on Personal Wireless Communications, PWC'98, 1998.

[PS97]   H. Peine and T. Stolpmann. The Architecture of the Ara Platform for Mobile Agents.
           In K. Rothermel and R. Popescu-Zeletin, editors, *Proc. of the 1st International Work-
           shop on Mobile Agents (MA '97)*, number 1219 in LNCS, pages 50–61. Springer,
           1997.

[RASS97]   M. Ranganathan, A. Acharya, S. Sharma, and J. Saltz. Network-aware Mobile Pro-
           grams. In *Proc. of the USENIX Annual Technical Conf.*, pages 91–103. USENIX,
           1997.

[She90]   A. H. Sherman. *C-Linda Reference Manual*. Scientific Computing Associates, Inc., 1990.

[Tho97]   T. Thorn. Programming Languages for Mobile Code. *ACM Computing Surveys*, 29(3):213–239, 1997. Also Technical Report 1083, University of Rennes IRISA.

[VJ99]   J. Vitek and C. Jensen, editors. *Secure Internet Programming: Security Issues for Mobile and Distributed Objects*, number 1603 in LNCS. Springer, 1999.

[VT97]   J. Vitek and C. Tschudin, editors. *Mobile Object Systems - Towards the Programmable Internet*, number 1222 in LNCS. Springer, 1997.

[Whi96]   J. E. White. Mobile Agents. In J. Bradshaw, editor, *Software Agents*. AAAI Press and MIT Press, 1996.

Dealing with Node Mobility in Ad Hoc Wireless Network

Mario Gerla, Ling-Jyh Chen, Yeng-Zhong Lee, Biao Zhou,
Jiwei Chen, Guang Yang, and Shirshanka Das

Computer Science Department, UCLA, Los Angeles, CA 90095, USA

1   Introduction

A Mobile "Ad hoc" wireless NETwork (MANET) is a network established for
a special, often extemporaneous service customized to applications. The ad hoc
network is typically set up for a limited period of time, in an environment that
may change from application to application. As a difference from the Internet
where the TCP/IP protocol suite supports a vast range of applications, in the
MANET the protocols are tuned to a specific customer and application (eg,
send a video stream across the battlefield; find out if there is a fire in the forest; establish a videoconference among several teams engaged in a rescue effort,
etc). The customers move and the environment may change dynamically and
unpredictably. For the MANET to retain its efficiency, the ad hoc protocols at
various layers may need to self-tune to adjust to environment, traffic and mission changes. From these properties emerges the vision of the MANET as an
extremely flexible, malleable and yet robust and formidable network architecture. Indeed, an architecture that can be deployed to monitor the habits of birds
in their natural habitat, and which, in other circumstances, can be organized to
interconnect rescue crews after a Tsunami disaster, or yet can be structured to
launch deadly attacks onto unsuspecting enemies.

MANETs are set apart from conventional wired or wireless infrastructure
type networks by a number of unique attributes and requirements. Perhaps the
two most critical attributes are self-configurability and mobility. A third important requirement (which is critically impacted by the first two) is scalability. We
review these attributes next:

Self-Organization: the MANET is deployed and managed independently of
any preexisting infrastructure. This is the most important prerequisite to qualify a wireless network as ad hoc. Consequently, the network must autonomously
determine its own configuration parameters including: addressing, routing, clustering, position identification, power control, etc. In some large networks, special
nodes (eg, mobile backbone nodes) coordinate their position and motion to provide coverage of disconnected islands. This way, an "infrastructure" may be
created within the ad hoc network itself.

Mobility: the fact that nodes move is probably the most important attribute of
MANETs. Mobility differentiates MANETs from their close cousins, the sensor

M. Bernardo and A. Bogliolo (Eds.): SFM-Moby 2005, LNCS 3465, pp. 69–106, 2005.

networks. Mobility dictates network and application level protocols. For example, rapid deployment in unexplored areas with no infrastructure may require that some of the nodes form scouting teams/swarms. These in turn coordinate among themselves to create a task force or a mission. Mobility may be in some cases a challenge for the designer, and may become part of the solution in other cases. We can have several types of mobility models: individual random mobility, group mobility, motion along preplanned routes, etc. The mobility model can have major impact on the selection of a routing scheme and can thus influence performance.

Scalability: in both military and civilian applications (eg, large battlefield deployments, urban vehicle grids, etc) the ad hoc network can grow to several thousands of nodes. For wireless infrastructure-type networks (eg, urban mesh networks) scalability is simply handled by a hierarchical construction. Mobility appears to be the discriminator between easy and difficult scaling. A hierarchical model is very scalable in static networks (as demonstrated by the Internet). Limited mobility in an infrastructure can be easily handled using Mobile IP or other handoff and re-direction techniques. Pure ad hoc networks, due to their self configuring nature and consequent unrestricted mobility, do not tolerate a classic hierarchy structure and a mobile IP approach. Thus, mobility, jointly with large scale is one of the most critical challenges in ad hoc designs.

In this chapter we will be studying the "mobility attribute" of ad hoc networks and its impact on protocols and operations. We will study mobility under two different aspects, namely: mobility as an enemy that must be fought, and; mobility as a friend that can help us design more efficient networks. To be more precise, we will first address the damage that mobility causes in terms of path breakage and connectivity partitioning, and will review approaches to alleviate such effects. Then, we will observe that mobility can actually harnessed to overcome some of the very problems originating from mobility itself - for example, the fact that nodes move in groups can be exploited to achieve a highly scalable routing design not possible with individual random mobility. This will lead to define situations where mobility "helps". An important factor that determines how dangerous or how helpful mobility can be is the mobility pattern. Thus, we advocate the need for accurate, comprehensive mobility models. Finally, we will introduce a case study, the Car Torrent, that illustrates the design of an application based on the mobility of cars in the urban grid.

Before we start, we will provide, in the next section, an overview of recent trends in the evolution of ad hoc networking. This section will serve as reference for the problems that will be introduced in later sections.

2   Setting the Context: The Evolving Ad Hoc Network Market

The concept of ad hoc wireless networking was born in the early 70's, just months after the successful deployment of the ARPANET. It was the US Army who first discovered the potential of wireless packet switching for their mobile tactical operations. The first packet radio systems were deployed in the early 70's, almost two decades earlier than any other cellular and wireless LAN technology. By the mid 70's, the packet radio concept was so familiar and so well understood that when Bob Metcalf (Xerox Park) came up with the Ethernet design in 1976, the word spread that this was a very ingenious way to demonstrate " ALOHA packet radio" technology on a cable!

In view of these early successes of the ad hoc network technology, one may ask how come there has not been any significant transfer of technology from military to commercial over the past 30 years. The main reason is that the original military applications scenarios had really nothing to do with "commodity" customers. The military solutions could not be easily adapted to commercial needs. In fact, until recently, the driving ad hoc network model has been the instant deployment in an unfriendly, remote infrastructure-less area. Battlefield, planet explorations, disaster recovery etc. have been an ideal match for that model. Early DARPA packet radio scenarios were consistently featuring dismounted soldiers, tanks and ambulances. If any transfer of the battlefield technology will occur, it will probably be to the areas of homeland security and civilian emergency recovery. In those applications, unmanned vehicles (UGVs and UAVs) are rapidly deployed in areas hostile to man, say, to establish communications before engaging agents and medical emergency personnel. Still, this is a far cry from commercial every day applications.

Yet, commercial ad hoc networking is finally emerging in many sectors of our society. Commercial networks will start small (one or two hops), as an extension of the wireless Internet infrastructure or of existing personal wireless LANs. They will not be very demanding in terms of QoS nor efficiency (they use unlicensed spectrum). Eventually, they may grow large (in fact, very large, in the urban grid case); but they do not need large size in order to attract the first customer! Early ad hoc networks will coexist and comply with whatever technology they will try to "opportunistically" extend, ie 802.11, Bluetooth, ZigBee, UWB etc. An important consequence of this trend (which is radically different from that followed by tactical networks) is the fact that commercial ad hoc nets will require new design criteria and new research in order to evolve efficiently. Some of the emerging commercial applications are:

- Indoor W-LAN extended coverage
- Hot spot (Mesh Networks) extensions
- Urban vehicle communications
- Campus networks
- Shopping malls, airport lounges

Of this set, we briefly review the last three scenarios, namely, the vehicle urban grid, the Campus network and the shopping malls. Starting with the **vehicle communications** scenario, cars communications today are mostly voice, to the fixed network, via the cellular system. The wireless data technology advances will stimulate an explosion of new car applications. To begin, **car to Internet** data communications will be greatly enhanced by **3G** and **mesh network** technologies. In addition to traditional Internet services, there are plenty of "mobile" Internet applications for cars, from resource discovery (restaurants, shops, tourist attractions) to entertainment (movie previews) and navigation safety. Extending the wireless LAN and 3G connections (to negotiate, say, radio signal propagation obstructions) via opportunistic car to car multihopping will be simple and very cost-effective. **Within the car**, short range wireless communications (e.g., PAN technology) and ad hoc networking will be used for monitoring and controlling the vehicle's mechanical components as well as for connecting the driver's headset to the cellular phone. However, by far the most innovative set of applications will be enabled by **car to car** communications. Potential applications include car to car road alerts, coordinated navigation, network video games, road "situation awareness" and other peer-to-peer interactions. To support these applications, an "opportunistic" **multihop** wireless network will evolve, which will connect cars among each other and to the wireless infrastructure spanning the urban grid and eventually extending also to intercity highways. This ad hoc network will alleviate the overload of the fixed wireless infrastructures (3G and hotspot networks), for example, by allowing direct car to car sharing of popular files. As shown in Fig. 1, the urban vehicle grid network can also offer an emergency backup in case of massive fixed infrastructure failures (e.g., terrorist attack, act of war, natural or industrial disaster, etc). The synergy of car multihop network, on-board PAN and cellular wireless infrastructure is a good example of **heterogeneous wireless network** aimed at cost savings, performance improvements and enhanced resilience to failures.

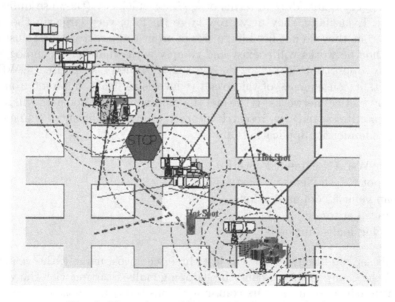

Fig. 1. The urban grid as an emergency network

The next scenario is the **Campus and shopping center**. For simplicity, we use the term "Campus" to refer to a place where people congregate for various cultural and social (possibly group) activities, thus including Amusement Park, Industrial Campus, Shopping Mall, etc. Today, on a typical Campus there are various wireless LAN access points in shops, hallways, street crossings, etc., that enable nomadic access to the Internet from various portable devices (e.g., laptops, notebooks, PDAs, etc.). Not all areas of a Campus or Mall are covered by department/shop wireless LANs. Thus, other wireless media (e.g., GPRS, 1xRTT, 3G, etc) may become useful to fill the gaps. There is a clear opportunity for multiple interfaces or agile radios that can automatically connect to the best available service. The Campus will also be ideal environment where group networking will emerge. For example, on a University Campus students will form small workgroups to keep track of their respective locations, to exchange files and to share presentations, results, etc. In an Amusement Park groups of youngsters will interconnect to play network games, etc. Their parents will network to exchange photo shots and video clips. To satisfy this type of close range networking applications, Personal Area Networks such as Bluetooth and IEEE 802.15 may be brought into the picture. As in the vehicular example, "opportunistic" ad hoc networking will extend access point coverage for Internet applications.

At this point it is appropriate to mention another type of wireless multihop network that is rapidly emerging in urban environments, namely, the **mesh network**. This architecture shares many of the characteristics of Wireless LANs and ad hoc networks at the same time. The MAC protocol is an extension of the IEEE802.11 family. The IEEE Committee is now working on the IEEE802.11s standard for such networks. Routing in the mesh is following the ad hoc network models (eg, AODV and DSR). Moreover, in an urban environment, mesh networks play an important role interconnecting the main types of commercial ad hoc networks we just described, namely, vehicular networks and the shopping malls. However, we must remember that the mesh network is actually an **"infrastructure"** network. It is a "permanent", public extension of institutional Wireless LANs. In this respect, the mesh network is similar to the cellular network - though faster to deploy. It would not be a surprise if in the future mesh networks will be regulated, tariffed and assigned a dedicated spectrum like other infrastructure networks. Yet, the design of mesh networks as multihop wireless architectures and topologies will radically differ from that of both the large scale battlefield designs and the smaller scale, very dynamic, opportunistic commercial network design. One can certainly argue that new design criteria and new research opportunities are present here as well.

Since our chapter is about mobility, the question is: how will this evolution from tactical, civilian networks to commercial networks affect our approach to mobility? The first answer is that in both scenarios the designer must protect the protocols from the damage of mobility (eg, path breakage, disconnection, etc). In this respect, the tactical and emergency networks are larger and have more stringent QoS requirements; thus, they will pose more challenges than the commercial counterparts. The second answer is that we also must look at opportunities to exploit mobility - namely, spontaneous, epidemic dissemination of information; flexible downloading from peers, etc. These opportunistic approaches generally make more sense in commercial than in tactical networks - in part because of the strict constraints of the latter. The reader should keep these considerations in mind while digesting the wealth of material presented in the rest of this chapter.

3   Motion Considered Harmful: How to Protect the Network

In this section, we view mobility as the "enemy", i.e. as the cause of damage and disruption in the ad hoc network. We identify three challenges caused by mobility:

1. **Path breakage** - we must prevent packet loss, for instance presetting backup paths etc
2. **Topology control traffic overhead** - one approach to combat path breakage is to "update" the topology very frequently. But, this can have dangerous side effects
3. **Long lasting disconnections** - how can we cope with network partitions caused be motion? One approach will be to design delay and disruption tolerant network protocols.

We address these challenges in the following sections.

3.1   Preventing Path Breakage

To start, we observe that the most visible problem is **path breakage**: as nodes move the previously computed path fails. Here several techniques come to our help. First, we can "prevent" path breakage by predicting when a link on the path will break (**link prediction**) and computing an anticipatory backup path "before" the first path fails. We can also be cautious when we compute the path, and just choose a path that will connect nodes that are sort of associated with each other by a common motion, e.g, they "travel" together (i.e., **Associative Based Routing**). The third approach consists of using geo-routing. With **geo-routing** there is no notion of path, rather, of direction to destination. There no state kept in the network (as in popular proactive and reactive schemes). As long as intermediate nodes can forward to destination, the integrity of forwarding is preserved, even if a stable path cannot be maintained because of high mobility.

Link Prediction. In typical mobile networks, nodes exhibit some degree of regularity in mobility patterns. For example, a car traveling on a road is likely to follow the path of the road and a tank traveling across a battlefield is likely to maintain its heading and speed for some period of time. By exploiting a mobile user non-random traveling pattern, we can **predict** the future state of the network topology and provide a transparent network access during the period of topology changes. Moreover, by using the predicted information, we can reduce the number of control packets needed to reconstruct routes and thus minimize overhead.

In this section, we present mobility prediction to enhance unicast and multicast routing protocols. The proposed scheme utilizes GPS location information [1]. In our protocol, GPS position information is piggybacked on data packets during a live connection and is used to estimate the expiration time of the link between two adjacent nodes. Based on this prediction, routes are reconfigured before they disconnect. Our goal is to provide a seamless connection service by reacting before the connection breaks.

We assume a free space propagation model [2], where the received signal strength solely depends on its distance to the transmitter. We also assume that all nodes in the network have their clock synchronized; for example, by using the NTP (Network Time Protocol) [3]. or the GPS clock itself. Therefore, if the motion parameters of two neighbors (such as speed, direction, and radio propagation range) are known, we can determine the duration of time these two nodes will remain connected. Assume two nodes i and j are within the transmission range T of each other. Let (x_i, y_i) be the coordinate of mobile host i and (x_j, y_j) be that of mobile host j. Also let v_i and v_j be the speeds, and θ_i and θ_j ($0 \leq \theta_i, \theta_j \leq 2\pi$) be the moving directions of nodes i and j , respectively. Then, the amount of time two mobile hosts will stay connected, D_t, is predicted by:

$$D_t = \frac{-(ab + cd) + \sqrt{(a^2 + c^2)r^2 - (ad - bc)^2}}{a^2 + c^2} \tag{1}$$

where $a = v_i \cos\theta_i - v_j \cos\theta_j$, $b = x_i - x_j$, $c = v_i \sin\theta_i - v_j \sin\theta_j$, and $d = y_i - y_j$. Note that when $v_i = v_j$ and $\theta_i = \theta_j$, D_t becomes ∞. The predicted value is the link expiration time (LET) between the two nodes.

Based on the above mechanism, we propose Distance Vector with Mobility Prediction (DV-MP) [4]. The protocol uses the route expiration time as the metric in the route table. Triggered update transmissions are eliminated because routes are established based on stability. Hence, routing update interval is relaxed and frequent updates are not required. In addition, using stable routes minimizes the disruption caused by mobility since a different route with a greater expiration time is used prior to a given route gets disconnected.

To utilize the prediction information, the mobility vector field is appended to the route update packet. In addition, the route expiration time (RET) metric is inserted into the routing table entry. Each node periodically broadcasts a route table. A sequence number is issued when generating updates, and it is incremented after each route table broadcast. The sequence number is associated with routing table entries for a particular origin of the route update. When node A receives a route table from its neighbor node B, the LET between nodes A and B is calculated based on the mobility vector contained in the received route table. Node A's route table is updated with the following rules:

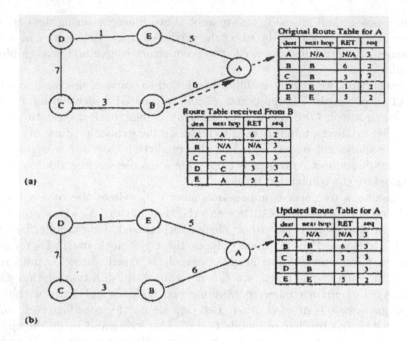

Original Route Table for A

dest	next hop	RET	seq
A	N/A	N/A	3
B	B	6	2
C	B	3	2
D	E	1	2
E	E	5	2

Route Table received From B

dest	next hop	RET	seq
A	A	6	2
B	N/A	N/A	3
C	C	3	3
D	C	3	3
E	A	5	2

(a)

Updated Route Table for A

dest	next hop	RET	seq
A	N/A	N/A	3
B	B	6	3
C	B	3	3
D	B	3	3
E	E	5	2

(b)

Fig. 2. A routing table update example

- If an entry for destination D with a better RET is received and the received sequence number is greater than or equal to the old entry's sequence number, node A's entry for destination D is updated.
- If an entry for destination D with a higher sequence number is received, node A's entry for destination D is updated.

Fig. 2 illustrates the route table updating process. Values shown next to each link are LETS. In Fig. 2(a), node A's next hop to node D is node E and the RET through node E is 1. After node A receives the route update packet from node B, it updates its next hop for destination D to node B as shown in Fig. 2(b) since the route via node B has a higher RET value of three.

There is a tradeoff between route distance and route stability. A route that has the largest RET will remain connected the longest, but may not have the shortest hop and/or delay.

Associativity-Based Routing. The problem at hand is to devise a scheme to compute routes that can adapt well to link changes. Conventional distributed routing schemes attempt to maintain consistent routing information in the face of motion by performing ever more frequent link and topology updates. These however are undesirable as they result in high transmission overhead (we will address overhead reduction strategies in a later section). An approach that attempts to overcome this problem is the Associativity Based Routing algorithm (ABR) [5]. ABR is based on a new metric called degree of association stability.

Every node monitors its 'Associativity' with its neighbor nodes in order to determine the best route. Stability is determined using beacon "ticks". Each node periodically transmits a beacon. The higher the number of ticks heard, the more stable the neighbor is. If all the mobiles along the route have high associativity ticks, the route is stable. The associativity ticks are reset when the neighbors or the node in question move out of proximity, not when the communication session is completed and the route made invalid. The distinctive feature of ABR, a unicast MANET routing protocol, is the use of 'associativity' as a primary metric in order to select more stable and thus long-lived routes. ABR is on-demand and maintains only the information for the desired routes. The route maintenance algorithm allows locally reconstructing a subsection of the route, instead of the entire route. There is no need for periodic route updates.

Geo-Routing and TCP. On-demand routing involves no periodic exchanges of route information but instead establishes routes when needed by flooding a route request to the network. This approach works well for small and moderate sized systems, and for large systems with relatively stable routes and limited communication patterns with significant destination locality. However, for large systems with bursty any-to-any communication patterns, and for systems with fast moving nodes, the overhead (and latency) of route discovery can become significant. In these cases, an interesting alternative is Geo-Routing. Geographic routing uses nodes locations as their addresses, and forwards packets (when possible) in a greedy manner towards the destination. Geographic routing is scalable, as nodes only keep state for their neighbors, and supports any-to-any communication pattern without explicit route establishment. Since there is no explicit path establishment, the scheme is by definition robust to path breakage. Namely, for successful forwarding it suffices that a neighbor is present in the direction to destination.

Geographic routing has been shown to dramatically improve the performance of TCP in ad hoc networks. Suppose that we need to set up a TCP connection over a mobile ad hoc network. As mentioned earlier, node mobility breaks routes forcing conventional routing schemes such as DSR or AODV to flood the network with discovery messages. Flooding is costly, and frequent flooding can saturate the network and thus degrade performance. A packet may experience significant long delay before discovering a new route. If the delay is larger than the RTO at the sender, the TCP sender times out, retransmits a packet, and experiences low throughput. On the other hand, if route discovery or reply message get lost, the packet will be dropped. In either case, the result is reduced TCP throughput. In a network where the route must be frequently recomputed due to node mobility, TCP will never get an opportunity to transmit at the optimal state and the congestion window will always be significantly small [6].

Since a node in geo-routing listens for neighbor's position updates, it passively estimates the moving velocity of its neighbors and infers immediately whether a neighbor is still reachable when transmission failure occurs. If the neighbor is estimated within transmission range, the packet could be "salvaged", ie transmitted to this neighbor again, or to other neighbors. This local repair is free of

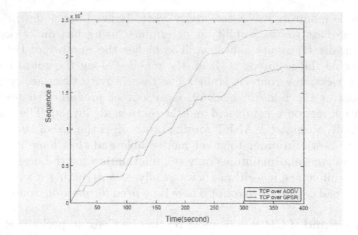

Fig. 3. Sequence Number of TCP over GPSR and AODV in Mobile Ad hoc Network

overhead and efficient. It is a network layer solution to flow contention and to random loss. With local repair, the packet transmission is robust to High BER, and can be lost only due to buffer overflow or route failure.

To demonstrate the efficacy of Geographic Perimeter Stateless Routing (GPSR) we run TCP-NewReno over GPSR [7]. The experiment consists of 20 nodes randomly placed within a 1000mx1000m area. Each node will continuously move within this area with speed randomly selected from 0 to 50m/s for 400 seconds. Random waypoint model is used for node mobility. In all simulations, we only show one TCP connection for clarity. The plot, as shown in Fig. 3, clearly shows that TCP over GPSR achieves much higher throughput than TCP over AODV.

3.2   Minimize the Control O/H Caused by Motion: Fisheye State Routing

As it became apparent in the previous sections, a common way to combat mobility is to refresh the routing tables very frequently. This however leads to another problem, namely, loss of performance due to high overhead. A solution to the refresh overhead problem is provided by Fisheye State Routing (FSR) [8] [9]. FSR introduces the notion of multi-level fisheye scope to reduce routing update overhead in large networks. Nodes exchange link state entries with their neighbors with a frequency that depends on distance to destination. From link state entries, nodes construct the topology map of the entire network and compute optimal routes.

FSR is an implicit hierarchical routing protocol. It uses the "fisheye" technique proposed by Kleinrock and Stevens [10], where the technique was used to reduce the size of information required to represent graphical data. The eye of a fish captures with high detail the pixels near the focal point. The detail decreases as the distance from the focal point increases. In routing, the fisheye

approach translates to maintaining accurate distance and path quality information about the immediate neighborhood of a node, with progressively less detail
as the distance increases.

FSR is functionally similar to LS (Link State) Routing in that it maintains
a topology map at each node. The key difference is the way in which routing information is disseminated. In LS, link state packets are generated and
flooded into the network whenever a node detects a topology change. In FSR,
link state packets are not flooded. Instead, nodes maintain a link state table
based on the up-to-date information received from neighboring nodes, and periodically exchange it with their local neighbors only (no flooding). Through this
exchange process, the table entries with larger sequence numbers replace the
ones with smaller sequence numbers. The FSR periodic table exchange resembles the vector exchange in Distributed Bellman-Ford (DBF) (or more precisely,
DSDV [11]) where the distances are updated according to the time stamp or sequence numbers assigned by the node originating the update. However, in FSR
link states rather than distance vectors are propagated. Moreover, like in LS, a
full topology map is kept at each node and shortest paths are computed using
this map.

In a wireless environment, a radio link between mobile nodes may experience
frequent disconnects and reconnects. The LS protocol releases a link state update
for each such change, which floods the network and causes excessive overhead.
FSR avoids this problem by using periodic, instead of event driven, exchange of
the topology map, greatly reducing the control message overhead.

When network size grows large, the update message could consume considerable amount of bandwidth, which depends on the update period. In order to reduce the size of update messages without seriously affecting routing
accuracy, FSR uses the Fisheye technique. Fig. 4 illustrates the application
of fisheye in a mobile, wireless network. The circles with different shades of
grey define the fisheye scopes with respect to the center node (node 11). The

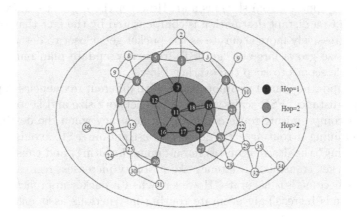

Fig. 4. Scope of fisheye

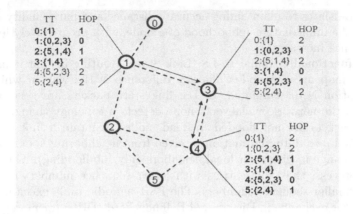

Fig. 5. Message reduction using fisheye

scope is defined as the set of nodes that can be reached within a given number of hops. In our case, three scopes are shown for 1, 2 and > 2 hops respectively. Nodes are color coded as black, grey and white accordingly. The number of levels and the radius of each scope will depend on the size of the network.

The reduction of routing update overhead is obtained by using different exchange periods for different entries in routing table. More precisely, entries corresponding to nodes within the smaller scope are propagated to the neighbors with the highest frequency. Referring to Fig. 5, entries in bold are exchanged most frequently. The rest of the entries are sent out at a lower frequency. As a result, a considerable fraction of link state entries are suppressed in a typical update, thus reducing the message size. This is exactly how FSR can handle high mobility with low O/H. In fact, FSR produces timely updates from near stations; it ignores the detailed motion of far nodes, and creates large latencies in the propagation of updates from stations afar. However the imprecise knowledge of the best path to a distant destination is compensated by the fact that the route becomes progressively more accurate as the packet gets closer to destination. As the network size grows large, a "graded" frequency update plan must be used across multiple scopes to keep the overhead low.

Through updating link state information with different frequencies depending on the scope distance, FSR scales well to large network size and keeps overhead low without compromising route computation accuracy when the destination is near. By retaining a routing entry for each destination, FSR avoids the extra work of "finding" the destination (as in on-demand routing) and thus maintains low single packet transmission latency. As mobility increases, routes to remote destinations become less accurate. However, when a packet approaches its destination, it finds increasingly accurate routing instructions as it enters sectors with a higher refresh rate.

3.3 Dealing with Long Term Disconnections: Disruption Tolerant Networking

There have been theoretical studies on the node density required for connectivity [12]. Low density and mobility combined can easily cause long lasting disconnections. When the ad hoc mobile network becomes partitioned, one may attempt to "reconnect" it, or simply to cope with the "temporary" disconnection. Several approaches have been proposed to reconnect the network. Li and Hou investigated how to deploy as few additional nodes as possible to improve the connectivity in [13]. The problem was formulated as NP-complete and heuristically solved with triangulation-based algorithms. Zhao et al proposed another solution called Message Ferrying to connect partitioned sub-networks [14]. Message ferries are special nodes that, with their mobility patterns and trajectories under control, relay packets between network partitions. Message Ferrying shares a similar idea with the work of Delay-Tolerant Networking Research Group [15] and DARPA Disruption Tolerant Networking [16] in that data is bundled and transmitted when intermittent connectivity is available.

In this section we outline another systematic solution to network partitioning, incorporating the concept of Disruption Tolerant Networking (DTN) with peer-to-peer (P2P) overlays [17] [18] [19] [20]. The main motivation stems from a paradox existing in current ad hoc networks. On the one hand, ad hoc networks are set up in emergency scenarios, e.g. a battlefield or disaster scene. Application data is in general important and cannot be lost. On the other hand, ad hoc networks often operate in an adverse environment and are much less reliable than the Internet or infrastructure-based wireless networks. To bridge the gap between application needs and network limitations, we propose to build a Disruption-Tolerant Storage (DTS) overlay on top of the ad hoc network.

The DTS overlay consists of nodes equipped with large storage and powerful CPUs. These nodes form a P2P overlay network and jointly provide safe data storage to connections affected by network partitioning. More specifically, when the network is partitioned, the routing protocol will detect it and notify the source of each affected connection. The source node then sets up a conversation with the closest DTS overlay peer and submits the data files for storage. The submitted files are indexed using distributed hash table (DHT) indexing techniques and are replicated to a set of peers. Data is delivered when the connection between a DTS overlay peer and the original destination node is stored. Two methods of data delivery exist: either a DTS peer pushes data to the destination, or the destination submits a query to the DHT index and pulls data from the DTS overlay.

Benefits of the DTS overlay solution are summarized as follows. First, it exploits node heterogeneity in ad hoc networks by storing data at nodes with large storage capacities. Second, data is replicated across the overlay and therefore more robust to node failures. Third, DTS overlay peers can process stored data, e.g. transcode video to an appropriate bit rate, before delivering to the destination. The DTS overlay thus provides safe and flexible storage services to important data that would otherwise be dropped when the network is partitioned.

4 Mobility Considered Helpful: Exploiting Mobility to our Advantage

In earlier sections we depicted mobility as a the necessary "evil" of the ad hoc network flexibility and selfconfigurability. We have shown ways to seek protection from path disruptions caused by mobility, and to make our applications operate correctly in spite of mobility. In reality, mobility can also be a "friend", in that it can be exploited to improve performance. In this section we show several examples of "friendly" mobility. To start, we show that **"group" mobility** can be harnessed via "landmarking" to lead to more scalable routing. Moreover, if **mobile backbone nodes** are deployed in the ad hoc network, connectivity can be enhanced. Related to the concept of conveniently relocatable nodes is **data ferrying** using data mules. Finally, **last encounter routing** exploits node motion and gossiping to achieve free dissemination of information.

4.1 Landmark Routing for Group Mobility

Typically, when wireless network size and mobility increase (beyond certain thresholds), current "flat" proactive routing schemes (i.e., distance vector and link state) become all together unfeasible because of line and processing O/H. In [21], we introduce a novel table driven routing protocol for wireless ad hoc networks - Landmark Ad Hoc Routing (LANMAR). LANMAR combines the features of Fisheye State Routing (FSR) [9] and Landmark routing [22]. The key novelty is the use of landmarks for groups of nodes that move together (e.g., a team of co-workers at a convention or a tank battalion in the battlefield) in order to reduce routing update overhead. Like in FSR, nodes exchange link state only with their neighbors. Routes within Fisheye scope are accurate, while routes to remote groups of nodes are "summarized" by the corresponding landmarks. A packet directed to a remote destination initially aims at the Landmark, as it gets closer to destination it eventually switches to the accurate route provided by Fisheye. In [23], we introduce an enhanced version of LANMAR which supports landmark election and provides a flexible way for the protocol to cope with a dynamic and mobile network without compromising scalability.

Network Model and Data Structures. Each node has a unique identifier, transmission range R, and landmark flag. Nodes move around and change speed and direction independently. An undirected link (i, j) connects two nodes i and j when the distance is less than or equal to the transmission R. For each node i, one list and three tables are maintained. They are: a neighbor list A_i, a topology table TT_i, a next hop table $NEXT_i$ and a distance table D_i. Each destination j within fisheye scope has an entry in table TT_i which contains two parts: $TT_i.LS(j)$ and $TT_i.SEQ(j)$. $TT_i.LS(j)$ denotes the link state information reported by node j. $TT_i.SEQ(j)$ denotes the time stamp indicating the time node j has generated this link state information. Similarly, for every destination j which is within its fisheye scope or which is a landmark node. $NEXT_i(j)$ denotes the next hop to forward packets destined to j on the shortest path, while $D_i(j)$ denotes the distance of the shortest path from i to j. The entries in next hop table $NEXT_i$ which point to landmarks form a new table called $LMDV_i$. Additionally, one or more link weight functions may be defined and used to compute the shortest path based on a specific metric, possibly with constraints. For instance, a bandwidth function can be used to support QoS routing. In this paper, we limit ourselves to mm hop paths, thus the link weight is 1.

Landmark Ad Hoc Routing Protocol(LANMAR). The key novelty in LANMAR is the notion of keeping track of logical subnets in which the members have a commonality of interests and are likely to move as a "group" (e.g., brigade in the battlefield, colleagues in the same organization, or a group of students from same class). Moreover, a "landmark" node is elected in each subnet. The scheme is an extension of FSR. It improves scalability by reducing routing table size and update traffic O/H. More precisely, It resolves the routing table scalability problem by using an approach similar to the landmark hierarchical routing proposed in [22] for wired networks. In the original landmark scheme, the hierarchical address of each node reflects its position within the hierarchy and helps finding a route to it. Each node has full knowledge of all the nodes within the immediate vicinity. At the same time each node keeps track of the next hop on the shortest path to various landmarks at different hierarchical levels. Routing is consistent with the landmark hierarchy and the path is gradually refined from top level hierarchy to low levels as a packet approaches destination.

We apply the above landmark concept to FSR to reduce routing update overhead for nodes that are far away. Each logical subnet has one node serving as "landmark". Beyond the fisheye scope the update frequency of the landmark nodes remains unaltered, while the update frequency of regular nodes is reduced to zero. As a result, each node will maintain accurate routing information about immediate neighborhood and as well as to landmark nodes. When a node needs to relay a packet, if the destination is within its neighbor scope as indicated in the routing table, the packet will be forwarded directly. Otherwise, the packet will be routed towards the landmark corresponding to the destination logical subnet. The packet does not need to go all way to the landmark. Rather, once the packet gets within the scope of the destination, it is routed to it directly.

The routing update exchange of LANMAR routing is similar to FSR. Each node periodically exchanges topology information with its immediate neighbors. In each update, the node sends entries within its fisheye scope. It will also piggyback a distance vector of all landmark nodes. Through this exchange process, the table entries with larger sequence numbers replace the ones with smaller sequence numbers. As a result, each node has detailed topology information about its neighborhood and has a distance and routing vector to all landmark nodes.

Typically, all members in a logical subnet are within the scope of the landmark, thus the landmark has a route to all members. It may happen, however, that some of the members "wonder" outside of the scope because of lack of coordination in the group mobility pattern. To keep track of such "outsiders", i.e. to make a route to them known to the landmark, the following modification to the routing table exchange was made. Each node, say i, on the shortest path between a landmark L and an "outsider" member l of such landmark keeps a distance vector entry to l. Note that if l is within scope of i, this entry is already included in the vector. When i transmits its distance vector to neighbor j, say, then j will retain the entry for member l only if $d(j, l) <$ scope or $d(j, L) < d(i, L)$. The latter condition occurs if j is on the shortest path from i (and therefore from l) to L.

Landmark Election. At the beginning of the execution, no landmark exists. Protocol LANMAR only uses the FSR functionality. As the FSR computation progresses, one of the nodes will learn (from the FSR table) that more than a certain number of group members (say, N) are in the FSR scope. It then proclaims itself as a landmark for this group. The landmark information will be broadcast to the neighbors jointly with the topology update packets. The landmark information is a status pair containing the ID of the landmark and the number of group members it can reach within the FSR scope. When more than one node declares itself as a landmark in the same group, the node with the largest number of group members wins the election. In case of tie, lowest ID breaks the tie. The competing nodes defer.

After the first few topology updates, nodes near the center of a group will have enough group members in their table to qualify as landmarks. These nodes will take the role of landmark, and build their LMDV. The landmark status pair and the LMDV will be broadcast to neighbors with the next FSR exchange packet. When its non-landmark neighbors receive this update message, they will update their LMDV using the incoming LMDV. If a neighbor is a landmark itself, a winner competition is performed. The landmark status pair and LMDV at this node is set up corresponding to the competition result. The updated LMDV and the node's landmark status pair will be propagated again jointly with the routing update packets. When the last landmark change information reaches every node, only one node will remain as landmark for each group. The election converges quite rapidly. At steady state, a landmark propagates its presence to all other nodes like a sink in DSDV [11].

In a mobile environment, an elected landmark may eventually lose its role. The role shifting is a frequent event. In a transient period, there exist several landmarks in a single group. The transient period may be actually the norm at high mobility. This transient behavior can be drastically reduced by using hysteresis.

A great advantage of landmark election in LANMAR is recovery from landmark failures. In a dynamic network, nodes may die and come up. When a landmark dies, its neighbors will detect the silence after a given timeout. The neighbors of the same group will then take charge as landmarks and broadcast this new landmark information. A new round of landmark election then starts over the entire network.

In conclusion, LANMAR is an extension of Fisheye Routing which exploits group mobility by "summarizing" the routes to the group members with a single route to a landmark. LANMAR provides an efficient, scalable solution for wireless, mobile ad-hoc network as well as a dramatic reduction in route table

storage overhead with respect to FSR leading to both line and storage overhead reduction.

4.2   GeoLANMAR: Geo Assisted Landmark Routing

GeoLANMAR routing protocol is based on LANMAR and extends LANMAR
by applying greedy forwarding to route data packet to remote landmark nodes
instead of relying on table driven forwarding using the routing info propagated
by DSDV. The main advantage of Geo LANMAR over LANMAR is **additional
robustness to mobility** (which is granted by the use of geo-forwarding - as
discussed earlier). The geo-routing scheme is used to route packet to the remote
landmark nodes (i.e. *geo-landmarks*) outside of the local scope. The number of
landmark nodes is typically much smaller than the total number of nodes in the
network. In GeoLANMAR, the geo-routing scheme offers much lower update
rate required for advertisements and more robust forwarding for long distance
routing, while local scope routing based on link state reduces update overhead.

In the greedy forwarding scheme applied to GeoLANMAR, intermediate
nodes do not have to store routing tables to landmark nodes. They do not need
to keep routing tables up-to-date either. The advantage of greedy forwarding is
to permit dynamic adjustment for update rate of landmark routing packets. The
dynamic update rate is determined by its movement and it offers GeoLANMAR
a better scalability than LANMAR in terms of control overhead, delivery ratio,
and throughput. Compared to geo-routing protocols, GeoLANMAR will overcome the inaccuracy of positions from the GPS devices since it uses link-state
routing for packets near destinations. GeoLANMAR does not need any location
service which is required by most geo-routing protocols.

A geo-landmark node is a special node dynamically elected by a group of
nodes that are moving together (e.g., a rescue team). The Geo-landmark node
propagates ID group, IP address and Geo-location to all other nodes in the
network. As depicted in Fig. 6, Geo-Landmark LM transmits the information of
its group to other nodes in the network.

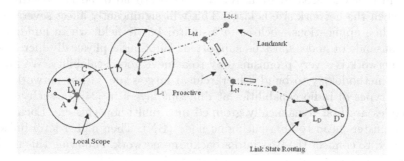

Fig. 6. Long distance Greedy forwarding applied through Landmarks as reference
points to reach the destination D

Referring to Fig. 6, if the source S wants to communicate with mobile node D, it verifies whether the destination D can be reached immediately through the local link-state routing. If there is no entry found in local routing table, it tries to send the data packet toward destination D through geo-forwarding. By virtue of landmark distance vector advertising, the GeoLANMAR protocol can get the position of the destination node D without using a Location Server (normally required in conventional geo-routing protocols). From the group ID, and from geo-location of destination D, one can apply geo-forwarding by using the knowledge of the destination landmark. When the packet reaches the local scope of destination D, the data packet can be directly sent to D through the table-driven forwarding.

To perform such management, each node needs to maintain the following tables: a local topology table, a local routing table, and a landmark table with the geo-location information and the group IDs of all landmarks in the networks. When a node needs to send a packet outside its local scope, it checks its local topology table and selects as the next hop the nearest to the destination landmark node.

For the management of very large network with group mobility, the GeoLANMAR protocol seems to offer a good solution. The drawback of the protocol is the distance vector periodic updating, which is required in order to maintain accurate landmark tables. Fortunately, because the number of landmarks is much lower than the total number of nodes inside the networks, this protocol can get a good trade-off for large size networks with group motion.

4.3   Mobile Backbone Network

A Mobile Ad Hoc Network (MANET) is usually assumed to be homogeneous, where each mobile node shares the same radio capacity. However, a homogeneous ad hoc network suffers from poor scalability. Recent research has demonstrated its performance bottleneck through both theoretical analysis and simulation experiments and testbed measurements. Poor scalability is due to the fact that in ad hoc networks, most bandwidth of a node is consumed by forwarding packets. This is further exacerbated by heavy routing overhead of ad hoc routing protocols when the network size is large. This will significantly affect several large scale ad hoc applications, such as in a digital battle field, where hundreds or even thousands of nodes must be supported. Building a physically hierarchical ad hoc network is a very promising way to achieve good scalability. We present a design methodology to build a hierarchical large-scale ad hoc network using different types of radio capabilities at different layers in [24]. In such a structure, nodes are first dynamically grouped into multi-hop clusters. Each group elects a cluster- head to be a backbone node (BN). Then higher-level links are established to connect the BNs into a backbone network. Following this method recursively, a multilevel hierarchical network can be established.

Mobile Backbone Network. The Mobile Backbone Network (MBN) is a hierarchical network in which a set of nodes functionally more capable than the

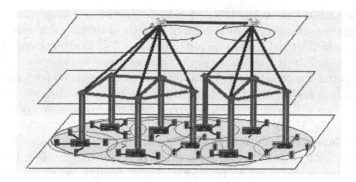

Fig. 7. Illustration of an ad hoc network with multilevel mobile backbones

ordinary nodes form the backbone. The basic scenario consists of a large numbers of mobile nodes deployed over a large area. Among these, the backbone nodes (BN) have the ability of forming multilevel backbone networks using long range radios. Usually, radios at each backbone level use some form of channel separation (eg, antenna directivity, different codes, different frequencies, or combinations thereof) in order to minimize interference across levels. Radios in the same level share the same frequency and channel resources. Unlike the wired network, the nodes in the mobile backbone network are also moving, thus the backbone topology is dynamically changing. In many scenarios such as the battlefield, the hierarchical structure is an inherent feature of the application. Different units have different communication devices and capacities. For example, the wireless radios installed in military vehicles have a more ample energy supply and thus are more powerful than those carried by the dismounted soldiers. Unmanned Aerial Vehicles (UAVs) and even satellites can be used for providing higher level and broader reach connections. Fig. 7 illustrates a three level hierarchy where the first level supports ground communications among soldiers; and second and third level are implemented using tanks and UAVs respectively. In this section, most of our discussions are based on a two level hierarchical architecture. However, the routing and clustering algorithms and protocols can be easily extended to multi-level hierarchical networks.

Hierarchical ad hoc networks have great potential in real time constrained applications, especially in the digitized battlefield. However, the backbone design is quite challenging if the nodes are mobile. Three critical issues are involved in building such a MBN, namely: optimal number of BNs, BN deployment and routing. In theory, a multi-level MBN can solve the scaling law problem observed in flat networks. However, MBNs with too many levels are not easy to operate and suffer from hardware limitations (e.g. each levels requires an additional radio). Thus, one generally opts for a MBN with a few levels (say, two) and must decide the number of BNs.

After the number of BNs is decided, the second issue is how to deploy them. The main difficulties are mobility and BN failures. Using a clustering scheme to elect the BNs is a natural choice. Clustering has been widely used to form

logically hierarchical networks [25] [26] and to partition a large scale network
into small groups. However, a drawback of current clustering schemes is cluster
instability, as indicated in many papers such as [25]. Conventional clustering
schemes work effectively only in networks with very low mobility or no mobility
at all, such as the sensor networks. Instability of the clusters and frequent changes
of BNs introduce high routing O/H and make the hierarchy difficult to operate.
In this paper, we will present a new clustering scheme to achieve good stability.

Routing is the third critical issue: The main requirement is to utilize the
wireless backbone links efficiently and in a robust way. The main challenge of
MBN routing with respect to the general Internet routing problem is mobility:
address prefixes would need to be continuously changed as nodes move! The
ensuing address management problem would be very complex and would offset
the hierarchy advantages.

Backbone Node Deployment and Clustering. After identifying the optimal number of BNs as a function of number of nodes and channel bandwidths,
the second critical issue is how to achieve an optimal BN deployment. The simplest way is to pre-assign backbone nodes and scatters them uniformly across the
field at initialization. However, such a static deployment has two main problems.
First, the BNs are constantly moving. Thus after some time, some BNs may congregate in small geographical areas, creating congestion; while other areas may
be depleted of BNs all together. This certainly is not a good scenario. The second
concern is fault tolerance. BNs may fail or even be destroyed (a likely event considering the emergency applications envisioned for MANETs). New BNs should
be deployed to replace the defunct ones. Static deployment cannot fulfill these
requirements. Our solution is to deploy a large enough number of backbone capable nodes (ie, nodes with long range radios) and to dynamically elect a proper
subset to BNs. When one BN is destroyed or moves out of a certain area, a
new BN will be selected from the backbone capable node pool. If two backbone
nodes move near to each other, one of them will give up its backbone role. The
backbone node election is completely distributed and dynamic. It must result in
a backbone node distribution that reflects the distribution of ordinary nodes. A
Distributed Clustering algorithm is the most common approach to this problem,
as described in [25] [26].

Ad Hoc Routing with Mobile Backbones. Once elected, the BNs establish
connections among each other using the long range radios. The next issue is
routing. The routing scheme in the MBN has a main requirement: it must be
able to exploit the high level backbone links, enhancing throughput and delay
with respect to scheme without a backbone. It must do so without compromising
(in fact, possibly enhancing) scalability and fault tolerance. In fact, considering
the emergency recovery, unfriendly or even hostile environments where ad hoc
networks are deployed, the backbone nodes can very possibly become disabled
or may fail to operate. Maintaining connectivity in the face of backbone node
failures is a strong requirement. Thus, the addressing and routing scheme cannot
be totally "dependent" on the health of the backbone. For this reason, a cellular

network like addressing and routing scheme will not work here. In a cellular
network, the HLR/VLR (Home Location Register/Visiting Location Register)
scheme will properly route the call request packet to the area where the roaming
user has now registered. This requires that the Home Location of the user is
up, and has a pointer to the Visited Location. In our Mobile Backbone Network
where BNs disappear and come up very frequently, there is no reliable Home
Location for any mobile. Redundant, robust Name Server schemes haven been
recently proposed [19]. But they are not appropriate for our application, as
their complexity would offset the advantages reaped by the hierarchical routing.
To meet the challenges of our extremely volatile environment, we extend the
Landmark Ad Hoc Routing (LANMAR) [21] [23] to operate in the MBN. We
call this solution Hierarchical LANMAR Routing (H-LANMAR).

Hierarchical Landmark Ad Hoc Routing (H-LANMAR). LANMAR can
be well integrated into the MBN by virtue of the fact that it is itself logically
hierarchical. Routing information to remote nodes is summarized by landmarks.
Now, we will extend such a logical hierarchical structure to utilize the physical
hierarchy. In the original LANMAR scheme, we route the packet toward the
corresponding remote landmark along a long multi-hop path. In the hierarchical MBN, we can route the packet to the nearest BN, which then forwards it
through a chain of MBN links to a remote BN near the remote landmark. Finally, the remote BN sends the packet to the remote landmark or directly to the
destination if it is within its scope. This will greatly reduce the number of hops.
The procedure is illustrated in Fig. 8. We can see that by utilizing the backbone
links, the 8-hop path is reduced to be 4 hops long, a great improvement!

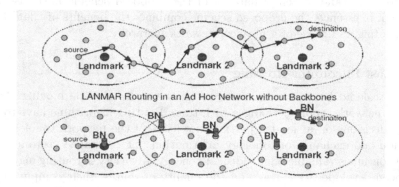

Fig. 8. Illustration of H-LANMAR routing in a MBN

We extend the LANMAR routing protocol so that it can take the "short cut"
described above. First, all mobile nodes, including ordinary nodes and BNs, are
running the original LANMAR routing via the short-range radios. This is the
foundation for falling back to "flat" multi-hop routing if BNs fail. Second, a BN
will broadcast the landmark distance vectors to neighbor BNs via the backbone

links. The neighbor BNs will treat this packet as a normal landmark update packet. Since this higher level path is usually shorter, it will win over (and thus replace) the long multi-hop path in the level 1 network. From landmark updates the ordinary nodes thus learn the best path to the remote landmarks, including the paths that utilize the backbone links.

One important feature of our routing scheme is reliability and fault tolerance. The ordinary nodes are prevented from knowing the backbone links explicitly. The backbone links are indirectly learned via BN routing broadcasts. Now, suppose a BN of one group is destroyed by enemies, the shorter paths via this BN will expire. Then new landmark information broadcasted from other nodes will replace the expired information. Thus, in the worst case, routing in this group goes back to original landmark routing while other groups with BNs can still benefit from backbone links among themselves. When all backbone capable nodes are disabled, the whole network becomes a "flat" ad hoc network running the original level 1 LANMAR routing, which can still provide connectivity, yet at lower performance.

In this section, we presented schemes to establish and operate a "physical" multi-level hierarchical ad hoc network with mobile backbones (MBN). The optimal numbers of backbone nodes at each layer are derived through theoretical analysis. A stable multihop clustering scheme is also proposed to elect required backbone nodes and organize the hierarchical network. For efficient routing in such a hierarchical structure, we proposed to use an extension of the LANMAR routing scheme. The LANMAR routing solution is key to the feasibility and efficiency of the hierarchical structure. It is robust to mobility and yet reaps the benefits of the hierarchy. For example, backbone links are automatically selected by the routing scheme if they can reduce hop distance to remote destinations. Fault tolerance and system reliability of the proposed scheme have also been discussed. In essence, the proposed scheme combines the benefits of "flat" LANMAR routing and those of a physical network hierarchy.

4.4   Last Encounter Routing

In large-scale ad hoc networks, some or all the nodes may be moving. Therefore, the network topology changes with time. Routing algorithms have to base routing decisions on at least a partial knowledge of the network topology. The collection and exchange of topology information (e.g., distance vectors or link states) consumes valuable bandwidth and energy. A variety of routing algorithms have been developed that trade off the quality of routes, their computing and transmission overhead, and the degree of permissible mobility [27].

An elegant way of reducing this cost is by exploiting the *distance effect* [28]: basically the precision with which the destination location must be known to make a good, albeit suboptimal, routing decision, decreases with distance. If the node is far away from the destination, an imprecise estimate is sufficient, and vice versa. Routing schemes such as DREAM [28] exploit this effect to develop more "lazy" approaches to maintaining location information about all the nodes in the network. This approach essentially amounts to trading off a smaller location

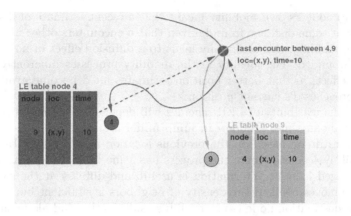

Fig. 9. A last encounter table in every node remembers the location and time of the last encounter with every other node in the network. In last encounter routing (LER), this table is queried by a packet to improve, if possible, its estimate of the location of its destination node

maintenance overhead, which is incurred continually with every topology change, for a slightly larger routing cost, as routes are in general suboptimal.

The authors of [29] go one step further and try to completely eliminate the cost to update location state. If nodes are not allowed to periodically relay any explicit location updates (as in Link State or Distance Vector), then the only topology information available at a node is the history of other nodes it has encountered in the past, i.e., nodes it has directly come into contact with. More specifically, we assume that every node remembers the time and location of its last encounter with every other node (i.e., when these two nodes last were directly connected neighbors; cf. Fig. 9). We call a routing algorithm a last encounter routing (LER) algorithm if at every node along a packet's route, the next hop decision depends only on (a) the time and location of that node's last encounter with the destination, and (b) auxiliary information carried by that packet. The main question we ask in this paper is the following: if all the nodes in the network are moving, is it possible for LER schemes to compute efficient routes, despite the absence of a location service? We show that, depending on the mobility processes, this is indeed possible. This is quite remarkable, given that LER invests no network capacity to track nodes, i.e., to maintain distributed location information.

The insight at the root of our investigation is the following. On the one hand, mobility of the nodes creates uncertainty about their location. On the other hand, consider some node d that is the destination of a packet. Some other node i that has encountered d in the past remembers the location of that last encounter. Three observations explain why LER routing can give rise to efficient routes: (a) the location of the last encounter is still a reasonably good estimate of the destination's location after some time; (b) the time of that encounter, or equivalently, the "age" of the estimator, is a measure for the precision of that estimate; (c) node i's own mobility means that a recent estimate of d's position is available at some distance from d; given that d encounters other nodes all the time due to mobility, this essentially leads to a diffusion effect of noisy position estimates around d. The locality in the mobility processes inherently leads to a distance effect, in that better position estimates for d become available as a packet approaches d's current position.

Clearly, the feasibility of LER schemes will depend on the mobility process. If at any point in time, a node can jump uniformly over the entire surface of interest, an estimate based on the previous location is of no help. However, in the more likely scenario where the process has some locality, such as a random walk, then aged location information is useful, and diffuses at the same speed as the node moves itself. If the density of neighbors is sufficient both along the path of the destination node (so as to diffuse sufficiently) and along the path of a packet moving towards the destination (to get enough new estimates), then LER routing can work well.

4.5   Data Ferrying with Mules

Routing in ad hoc networks has been an active research field in recent years. However, most of the existing work focuses on connected networks where an end-to-end path exists between any two nodes in the network. In this section, we focus on mobile networks where nodes are sparsely distributed such that network partitions can last for a significant period. Sparse networks naturally arise in a variety of applications. For example, imagine the following hypothetical disaster scenario. A severe earthquake has occurred which collapses buildings, traps people in the debris, damages utilities and roads, and causes fires and explosions. Under this situation, the ability to communicate, even at low rates, is extremely valuable for sharing vital information (such as the number and locations of survivors, damages and potential hazards) and coordinating rescue efforts. However, providing communication capacity is difficult. First, fixed and stable communication infrastructure might be destroyed. Even if some infrastructure is usable, most rescue participants and victims may not have access to it. Second, available devices such as cell phones or PDAs can only communicate within a limited range. Due to the size of the area affected, a connected ad hoc network cannot be formed using these devices alone. To overcome partitions in sparse networks, a straightforward approach is to use radios with longer transmission ranges and maintain persistent network connectivity. However, since many mobile nodes use batteries for power supply, the use of a long range radio leads to excessive energy consumption. In addition, the availability of such devices in critical scenarios would be questionable.

To help overcome disconnection problems like discussed above, a Message Ferrying (MF) approach for data delivery in sparse networks is proposed [8]. Referring to Fig. 10, MF is a proactive mobility assisted approach which utilizes a set of special mobile nodes called message ferries (or ferries for short) to provide communication services for nodes in the network. Similar to their real life analog, message ferries move around the deployment area and take responsibility for carrying data between nodes. The main idea behind the Message Ferrying

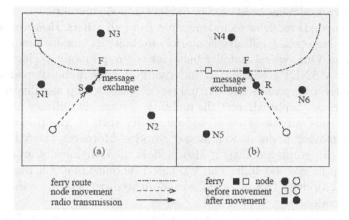

Fig. 10. An example of message delivery in the node-initiated MF scheme

approach is to introduce non-randomness in the movement of nodes and exploit such non-randomness to help deliver data. Message ferrying can be used effectively in a variety of applications including battlefields, disaster relief, wide area sensing, non-interactive Internet access and anonymous communication. For example, in the earthquake disaster scenario, unmanned aerial vehicles or ground vehicles that are equipped with large storage and short range radios can be used as message ferries to gather and carry data among disconnected areas. This enables rescue participants and victims to use available devices such as cell phones, PDAs or smart tags for communication.

While the previous paper [30] has studied the idea of Message Ferrying in networks with stationary nodes, [14] considers networks with mobile nodes. More specifically, [14] develops two variations of the MF schemes, depending on whether ferries or nodes initiate non-random proactive movement. In the Node-Initiated MF (NIMF) scheme, ferries move around the deployed area according to known routes and communicate with other nodes they meet. With knowledge of ferry routes, nodes periodically move close to a ferry and communicate with the ferry. In the Ferry-Initiated MF (FIMF) scheme, ferries move proactively to meet nodes. When a node wants to send packets to other nodes or receive packets, it generates a service request and transmits it to a chosen ferry using a long range radio. Upon reception of a service request, the ferry will adjust its trajectory to meet up with the node and exchange packets using short range radios. In both schemes, nodes can communicate with distant nodes that are out of range by using ferries as relays.

5 Mobility Modeling: A Virtual Track Markov Chain Approach

The mobility model is one of the most important factors that impact the performance of a mobile ad hoc network (MANET). Traditionally, the random waypoint mobility model has been used to model the node mobility, where the movement of one node is modeled as independent from all others. However, in reality, especially in large scale military scenarios, mobility coherence among nodes is quite common. One typical mobility behavior is group mobility. Thus, to investigate military MANET scenarios, an underlying realistic mobility model is highly desired. We recently proposed a "virtual track" based group mobility model (VT model) that closely approximates the mobility patterns in military MANET scenarios. It models various types of node mobility such as group moving nodes, individually moving nodes as well as static nodes. Moreover, the VT model not only models the group mobility, it also models the dynamics of group mobility such as group merge and split. The VT based mobility model is one of Markov Chain Driven Models. This model uses random seeds to determine the speed and direction of nodes.

Group mobility models have drawn a lot of interest recently. The mobility models proposed so far in the literature assume some kind of permanent group affiliation. Also they require that each node belong to a single group. In reality in a typical military scenario, a much more complex mobility behavior is observed. Some nodes move in groups; while others move individually and independently; a fraction of nodes are static. Moreover, the group affiliation is not permanent. The mobile groups can dynamically re-configure themselves triggering group split and mergence. All these different mobility behaviors coexist in military scenarios. A good realistic mobility model must capture all these mobility dynamics in order to yield realistic performance evaluation results, which, unfortunately, is not satisfactorily captured in any of the existing models.

We refer to the non-uniform, dynamic changing scenario described above as "heterogeneous" group mobility scenario. Here, different mobility behaviors such as group motion (including group merge and split), individual motion as well no motion can all coexist. Our proposed "virtual track" based group mobility model (VT model) handles all these heterogeneous mobility behaviors. In this model, a certain number of "switch stations" are randomly placed in the field. These stations are all interconnected by "virtual tracks" with given track width. Groups move along the virtual tracks towards the stations. At a station, a group can then be split into multiple groups heading to different stations (e.g. swarming). Groups entering the same station may also merge into one group. The individually moving nodes are then modeled as random moves (using the waypoint model) without the constraint of the virtual tracks.

The key idea of the proposed model is to use some "virtual tracks" to model the dynamics of group mobility. Some "switch stations" are first randomly deployed in the field. These stations are then connected via virtual tracks with given track width. The grouped nodes must move following the constraint of the tracks. At the switch stations, a group can then be split into multiple smaller groups; some groups may be even merged into a bigger group. Such group dynamics happen randomly under the control of configured split and merge probabilities. Nodes in the same group move along the same track. They also share the same group movement towards the next switch station. In addition, each group mem-

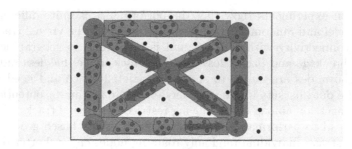

Fig. 11. Overview of Virtual Track Based Group Mobility Model

ber will also have an internal random mobility within the scope of a group. The mobility speeds of these groups are randomly selected between the configured minimum and maximum mobility speeds. One can also define multiple classes of mobile nodes, such as pedestrians, cars, UGVs, and UAVs, etc. Each class of nodes has different requirements: such as moving speed etc. In such cases, only nodes belonging to the same class can merge into a group.

The proposed VT model is also capable to model randomly and individually moving nodes as well as static nodes (such as sensors). Such non-grouped nodes are not restricted by the switch stations and virtual tracks. Instead, their movements are modeled as random moves in the whole field.

Fig. 11 illustrates a main idea of the proposed virtual track based group mobility model. In this example, 5 switch stations are randomly placed in the field connected via 8 virtual tracks with equal track width. Group moving nodes are moving towards switch stations along the tracks. They split and merge at switch stations as shown in the figure. The black nodes in Fig. 11 represent the individually moving nodes and static nodes. They are placed and move independent of tracks and switch stations.

The proposed VT mobility model is suitable for both military and urban environment. In the battlefield, the "switch stations" can be viewed as the gathering points or hot spots of military forces. The virtual tracks are roads or trails or valleys connecting those hot spots. The troops usually move following the predefined track. In the urban environment, the virtual tracks can be viewed as the streets. The switch stations are then the intersections of the streets. In a suburban scenario, the virtual tracks can represent the highways. The switch stations are then viewed as the inter-sections of the highway. The mobile nodes are then the cars running on the highway (e.g. under the constraint of the tracks). The convoys of cars on the highway can only split at the intersections.

Groups split and merge happen at the switch stations. Each group is defined with a group stability threshold value. When at the switch stations, each node in the group will check whether its stability value is beyond its group stability threshold value. If it is true, this node will choose a different track from its group. A group split happens. When several groups arrive at the same station and select the same track for the next movement, naturally, they will be merged into one bigger group.

Simulation experiments show that the performance is quite different under the track model and random waypoint mobility models. The virtual track model has better connectivity within groups and is less prone to geographic separation, route breakage and packet loss. But the track model has less radio space resource. The nodes are forced to share a restricted space and need a longer path to route data packets in the track model. There are more contention, collisions and congestion among nodes moving restriced in virtual tracks. The above constraints lead to performance degradation in the track based group mobility model. In contrast, individual randomly roaming nodes enjoy shorter paths and lower contention, which gives the random waypoint model a better performance.

From the simulations, it is also observed that the performance under the virtual track group mobility model can be enhanced by the introduction of individual nodes and static nodes. The reason is that the connectivity among multiple groups is increased by the roaming nodes outside of the virtual tracks. The above phenamon has a practical implication: the deployment of "relay" nodes in a group mobility environment can significantly improve performance, for example, the Mobile Backbone Overlay, etc.

6   Case Study: Car Torrent - Opportunistic File Downloading in the Urban Grid

In this section we report a rather extensive case study that illustrates the limits, trade-offs and opportunities associated with mobility. The application is about downloading files to a moving car from the Internet. While going through the details of the "Car Torrent" protocol, the careful reader should notice that the car to car download, if done efficiently, allows to utilize the unused bandwidth between hot spots. In fact, this is an excellent example where car **mobility helps** expand systems capacity. Without Car Torrent, each car should park at the "hot spot kiosk" and wait until it gets served. With popular file distribution, this may easily exceed hot spot capacity!

6.1   Cooperative Downloading in Vehicular Ad-Hoc Wireless Networks

Future vehicular networks are expected to deploy short range communication technology for inter-vehicle communication. In addition to vehicle-to-vehicle communication, users will be interested in accessing the multimedia-rich Internet from within the vehicular network. This motivates a compelling application of Co-operative Networking in the Vehicular Ad-Hoc network (VANET) where the Ad Hoc network extends and complements the Internet.

Consider a VANET with short-range communication technology. Given an average speed of 50 miles per hour and a gateway radio range of 500 meters, a simple calculation gives a car a transmission window to and from a fixed Internet access point on the order of a minute at the most. Taking into account contention from other cars, there may not be enough bandwidth to allow each user to download email, songs, as well as browse multimedia rich web-sites in the short time that they are connected to the gateway. Another practical issue is that on intercity highways, the gateways will be hosted by gas stations and food concessions, and thus will be less frequent; say every 5-10 miles. Thus the vehicle would be connected for about a minute to the Internet before being disconnected for around 5 minutes. As we shall see, the high mobility of nodes in VANETs coupled with the intermittent connectivity to the Internet provides an incentive for individual nodes to cooperate while accessing the Internet to achieve some level of seamless connectivity.

For the above reasons, an interesting problem is the design of cooperative protocols to improve client perceived performance of the vehicular network as a whole. The key contributions of CarTorrent are as follows:

1. A gossip mechanism to propagate content availability information,
2. A proximity driven content selection strategy (which takes into account the fact that transport-layer throughput degrades over multi-hop wireless connections), and
3. Leveraging the broadcast nature of wireless networks to reduce redundant message transmission.

6.2   Preliminaries

The network consists of a set of N nodes with same computation and transmission capabilities, communicating through bidirectional wireless links between each other. This is the infrastructure-less ad-hoc mode of operation. There are wireless gateways at regular intervals providing access to the rest of the Internet using infrastructure support (either wired or multi-hop wireless). A unicast routing protocol is available to support packet transmissions between the network nodes. Nodes may or may not run the peer-to-peer application protocol. Nodes use TCP for reliable transfer of data and UDP for dissemination of *gossip* messages for content availability. The data unit for the swarming protocol is a *chunk*. That is, the content is broken up into equal sized *chunks* each with their unique identity. These chunks are shared and transferred among the peers. The terms chunks and pieces are used interchangeably throughout this article and have the same meaning. The problem is to design an application level protocol for vehicular ad hoc networks that disseminates data over this network in an efficient and scalable fashion and improves client perceived performance in the presence of transient connectivity.

We propose *CarTorrent* which builds on the fundamental mechanisms of partial downloading and sharing of content in *BitTorrent* but adapts to the wireless scenario by using different mechanisms for peer discovery, selection and content delivery.

6.3   The Protocol

CarTorrent has the same generic structure of any swarming protocol. Peers downloading a file form a mesh and exchange pieces of the file amongst them-

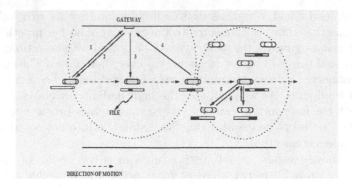

Fig. 12. Evolution of a file in a node using the SPAWN protocol. (1) A car arrives in the range of a gateway, (2) initiates a download (3) downloads a piece of the file. (4) After getting out of range, (5) starts to gossip with its neighbors about content availability and (6) exchanges pieces of the file, thereby getting a larger portion of the file as opposed to waiting for the next gateway to resume the download

selves. However the wireless setting of VANETs, characterized by limited capacity, intermittent connectivity and high degree of churn in nodes (cars) requires it to adapt in specific ways. Fig. 12 and the pseudo-code describe the basic operation of the *CarTorrent* protocol.

There are several components to the operation of the *CarTorrent* protocol like Peer Discovery, Peer and Content Selection, and Content Discovery and Selection.

6.4   Peer Discovery

When a new car enters the vehicular network (such as entering a freeway or a section of freeway with access points), it requests the Gateway for the particular file. If the Gateway has the file in its cache, it starts uploading a chunk to the node. Decision policies with respect to chunk choice are discussed later. The node starts downloading chunks from the Gateway while it is in range. The Gateway also bootstraps it with a list of the last known peers (cars) who requested for the same file. Thus the car has an idea of how popular the file is and how likely it is to benefit from cooperative strategies.

The centralized approach to peer discovery in *BitTorrent* has several disadvantages (beyond the most obvious disadvantage of having a central point of failure). In our scenario, the Gateway can only bootstrap an incoming peer with the last few peers that passed by and were interested in the same file. This set is too small for efficient sharing/downloading. We propose a decentralized mechanism for peer discovery to be carried out en route. We utilize the broadcast medium of the wireless channel to gossip information about the content availability at neighbors.

In *CarTorrent*, the centralized approach and the gossiping mechanism can be used in conjunction to construct the mesh of peers and update connectivity information continuously.

Gossip is the mechanism used to advertise the chunks that a particular peer possesses. A Gossip Message contains information to identify the file being distributed by the Gateway, and representing the list of chunks that the originator possesses, a timestamp indicating when it was originated, and a list of node-ids indicating which nodes processed it along the route. All nodes within range will hear it and process it depending on their type. We evaluate various gossiping schemes which we describe in this section.

Probabilistic Spawn. Spawners not interested in the particular file listen to gossip messages of that file and forward them with a low probability. *Interested Spawners* listen to those gossip messages and forward them with a higher probability after stamping the route-list of the packet with their own id. An *Interested spawner* who is currently downloading a file will generate Gossip messages on completion of downloading a new piece.

Rate-Limited Spawn. Each *Spawner* maintains two caches, a Non-Interested cache of gossip messages about files that it is not interested in, and an Interested cache. Periodically, gossip messages are picked up from one of the caches and re-broadcasted (without updating the origination time-stamp). Interested cache messages are selected at a higher frequency. The decision about which message to select from a particular cache can be made in different ways.

1. **Rate-Limited-Recent Spawn:** The gossip message with the most recent origination time-stamp is forwarded.
2. **Rate-Limited-Random Spawn:** The gossip message is selected at random from the relevant table.

6.5   Peer and Content Selection

TCP connections spanning fewer hops perform better in multi-hop wireless networks. To that end, *CarTorrent* does some intelligent Peer Selection based on the distance of the peer possessing a certain piece it intends to download. This information is gathered from the gossip messages. One could also gather this information from GPS enabled traffic-safety messages that are likely to become "standard" applications running on vehicles in the future. However we decided to keep our "inference" methodology independent of other applications that may co-exist on the same node.

We introduce a *proximity-driven piece selection* strategy. It uses several distinct strategies to choose which piece to download, based on how much has been downloaded already. Selecting pieces to download in an order that reduces contention at the peer serving the piece has a definite impact on performance as observed earlier. We employ several strategies that might perform better in the wireless setting. We estimate proximity based on hop-count. Other approaches to estimate proximity can be using ping messages to measure round-trip times, however this approach inadvertently introduces more delay and message overhead.

Our hop-count based estimate performs well in a mobile wireless scenario. By bringing proximity awareness to content selection, users will experience seamless downloads. We refer the interested reader to a more detailed paper [31].

6.6   Design Rationale

It has been argued that the key deciding factor to whether a large ad hoc network is feasible is the locality of traffic. The effect of traffic locality determines to a large extent the scalability of per node capacity. *CarTorrent* tries to minimize the peer-side wall clock time taken to download a large file. *CarTorrent* like all swarming protocols is motivated by the fact that for popular files, the content distributor becomes the bottleneck as far as bandwidth and processing is concerned while the downloaders have ample spare capacity. In vehicular networks this problem is further exacerbated due to the intermittent and short-lived connectivity to the infrastructure. This form of cooperative data transfer encourages locality in network traffic and consequently scales while at the same time providing extended perceived connectivity. We prove it more formally using simulation and analysis in [31].

6.7   Simulation

In this section we describe the simulations we performed to evaluate the gossip schemes proposed. We implemented the gossip schemes in *Nab* a network simulator written in *Ocaml*. *Nab* [32] is a fast (For example, a 100 node simulation run for 300 simulated seconds completes in 4 minutes), flexible and scalable simulator for ad-hoc networks. We incorporated our mobility model, and a simple traffic model into the simulator. The car arrival process at the access point follows a poisson distribution with the average interarrival time varying from 0.5 to 4 seconds. We consider only one direction of vehicle motion in the highway. The peer group is maintained among cars driving in the same direction. When a car comes within range of the gateway, it starts downloading random pieces of the file. The tracker running on the gateway bootstraps the car with a set of 6 peers who last crossed that gateway and were interested in the same file. Each car possesses an initial speed which is varied at random by a small amount every 5 seconds. Cars maintain the same direction throughout and are not affected by the speeds of cars around them. The simulation parameters are as follows: File Size is 5MB, the piece size is 64KB and the velocity varies from 40-80mph.

We used a simplified version of the 802.11 DCF protocol implemented in the NAB simulator. In particular, the gossip messages are broadcast in the CSMA mode of 802.11. At the network layer we used AODV (Ad-Hoc On-Demand Distance Vector Routing). There are other on demand routing protocols such as DSR (Dynamic Source Routing) which can be potentially used in Vehicular Ad-Hoc Networks. Moreover, proactive routing protocols (e.g. OLSR) could also be used. The optimal choice of routing scheme is clearly an important issue. However since the focus of this paper is to evaluate application layer strategies, we will keep our study routing protocol agnostic. Leveraging routing protocol spe-

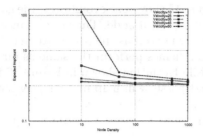

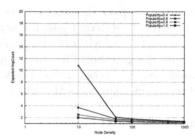

Fig. 13. Impact of Average Velocity on the Expected # of Application Hops needed to find a peer, with varying node densities

Fig. 14. Impact of Popularity of the File on the Expected # of Application Hops needed to find a peer with the file, with varying node densities

cific messages(for instance coupling our gossip messages with RREQ messages for efficiency purposes is part of continuing research effort). For channel data transfer rate we assume the typical 802.11a data transfer rate. This is a conservative assumption given that DSRC has a rate varying from 6-27Mbps. We are interested in the efficiency of the gossip schemes, the message overhead each scheme introduces. We analyze the impact of each of the simulation and traffic model parameters on the performance of the gossip schemes.

6.8   Analysis of Gossip Schemes

There are essentially three characteristics which we observe while evaluating the gossip mechanisms: (a) Good Peer Set Length: "Good Peer" is defined as the set of peers that are within k hops of a particular node. In all our simulations we set k to be 3. (b) Local File Downloaded (c) Peer-Space File Downloaded: the total fraction of the file that is present at a node and its Peer-List nodes.

We are interested in the Peer-Space File Evolution since this is the upper bound for the achievable fraction of the file for a particular car at a particular instant. The number of Good Peers in the Peer-List is a measure of the locality

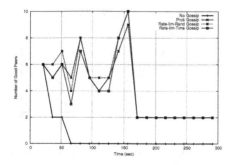

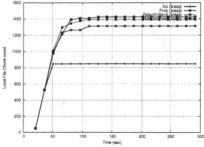

Fig. 15. Number of Good Peers

Fig. 16. Local File-Chunk Evolution

awareness of the peer discovery scheme. Figure 15 shows the evolution of the good peer list with the different gossip schemes at a typical node. The performance of a swarming protocol without any gossip clearly falls off as the peer starts moving away from the gateway. The various gossip schemes perform the same as far as the good peer set is concerned. The local File Evolution shown in Figure 16 for different schemes supports the intuition that gossip will help in retrieving more pieces of the file. The Peer-Space File Evolution in Figure 18 depicts that the gossip does enable robust peer discovery in the presence of high churn of peers.

6.9   Message Overhead

The advantages of gossip are clearly visible in the simulation results we presented. A natural question to ask is what is the cost of this robustness and location awareness? We ran simulations to analyze the Message Overhead of each of the gossip schemes. One of the simulation parameters that would have an impact on the overhead is the Forwarding Interval of the gossip messages. Figures 17 and 19 show that by varying the forwarding interval the overhead re-

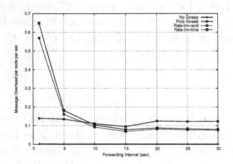

Fig. 17. Message Overhead with Forwarding Interval

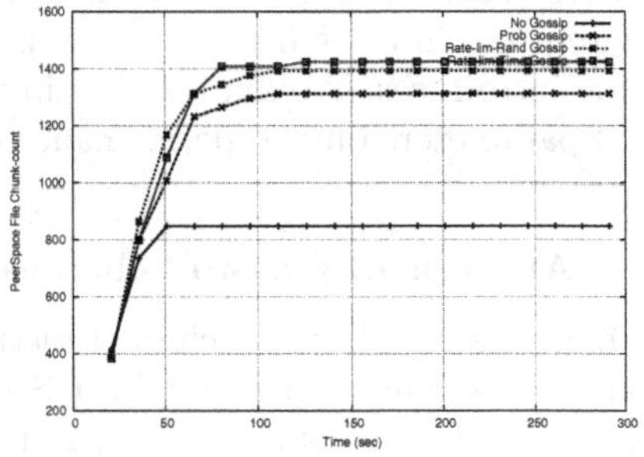

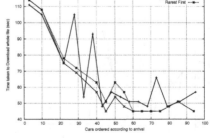

Fig. 18. Peer-Space File-Chunk Evolution

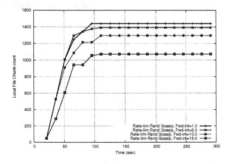

Fig. 19. Effect of Forwarding Interval on Chunk Evolution

Fig. 20.   Different   PieceSelection Strategies

duces considerably while still keeping the local File- Chunk evolution relatively stable. For our simulation runs, a forwarding interval of 1 second provided low message overhead and decent evolution rate.

6.10   Piece Selection Strategy

We experimented with three different piece selection strategies: *First Available*, *Rarest First* and *Rarest Closest*. First Available tries to fill the first empty chunk in the bit-field that can be filled. The search procedure is from low index to high, so lower index bitfields get filled up faster. Such a strategy is useful for files which have partial content usefulness. Some Mpeg files will play parts of the file if you have the partial file, so in these cases it would be advantageous to assemble the initial parts of the file first. Rarest First is the BitTorrent policy of searching for the rarest bit-field in your peerlist and downloading it. In wireless networks this could suffer from problems such as trying to download a rare piece from someone quite far away, while a slightly less rare piece is located very close to you. Connections to far away hosts are likely be unstable and lossy so we experiment with a variation of the rarest first scheme called Rarest Closest which weighs the rare pieces based on the distance to the closest peer who has that piece. Rare pieces which are situated closer to the node are preferred.

A node can guess the distance of a particular peer by looking at the gossip message of the peer, and calculating the number of nodes which have stamped the packet from the relevant field. Figure 20 shows the experienced download times for the three strategies; it is clear that Rarest Closest consistently gives shorter download times than Rarest First. First Available does the worst since it encourages determinism and reduces the entropy of the system.

6.11   Popularity Index

One of the critical factors in determining the download time of a file is its popularity. We varied the popularity index of the file (the percentage of cars that are interested in this file) from 20% to 80%. Figure 21 shows the percentage of the file that is downloaded by the cars in the allotted 300 seconds time. It is

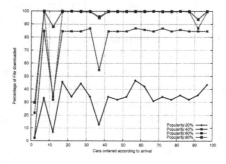

Fig. 21. Popularity works !

clear that low popularity files are slow to download, however the speed ramps up pretty fast and gets bottlenecked by the capacity of the wireless channel at around 60% popularity. From there on, there are always "enough" new chunks for cars to keep downloading until they finish.

6.12   The Future of VANETs

We looked at vehicular ad-hoc wireless networks and how advances in peer-to-peer research can be adapted to these settings to improve the perceived throughput of the network. We gave a brief overview of the product of our research, the *CarTorrent* protocol which tries to achieve the design goals of scalability in wireless networks, improved perceived performance for individual clients using co-operation in highly mobile scenario. Research in vehicular networks has made tremendous strides over the past decade. Prominent players like BMW, Daimler-Chrysler, and Toyota, are looking at this area very carefully to determine the right mix of ingredients which makes life easier for the driver without taking away personal control or jeopardizing privacy. Infotainment within the vehicle is again one of the grey areas, where it is difficult to determine when entertainment becomes distraction.

We envision the day when you are zipping down the highway listening to your favorite radio station when you hear a really good song. You hit the download button on your player. As you pass a gateway, the player initiates a *CarTorrent* download of the file. After you cross the gateway, your player starts gossiping with neighboring cars advertising your interest in the file. You also hear other cars advertising some pieces and start downloading pieces from them. In about 5-10 minutes, you've assembled all the pieces of the file with a combination of downloading through the gateway and exchanging pieces with your neighboring cars. From then on, you can keep playing that song until you get it out of your head. Until that day, research on vehicular networks will continue to strive towards getting information to the car faster, swifter, and better.

7   Conclusions and Future Trends

In this chapter we have looked at the "mobility attribute" of ad hoc networks under two different aspects, namely: mobility as an enemy that must be fought, and; mobility as a friend that can help us design more efficient networks. These two aspects are often intertwined, as shown in the Car Torrent case study. The exploitation of mobility to assist routing via epidemic dissemination and the use of "data mules" to help with long lasting disconnections are very novel, and perhaps a bit "controversial" concepts. The epidemic dissemination in particular requires the willingness of third parties to help as store and forwarders. Looking into the future, as ad hoc networks will move from battlefield to commercial scenarios, we will witness a shift from large scale, reliable, structured, preplanned operations to smaller scale, spontaneous, casual interaction between nomadic users. This will lead to an increase in popularity of "opportunistic", epidemic, peer to peer routing and information dissemination schemes. In this opportunistic, "autonomic" world, it will be indeed essential to deal with mobility - starting with realistic individual and group models of mobility, and also make any possible effort to harness mobility to advantage. We expect that in future ad hoc network studies the mobility "variable" will receive at least as much attention as other important parameters such as time varying channel characteristics, traffic distribution, node distribution, Quality of Service requirements and energy constraints.

References

1. Kaplan, E.: Understanding the gps: Principles and applications (1996)
2. Rappaport, T.: Wireless communications: Principles and practice (1995)
3. Mills, D.: Internet time synchronization: the network time protocol. IEEE Transactions on Communications **39** (1991) 1482–1493
4. Su, W.: Motion Prediction in MobileNireless Networks. PhD thesis, UCLA, Computer Science Department (1999)
5. Toh, C.: Associativity-based routing for ad-hoc mobile networks. Wireless Personal Communications **4** (1997) 103–139
6. Liu, J., Singh, S.: Atcp: Tcp for mobile ad hoc networks. IEEE Journal on Selected Areas in Communications **19** (2001) 1300–1315
7. Karp, B., Kung, H.T.: Greedy perimeter stateless routing for wireless networks. In: ACM MobiCom. (2000) 243–254
8. Pei, G., Gerla, M., Chen, T.W.: Fisheye state routing in mobile ad hoc networks. In: ICDCS Workshop on Wireless Networks and Mobile Computing. (2000)
9. Pei, G., Gerla, M., Chen, T.W.: Fisheye state routing: A routing scheme for ad hoc wireless networks. In: IEEE ICC. (2000)
10. Kleinrock, L., Stevens, K.: Fisheye: A lenslike computer display transformation. Technical report, UCLA Computer Science Department (1971)
11. Perkins, C., Bhagwat, P.: Highly dynamic destionation-sequenced distance-vector routing (dsdv) for mobilie computers. In: ACM SIGCOMM. (1994)
12. Xue, F., Kumar, P.R.: The number of neighbors needed for connectivity of wireless networks. Wireless Networks **10** (2004)
13. Li, N., Hou, J.C.: Improving connectivity of wireless ad-hoc networks. Technical Report UIUCDCS-R-2004-2485, UIUC DCS (2004)
14. Zhao, W., Ammar, M., Zegura, E.: A message ferrying approach for data delivery in sparse mobile ad hoc networks. In: ACM MobiHoc. (2004)
15. DTNRG: Delay tolerant networking research group. (http://www.dtnrg.org/)
16. DTN: Disruption tolerant networking. (http://www.darpa.mil/ato/solicit/DTN/)
17. Ratnasamy, S., Francis, P., Handley, M., Karp, R., Shenker, S.: A scalable content-addressable network. In: ACM SIGCOMM. (2001)
18. Rowstron, A., Druschel, P.: Pastry: Scalable, decentralized object location and routing for large-scale peer-to-peer systems. In: 18th IFIP/ACM International Conference on Distributed Systems Platforms (Middleware 2001). (2001)
19. Stoica, I., Morris, R., Karger, D., Kaashoek, M.F., Balakrishnan, H.: Chord: A scalable peer-to-peer lookup service for internet applications. In: ACM SIGCOMM. (2001)

20. Zhao, B.Y., Huang, L., Stribling, J., Rhea, S.C., Joseph, A.D., Kubiatowicz, J.D.: Tapestry: A resilient global-scale overlay for service deployment. IEEE JSAC **22** (2004)
21. Pei, G., Gerla, M., Hong, X.: Lanmar: Landmark routing for large scale wireless ad hoc networks with group mobility. In: ACM MobiHoc. (2000)
22. Tsuchiya, P.F.: The landmark hierarchy: a new hierarchy for routing in very large networks. ACM Computer Communication Review **18** (1988) 35–42
23. Gerla, M., Hong, X., Pei, G.: Landmark routing for large ad hoc wireless networks. In: IEEE Globecom. (2000)
24. Xu, K., Hong, X., Gerla, M.: Landmark routing in ad hoc networks with mobile backbones. Journal of Parallel and Distributed Computing (JPDC), Special Issues on Ad Hoc Networks (2003) 110–123
25. Banerjee, S., Khuller, S.: A clustering scheme for hierarchical control in multi-hop wireless networks. In: IEEE Infocom. (2001)
26. Sinha, P., Sivakumar, R., Bharghavan, V.: Enhancing ad hoc routing with dynamic virtual infrastructures. In: IEEE Infocom. (2001)
27. Perkins, C.E.: Ad hoc networking (2001)
28. Basagni, S., Chlamtac, I., Syrotiuk, V.R.: A distance routing effect algorithm for mobility (dream). In: ACM MobiCom. (1998)
29. Grossglauser, M., Vetterli, M.: Locating nodes with ease: Last encounter routing in ad hoc networks through mobility diffusion. In: IEEE Infocom. (2003)
30. Zhao, W., Ammar, M.: Proactive routing in highly-partitioned wireless ad hoc networks. In: 9th IEEE International Workshop on Future Trends of Distributed Computing Systems. (2003)
31. Nandan, A., Das, S., Pau, G., Sanadidi, M.Y., Gerla, M.: Cooperative downloading in vehicular ad-hoc wireless networks. In: Wireless On-Demand Network and Services. (2005)
32. Ferriere, H.D.: Nab (network in a box). (http://nab.epfl.ch/)

Performance Analysis of Mobile Systems

Vincenzo Grassi

Dipartimento di Informatica, Sistemi e Produzione,
Università di Roma "Tor Vergata", Italy
vgrassi@info.uniroma2.it

Abstract. Mobile systems, where both computing nodes and software components can dynamically change their location, are already a reality, thanks to technological advances in several related fields. The high variability and heterogeneity of these systems raises severe performance problems, thus requiring a careful planning of any performance validation activity concerning these systems. This paper reviews some approaches that have been proposed to this end, presenting them within a general framework aimed at supporting a systematic approach to the validation of non functional attributes. In this framework we emphasize that one of the key points for the actual and effective introduction of non-functional attributes validation since the early design phases is the definition of *model-based transformations* from design-oriented models to analysis-oriented models.

1 Introduction

Two kinds of technological advances are having a profound impact on the way software applications are designed. On one side, advances in wired and wireless communication technologies are leading to the pervasive deployment of large-scale and ubiquitous networking infrastructures, providing support for *wide area computing*, where application components are spread and cooperate over geographical distance. On the other side, advances in component miniaturization are leading to the increasing diffusion of portable computing and communication devices, providing support (in conjunction with wireless technologies) to *mobile computing*, where some of the application components are hosted by mobile devices. As a consequence, the execution environment of a distributed application is likely to be characterized by a high dynamicity and variance in both the computing capacity of the hosting nodes, that span powerful fixed hosts and less powerful portable devices, and in the communication bandwidth and latency, with the former ranging from tens of Kbps to tens of Mbps, depending on the type of wireless or wired network [49], and the latter ranging from negligible to non negligible values in case of geographically distant nodes.

The high variability and heterogeneity of wide area and mobile computing environments rises problems that could be considered negligible in the local area environments considered in the past as the usual target for distributed applications. In particular, it can have a profound impact on the quality of service (e.g. performance or reliability) experienced by the end users.

M. Bernardo and A. Bogliolo (Eds.): SFM-Moby 2005, LNCS 3465, pp. 107–154, 2005.
© Springer-Verlag Berlin Heidelberg 2005

The addition of adaptation features to distributed applications can be a viable way to cope with these problems [24, 29, 36]. In this respect, the technologies, architectures and methodologies traditionally used to develop distributed applications in local area environments, usually based on the notion of *location transparency*, do not provide an adequate support. On the contrary, *location awareness* (or, more generally, *context awareness*) has been suggested as a more suitable approach to support since the early design phases the reasoning about possible adaptation strategies for wide area and mobile computing applications. In particular, explicitly considering components location at the application level straightforwardly leads to exploit the location change as a new dimension in the design and implementation of distributed applications. Indeed, *mobile code* design paradigms and technologies, based on the ability of moving code across the nodes of a network, have been introduced.[1] Thanks to the mobility of its components, a distributed application can adapt to the changing conditions of its environment by, for example, modifying the load at some of the hosting nodes or the traffic intensity on some network links.

Hence, a wide area or mobile computing application may be generally involved in two types of mobility: the *physical mobility* of some of the hosting nodes, and the *virtual mobility* of some of its components. We call *mobile system* any computing system where at least one of them is present.

Both these kinds of mobility can have a large impact on quality attributes of a distributed application. In this paper, we focus on attributes related to the application *performance*. In this respect, physical mobility can cause a mobile node to connect to resources with different performance capabilities and possibly belonging to different administrative domains, with the consequent overhead for access and security controls. Moreover, a mobile node can enter zones covered by wireless networks with reduced or intermittent bandwidth, or not covered at all, thus causing variable communication delays.

On the other hand, using virtual mobility different but functionally equivalent software architectures can be designed and implemented. For example, remote resources must no longer be accessed remotely; instead, (part of) the application can move to use the resources locally. Under the right circumstances, this can reduce both network traffic and network protocol overhead, so reducing the total amount of work done by the system, and improving the performance of the entire system. On the other hand, under the wrong circumstances, the entire system slows down, e.g. because of excessive migration traffic, or increased load at already congested nodes.

Hence, the validation of mobile systems against specific performance attributes is necessary, and calls for a careful planning of this activity.

The main goal of this paper is to discuss the performance validation of mobile systems. Toward this end, we first provide in section 2 some general guidelines for a systematic approach to the validation of performance (or, more generally, of some non functional attribute) of a software system. In section 2 we emphasize that one of

---

[1] Proposed paradigms differ in the definition of the movement "initiator" (code can move autonomously or upon request) and the type of moving entities (that span code fragments and whole execution units).

the key points for the actual and effective introduction of performance validation since the early design phases, is the definition of *model-based transformations* from design-oriented models to analysis-oriented models. Then, the performance validation of mobile systems will be presented in the next sections as an "instance" of the general framework outlined in section 2.

In section 3 we discuss the basic elements that characterize the domain of mobile systems. In section 4 we present modeling frameworks that have been proposed for mobile system. Then, in section 5, we present transformations from models defined within these frameworks to suitable analysis models. In both section 4 and 5 we present a general overview of some proposals that have appeared in the literature, and then discuss in some detail a particular proposal we have made.

Finally, section 6 concludes the paper and provides hints for future research.

2 Non Functional Requirements Validation

The validation of software systems can be performed versus functional and/or non-functional requirements (NFR). Approaches basically differ in the two cases, as the former are statements of services the software system should provide, how it should react to particular inputs and behave in particular situations (what the system does), whereas NFR are constraints on the quality of the services offered by the software system (how the system does what it does, e.g. with which performance or reliability).

It has been widely argued that NFR validation should be performed since the early design phases, before the system is actually implemented, to provide guidelines for further design refinements and to reduce the costs of late problem fixing [45, 46]. As an obvious implication of this argument, NFR validation must be based on *predictive* analysis methodologies applied to some suitable system model. In the past, the construction of such models has been often considered as an "art" that required special skills. This is at least partially true, but it has not contributed (together with other reasons dictated by, for example, short time to market) to the acceptance of NFR validation within the software community, where such skills could be absent. As a consequence, NFR validation is often neglected in software development.

To get a wider acceptance, we think that it is more convenient to give a definition of NFR validation as a systematic activity with some clearly identified key steps (where some "creativity" is of course allowed!), rather than as some unstructured "artistic" activity.

As a contribution in this direction, we identify as a first step a grid of "dimensions" along which a NFR validation methodology can be classified, so that any methodology can be seen as a particular instance within this grid. Then, to give some guidelines toward a systematic approach to NFR validation, we argue that values along different dimensions cannot be freely selected, but some dependencies exist among some of them, that restrict the set of possible "values" and suggest a path to be followed in selecting those values.

The dimensions along which we classify NFR validation methodologies are as follows:

system domain (**SD**) - the relevant characteristics of the system to be analyzed, that include, for example, its architectural style and its structure (e.g. client-server, peer-to-peer, ..., local area, wide area, ...);

starting model notation (**SMN**) - the notation used to express a model of the system at some stage of its development process (e.g. UML, process algebra, ..) ;

non-functional attribute (**NFA**) – the non-functional attribute that is concerned with the set of requirements that the software system must fulfill (e.g., reliability, performance, safety, etc.);

missing information (**MI**) – the information that is lacking in the software system description expressed using the selected SMN, which is rather crucial for the type of validation that is pursued (e.g., number of invocations of a component within a certain scenario, mapping of components to platform sites, etc.[2]);

collection technique (**CT**) – the technique adopted to collect the missing information (e.g., prototype execution, retrieving from a repository of projects);

target model notation (**TMN**) – the notation adopted for representing the model whose solution provides the non-functional attribute values useful for the validation task (e.g., Petri Nets, Queuing Networks, etc.);

solution technique (**ST**) – the technique adopted to process the target model expressed using the selected TMN, and obtain a numerical solution (e.g., simulation, analytical, etc.).

Every validation methodology can be reduced to a selection of values along the above dimensions. For example, in a Bayesian approach to the reliability validation of some software system whose design is expressed using UML, and where the operational profile and the failure probabilities are missing, the following values may be selected:

   system domain (**SD**) = "don't care";
   starting model notation (**SMN**) = Unified Modeling Language;
   non-functional attribute (**NFA**) = reliability;
   missing information (**MI**) = operational profile, failure probabilities;
     collection technique (**CT**) = repository (operational profile), unit testing (failure probabilities);
   target model notation (**TMN**) = Bayesian stochastic model;
   solution technique (**ST**) = numerical simulation.

The choice of a value along some dimension is not always independent of the choices of the other ones. In many cases the domain of a choice is restricted to a subset of potential values as a consequence of a value selected along a different dimension. For example, in case a reliability validation has to be performed (i.e., NFA=reliability), it is quite inconvenient to choose a Queuing Model as target (i.e., TMN=Queueing Model), because queues are suitable to represent delays and contentions, and they badly work to combine failure probabilities.

---

[2] Usually the missing information appears (in the whole approach) either as annotations on the available software system description or as an integration of the description itself (in the latter case, for example, in the transition from process algebras to stochastic process algebras).

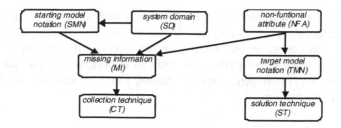

Fig. 1. Graph of dependencies among dimensions for NFR validation

In figure 1 we propose a dependency graph, where each node represents one of the above dimensions. An arrow from node *i* to node *j* suggests that the *j* depends in some way on *i*. This means that it would be better choosing the value of *j* after choosing the value of *i*; in other words, the value assigned to *i* helps the validation team to better understand which would be the more appropriate choice for *j*. Hence, this dependency graph suggests a partial order in the choices that a validation team has to perform in order to accomplish its validation task. However, we point out that this partial order is not mandatory, as other considerations could influence the selection of some values.

According to figure 1, the first steps in a validation activity consists quite obviously in identifying the domain of interest (SD) for the validation activity itself and the type of validation to perform (NFA).

Then, the selection of SMN should be driven by SD, as the SMN should be suitable to express the relevant aspects of the system to be analyzed, e.g. its architectural style.

The value of MI depends on SMN, SD and NFA. It depends on NFA since the information lacking in the system design may heavily differ depending on the type of non-functional attribute to validate. On the other hand, the dependency from SMN stems from the consideration that the adopted SMN determines the set of items and relationships that are available to model the software system, hence determines also the set of missing items and relationships, depending on the type of validation to perform. Finally, the dependency from SD takes into account the fact that the architectural style may help to determine the missing information.

The dependency between NFA and TMN derives from the consideration that the same non-functional attribute can be validated using different types of model (e.g. Petri Nets and Queuing Models are suitable models for performance evaluation), but the complexity of the validation process may heavily change by using a notation rather than another, and this depends on the specific non-functional requirements under validation.

Finally, ST depends on TMN since a certain type of model can be solved (almost in all cases) by different techniques with different solution process complexity. Therefore, it is generally better to delay the choice of a solution technique after the selection of the model notation, in order to be able to use the technique with lowest complexity. Analogously, CT depends on MI, as if we know what type of information has to be collected then we can devise a much effective technique for the CT task.

For any pair of dimensions without a connecting path in the graph of figure 1, no evident dependency occurs, namely their values can be concurrently selected because one value does not bring any information on the other one. For example, there is no dependency between CT and TMN, as the way we collect the missing information is not affected by the type of target model notation, which affects, instead, the way we represent that information.

The sort of "task graph" depicted in figure 1 provides suggestions for a more systematic approach to NFR validation, but this is likely to be not enough to make NFR validation fully accepted within the software design process. In particular, once a specific SMN and TMN have been selected, a further problem to be faced is the transition from a design-oriented model (i.e. a model produced during the "normal" development process) expressed using SMN to a representative analysis-oriented model (i.e. a model that lends itself to the application of some analysis methodology [22]) expressed using TMN. This task is not trivial at all and could require some specific expertise.

Hence, it seems reasonable that any approach to the validation of NFR should also require a minimal effort to the design team to conduct predictive analysis of non-functional attributes. This requirement calls for the development of *model transformation* tools, that take as input some design-oriented model of the software system and (almost) automatically generate an analysis-oriented model. In this way, the specific expertise needed to build an analysis-oriented model is embedded within the transformation tool, and only a limited knowledge about this point is required to? the design team.

The general problem of defining model transformations and designing tools that implement them is considered in the framework of Model Driven Development (MDD) [30, 32, 33]. For the particular type of model transformations we are interested in here, a thorough review of approaches to the generation of performance models from design models can be found in [44]. These approaches differ in the assumed notation for the design-oriented model (SMN in our classification), and in the generated analysis-oriented models (TMN), spanning queueing networks, Petri nets, Markov processes, simulation models. Hence, for what concerns the selection of a SMN, a further criterion that could drive this selection, besides being suitable for the domain of interest, is the availability of a transformation methodology toward the selected TMN.

However, in the perspective of a smooth integration of NFR validation within the software design process, we point out that suitability for the domain of interest and availability of a transformation methodology towards some TMN are not the only criteria to be considered for the selection of a SMN. A further criterion should be based on the consideration of a minimal affection on the software notation and the software process usually adopted by a design team. From this viewpoint, the selection of SMN could also be driven by the expertise in some particular modeling notation accumulated in the past by the design and validation team.

The track of this paper is to look, within the framework introduced in this section, at the software validation approaches having SD in the domain of *mobile systems* and NFA in the domain of *performance*. Starting from this selection for SD and NFA, we will only discuss issues concerning the definition of a suitable SMN and of the related MI needed to support performance analysis, and the transformation to some suitable TMN. We will not discuss issues concerning the ST and CT dimensions.

3   The Mobile Systems Domain (SD = "Mobile System")

In this section we discuss the relevant aspects that characterize a mobile system, to provide a reference framework for the modeling approaches that will be reviewed in section 4.

As already discussed in the introduction, what basically characterizes a mobile system is the presence of *virtual* or *physical mobile entities*.

Virtual mobile entities can be, in principle, any kind of software artifact (run time entity), intended as the manifestation of a software component (design time entity). On the other hand, the physical mobile entities we are basically interested in are computing nodes (and the execution environments inside them). However, we could also be interested in other kinds of physical mobile entities, whose movement causes the actual mobility of computing nodes (e.g. vehicles, persons).

To reason about the movement of mobile entities, we have to define some underlying concept of *location*. Basically, the location of a virtual entity is the computing node that hosts it, while the location of a physical entity is some point in a physical (2- or 3-dimensional) space. Hence, virtual and physical entities move in a discrete and continuous space of locations, respectively. However, for what concerns physical entities, we could not be interested in such a fine-grained notion of location. Often, we are interested in a coarser notion, where the location of a physical entity is defined as a region of the physical space delimited in some suitable way (e.g. a room in a building, delimited by its walls; a cell in a cellular system, delimited by the coverage range of its antenna). As a consequence, discrete spaces of locations could be suitable to describe the movement of both physical and virtual entities.

Given a space of locations, movement is usually not free within it, but is generally constrained by the existence of a *channel* between the location where the moving entity currently is and the destination location. This concept of channel is very generic, and applies to both virtual and physical movements. In the virtual case, it could correspond to a network link between two workstations, that allows software components located at one of them to migrate towards the other workstation. In the physical case, it could correspond to a corridor between two rooms, that allows a mobile device (the person holding it) to move from a room to the other.

Finally, nesting relationships may exist among both virtual and physical entities. A virtual entity may be embedded within another virtual entity (e.g. a class within a class closure). A physical entity may be nested within another physical entity (e.g. a portable computing device within a person holding it, a person within some vehicle). Moreover, at the boundary between the virtual and physical "worlds", the notion itself of location of a virtual entity could be thought of as a nesting relationship between that entity and the computing node (execution environment) it is directly allocated to.

Nesting relationships have a twofold implication. They introduce the need of a hierarchical concept of location (for example, depending on the context, the location of a software sub-component could be better defined as the component it is part of, the computing node where that component is allocated, or the physical space region where that node presently resides). Moreover, the movement of some entity indirectly causes the movement of all the entities that are nested within it.

Up to now we have discussed indifferently of physical and virtual mobility. However, it could be useful to point out that they play different roles from the viewpoint of an application designer. Indeed, physical mobility is an environment feature that is generally out of the control of the designer; in other words, it is a sort of constraint she has to deal with, to meet the application requirements. On the other hand, logical mobility is really a tool in her hands, that she can exploit to better adapt the application to the environment where it will be deployed. In this respect, we point out that code mobility, as it is intended in this perspective, should not be confused with the well known concept of process migration, even if the adopted mechanisms to implement them may be similar. Process migration is a (distributed) OS issue, realized transparently to the application (usually to get load balancing), and hence does not represent a tool in the hands of the application designer; on the contrary, code mobility is intended to bring the ability of changing location under the control of the designer, so representing a new tool she can exploit to accomplish quality requirements.

In particular, for what concerns virtual mobility, some basic patterns have been identified, that can be followed by the application designer to implement some application level adaptation policy based on code mobility: the Code on Demand (COD), Remote Evaluation (REV) and Mobile Agent pattern (MA) [13].

The COD and REV patterns can be defined as the "location-aware" extensions of the basic "location-unaware" client-server (CS) interaction pattern. Indeed, in the CS case, we have some software component that invokes an operation implemented by some other software artifact; the operation result is then sent back to the caller. This interaction pattern is realized independently of the location of the two partners, that does not change during the interaction.

In the COD case, upon invocation of the operation, if the artifact that implements the operation is remotely located, a copy of it is first moved to the caller location and then executed.

Conversely, in the REV case, upon invocation of a locally available software artifact, a copy of it is first sent to a specified remote location, where it is executed.

In both the COD and REV patterns only "passive" code is sent to some location. On the contrary, in the MA pattern an active software artifact moves together with its state, at some point of its execution, to a different location where it will resume its execution. The state which is moved may consists of internal variables only (*weak* mobility) or it may include also the program counter and execution stack (*strong* mobility). In the latter case the moving artifact can resume its execution from the exact point where it was stopped, while in the former case some convention must be established about the execution resumption point.

To conclude this section, we note that, for a computing system, the movement of some of its parts (be they virtual or physical) is not relevant per se, but because it can change their *context*, i.e. the type, quality and number of resources (e.g. computing devices, communication links, access rights) that are available at the location where they reside. These context changes can have on impact on the functions the system can perform and on their quality.

In this respect, we should note that the context can change not only along a spatial dimension (because of different available resources at different locations) but also along a temporal dimension independently of any movement (because of changes in the available resources at the same location). Examples of the latter case are a wireless link with variable bandwidth because of interference, or a computing device that is switched on and off by its owner.

As a consequence, we may also consider the mobile systems as a special case of more general *variable context systems*, where mobility is only one of the possible causes of context variability. According to this different perspective, one could argue that we should focus directly on context changes rather than viewing them as a consequence of mobility, to deal uniformly with all the types of variable context systems.

4 Mobile Systems Models (Which SMN When SD = "Mobile System"?)

In this section we review some modeling frameworks that have been proposed for mobile systems. This review does not intend to be complete, but we hope that it is representative of approaches that have been and are currently pursued in this field. In this respect, we point out that we are only interested in the modeling of mobility from an "application level" perspective, since our viewpoint is that of the software designer. We will not discuss issues concerning the modeling of "low level" mobility aspects (e.g. routing protocols, link layer communication).

The considerations made in section 3 can be used to discuss the merits of each SMN that will be reviewed. To summarize those considerations, a SMN for mobile systems should be able to deal with space of locations that are generally discrete and hierarchical (with, in principle, no limit to the depth of the hierarchy), where movement is allowed only among locations connected by suitable channels. Moreover, it should be able to represent both "involuntary" (physical) and "voluntary" (virtual) mobility. In the latter case, it should provide support for the modeling of "standard" mobility patterns (COD, REV, MA).

However, besides the ability of representing the various facets of a mobile system, a SMN should also be judged with respect to the issues raised in section 2, that can be summarized around the concept of "usability". Usability itself has several facets. One of them is related with the degree of integration of a given SMN for mobile systems with other notations used by a design team. Another one is related with "decomposability" issues in system design (also known as "separation of concerns"), i.e. the offered support for the modeling of different views of a system that are to some extent independent of each other. An example of this in the case of mobile systems is the separation that exists between the core "business logic" implemented by the system, and its mobility characteristics, which are often largely independent of each other (even if together contribute, for example, to its performance properties). A SMN that allows to separately modeling, as long as possible, these two aspects is likely to be more usable, as it may allow the designer to easily change a part of the design model (for example the one concerning the system mobility) without touching the other one. This could facilitate, for example, "what-if" experiments about the impact of different types of mobility (both physical and virtual) on the overall system performance.

We will classify the reviewed proposals into two broad classes: those based on formal modeling notations, and those based on somewhat less formal notations that are more used in the practice of system design. In the former case we will focus in particular on some proposals based on the use of suitable *process algebras*, since this is the kind of notation for which we are aware of an explicit translation methodology towards some TMN. However, we will also briefly mention other formal modeling proposals.

In the latter case, we will focus on proposals based on the *Unified Modeling Language* (UML) which is a de-facto standard notation in the industrial software development process.

Example 1. To illustrate some of the reviewed modeling proposals, we will use a simple application example based on a travel agency scenario, where a travel agency periodically contacts K airlines to get information about the cost of a ticket for some itinerary. The agency exchanges a sequence of N messages with each airline, to collect the required information. Using a traditional client-server approach, this means that the agency should explicitly establish N RPCs with each airline to complete the task. On the other hand, with a REV approach, the agency could send a code encompassing all the N messages along with some gluing operations, to be executed by each airline, getting only the final reply. Within a COD approach, we could think that the agency makes an overall request to each company, and that it is the responsibility of each airline to possibly get somewhere the needed code to fulfill the request. Finally, in an MA approach, the agency could deliver an agent that travels along all the K airlines getting locally the information, and then reports it back to the agency. Note that only virtual mobility is taken into consideration, but we think that it is sufficient for the purposes of this example. *EndOfExample1*

4.1 Formal SMN for Mobile Systems: Process Algebras Based Notations

The modeling approaches considered in this section are based on the selection of a process algebra as SMN. Process algebras are well-known formalisms for the modelling and analysis of parallel and distributed systems. What makes them attractive as SMN for the evaluation of large and complex systems, are mainly their compositional and abstraction features, that facilitate building complex system models from smaller ones. Moreover, they are equipped with a formal semantics, that allows a non ambiguous system specification, and a calculus that allows to prove rigorously whether some functional properties hold. We defer to the vast available literature for details about the general characteristics of these formalisms (e.g., [35]), and focus in this section on process algebras for the modeling of mobile software architectures. We only provide their (partial) formal syntax and informal descriptions of the corresponding semantics, aimed at illustrating the salient features of different approaches to formal modeling of mobile systems.

A process algebra is a formal language, whose syntax basically appears like this:

$$P ::= \mathbf{0} \mid \pi.P \mid P + P \mid P \parallel P \mid \dots {}^3$$

where $\mathbf{0}$ denotes the "null" (terminated) process that cannot perform any action, $+$ and $\parallel$ denote process composition by non-deterministic alternative or parallelism, respectively, and $\pi.P$ denotes the process that performs *action* π *Act,* and then behaves as P (where *Act* is a set of possible actions). Process algebras for mobility modeling basically differ in the set *Act* of actions the defined processes can perform. We group them into two sections, based on the way used to model the location of components.

Notations Without Explicit Location Specification. Algebras listed in this section can be considered as a direct derivation from CCS-like algebras [34], and are characterized by the lack of any explicit modeling of the location concept. What they model instead is a change in the links that connect processes, and that can be used to make them communicate to each other. Note that a change in the communication links "seen" by a process can be both the consequence of some kind of mobility (that leads the entity modeled by that process to a location characterized by different communication channels) or of other events (e.g. an interference that changes the quality of a channel). Hence, according to the considerations made at the end of section 3, these process algebras model variable context systems rather than just mobile systems, albeit with a notion of context restricted to communication channels only.

Before reviewing them, we briefly illustrate a basic CCS-like algebra. In this case, we have π $\{ \tau_i \ (i = 1, 2, \dots),$ **in**$x,$ **out**$x\}$, where τ_i denotes a "silent" (internal) action of a process[4], while **in** and **out** are input and output actions, respectively, along the link named x, that can be used to synchronize a process with another parallel process that executes their output or input counterparts along the same link. For example, if two processes are specified as follows:

$$P := \mathbf{out}a.P_1 \qquad\qquad Q := \mathbf{in}a.Q_1$$

from these definitions we get that $P \parallel Q$ evolves into $P_1 \parallel Q_1$, that is, processes P and Q synchronize (i.e., wait for each other) thanks to a communication along link a, and then prosecute in parallel (possibly independently of each other, if no other synchronizing communication takes place in their following behavior).

---

[3] Note that, for the sake of simplicity, this syntax is incomplete, since we are omitting constructs to define abstraction mechanisms, or recursive behavior, etc.

[4] Subscript i is used to distinguish different internal actions, which is useful for modeling purposes.

π-calculus [34]. This algebra, besides synchronization between parallel processes, allows also link names communication, so that we can change the links a process uses to communicate with other processes. The possible system actions are π {τ_i ($i = 1$, 2, ...), **in**x, **out**x, **in**$x(y)$, **out**$x(Y)$}, where in addition to the above definitions, Y (y) is a "link name" (link variable), sent (received) over the link named x. For example, with the following specifications:

$M := \textbf{out}a(b).\textbf{out}a(c).M$ $Q := \textbf{in}a(y).\textbf{out}y.Q$
$P_1 := \textbf{in}b.P_1$ $P_2 := \textbf{in}c.P_2$

we get that $M \parallel Q \parallel P_1 \parallel P_2$ evolves as a system where Q alternatively sees (and communicates with) P_1 and P_2, according to the link name sent to it by M along the channel a. Focusing on mobility modeling, this behavior could model a mobility pattern of Q that brings it alternatively close to P_1 and P_2. The same mechanism (in particular, the definition of M, that acts as a sort of controller of the mobility of Q) can be used to model both physical and virtual mobility. What changes is that in the former case the sending of a new link name models the effect of some physically observable mobility behavior that is out of the control of the system designer, while in the latter it is meant to model a mobility behavior which is under the control of the designer.

HOπ-calculus [43]. Besides the operations of π-calculus, this algebra allows also the communication of process names, so that we can change the behavior of the receiving process. The possible system actions are again π {τ_i ($i = 1, 2, ...$), **in**x, **out**x, **in**$x(y)$, **out**$x(Y)$)}, but, in addition to the above definitions, Y (y) may also be a "process name" (process variable) besides a link name (variable), sent (received) over the link named x. For example, with the following specifications:

$M := \textbf{out}a(b).\textbf{out}a(c).M$ $Q := \textbf{in}a(y).\textbf{out}y(R).Q$ $R := ...$
$P_1 := \textbf{in}b(w).w.P_1$ $P_2 := \textbf{in}c(z).z.P_2$

we get that $M \parallel Q \parallel P_1 \parallel P_2$ evolves as a system where process R is executed alternatively within P_1 and $|P_2$. With respect to π-calculus, the extension introduced in the HOπ-calculus allows a more direct mobility modeling (someone could argue: a more "intuitive" modeling): some processes (with each process seeing different links) could play the role of "locations", so that sending a process to one of this special processes can be used to model its movement to that location.

Example 2[5]. Let us consider the system of example 1 in the case of K=2 airlines, with Ai and ai (i=1, 2) denoting an airline and the channel used to communicate with it, C denoting the overall code corresponding to the N "low level" interactions, Ri the overall response collected at airline Ai, and *SelectBest* the operations to select the best ticket offer. Using HOπ-calculus, this application could be modeled as follows, in the case of the REV pattern (where *Sys* models the overall application):

$TravAg := \textbf{out}a1(C).\textbf{in}a1(x).\textbf{out}a2(C).\textbf{in}a2(x).SelectBest.TravAg$
$Ai := \textbf{in}ai(z).z.\textbf{out}ai(Ri).Ai$

---

[5] Adapted from [37].

SelectBest := ...
Sys := TravAg || A1 || A2

Note that in this example the Ai's play the role of location processes. *EndOfExample2.*

Notations with Explicit Location Specification. The above approaches suggest as SMN for the modeling of mobile systems a process algebra where the location of a process is indirectly defined in terms of its connectivity, i.e. the link names it sees and the identity of the processes it can communicate with at a given instant of time using those links; hence, the location of a process can be changed by changing the links it sees (by sending it new link names, as in the π-calculus, or by sending the process itself, i.e., its name, as in the HOπ-calculus to a receiving process that has a different location (again, defined by its connectivity)). Other process algebras approaches have been defined where the location of processes is directly and explicitly defined, giving it a first class status, so allowing for a more direct modeling and reasoning about problems related to locations, such as access rights or code mobility, thus making these algebras somewhat more appealing as SMN for mobile systems. Two of these approaches are the *Ambient* and the *KLAIM* calculus. In the following we briefly outline some of their features. As before, the presentation is far from complete, with the main goal of only giving some flavor of the way they adopt to model process location and mobility in a process algebras setting.

Ambient calculus [8]. In this formalism the concept of *ambient* is added to the basic constructs for processes definition and composition described above. An ambient has a *name* that specifies its identity, and can be thought of as a sort of boundary that encloses a set of running processes. Ambients, denoted as $n[P]$, where n is the ambient name and P is the enclosed process, can be entered, exited or opened (i.e., dissolved) by appropriate operations executed by a process, so allowing to model movement as the crossing of ambient boundaries. Ambients are hierarchically nested, and a process can only enter an ambient which is sibling of its ambient in the hierarchy, and can exit only into the parent ambient of its ambient; hence, moving to a "far" ambient in the ambients hierarchy requires, in this formalism, the explicit crossing of multiple ambients. The mobility operations for an ambient $n[.]$ are denoted by **inamb**n, **outamb**n, **open**n, respectively[6]. In general, a process cannot forge them by itself, but receives them thanks to the communication operations **in** and **out**. Hence, a process receiving one of such operations through a communication actually receives a capability for it, being allowed to execute the corresponding operation on the named ambient. The (partial) formal syntax of this algebra is then as follows:

$$P ::= \mathbf{0} \mid \pi.P \mid P + P \mid P \| P \mid n[P] \mid \dots$$

with π $\{\tau_i\ (i = 1, 2, \dots)$, **in**$(x)$, **out**$(M)$, **inamb**$n$, **outamb**$n$, **open**$n\}$, where x is a variable and M stands for either an ambient name (n), or a capability for an ambient

---

[6] Note that the ambient operations are named **in**, **out** and **open** in the original paper [8]; we have renamed them to avoid confusion with the names used in this paper to denote the mesage passing communication operations.

(either **inamb***n*, or **outamb***n*, or **open***n*). Communication is restricted to be local, i.e. only between processes enclosed in the same ambient. Communication between non local processes requires the definition of some sort of "messenger" agent that explicitly crosses the required ambient boundaries bringing with itself the information to be communicated. Alternatively, a process can move itself to the ambient of its partner before (locally) communicating with it. In both cases, the messenger or the moving process must possess the needed capabilities.

KLAIM (Kernel Language for Agents Interaction and Mobility) [11]. This formalism allows to define a net of locations that are basically not nested into each other, with direct communication possible, in principle, between processes located at any location, differently from the ambient calculus (anyway, the extension to nested locations is possible). Another remarkable difference with the ambient calculus, and with all the previously mentioned algebras, consists in the adoption of a *generative* (rather than message passing) style of communication, based on the use of *tuple spaces* and the communication primitives of the *Linda* coordination language [9]. Tuple spaces are linked to locations, and interaction between processes located at different locations can happen by putting or retrieving the opportune tuple into the tuple space at a given location. Again, the (partial) formal syntax of this algebra is as follows:

$$P ::= \mathbf{0} \mid \pi.P \mid P + P \mid P \parallel P \mid \dots$$

with π $\{\tau_i$ $(i = 1, 2, \dots)$, **in_t**$(t)@l$, **read_t**$(t)@l$, **out_t**$(t)@l$, **eval_t**$(t)@l$, **newloc**$(u)\}$, where the indicated operations are the usual Linda-like operations on a tuple t, restricted to operate on the tuple space associated to the l location[7]. Moreover, the **newloc**(u) operation allows a process to create a new (initially private) location that can be accessed through the name u. Note that the fields of a tuple may be either values, or processes, or localities, or variables of the previous types. This allows a simple modelling of all the mobile code patterns (namely REV, COD and MA), as shown in [11].

Example 3. Adopting the same notation of example 2, the travel agency system adopting the REV pattern can be modeled in KLAIM as follows, where loc_i denotes explicitly the location of the A_i airline, and "inforeq" and "inforeply" are keys used for the tuple matching:

$TravAg :=$ **out_t**$([C, "inforeq"])@loc_1.$**in_t**$([x, "inforeply"])@loc_1.$
        out_t$([C, "inforeq"])@loc_2.$**in_t**$([x, "inforeply"])@loc_2.$
        SelectBest.TravAg
$A_i :=$ **in_t**$([y, "inforeq"])@self.y.$**out_t**$([R_i, "inforeply"])@self.A_i$
$SelectBest := \dots$
$Sys := TravAg \parallel A_1 \parallel A_2$
$EndOfExample3.$

---

[7] Note that the tuple operations are named **in**, **out**, **read** and **eval** in the original paper [11]; we have renamed them to avoid confusion with the names used in this paper to denote the message passing communication operations.

Other Formal Notations. Besides the notations reviewed above, other notations for mobility modeling (and formal verification of functional requirements for mobile systems) have been proposed, not based on a process algebras framework; examples are MobileUNITY [41] and Mob$_{adtl}$ [12], both with an explicit notion of location, and a temporal logic based semantics.

As a general comment about all the formal notations we have reviewed, they are quite low-level notations, and using them to directly model a system of even average complexity would be quite cumbersome. Hence their score would be quite low if we evaluate them on the usability scale. One approach that have been pursued to get a higher usability consists in using them to provide a foundation to higher level formalisms, that are closer to the practice of system design. An example of this approach is the π-ADL language [38] which is built over the π-calculus and HOπ-calculus and supports the definition of system models following an architecture-based approach, where a system is modeled in terms of components, connectors and their composition [3].

Another example is the X-Klaim language [6], whose underlying semantics is based on the KLAIM calculus, and that supports the implementation of object-oriented applications with mobile components.

Along a different direction, other approaches have pursued the usability goal stressing the need of supporting the separation of concerns between the modeling of location and mobility aspects of a system on one hand, and the modeling of its location-independent aspects on the other hand, as discussed at the beginning of this section. An example is the BasicSail calculus [39] that derives from the Ambient calculus the idea of a hierarchical location space, where each location can be thought of as a process container, and processes can enter and exit locations following the hierarchical structure. However, differently from the Ambient calculus, the goal of BasicSail is to keep independent the modeling of topological variations (i.e. changes in the process location) from the modeling of the computation performed by the system. However, to achieve this goal, the resulting calculus is somewhat less powerful than the Ambient calculus (see [39] for details).

Another example is the CommUnity language [27], that has a Category Theory theoretical background. Similarly to the π-ADL language briefly reviewed above, also CommUnity aims at providing support for the modeling of systems following an architecture-based approach. The specific goal of CommUnity is to extend the principle of separation of concerns, already pursued by architecture-based approaches between intra-component behaviors and inter-component interactions, also to location and mobility aspects. Another noteworthy aspect of CommUnity is the explicit support it provides for a general notion of *context*.

4.2 Semi-formal SMN for Mobile Systems: UML Based Notations

SMNs based on process algebras or other types of formal notations support a rigorous and non ambiguous modeling activity. However, the use of these formal notations does not have yet gained widespread acceptance in the practice of software development. On the contrary, a semi-formal notation like the Unified Modeling

Language (UML) [7, 47] lacks some of the formal rigor of the notations considered in the previous section, but has quickly become a de-facto standard in the industrial software development process. Some of the reasons for the UML success may be summarized as follows:

It allows to embed into the model static and dynamic aspects of the software by using different diagrams, each representing a different view of the software system. Each view captures a different set of concerns and aspects regarding the subject. Therefore it is broadly applicable to different types of domains or subject areas.

The same conceptual framework and the same notation can be used from specification through design to implementation.

It is widely supported by a broad set of tools. By having a set of tools that support UML, knowledge may be more readily captured and manipulated to meet an organization's objectives.

UML consists of two parts: a *notation*, used to describe a set of diagrams (also called the syntax of the language and that provides the "tools" to define user level *models*) and a *metamodel* (also called the semantics of the language) that specifies the abstract integrated semantics of UML modeling concepts. The UML notation encompasses several kinds of diagrams, most of them belonging to previous methodologies, that provide specific views of the system. Examples of UML diagrams are static diagrams, like the Use Case, Class and Object Diagrams, behavioral diagrams like the Activity and State Diagrams, interaction diagrams like the Sequence and Collaboration Diagrams, and implementation diagrams like the Deployment Diagram.

A further reason for the UML success is due to its extensibility mechanisms, that allow to customize and tailor it to particular system types, domains, and methods/processes. Extensions can be introduced at two different levels: as *lightweight* extensions (based on the *profile* mechanism) that does not modify the UML metamodel, and *heavyweight* extensions, that do modify the metamodel. The latter kind of extensions allows greater expressive power and flexibility, but they generally introduce incompatibilities with tools based on the original metamodel, thus causing usability problems.

UML has recently undergone a complete revision, that has led to the definition of the UML 2.0 version [47], where some aspects of the previous versions have been clarified and new diagrams have been included, to better support recent trends in system design (e.g. component-based design).

UML by itself does provide only a limited support for the modeling of mobile systems. Hence, suitable customizations of UML have been proposed. We classify them according to the degree of extension they introduce with respect to the "standard" UML notation. Some of them cannot be actually defined as UML extensions, as they only suggest guidelines for using standard diagrams in the modeling of mobile systems. Others do introduce heavyweight or lightweight extensions. In the following we briefly review some of these proposals, and then we illustrate in greater detail one of them in section 4.3.

Notations Based on the "Standard" UML. The two proposals presented in this section differ in the type of UML diagrams they suggest to use for the modeling of mobile systems. For both of them, methodologies have been suggested for the transformation from the design model to an analysis oriented model. These methodologies will be presented in section 5.

Merseguer et al. model [31]. This proposal suggests the use of State Diagrams (SD) to model the internal behavior of each component of a software application, and of Sequence Diagrams to model interaction scenarios among components. The modeling of component mobility simply consists in the addition at suitable points of its SD of a state whose dispatched action (*goto* action) moves that component to a different location. Figure 2 depicts the addition of a component movement between the transition from a state to another state. This way of modeling mobility appears more oriented to virtual mobility only. Moreover, what seems to be actually modeled is a MA mobility pattern only. No suggestion about how other patterns could be modeled is given in [31]. Also the modeling of nested locations is not explicitly discussed.

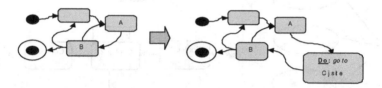

Fig. 2. Adding mobility within a State Diagram

Example 4. Using the notation proposed by Merseguer et al., the travel agency application with an MA mobility pattern could be modeled as depicted in figures 3 and 4, that show the interaction scenario and the internal behavior of each component, respectively. The *collector* component models the interaction logic with each airline. For the sake of generality, we have modeled the *collector* as an agent that can decide whether to move to the location of an airline before interacting with it.

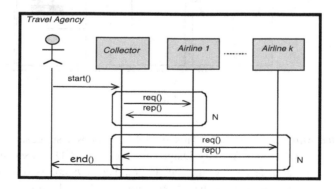

Fig. 3. Interaction scenario model

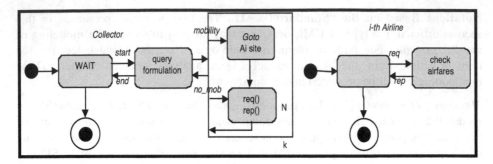

Fig. 4. Components internal behavior

EndOfExample4

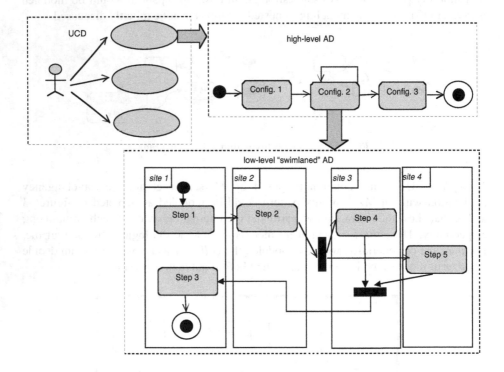

Fig. 5

Balsamo and Marzolla model [2]. This modeling proposal suggests the use of Use Case Diagrams (UCD and Activity Diagrams (AD). A UCD is used to express the possible presence of different mobility behaviors. The ADs are used to represent both the effect of mobility on the system configuration (location of entities belonging to it) and the internal activities of each system entity. For this purpose, a "high level" AD is used to model configuration changes; each node of this AD corresponds to a particular configuration and models mobility activities that leads to a configuration change. Associated with each node of this high level AD there is also a "low level" AD that models the activities performed by the system when it is in that configuration. This low level AD is "swimlaned", where each swimlane identifies the location where the activities it embeds are performed. Figure 5 depicts an example of use of this notation, with a UCD modeling three different mobility scenarios. For the first scenario figure 5 includes the corresponding high level AD, showing that in this scenario the system may assume three different configurations. When the system is in one of these configurations (the second one) the figure also shows which are the system activities and at which location they are performed.

This notation is suitable to model both physical and virtual mobility, as each configuration may be the result of movements involving both physical and virtual entities. No explicit support is provided for the modeling of different virtual mobility patterns. Moreover, also the concept of hierarchical locations is not explicitly supported.

Example 5. Using the notation of Balsamo and Marzolla, the travel agency application may be modeled as follows, using an MA virtual mobility pattern. The UCD in figure 6 models two different scenarios for the implementation of this application, based on the use of virtual mobility (according to an MA pattern), or no mobility (according to a static client-server pattern), respectively. Figure 6 also shows the high level ADs for these two scenarios, where, as one could expect only one configuration is possible in the case of no mobility, while in the mobility case the configurations B1 ... Bk model the presence of the mobile agent at each airline site, while configurations B' and B" model the presence of the mobile agent at the travel agency site, at the beginning and

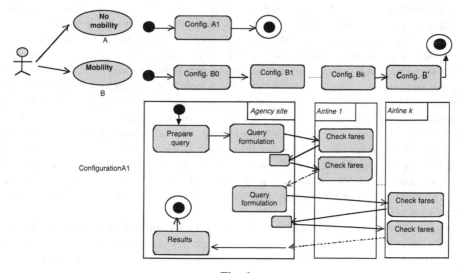

Fig. 6

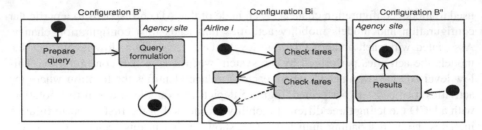

Fig. 7

end of its trip, respectively. Moreover, figure 6 also depicts the low level AD for the no mobility scenario. The low level ADs for the different configurations of the mobility scenario are depicted in figure 7.

EndOfExample5

Notations based on UML lightweight extensions. The two proposals presented in this section extend the standard UML notation through the introduction of attributes for some classes and of new stereotypes that can be used to label modeling elements. Methodologies for the transformation from the design model to analysis oriented models have been suggested only the first of these proposals. These methodologies will be presented in section 5.

Grassi and Mirandola model [15, 18]. This notation pursues the goal of separation of concerns in the modeling of a mobile system. For this purpose, it is based on the use of a Sequence Diagram (SD) to model the interaction logic among components of an application, independently of any mobility aspect, and of a Collaboration Diagram (CD) to model the interaction structure only (i.e. who interacts with whom). To model the possible presence of virtual mobility, a moveTo stereotype is introduced that applies to the (directional) links of the CD. Where present, moveTo indicates that the source component of the link moves to the location of its target before starting a sequence of consecutive interactions with it. If no other information is present, this style applies to each sequence of interactions shown in the associated SD, between the source and target components of the moveTo labeled link; otherwise a condition can be added to restrict this style to a subset of interactions between two components. Alternatively, a question mark can be used as suffix of moveTo, yielding a new moveTo? stereotype, to model the uncertainty about the moblity of a component. When a link between two components in a CD is labeled with moveTo?, this means that the source component "could" move to the location of its target at the beginning of a sequence of interactions with it. In other words, the designer does not have enough information at that design stage to decide whether virtual mobility is really beneficial.

Physical mobility is modeled instead using a Deployment Diagram (DD) where a mobile physical node is modeled introducing as many replicas of that node as the different locations where it can stay, each labeled with a different location attribute, and connected to other replicas by suitable become labeled messages to model some movement pattern.

This notations appears suitable to model mobile system where virtual mobility occurs according to the MA pattern only.

Example 6. According to the adopted modeling framework, the travel agency example application can be modeled as shown in figure 8.

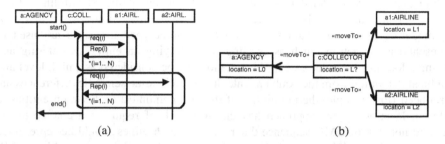

(a)   (b)

Fig. 8. Travel agency example: (a) interaction logic, (b) interaction style

Figure 8.a shows a SD that describes in detail the "logic" of the interaction, i.e. the sequence of messages exchanged among the components. In this diagram no information is present about whether or not some component changes location during the interactions. This information is provided by the CD in figure 8.b. The diagram shows that only c can change location, and according to the moveTo semantics described above, it moves to the location of a, a1 or a2 before interacting with them. Note that in figure 8.b the location of c is left unspecified (L?), since it can dynamically change. In general, it is possible to give it a specified value in the diagram, that would show the "initial" location of the mobile object in an initial deployment configuration. *EndOfExample6*

Baumeister et al. model [4]. This notation is based on an extension of UML Class Diagrams and Activity Diagrams to represent mobility. New stereotypes are defined for identifying mobile objects and locations. Stereotypes are also defined for moving and cloning activities that can be included in Activity Diagrams to represent location changes. Mobile systems are then represented by Activity Diagrams using either a "responsibility centered notation", which focuses on who is performing actions, and a "location centered notation" which focuses on where actions are being executed and how activities change their location.

This notation can be used to model both physical and virtual mobility. For the latter, no explicit mention is made in [4] about the modeling of different patterns. They should be modeled by suitable combinations of moving and cloning actions. A possible shortcoming of this notation is that it represents in the same Activity Diagram both the mobility model (how objects change their location) and the computation model (what kind of computations the objects perform). For large models this could render the diagrams difficult to understand.

Notations Based on UML Heavyweight Extensions. These notations introduce modifications at the level of the UML metamodel. As already remarked at the beginning of this section, their main drawback is their poor integration with standard UML compliant tools. Apart from this, they provide valuable suggestions about possible approaches to mobility modeling.

Kosiuczenko model [25]. This notation extends UML Sequence Diagrams (SD) to represent the dynamics of a mobile system (with both physical and virtual mobility). Mobile entities are modeled using an extended version of the SD lifelines. Each lifeline is represented as a box that can contain other entities (lifelines). In this way, the modeling of nested locations is supported. Stereotyped messages are used to represent various actions such as creating or destroying an entity, or entering and leaving a location. To some extent, this notation can be considered as a high level and graphical derivation from the Ambient calculus, even if some semantic differences are introduced (for example, the possibility of direct communication between entities at different locations). This approach has the drawback of requiring a change in the standard notation of UML Sequence diagrams, that is, lifelines should be represented as boxes, with possibly other Sequence diagrams inside. Existing graphical UML editors and processors need to be modified in order to support the new notation.

Manson et al. model [28]. This notation has been proposed within the framework of the FIPA (Foundation for Intelligent Physical Agents) initiative. Hence, it is specifically aimed at the modeling of multi-agent distributed systems, where some of them may be mobile agents. As a consequence, the only virtual mobility pattern this notation is explicitly interested in is the MA pattern. To model a mobile system, this notation introduce modifications to both UML Deployment Diagrams (DD) and Activity Diagrams (AD). The DDs are modified to model not only the deployment of agents to physical nodes (and the existence of physical connections among these nodes) but also the "acquaintance" relationships among agents, that are used to specify which other agents an agent knows and may communicate with. The ADs are modified to model not only the sequence of activities of agents, but also the paths they can follow when moving to the locations of other agents they want to interact with.

4.3 A Semi-formal SMN: UML Profile for Mobile Systems (UML-PMS)

In this section we present the fundamental characteristics of a SMN we have proposed for mobile systems [19]. This notation is intended to model both virtual and physical mobility. It takes into account the case of nested locations, and offers explicit support for the modeling of different virtual mobility patterns. Moreover, usability has been one of the guidelines we have followed in its definition. For this purpose, it has been defined as a lightweight UML extension (UML profile for mobile systems: UML-PMS), compliant with the latest UML 2.0 version [47], and supports a separation of concerns approach, keeping the modeling of the virtual and physical mobility as much as possible separated from the modeling of other system aspects like its application logic. In the following we present the extensions we have introduced to model three basic concepts: *locations*; *mobile entities* and *entity movement*; *movement "control"*. We refer to [19] for details about these extensions. Then, we show how these extension can be used to model "standard" virtual mobility patterns (namely COD, REV and MA).

Locations. We adopt a discrete and hierarchical locations space for both virtual and physical mobility, modeling the *location* concept as a relationship between two entities, where one acts as a container for the other. This model is inspired by the Ambient calculus model. However, differently from the Ambient model, we have implemented in two different ways this basic idea for physical and virtual entities, to remain compliant with the UML 2.0 metamodel.

A physical entity (such as a computing device) is located in a *place* (such as a room, a building, a vehicle or even a person), and places themselves can be located in other places (such as a room in a building). Hence, we have introduced the stereotype <<Place>> that extends the UML 2.0 metaclass *Node* to encompass all these concepts, and the stereotype <<NodeLocation>> that applies to association instances (i.e. links) between places to explicitly express their location at some place. Figure 9 depicts an example of <<NodeLocation>> relationship among instances of a PDA computing device, a person who holds it and a room that person is in.

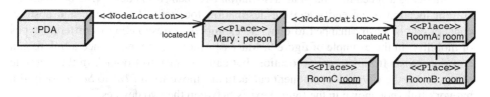

Fig. 9. Example of location relationships among nodes and places

The location of a virtual entity can be an execution environment or a computing device (i.e. a *Node* in the UML metamodel), or some other virtual entity where it is embedded. This latter case is simply modeled using the structural relationships provided by UML to model components and subcomponents. For the former case, we extend the UML *Deployment* relationship through two new stereotypes <<CurrentDeployment>> and <<AllowedDeployment>>, using the former to specify the location where a virtual entity is currently deployed to, while using the latter to specify multiple relationships with locations where a virtual entity can possibly be deployed to. The rationale for this latter stereotype is to introduce the possibility of specifying constraints (e.g. due to administrative or security concerns) for the locations of a component (in particular a mobile one). Figure 10 shows an example where a *Comp_B* software component is currently located at a *PDA* place, but it has also a *Server* place as possible deployment location. Also note that the *PDA* itself is marked as mobile, so that also its location (not shown here) can change.

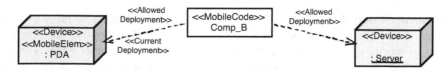

Fig. 10. Example of deployment relationships for a mobile logical element

Mobile Entities and Entity Movement. A mobile entity is an entity whose location can change. We define two stereotypes <<MobileElement>> and <<MobileCode>> to mark as mobile a physical and virtual entity, respectively. We model the movement of a mobile entity as a change in the relationship between the entity itself and its container. This change is caused by the execution of stereotyped <<PhysicalMove>> and <VirtualMove> activities, that we have defined in our profile. For physical entities (i.e. nodes) the move activity corresponds to changing the association (stereotyped as <<NodeLocation>>) with their container node, whereas for logical entities it corresponds to updating the <<CurrentDeployment>> dependency. The execution of a move activity is subject to some constraints. First of all, its subject must be a mobile entity. Then, in the case of <<MobileCode>> entities, an <<AllowedDeployment>> dependency must exist between the subject and the destination place. Finally, as a general rule, it can be performed only if a *CommunicationPath*, defined in the UML metamodel as a specialization of an association between two nodes, exists between the current location of an entity and the destination location. This generic and abstract concept can be easily mapped to concrete examples corresponding to different types of mobility. In the example of figure 9, Mary can move to RoomB, since a link (e.g. a corridor) exists from its current location, but cannot move to RoomC. In the example of figure 10, the *Comp_B* component can actually move from *PDA* to *Server* only if a network link (not shown in the figure) exists between the two devices.

Besides these basic mobility activities, we have introduced in our profile other mobility related activities, listed below, that refer specifically to virtual mobile entities, and allow a more complete modeling of different mobile code patterns:

- <<BeforeMove>> : this stereotype is used to define the activities that prepare a <<MobileCode>> element to be copied or moved (e.g. the serialization of a component, the handling of bindings to resources or local data, the encryption of confidential data that must cross untrusted channels);
- <<AfterMove>> : this stereotype is used for activities that operate on a <<MobileCode>> element after its migration to a new execution environment (e.g. the regeneration of a component able to run again out of its serialized form, the recreation of the data structures and execution context the component expects to find upon resuming its execution);
- <<AllowDeployment>> : an activity stereotyped in this way is a *CreateLinkAction* (see the UML metamodel) that adds a deployment to the set of allowed deployments for a given *DeployedArtifact*;
- <<DenyDeployment>> : an activity stereotyped in this way is the complementary of a <<AllowDeployment>> activity, and is used to remove a deployment from the set of allowed deployments for a given *DeployedArtifact*.

Movement "Control". The modeling elements we have presented so far show how we can model the manifestation of a mobility behavior, but they do not give any means to specify what "triggers" such a behavior. We model this latter issue by means of the *mobility manager* concept, whose main purpose is to encapsulate all the logic of mobility, separating it from any other modeling concern, and in particular from the intrinsic software application logic. The interaction between a mobility manager and the other parts of the modeled system is possible by giving to the manager the ability to perceive events that occur in its "environment" (which can be composed by both physical and logical elements) and to react to them by firing mobility activities, as those listed above. To this end, a mobility manager is modeled as a state machine stereotyped as <<MobilityManager>>, whose main characteristics is that it can dispatch "mobility activities" defined, in general, as a suitable composition of the activities listed above. Its initial state is entered as soon as the system is started. A state transition fires when the event specified in the transition label occurs, provided that the guard condition specified in the same label is satisfied. Hence, by properly defining the guard condition and the firing event in terms of conditions and events that occur in the manager environment we can model suitable interactions between the manager and its environment. We adopt the same concept for both physical and virtual mobility.

We recall that in the Grassi-Mirandola model reviewed in section 4.2 it was introduced the possibility of explicitly modeling the designer uncertainty about the introduction of mobility (albeit limited, in that model, to the MA mobility pattern), by introducing an *ad hoc* stereotype. In the model we are reviewing here, the same effect can be reached (for all kinds of mobility) by the use of a nondeterministic state machine as mobility manager: given a mobility manager, the uncertainty about some mobility behavior can be modeled by adding for each transition dispatching that behavior another transition enabled and triggered by the same conditions and events, but that does not dispatch any mobility activity.

Finally, we point out that, in principle, a mobility manager should be mainly intended as a "modeling artifact", that could not directly correspond to some specific entity in a real implementation of the system we are modeling, or whose responsibilities can be shared among several different entities; its modeling utility actually consists in giving the possibility of providing an easily identifiable entity that encapsulates the logic that drives mobility. In this way different mobility managers, each modeling a different mobility behavior or policy, can be modularly plugged into some physical environment or software application model, to experiment with different environment dynamics and/or adaptation policies. Of course, once a virtual mobility policy modeled by some manager is selected to be incorporated in a system implementation, it remains the open design problem of how implementing it into the "real" system components.

Models of Virtual Mobility Patterns. In this section we show how "standard" patterns for virtual mobility can be modeled, using our profile, by a suitable definition of the event that triggers a state transition of some mobility manager, and of the code mobility activity dispatched by this state transition, where this activity is defined by a suitable composition of the basic activities defined in the profile.

The COD interaction pattern can be modeled by defining the triggering event of the mobility manager as the invocation of the operation implemented by the remotely located code, possibly conditioned by some other guard condition (see figure 11(b)), while the dispatched mobility activity is the sequence of "grey" activities shown in figure 11(a). Figure 11(a) also shows the whole activity diagram fragment obtained by plugging the COD pattern into a basic location unaware interaction pattern ("white" activities).

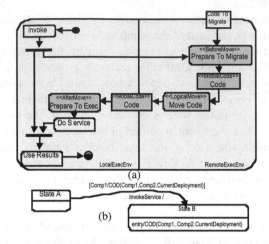

Fig. 11. UML-PMS model of the COD pattern

On the other hand, in the REV case, the triggering event is again the operation invocation (see figure 12(b)), while, analogously to figure 11(b), the corresponding sequence of activities and the result of plugging them into a basic location unaware interaction pattern are shown in figure 12(a).

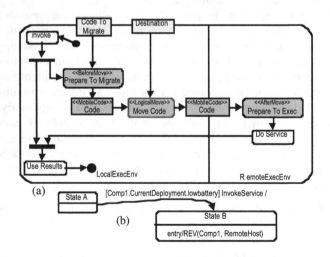

Fig. 12. UML-PMS model of the REV pattern

Finally, in the MA pattern the triggering event in the mobility manager can be any suitable event occurring in the software application or its environment (according to some mobility policy the designer wants to model). Figure 13(a) depicts an activity diagram fragment modeling the location unaware behavior of some component, while figure 13(c) shows the result of plugging into it the MA pattern triggered by the mobility manager fragment depicted in figure 13(b).

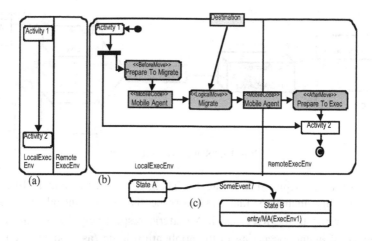

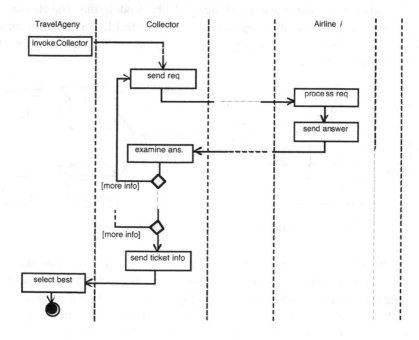

Fig. 13. UML-PMS model of the MA pattern

Example 7. The travel agency application can be modeled as follows using our UML profile for mobile systems. Figure 14 depicts a location unaware model of the application logic, defined by an Activity Diagram, and figure 15 depicts a model (Deployment Diagram) of the supporting platform and of application components deployment (in the case of two Airline sites). We can "plug" mobility into this model by first suitably labeling the application and platform components, using suitable

Fig. 14. Location unaware model of the application logic

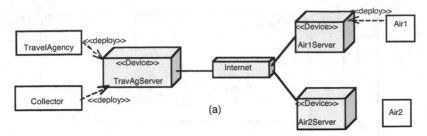

Fig. 15. "Static" system model

profile elements, as depicted in figure 16. Then, figures 17(a) and 17(b) depict two different mobility managers that model, respectively, the introduction of virtual mobility according to the REV and MA pattern, respectively. These managers, as a consequence of events occurring in the application logic (as modeled by the AD of figure 14) trigger suitable mobility behaviors (as specified by the "grey" activities of figure 12 and 13, respectively). Note that, actually, only the manager of figure 17(a) is compatible with the platform model of figure 16. The manager of figure 17(b) would cause an "error" because the "TravelAgency" component has not been declared as "mobile". This error can be corrected by labeling also this component as <<MobileCode>> (or by giving up the MA pattern). In particular, the manager of figure 17(a) models the transfer from the travel agency site and remote execution at each airline site of a copy of the Collector component, according to the REV pattern. On the other hand, the manager of figure 17(b) models the TravelAgency and Collector components traveling together, according to the MA pattern, from an airline site to the next one, locally collecting the necessary information, and then reporting it back to the travel agency site.

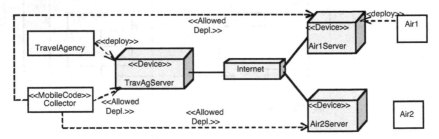

Fig. 16. Adding mobility to the system model

Finally, figure 18 is an example of mobility managers that include the modeling of the designer uncertainty about the opportunity of moving the collector component, as discussed above. Differently from the mobility managers of figure 17, in each of the figure 18 managers the "invoke(Collector)" event triggers non deterministically two transitions to two "twin" states, where in only one of them the REV or MA behavior is dispatched.

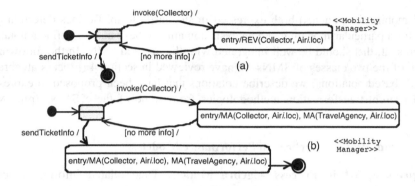

Fig. 17. Two different mobility managers

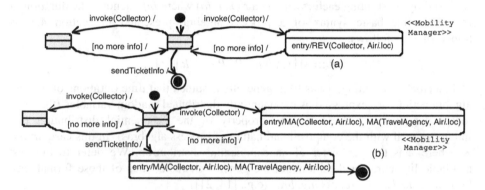

Fig. 18. Non deterministic mobility managers

EndOfExample7

5   From Design Models to Performance Analysis Models (SMN (+ MI) --> TMN)

In this section we outline transformation methodologies to suitable TMNs that have been proposed for some of the SMNs reviewed in section 4. In this review, we limit ourselves to TMNs that support *stochastic* performance analysis of mobile systems (hence, we do not consider TMNs that support, for example, deterministic performance analysis like worst case execution time). TMNs that have been considered to this end include Markov and Markov Decision processes, Petri nets, Queueing Networks and simulation models. To support any of these transformations, models expressed using the notations of section 4 must be enriched with some information, that is what we have called MI in the general modeling framework presented in section 2. When NFA="performance", this information includes time-related (e.g. frequency and/or duration of events of interest) and non time-related information (e.g. selection of alternative execution paths, size of exchanged messages and mobile components) both expressed in stochastic form. Besides determining the MI for a particular modeling and analysis domain, we have also to define a notation to express it, that should be well integrated with the adopted SMN. In the following, for each of the two classes of SMNs we have reviewed in section 4 (process algebras and UML based notations) we describe notations that have been proposed to express MI, and present transformation methodologies from some of these SMNs (plus MI) to some TMN.

5.1   From Process Algebras to Performance Models

Expressing MI in Process Algebra Models. Time related information can be introduced in a process algebra based SMN by associating a duration to each action modeled in that algebra (i.e. to each π Act). From a notational viewpoint, this is achieved by substituting each π with a pair (π, info) where info denotes the duration of π. Hence, the basic syntax of a process algebra, presented in section 4.1, is transformed as follows:

$$P ::= \mathbf{0} \mid (\pi, info).P \mid P + P \mid P \parallel P \mid \dots$$

In a stochastic setting, it has been generally assumed that time durations of process algebra actions are expressed as exponentially distributed random variables (the main reason for this is the memoryless property of the exponential distribution that integrates well with the compositional nature of process algebras). In this case, info = λ, where λ is the parameter of an exponential distribution. We defer to the vast available literature for details about the general characteristics of these formalisms, known as *stochastic process algebras* (e.g., [14, 21]).

Besides time related information like action duration, other information could belong to the MI needed to carry out a performance analysis: this information could include, for example, the size of an exchanged message, or the energy consumption associated with a given action. This kind of information may be generally expressed in the form of a *reward* (or *cost*) associated with the system actions, which is accumulated when those actions are performed. Hence, from a notational viewpoint, this may be expressed by setting info = (λ, r) where r is the reward of the associated action. Also in this case, we defer to available literature for details (e.g. [5, 19]).

Transformation Methodology. The selected TMN for the transformation methodology we are going to outline is a *continuous time Markov Process* (CTMP). The transformation methodology exploits the operational semantics associated with a process algebra. Hence, besides the process algebra based notations reviewed in section 4.1, this methodology can be applied to any formal notation with an operational semantics. We start with a brief review of operational semantics.

The operational semantics of a process specified using the syntax of a given process algebra is given by a *labeled transition system*, i.e. (informally) a graph that represents all the possible system evolutions; each node of the graph represents a particular system state, while a transition represents a state change, and the label associated with a transition provides information about the "activities" that cause the corresponding state change. The transition relation (i.e. which are the states reachable in one step from a given state, and the associated labels) is specified by giving a set of syntax-driven rules, in the sense that they are associated to the syntactic rules of the algebra. Each rule takes the form $\dfrac{Premises}{Conclusion}$ whose meaning is that whenever the premises (that can be interpreted as a given computational step) occur, then the conclusion will occur as well. (Simplified) examples of such rules are the following:

$$\frac{}{\pi.P \xrightarrow{\pi} P}, \quad \frac{P \xrightarrow{\pi} P'}{P+Q \xrightarrow{\pi} P'}, \quad \frac{P \xrightarrow{\pi} P'}{P \| Q \xrightarrow{\pi} P' \| Q}, \quad \frac{P \xrightarrow{out x} P', Q \xrightarrow{in x} Q'}{P \| Q \xrightarrow{\tau} P' \| Q'}$$

Note that the third rule specifies a transition relation for parallel independent processes, while the fourth rule specifies a transition relation for parallel processes that synchronize themselves through a communication operation[8].

Example 8. The transition graph obtained applying rules as the ones specified above to the *Sys* model of example 2 (using HOπ-calculus) is given by (assuming C = $(\tau_1 + \tau_2).0$):

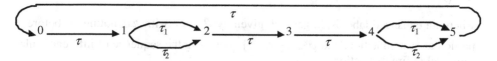

EndOfExample8

The state transition graph obtained in this way can be considered as the "skeleton" of a CTMP, providing information about possible state transitions. The only thing we need to get a complete CTMP is to associate an exponential rate with each state transition. These rates can be easily derived from the rates specified in the labels of the actions involved in a state transition (see for example [21]).[9] We note that, as a consequence, from the viewpoint of the obtained model representativeness, the transition rate values cannot be more accurate than the rate associated with each single action. The accuracy of the action rates depends on the adopted technique of information collection (CT in the general framework of section 2). However, the discussion of CT issues is beyond the scope of this paper. In the following, we rather present a methodology aimed at improving the basic technique used to build state transition rates starting from action rates (which are hence assumed as given) [37]. This methodology has been presented in the framework of π-calculus and HOπ-calculus, but it is applicable to any formalism with an operational semantics

---

[8] In the "standard" semantics of process algebras [35], the label of this latter rule is equal to τ, that is an invisible action, since the two matching input and output operations "consume" each other, making them unobservable for an external "observer" (e.g. a process running in parallel).

[9] Transformation methodologies that have been proposed basically differ only in the way adopted to calculate the rate of synchronization (i.e., communication) operations; for a discussion of this topic, see [21].

The idea of [37], is to associate with each transition a label that does not merely register the action associated to that transition (e.g., τ_1, as in example 8), but also the inference rules used during the deduction of the transition, so to keep trace of the "underlying operations" that lead to the execution of that action. For instance, in example 8 the operation underlying the execution of action τ_1 is a selection operation between the two concurrently enabled operation τ_1 and τ_2. These "enhanced" labels can be used to define a systematic way for deriving the rates to be associated with the system transitions. The enhanced labels are built using symbols from a suitable alphabet (e.g., $\{+, \parallel, \dots\}$), to record the inference rules used during the derivation of the transitions. For example, the transition rules given above would be rewritten as follows to get enhanced labels[10]:

$$\frac{}{\pi.P \xrightarrow{\pi} P}, \quad \frac{P \xrightarrow{\theta} P'}{P+Q \xrightarrow{+\theta} P}, \quad \frac{P \xrightarrow{\theta} P'}{P \parallel Q \xrightarrow{\parallel\theta} P' \parallel Q},$$

$$\frac{P \xrightarrow{\vartheta\text{out } x} P', Q \xrightarrow{\vartheta'\text{in } x} Q'}{P \parallel Q \xrightarrow{\langle\parallel\vartheta\text{out } x, \vartheta'\text{in } x\rangle} P' \parallel Q'},$$

where an enhanced label is, in general, given by $\theta = \vartheta\pi$, with π denoting, as before, a particular system action, and $\vartheta \in \{+, \parallel, \dots\}^*$ denoting the sequence of inference rules followed to fire that action.

Example 9. The transition system of example 8 would be enhanced as follows:

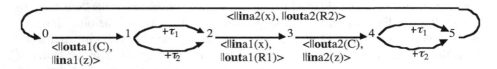

EndOfExample9

Using the enhanced labels, the rate of a transition can be calculated by defining suitable functions, as follows:

$$\$_b : Act \to \mathfrak{R}^+, \qquad \$_s : \{+, \parallel, \dots\} \to \mathfrak{R}^+, \qquad \$: \{+, \parallel, \dots\}^* \blacktriangleleft Act \to \mathfrak{R}^+$$

where $\blacktriangleleft$ denotes the concatenation operator, $\$_b$ defines the basic exponential rate of an action (i.e. the λ value associated with that action) in a reference architecture dedicated only to the execution of that action without any interference, while $\$_s$ defines a slowing factor in the execution of an action due to the execution of some underlying operation in the target architecture where the action is actually executed. $\$$ is the function that calculates the actual exponential rate of the transition, taking into

---

10 Again, we are introducing a simplification: in a complete specification different symbols should be used to distinguish the selection of the left or right alternative in a parallel or alternative choice composition (see [37]).

account all possible interferences, and can be basically recursively defined using $\$_b$ and $\$_s$, as follows:

$$\$(\pi) = \$_b(\pi), \qquad \$(\sigma\vartheta\pi) = \$_s(\sigma)\$(\vartheta\pi), \qquad \sigma \in \{+, \|, ...\}, \; \vartheta \in \{+, \|, ...\}^*$$

By suitably defining the functions $\$_b$ and $\$_s$, we can limit the problem of calculating meaningful transition rates to the problem of defining only the cost of the "primitive" system actions, and of the slowing factors caused by a particular target architecture (but it should be remarked that the definition of the above functions and the collection of the "primitive" rates are, in general, non trivial tasks). Moreover, by changing the definition of $\$_s$, we can also analyze the impact on performance of different target architectures.

Once the rates of all the possible transitions from a given state (representing the system behaving like process P_i) have been determined, the overall rate from state P_i to another state P_j which is one-step successor of state P_i is given by:

$$q(P_i, P_j) = \sum_{P_i \xrightarrow{\vartheta\pi} P_j} \$(\vartheta\pi)$$

(note that, in general, more than one transition from state P_i to state P_j may be present in the graph of the transition system).

The presented methodology concerns the derivation of transition rates of a CTMP. A similar approach can be followed also to calculate the rewards when TMN is a *Markov Reward process*, exploiting the rewards specified in the starting SMN [5, 37].

5.2   From UML Based Models to Performance Models

Expressing MI in UML Based Models. The OMG has defined a standard set of concepts and notations that can be used to enrich a UML based model with time related information, collecting them in the standard *Profile for Schedulability, Performance and Time* (SPT) [48]. At the core of the profile is the *general resource modeling* (GRM) framework, which provides a common model of resources and of their Quality of Service (QoS) attributes. The GRM includes several aspects that are grouped in different models (*Core Resource, Causality, Resource Usage, Resource Type, Realization or Deployment*). Based on the GRM, more specific sub-profiles are defined in SPT, whose purpose is to specialize the general concepts of GRM to better represent the needs of a specific domain. Since our domain of interest is performance we focus in particular on the SPT *performance analysis sub-profile* (PA).

The SPT-PA profile extends the UML notation to deal with the performance specific basic notions of *scenario*, *resource*, and *workload*, and the associated attributes (in the following, PA attributes), to support extensive and wide-ranging performance analysis: the *scenario*, i.e., an ordered sequences of steps, describes various dynamic situations involving the usage of a specified set of both processing and passive resources under specified workloads; the *resource* describes a server in a performance model, that can be active or passive; finally, the *workload* describes the load intensity and the required or estimated response time for a scenario. We do not give here details about these notations (see [48] for details). In the rest of this section, we outline transformation methodologies for some of the UML based SMNs reviewed in section 4.2, assuming that they have been enriched with suitable MI represented using the notations of the SPT-PA profile. Then, in section 5.3, we focus on the UML based SMN presented in section 4.3 (UML profile for mobile systems), showing explicitly how the notations defined in the SPT-PA profile can be used to embed the performance related MI within this SMN for mobile system, and how we can derive performance models from design models expressed in this enriched notation.

Transformation Methodologies. Differently from process algebras based SMNs, that basically share a single transformation methodology to a single TMN (Markov process), the situation is less homogeneous for UML based SMNs, for both the proposed transformation methodology itself and the adopted TMN.

Merseguer et al. model [31]. In this case the adopted TMN is a Generalized Stochastic Petri Net. The methodology defines a way for building a Petri net from each State Diagram describing a single component, and then an overall Petri Net using information extracted from the Sequence Diagram that models an interaction scenario.

Example 10. Let us consider the model presented in the example 5. The MI that must be added to that model to carry out performance analysis includes the (exponentially distributed) duration of system actions, the size of the *Collector* component and of the *request* and *reply* messages, and the probability of selecting the "moving" or "not moving" alternative for the interaction with an airline site. Using this MI, we get the following Stochastic Petri net:

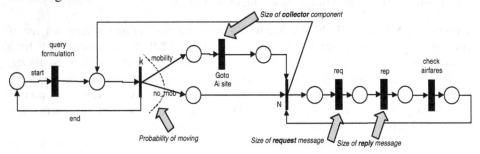

EndOfExample10

Balsamo and Marzolla model [2]. The adopted TMN is a process-oriented simulation model, implemented as a discrete-event C++ simulation program. The transformation methodology is close to a one-to-one mapping from elements of UML model (enriched with SPT-PA annotations) to elements of the simulator, so that the structure and the dynamics of the simulator closely follows the structure and the behavior of the UML model.

Grassi and Mirandola model [15, 17, 18]. We recall that this notation supports the modeling of systems with physical and virtual mobility, with the latter restricted to the MA pattern. Moreover, it also supports the explicitly modeling of the designer uncertainty about virtual mobility, through the use of the `moveTo?` stereotype. Hence the goal of the proposed transformation methodology is to build models whose solution gives to the designer insight about the effectiveness of virtual mobility. In terms of the proposed SMN, the gained insights should allow the designer to substitute the `moveTo?` labels in the preliminary CD with (possibly constrained) `moveTo` labels, or with no such label at all, if the obtained insights provide evidence that a static architectural style is more advantageous. Two different transformation methodologies have been proposed to this end [15, 17, 18] that derive two different TMNs, namely, a Markov Decision model [42] or a "non deterministic" ExecutionGraph/Queueing Network model (see later). When no `moveTo?` label is present in the starting design model (i.e. when there is no uncertainty about the design to be adopted), the derived models reduce to Markov Reward and ExecutionGraph/ Extended Queueing Network models, respectively [23, 45]. In the following we briefly present these two methodologies.

The first methodology is suitable for cases when the NFAs of interest are mainly interaction-related measures (e.g., generated network traffic) without considering possible contention with other applications.

The second one, based on classic SPE technique [45, 46], is suitable for cases where the NFAs of interest are measures like throughput or response time and we are possibly interested in considering contention with other applications on the use of system resources. Two different TMNs are taken into account, namely, Execution Graphs and Extended Queueing Network Models for NFAs with and without consideration to the impact of contention, respectively.

Let us consider the first methodology. In general, a Markov Reward Process (MRP) models a state transition system, where the next state is selected according to a transition probability that only depends on the current state. Moreover, each time a state is visited or a transition occurs, a reward is accumulated, that depends on the involved state or transition. Typical measures that can be derived from such a model are the reward accumulated in a given time interval, or the reward accumulation rate in the long period. A Markov Decision Process (MDP) extends the MRP model by associating to each state a set of alternative *decisions*, where both the rewards and the transitions associated with that state are decision dependent. A *policy* for a MDP consists in a selection, for each state, of one of the associated decisions, that will be taken each time that state is visited. Hence, different policies lead to different system behaviors and to different accumulated rewards. In other words, a MDP defines a family of MRPs, one for each different policy that can be determined. Algorithms exist to determine the optimal policy with respect to some optimality criterion (e.g. minimization of the accumulated reward) [42].

In the translation methodology adopted in [15, 18], a MRP/MDP state corresponds to a possible configuration of the components location, while a state transition models the occurrence of an interaction between components or a location change, and the associated reward is the "cost" (e.g. number of transmitted bytes, energy consumption) of that interaction. In case of MDP, the decisions associated with states model the alternative choices of virtual mobility or no virtual mobility as software architectural style, for those components that are the source of a `moveTo?` labeled link.

The translation method from the extended UML to this TMN consists of the definition of some elementary generation rules, and then in the use of these rules to define a MDP generation algorithm [15, 18].

Once the MDP has been generated, it can be solved to determine the optimal policy, that is the selection of a decision in each state that optimizes the reward accumulated in the corresponding MRP. Of course, the optimal policy depends on the values given to the system parameters (e.g., the size of the messages and of the possibly mobile component). Different values for these parameters model different scenarios.

Now, let us consider the second methodology [17], based on SPE techniques and having Execution Graphs (EG) and Extended Queueing Network (EQN) models as TMN.

We start by briefly reviewing SPE. Its basic concept is the separation of the software model (SM) from its execution environment model (i.e., hardware platform model or machinery model, MM). The SM captures the essential aspects of software behavior; and is usually represented by means of Execution Graphs (EG). An EG is a graph whose nodes represent software workload components and whose edges represent transfers of control. Each node is weighted by a demand vector that represents the resource usage of the node (i.e., the demand for each resource).

The MM models the hardware platform and is based on an EQN model. To specify an EQN, we need to define: the components (i.e., service centers), the topology (i.e., the connections among centers) and some relevant parameters (such as job classes, job routing among centers, scheduling discipline at service centers, service demand at service centers). Component and topology specification is performed according to the system description, while parameters specification is obtained from information derived by EGs and from knowledge of resource capabilities. Once the EQN is completely specified, it can be analyzed by use of classical solution techniques (simulation, analytical technique, hybrid simulation) to obtain performance indices such as the mean network response time or the utilization index.

To cope with mobility, in the methodology proposed in [17], well-known formalisms such as EG and EQN have been extended by defining the *mob?*-EG and *mob?*-EQN formalisms with the goal of modelling code mobility and the uncertainty about its possible adoption, within a model of the system dynamics.

To include the information about possible component mobility expressed in the CDs by `moveTo?` labeled links, a new kind of EG called *mob?*–EG is derived [17]. The *mob?*-EG modifies the original EG by introducing *mv* nodes that model the "cost" (typically, processing and communication) of code mobility. Moreover, the *mob?*-EG extends the EG formalism by introducing a new kind of node, called *mob?*, characterized by two different outcomes, "*yes*" and "*no*", that can be non-deterministically selected, followed by two possible EGs. The EG corresponding to branch "*yes*" models the selection of component mobility style, while the EG of the branch "*no*" models the static case.

Example 11. The structure (without labels showing performance related information) of the *mob?*-EG derived from the SD and CD of example 6 is depicted in the following figure.

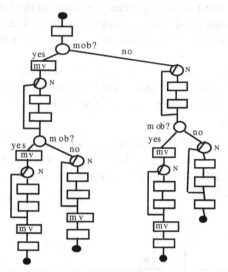

EndOfExample11

Mob?-EG can be considered by itself as the TMN for a first kind of performance evaluation corresponding to the special case of a stand-alone application where the application under study is the unique in the execution environment (therefore there is no resource contention). In this case performance evaluation can be carried out by standard graph analysis techniques [45] to associate an overall "cost" to each path in the *mob?*-EG as a function of the cost of each node that belongs to that path. Note that each path in the *mob?*–EG corresponds to a different mobility strategy, concerning when and where components move. Hence these results provide an optimal bound on the expected performance for each strategy, and can help the designer in selecting a subset of the possible mobility strategies that deserve further investigation in a more realistic setting of competition with other applications.

The complete application of SPE techniques implies the definition of a target performance model obtained from the merging of the *mob?*-EG with a QN modeling the executing platform. The merging leads to the complete specification of a EQN by defining job classes and routing, using information from the blocks and parameters of the *mob?*-EG. However, well known translation methodologies [10, 45] are not sufficient to perform this merging because of the presence of the *mob?* nodes with non-deterministic semantics in the *mob?*-EG; hence it is necessary to give a new translation rule to cope with this kind of nodes. To this end an extension of classical EQN models has been proposed in [17], to be used as TMN. The extension is based on the definition of new service centers, called *r?(outing)*, that model the possibility, after the visit of a service center (and therefore the completion of a software block) of choosing, in a non-deterministic way, which is the routing to follow: the one modelling the static strategy or the one modelling the mobile strategy.

In such a way, a job visiting center *r?* generates two different mutually exclusive paths: one path models the job routing when the component changes its location, the other one models the routing of a static component. Note that, as node *mob?* in the EG, nodes *r?* are characterized by a null service time, since they only represent a routing selection point. The obtained model is called *mob?*-EQN and is characterized by different routing chains starting from nodes *r?*. Note that these different routing chains are mutually exclusive; in other words a *mob?*-EQNM actually models a family of EQNs, one for each different path through the *r?* nodes, corresponding to a different mobility policy.

Example 12. The following figure illustrates an example of *mob?*-EQN derived from the *mob?*-EG of example 11, exploiting also information about the execution platform (e.g., obtained from a UML Deployment Diagram). The figure evidences the mutually exclusive routing chains.

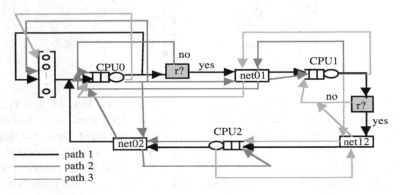

EndOfExample12

When the *mob?*-EQN is the TMN, the ST suggested in [17] for contention based analysis is based on solving the *mob?*-EQN through well assessed techniques [23, 45], separately considering each different EQN belonging to the family modeled by the *mob?*-EQN. When the number of different EQN models is high, this solution approach could result in a high computation complexity. This problem can be alleviated by exploiting results from the stand-alone analysis. It is still an open problem how to devise more efficient solution methods. Starting from the obtained results it is possible to choose the mobility strategy which is *optimal* according to the selected criterion, for example the one that minimizes the response time.

5.3   UML Profile for Mobile Systems: Performance Annotations and Transformation to Performance Models

Adding MI to the UML Profile for Mobile Systems. In this section we show how elements of the SPT-PA profile can be used to add performance related MI to the design model of a mobile system expressed using the SMN described in section 4.3

(UML-PMS) [19]. We recall that the UML-PMS goal is to provide the means for "plugging" mobility features into a pre-existing, mobility unaware, UML based design. Hence, we only focus on the MI that must be added to model elements directly involved in mobility. Of course, to carry out performance analysis, it could be necessary to enrich with suitable performance related annotations also elements of the original model (expressed using the "standard" UML) not directly involved in mobility.

For what concerns entities belonging to the physical platform of the system, we have to specify performance features of those nodes that play a significant role in the execution of (parts of) an application. For example, this is the case of the nodes that correspond to processing or communication devices. According to the SPT profile, this can be achieved by labeling these nodes with the <<PAhost>> or <<PAresource>> stereotypes, depending on whether they play the role of "processing resource" or "passive resource", respectively.[11] These stereotypes add to the node they are associated with a list of attributes that can be used to specify performance related information (e.g.: scheduling policy, processing rate). Figure 19 shows two nodes (one of which is also stereotyped as mobile) stereotyped as <<PAhost>>, so allowing the addition of performance attributes (graphically expressed by the "notes" attached to these nodes).

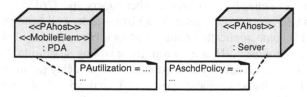

Fig. 19. Performance annotations for computing nodes in a UML-PMS model of a mobile system

Then, we must take into account the impact on the overall system performance of "mobility activities" defined in UML-PMS. The only activities that are relevant to this end are <<PhysicalMove>>, <VirtualMove>>, <<BeforeMove>>, and <<AfterMove>. As a consequence, as depicted in figure 20, these activities are labeled with the SPT-PA <<PAstep>> stereotype, to have the possibility of exploiting the list of attributes associated with this stereotype.[12] However, only a part of these attributes is meaningful for some of these activities, as discussed below.

---

[11] A *processing resource* is a device where a computation ("processing step" in the SPT-PA terminology) can be allocated; a *passive resource* is a resource that can be accessed during a computation.

[12] We introduce in figure 20 a little abuse of notation, as the performance annotations should be actually associated with the stereotyped activities, and not with the stereotypes themselves.

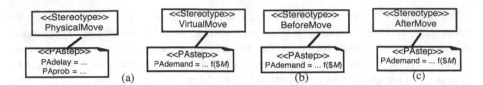

Fig. 20. Performance characterization of mobility activities

A <<PhysicalMove>> refers to a physical entity and denotes the occurrence of an event which is out of the control of the designer. Hence, from a performance viewpoint, the typical information we may want to associate with this activity is when it will occur (once a given state of a mobility manager has been entered), or which is the probability of its occurrence, given that some event has occurred. This activity does not have a direct performance cost, since its "execution" does not require the intervention of computing or communication resources. As a consequence, we are interested in the *PAdelay* or *PAprob* attributes associated with the <<PAstep>> stereotype, that are used to denote, respectively, the delay or the probability to dispatch the activity, once it is enabled. *PAdelay* can be defined as a random variable, to model the uncertainty about the delay length. Note that the introduction of stochastic aspects in a state machine requires a careful definition of its semantics. We do not discuss here this issue, that has been already considered in other papers, like [26].

A <<VirtualMove>> activity refers to a virtual entity and denotes the firing of virtual mobility for some application component as a consequence of some event in the application environment. Hence, when its enabling condition holds and its triggering event occurs, this activity is dispatched with no delay (apart from the delay indirectly caused by shared resource contention), and with probability one. This activity has also a direct performance cost, corresponding to the traversal of the communication link from the source to the destination location (that involves the use of communication and computing resources): it is reasonable to assume that this cost is proportional to the size of the moving entity. Based on these considerations, a <<VirtualMove>> exploits only the *PAdemand* attribute of the <<PAstep>> stereotype, that denotes the demand of communication and computing resources caused by the movement of some logical entity. This demand is parametric with respect to the size M of the moving entity, and will be mapped to the communication and computing resources used to connect the source and destination location.

Let us now consider the <<BeforeMove>> and <<AfterMove>> activities. The only <<PAstep>> attribute they exploit is *PAdemand*, that denotes the demand of computing resources needed to perform them (figures 20(b) and 20(c)). This demand is again parametric with respect to the size M of the moving entity, and will be mapped to the computing resources of the source and destination location, respectively.

Adding MI to virtual mobility pattern models. Figures 21, 22 and 23 depict how the "general rules" outlined above can be exploited to embed performance related information in the models of virtual mobility patterns described in section 4.3.

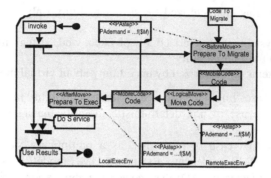

Fig. 21. Performance characterization of the COD pattern

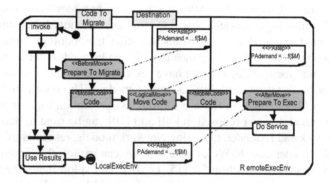

Fig. 22. Performance characterization of the REV pattern

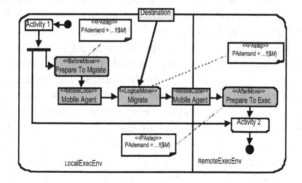

Fig. 23. Performance characterization of the MA pattern

Transformation to Performance Models. In this section, rather than presenting transformation methodologies built from scratch for UML-PMS models, we discuss how we can exploit existing methodologies. We distinguish three different uses of UML-PMS (with the SPT based performance annotations outlined above):

a) modeling of systems characterized by virtual mobility only, with no uncertainty about mobility;

b) modeling of systems characterized by physical and virtual mobility, with no uncertainty about virtual mobility;

c) modeling of systems characterized by uncertainty about virtual mobility.

The former two cases imply the use of deterministic mobility managers only, while the latter implies the use of non deterministic mobility managers, as discussed in section 4.3.

Let us consider first case *a*. Note that, as a preliminary step, we may easily transform the UML-PMS model into a standard UML model, by simply navigating through the Activity Diagram (AD) that models the application logic and "weaving" into it, at suitable points (corresponding to triggering events for mobility managers of the UML-PMS model) the AD fragments that model the adopted virtual mobility pattern (see figures 20, 21 and 22). After this weaving has been completed, what we get is an application logic model consisting only of a standard AD with SPT-PA performance annotations. Hence, any transformation methodology from UML and SPT-PA compliant models to performance models can be used to derive performance models, even if that methodology do not have been defined having in mind models of mobile systems (with virtual mobility) as source models. The only constraint is that the methodology should support the use of ADs as application logic models. As an example, the methodologies proposed in [40] and [10] can be used to derive Layered Queueing Network and Extended Queueing Network models, respectively.

Now, let us consider case *b*. We discuss how we can exploit the Grassi-Mirandola methodologies presented in section 5.2 [15, 17, 18]. To exploit them, the UML-PMS model must satisfy the following constraints: only the MA virtual mobility pattern is used, and triggering events for virtual mobility managers consists only of a subsets of "start interaction" events among pairs of software components. If these constraints hold, we note that it is relatively simple to map an AD (like the AD modeling the mobility unaware application logic in the UML-PMS model) onto an equivalent Sequence Diagram (SD), thus obtaining the SD used in [15, 17, 18] as mobility unaware application logic model. Then, we can build the Collaboration Diagram (CD) modeling the "interaction structure" by simply drawing the "boxes" modeling the application components and linking together all the boxes corresponding to pairs of directly interacting components (which components directly interact can be determined by inspecting the SD); some of these links will be labeled with the (possibly constrained) moveTo stereotype if some "start interaction" event between the pair of linked components belong to the set of triggering events for mobility managers of the original UML-PMS model. Finally, starting from the Deployment Diagram (DD) and the associated mobility manager (if physical mobility is present) of the UML-PMS model, we can easily build a DD where physical location changes are represented by different instances of the moving entity connected by become labeled links, as assumed in the [18] methodology. Figure 24 depicts an example of this latter transformation. After these transformations have been performed, we can build either a Markov Reward or an Extended Queueing Network model, following the methodologies outlined in section 5.2 [15, 17, 18]. We point out that the exploitation of other methodologies presented in section 5.2 (like the Balsamo-Marzolla methodology) appears less immediate.

Finally, let us consider case *c*. With respect to case *b*, the only difference is the presence in the UML-PMS model of non deterministic mobility managers controlling virtual mobility. As explained in previous sections, the explicit modeling of the designer uncertainty has been already considered in the already reviewed Grassi-Mirandola approach. We can exploit the transformation methodologies of that approach also in this case, following a similar procedure as for case *b* above. The only difference is that for those pairs of interacting components whose "start interaction" events trigger non deterministic transitions in the UML-PMS mobility manager, the corresponding link in the CD must be labeled with a `moveTo?` rather than `moveTo` stereotype.

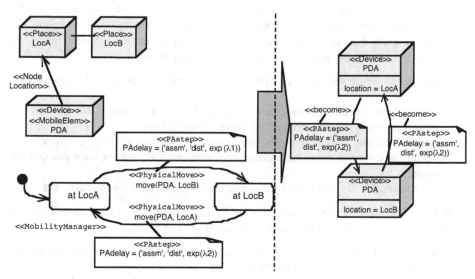

Fig. 24. Transformation from a UML-PMS to a [18] model of physical mobility

Example 13. Let us consider the UML-PMS model of the travel agency example presented in Example 7, restricting ourselves to the virtual mobility strategy modeled by the mobility manager of figure 18(b). Since that manager includes non deterministic transitions, we are in the case *c* discussed above. Hence, we can apply the transformation methodologies presented in [15, 17, 18].

For this purpose, we make the following assumptions about the system:

- total size of the Travel Agency and Collector components: 1000;
- size of each *request* or *reply* message: 1;
- number of airline sites: 2;
- number of consecutive *request-replay* interaction between the collector and an airline: $N \geq 1$.

This information must be embedded within the original model using appropriate SPT-PA annotations (not shown here). Our goal is to determine whether an MA based virtual mobility strategy improves the system performance.

Let us consider the methodology presented in [15, 18]. The adopted TMN is a Markov Decision Process (MDP), and the NFA we are interested in is the generated network traffic. For this example, the derived MDP has three states, corresponding to the three possible locations of the TravelAgency and Collector components (note that, according to the strategy depicted in figure 18(b), these two components move together). Solving the MDP model, we get the following results:

- if $N \leq 500$, then the network traffic is minimized when no virtual mobility is introduced in the system;
- if $N > 500$, then the network traffic is minimized when virtual mobility is introduced in the system, with the Travel Agency and Collector components moving to each airline site they have to interact with.

Then, let us consider the methodology presented in [17]. In this case, the adopted TMN is a *mob?*-EQN, and the NFA we are interested in is the system throughput. To take into account the impact of contention on system resources, we introduce these further system characterizations, besides those reported above:

- number of ticket information requests contemporarily present in the system: $K = 3, 5, 10$;
- the relative speeds of the processing nodes at the three sites and of the communication network connecting them are as follow:
  - configuration $C1$: the three processing nodes are slower than the network;
  - configuration $C2$: the three processing nodes and the network have comparable speed;
  - configuration $C3$: the three processing nodes are faster than the network;

Solving the *mob?*-EQN model (reported in example 12) we get the following results (limiting the analysis to values of N less than 2000):

- in configuration $C1$, for any $N \leq 2000$ and $K = 3, 5, 10$, the system throughput is maximized when no virtual mobility is introduced in the system;
- in configuration $C3$, for any $N \leq 2000$ and $K = 3, 5, 10$, the system throughput is maximized when virtual mobility is introduced in the system, with the Travel Agency and Collector components moving to each airline site they have to interact with;
- in configuration $C2$, for any $N \leq 2000$ and $K = 3$, the system throughput is maximized following the optimal strategy for configuration $C1$; on the other hand, for $K = 5, 10$, the system throughput is maximized following the optimal strategy for configuration $C3$.

EndOfExample13

6   Conclusions

The primary goal of this tutorial has been to provide a structured view within the domain of performance validation of mobile systems. The classification of the presented approaches has been supported by a general framework (section 2) classifying the "dimensions" each approach has to deal with.

This review have been focused on two kinds of approaches for the systematic modeling and analysis of NFA in mobile systems, based on the use of formal or semi-formal SMNs.

The merit of formal languages comes primarily from their lack of ambiguity, and their precise compositional features. One of the main drawbacks comes from the gap between the skills they require to be used and the skills usually present in software design teams. However, to be fair, we have to point out that all the notations presented in section 4.1 are quite low level, as already remarked at the end of that section, so that it can be hardly suggested to use them directly in the modeling of realistic systems. Also the "high level" formal SMNs that have been briefly mentioned in section 4.1 [6, 38] basically share the same problem. Probably, these notations can play a significant role in providing as underlying model for more "user friendly" SMNs (such as those based on the use of UML), giving them a sound semantics. As an example, an attempt to bridge the gap between formal and semi-formal SMNs can be found in [1] that defines a π-ADL based UML profile.

On the other hand, the use of UML as SMN from which to derive performance models is not immune from problems as well, so the general problem of deriving meaningful performance models from UML artifacts deserves further investigation by itself. One of the problems comes from the fact that all the transformation methodologies reviewed in section 5.2 (differently from that described in section 5.1) have been basically empirically defined. This make difficult, for example, to reason about the consistency among performance models derived from the same source model using different methodologies. A promising way that could be pursued to deal with this problem is the exploitation of the *model driven* methodologies, languages and tools that have been and are going to be developed, aimed at providing a sound basis to the problem of building and transforming software systems models [30, 32, 33].

Acknowledgements

This work is based on materials taken from [16, 19, 20]. The author would like to thank his co-authors of those papers, Vittorio Cortellessa, Raffaela Mirandola and Antonino Sabetta, for their contribution and for insightful discussions.

References

1. L. Alloui, F. Oquendo "The ArchWare architecture description language: UML profile for architecting with ArchWare ADL" Deliverable DI.4b, ArchWare European RTD Project, IST-2001-32360, June 2003.
2. S. Balsamo, M. Marzolla "Towards performance evaluation of mobile systems in UML", in *Proc. of ESM'03*, Napoli, Italy, October 2003, pp. 61-68.
3. L. Bass, P. Clements, R. Kazman, *Software Architectures in Practice*, Addison-Wesley, New York, NY, 1998.
4. H. Baumeister, N. Koch, P. Kosiuczenko, and M. Wirsing "Extending activity diagrams to model mobile systems" in *NetObject-Days* 2002 (M. Aksit, M. Mezini, R. Unland Eds.), LNCS 2591, pp. 278-293, 2003.

5. M. Bernardo "An algebra-based method to associate rewards with EMPA terms" (P. Degano and R. Gorrieri eds.), LNCS 1256, Springer Verlag, 1997.
6. L. Bettini "Linguistic Constructs for Object-Oriented Mobile Code Programming & their Implementations" PhD Thesis, Dip. di Matematica, Università di Siena, Italy, Feb. 2003, on line at: http://music.dsi.unifi.it/xklaim/index.html.
7. G. Booch, J. Rumbaugh, and I.Jacobson, *The Unified Modeling Language User Guide*, Addison Wesley, New York, 1999.
8. L. Cardelli, A.D. Gordon "Mobile ambients" *Foundations of Software Science and Computational Structures* (M. Nivat ed.), LNCS 1378, Springer-Verlag, 1998, pp. 140-155
9. N. Carriero, D. Gelernter "Linda in context" *Communications of the ACM*, vol. 32, no.4, 1989, pp. 444-458.
10. V. Cortellessa, R. Mirandola "PRIMA-UML: a performance validation incremental methodology on early UML diagrams" *Science of Computer Programming*, Elsevier Science, vol 44, n.1, pp 101-129, July 2002.
11. R. De Nicola, G. Ferrari, R. Pugliese, B. Venneri "KLAIM: a kernel language for agents interaction and mobility" *IEEE Trans. on Software Engineering*, vol. 24, no. 5, May 1998, pp. 315-330
12. G. Ferrari, C. Montangero, L. Semini, S. Semprini "Mobile agents coordination in Mob$_{adtl}$" Proc. of *4th Int. Conf. on Coordination Models and Languages (COORDINATION'00)*, (A. Porto and G.-C. Roman eds.), Springer-Verlag, Limassol, Cyprus, Sept. 2000.
13. A. Fuggetta, G.P. Picco, G. Vigna "Understanding code mobility" *IEEE Trans. on Software Engineering*, vol. 24, no. 5, May 1998, pp. 342-361.
14. N. Gotz, U. Herzog, M. Rettelbach "Multiprocessor system design: the integration of functional specification and performance analysis using stochastic process algebras" in *Performance Evaluation of Computer and Communication Systems* (L. Donatiello and R. Nelson eds.), LNCS 729, Springer-Verlag, 1993.
15. V. Grassi, R. Mirandola, "Modeling and performance analysis of mobile software architectures in a UML framework" in *Proc. <<UML2001>> Conference*, LNCS 2185, Springer Verlag, October 2001.
16. V. Grassi, V. Cortellessa, R. Mirandola "Performance validation of mobile software architectures" LNCS 2495, Springer Verlag, 2002, pp. 346-373.
17. V. Grassi, R. Mirandola, "PRIMAmob-UML: a methodology for performance analysis of mobile software architectures", in *WOSP 2002, Third International Conference on Software and Performance*, ACM, July 2002.
18. V. Grassi, R. Mirandola "Derivation of Markov Models for Effectiveness Analysis of Adaptable Software Architectures for Mobile Computing" *IEEE Trans. on Mobile Computing*, vol. 2, no. 2, Apr.-June 2003, pp. 114-131.
19. V. Grassi, R. Mirandola, A. Sabetta "A UML profile for mobile systems" in *Proc. <<UML2004>> Conference*, LNCS 3273, Springer Verlag, Sept. 2004, pp. 128-142.
20. V. Grassi, R. Mirandola, A. Sabetta "UML based modeling and performance analysis of mobile systems" in *Proc. ACM Workshop on Modeling and Simulation of Wireless and Mobile Systems*, Oct. 2004.
21. H. Hermanns, U. Herzog, J.-P. Katoen "Process algebras for performance evaluation", *Theoretical Computer Science*, vol. 274, no. 1-2, 2002, pp. 43-87.
22. S.A.Hissam, G. Moreno, J. Stafford, K. Wallnau "Enabling Predictable Assembly" *Journal of Systems and Software*, vol. 65, 2003, pp. 185-198.
23. R. Jain, *Art of Computer Systems Performance Analysis*, Wiley, New York, 1990.
24. A.D. Joseph, J.A. Tauber, M.F. Kaashoek "Mobile computing with the Rover toolkit" *IEEE Trans. on Computers*, Feb. 1997

25. P. Kosiuczenko "Sequence diagrams for mobility" in Proc. of *MobIMod Workshop* (J. Krogstie editor), Tampere, Finland, October 2003.
26. C. Lindemann, A. Thummler "Performance analysis of time-enhanced UML diagrams based on stochastic processes" in Proc. of *3rd Int. Workshop on Software and Performance* (WOSP 2002), Roma, Italy, July 2002, pp. 25-34.
27. A. Lopes, J.L. Fiadeiro "Adding mobility to software architectures" in *Proc. FOCLASA 2003: Foundations of Coordination Languages and Software Architectures*, Sept. 2003.
28. G. Manson et al. "FIPA Modeling Areas: Deployment and Mobility" on line at: www.auml.org/auml/documents/DeploymentMobility.zip.
29. M. Margaritidis, G.C. Polyzos "Adaptation techniques for ubiquitous internet multimedia" *Wireless Communication and Mobile Computing*, vol. 1, no.2, Apr.-June 2001, pp. 141-163
30. "MDA Guide Version 1.0.1" *OMGDocument omg/03-06-01*, on line at: www.omg.org/docs/omg/03-06-01.pdf.
31. J. Merseguer, J. Campos, E. Mena "Evaluating performance on mobile agents software design", in *Actas de las VIII Jornadas de Concurrencia*, pages 291-307. Cuenca, Spain: Universidad de Castilla-la Mancha, June 2000.
32. "Meta Object Facility (MOF) 2.0 Core Specification", *OMG Adopted Specification ptc/03-10-04*, on line at: www.omg.org/docs/ptc/03-10-04.pdf.
33. "MOF 2.0 Query/Views/Transformations RFP", *OMG Document ad/2002-04-10*, on line at: www.omg.org/docs/ad/02-04-10.pdf.
34. R. Milner, *Communication and Concurrency*, Prentice Hall, 1989.
35. R. Milner, *Communicating and Mobile Systems: the π-calculus*, Cambridge Univ. Press, 1999.
36. B.D. Noble, M. Satyanarayanan, G.T. Nguyen, D.Narayanan, J.E. Tilton, J. Flinn, K.R. Walker "Agile application-aware adaptation for mobility" in *Proc. 16th ACM Symp. on Operating Systems Principles*, pp. 276-287, Oct. 1997
37. C. Nottegar, C. Priami, P. Degano "Performance evaluation of mobile processes via abstract machines" *IEEE Trans. on Software Engineering*, vol. 27, no. 10, Oct. 2001, pp. 867-889.
38. F. Oquendo "π-ADL: an architecture description language based on the high-order typed π-calculus for specifying dynamic and mobile software architectures" *ACM Software Engineering Notes*, vol. 29, no. 4, May 2004.
39. D. Pattinson, M. Wirsig "Making components move: a separation of concerns approach" in *Proc. First Int. Symposium on Formal Methods for Components and Objects (FMCO 2002)*.
40. D.C. Petriu, H. Shen "Applying the UML Performance Profile: Graph Grammar-based derivation of LQN models from UML specification". Proc. of *Performance TOOLS 2002*, London, England, April 14-17 2002, LNCS 2324, Springer Verlag.
41. G.P. Picco, G.-C. Roman, P.J. McCann "Reasoning about code mobility in Mobile UNITY" *ACM Transactions on Software Engineering and Methodology*, vol. 10, no. 3, July 2001, pp. 338-395.
42. M.L. Puterman, *Markov Decision Processes*, J. Wiley and Sons, 1994.
43. D. Sangiorgi "Expressing mobility in process algebras: first-order and higher-order paradigms" PhD thesis, Univ. of Edinburgh, 1992.
44. M. Simeoni, P. Inverardi, A. Di Marco, S. Balsamo "Model-Based Performance Prediction in Software Development: A Survey" *IEEE Trans. on Software Engineering*, Vol. 30, no. 5, May 2004, pp. 295- 310.

45. C.U. Smith, *Performance Engineering of Software Systems*, Addison-Wesley, Reading, MA, 1990.
46. C.U. Smith, L. Williams. *Performance solutions: A Practical Guide to Creating Responsive, Scalable Software.* Addison Wesley, 2002.
47. "UML 2.0 Superstructure Specification" *OMG Adopted Specification ptc/03-08-02*, on line at: www.omg.org/docs/ptc/03-08-02.pdf.
48. "UML Profile for Schedulability, Performance, and Time Specification", *OMG Adopted Specification ptc/02-03-02*, on line at: www.omg.org/docs/ptc/02-03-02.pdf.
49. U. Varshney and R. Vetter "Emerging mobile and wireless networks" *Communications of ACM*, 43(6), pp. 73-81, June 2000.

A Methodology Based on Formal Methods for Predicting the Impact of Dynamic Power Management*

A. Acquaviva, A. Aldini, M. Bernardo, A. Bogliolo,
E. Bontà, and E. Lattanzi

Università di Urbino "Carlo Bo",
Istituto di Scienze e Tecnologie dell'Informazione,
Piazza della Repubblica 13, 61029 Urbino, Italy
{acquaviva, aldini, bernardo, bogliolo, bonta, lattanzi}@sti.uniurb.it

Abstract. One of the major issues in the design of a mobile computing device is reducing its power consumption. A commonly used technique is the adoption of a dynamic power management policy, which modifies the power consumption of the device based on certain run time conditions. The introduction of the dynamic power management within a battery-powered device may not be transparent, as it may alter the overall system behavior and efficiency. Here we present a methodology that can be used in the early stages of the system design to predict the impact of the dynamic power management on the system functionality and performance. The predictive methodology, which relies on formal methods to compare the properties of the system without and with dynamic power management, is illustrated through the application of its various phases to a simple example of power-manageable system.

1 Introduction

Reducing the power consumption is a fundamental criterion in the design of battery-powered devices typical of modern mobile embedded systems. Significant power savings can be achieved at run time through the application of dynamic power management (DPM) techniques [3], i.e. techniques that – based on run time conditions – modify the power consumption of the devices by changing their state or by scaling their voltage or frequency.

The approaches to DPM proposed in the literature have been classified into deterministic schemes, predictive schemes, and stochastic optimum control schemes. The schemes of the first class schedule the shutdown periods at fixed time instants, possibly depending on the occurrence of some event. Instead, the schemes of the second class attempt to predict the device usage behavior in the future based on historical data patterns. Finally, the schemes of the third class

---

* Co-financed by Regione Marche within the CIPE 36/2002 framework.

M. Bernardo and A. Bogliolo (Eds.): SFM-Moby 2005, LNCS 3465, pp. 155–189, 2005.

make probabilistic assumptions – based on observations – about usage patterns to formulate an optimization problem.

Whatever scheme is adopted, the introduction of the DPM within a mobile computing device may have a non negligible impact on the overall system functionality and performance. It is therefore of paramount importance to assess such an impact before the DPM is introduced, in order to make sure that the system behavior will not be significantly altered and that the quality of service will not go below an acceptable threshold.

This objective can be achieved by following a methodology that helps predicting the effect of the DPM through the comparison of the functional and performance characteristics of the system without and with DPM. Since it should be applied in the early stages of the system design – in which a high level of abstraction is admitted that favors the task of verifying properties – the predictive methodology can take advantage of formal description techniques, like e.g. stochastic process algebras [7] and stochastic Petri nets [2], as well as formal analysis techniques, like e.g. equivalence checking [11] and model checking [10]. This paper describes and discusses a formal methodology introduced by the same authors for predicting the impact of the application of a DPM strategy [1].

The rest of the paper is organized as follows. In Sect. 2 we present an introduction to DPM including a brief survey of the most frequently adopted techniques. In Sect. 3 we discuss the methodology based on formal methods to predict the impact of the DPM on the system functionality and performance. After recalling in Sect. 4 a particular specification language that provides all the ingredients that are needed to support the predictive methodology, an application of the methodology itself to a simple power-manageable mobile device is illustrated in Sect. 5, 6, and 7. Finally, in Sect. 8 we draw some conclusions.

2   Dynamic Power Management

Electronic systems are designed to deliver peak performance, but they spend most of their time executing tasks that do not require such a performance level. For instance, hand-held personal digital assistants are mainly used to run interactive applications (such as personal organizers and text editors) whose main task is capturing sparse input events, while cellular phones are reactive systems that are usually idle waiting for incoming calls or user commands.

In general, electronic systems are subject to time-varying workloads. Since there is a close relation between power consumption and performance, the capability of tuning at run time the performance of a system to its workload provides great opportunity to save power.

Dynamic power management (DPM) techniques dynamically reconfigure an electronic system by changing its operating mode and by turning its components on and off in order to provide at any time the minimum performance/functionality required by the workload while consuming the minimum amount of power.

The application of DPM techniques requires i) power-manageable components providing multiple operating modes, ii) a power manager having run-time control of the operating mode of the power-manageable components, and iii) a DPM policy specifying the control rules to be implemented by the power manager.

The simplest example of power-manageable hardware is a device that can be dynamically turned on and off by a power manager that issues shutdown and wakeup commands according to a given policy. When turned on, the device is active and provides a given performance at the cost of a given power consumption. When turned off, the device is inactive, hence provides no performance and consumes no power. The workload of the device is a sequence of service requests issued by a generic client.

If the workload keeps the device busy for 30% of time, up to 70% of energy can be saved by turning the device off during idle periods. Under the assumption that the device can be switched on and off instantaneously at no cost, the maximum power saving can be achieved without performance penalty by means of a greedy policy turning off the device right after each service accomplishment and turning it on upon each incoming service request.

In all cases of practical interest, however, shutdown and wakeup transitions have non-negligible costs both in terms of energy and in terms of time. Transition costs make the design of DPM policies a non-trivial task for two main reasons. First, a shutdown can be counterproductive if the idle period is not long enough to compensate for the transition energy. Second, if a service request is issued when the device is inactive, the wakeup time adds a delay to the service time that may cause an unacceptable performance degradation.

In practice, transition costs limit the actual exploitability of low power states and make it necessary to predict user idleness to take DPM decisions. In the rest of this section we show how to describe a DPM system as a power state machine, we provide a formal definition of exploitability of a low power state, we discuss the issue of workload prediction, we briefly outline typical DPM strategies, and we introduce a simple case study that will be used throughout the paper.

2.1   Power State Machine

As far as DPM is concerned, a power-manageable system (or component) can be represented as a power state machine (PSM). Power states are operating modes characterized by average performance and power values. They are called active if they provide positive performance, inactive otherwise. Transitions among power states are characterized by their costs (transition time and energy) and triggered by DPM commands or service requests.

Many power-manageable components have only two power states and can be represented by a PSM like the one shown in Fig. 1.a). Transitions from the active state (on) to the inactive state (off) are triggered by a shutdown command issued by the power manager, while wakeup transitions are triggered by incoming service requests issued by the client.

Fig. 1.b) shows a more complex PSM with multiple active and inactive states, representing a server with two processing units. The server is sensitive to shutdown commands (sd) when idle. Wakeup transitions are triggered by incoming

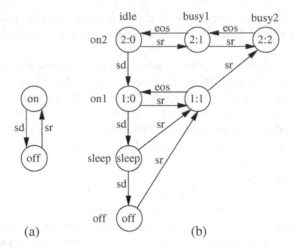

Fig. 1. a) Power state machine of a two-state power-manageable system; b) power state machine of a power-manageable system with 5 active states (labeled x:y, where x is the number of active servers and y is the number of requests under processing) and 2 inactive states (sleep and off), representing a server with 2 CPUs

service requests (sr). The active states span the tradeoff between power and performance, while the inactive states provide different tradeoffs between stand-by power and wakeup cost.

2.2   Exploitability of Low Power States

We now define and discuss the exploitability of the inactive states of a power-manageable component. Since any component needs to be active to deliver its service, the inherent cost of putting it into an inactive state can be computed as the sum of the costs of the shutdown and wakeup transitions needed to enter and exit the inactive state starting from the closest active one:

$$T_{tr} = T_{shutdown} + T_{wakeup} \tag{1}$$

$$P_{tr} = \frac{T_{shutdown} \cdot P_{shutdown} + T_{wakeup} \cdot P_{wakeup}}{T_{tr}} \tag{2}$$

where T_{tr} is the overall transition time and P_{tr} is the average transition power. If the transition power is greater than the active power (P_{on}), the transition to the inactive state provides a power reduction if and only if the time spent in the inactive state is long enough to compensate for the extra transition power. If this is not the case, the transition is counterproductive. The minimum idle period that makes it convenient to go to the inactive state is called break-even time (T_{be}) and can be computed as follows:

$$T_{be} = T_{tr} + T_{tr} \cdot \frac{P_{tr} + P_{on}}{P_{on} - P_{off}} \tag{3}$$

The break-even time of an inactive state is closely related to its exploitability: An inactive state is exploitable if and only if the workload contains idle periods longer than its break-even time. Notice that the break-even time is a property of the inactive state independent of the workload, while the exploitability depends both on the break-even time and on workload statistics. For a given workload, the lower the break-even time of an inactive state, the higher its exploitability.

The average power saved by entering an inactive state (off) during an idle period of length $T_{idle} > T_{be}$ can be expressed as:

$$P_{saved,off}(T_{idle}) = (P_{on} - P_{off}) \cdot \frac{T_{idle} - T_{be}}{T_{idle}} \tag{4}$$

Needless to say, the lower the break-even time and the lower the power consumption of the inactive state, the higher the energy saving. If multiple inactive states are available, their exploitability and energy saving need to be evaluated at each idle period. Given two inactive states (off1 and off2) of the same component, if off2 has a longer break-even time and a higher power consumption than off1 we say it is dominated by off1 since off1 is always more convenient than off2.

Fig. 2 shows the average power consumed by a system during an idle period of length T_{idle} under the assumption that its low power states are carefully exploited by an ideal power manager. The four curves refer to the four different inactive states of the system. Notice that for $T_{idle} < 5$ no inactive state is exploitable and the average power consumption is P_{on}. For larger idle periods, inactive states ca͏ ͏
rel͏

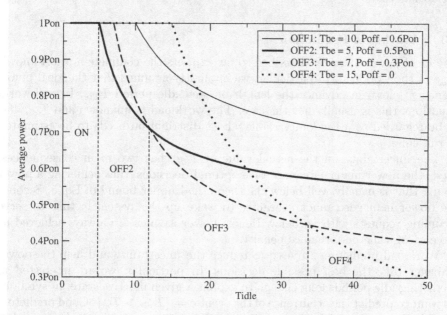

Fig. 2. Average power consumption during an idle period of length T_{idle} achieved by exploiting four different inactive states

for $5 < T_{idle} < 12$ the best choice is off2, for $12 < T_{idle} < 34$ the best choice is off3, for $T_{dile} > 33$ the best choice is off4. The inactive state off1 is never the best choice since it is dominated by off2, which has a lower power consumption and a shorter break-even time.

The inactive states of properly designed power-manageable components do not dominate each other, rather, they provide different tradeoffs between break-even time and power consumption.

Given a power-manageable system, an ideal power manager achieves the best energy saving from each idle period. To this purpose, it needs to evaluate the exploitability and energy savings of all inactive states, then chooses the exploitable state (if any) providing the highest savings. In addition, if no performance degradation is tolerated, the power manager needs to wake up the system right in time to serve the next service request. Similar considerations apply to the choice of the best active state to be used to serve each request.

Referring, for the sake of simplicity, to the two-state power-manageable system of Fig. 1.a), the average power saving achieved by the ideal power manager without impairing performance can be expressed by:

$$P_{saved,off} = (P_{on} - P_{off}) \cdot \frac{T^{avg}_{idle>T_{be}} - T_{be}}{T^{avg}_{idle}} \cdot (1 - F_{T_{idle}}(T_{be})) \tag{5}$$

where $T^{avg}_{idle>T_{be}}$ is the average length of idle periods longer than T_{be}, T^{avg}_{idle} is the average length of all idle periods, and $F_{T_{idle}}(T_{be})$ is the probability of idle periods shorter than T_{be} ($F_{T_{idle}}$ being the probability distribution of the idle period lengths).

2.3   Workload Prediction

The ideal power manager described so far exploits the complete a priori knowledge of the workload. In particular, we implicitly assumed that the ideal power manager knows in advance the length of each idle period T_{idle}. In real-world situations this is usually not the case. The workload is unknown and T_{idle} has to be regarded as a random variable whose distribution needs to be estimated at run time.

The uncertainty on the actual value of T_{idle} has two main consequences. First, the power manager cannot take optimal decisions, thus achieving a power saving that is usually well below the theoretical upper bound of Eq. 5. Second, the power manager cannot guarantee to wake up the system in time to serve incoming requests with no delay. Hence, power savings are always achieved at the cost of some performance penalty.

Workload predictors are used to reduce the uncertainty and help the power manager take the best possible decisions. In particular, we are interested in predicting idle periods long enough to exploit a given inactive state. In symbols, we want to predict the occurrence of the event $e = \{T_{idle} > T_{be}\}$. Good predictors should minimize the risk of mispredictions. We call over-prediction (resp. under-prediction) a predicted idle period longer (resp. shorter) than the actual one.

Over-predictions give rise to performance penalties, while under-predictions give rise to power waste.

The quality of an estimator can be expressed in terms of safety, that is the complement of the probability of over-predictions, and efficiency, that is the complement of the probability of under-predictions.

In general, the prediction of an incoming event (e) is based on the observation of a past event (o) under the assumption that the conditional probability $\Pr(e|o)$ is greater than the marginal probability $\Pr(e)$. A totally safe predictor never makes over-predictions ($\Pr(e|o) = 1$), while a totally efficient predictor never makes under-predictions ($\Pr(o|e) = 1$) [3, 17, 20].

Since no ideal predictors exist, DPM trades off performance for power. The problem of designing optimal DPM policies can be formulated either as a multi-objective optimization problem (finding the policy that minimizes a cost function that takes both power and performance into account) or as a constrained optimization problem (finding the policy that minimizes the power consumption under given performance constraints).

We remark that predictors exploit the correlation between the observed event o and the target (future) event e. If the workload is memoryless there is no correlation between past and future input events (in symbols, $\Pr(e|o) = \Pr(e)$) making any predictor ineffective.

2.4   Survey of DPM Strategies

Providing a thorough overview of existing approaches to DPM is beyond the scope of this paper [3, 8]. Here we only propose general classification criteria derived from the discussion conducted so far and we use them to describe and compare the most commonly used DPM strategies.

We classify DPM techniques on the basis of i) the predictor they use, ii) the degree of control granted to the power manager, and iii) the nature of the decisions it takes.

Existing predictors differ from each other both for the target of the prediction and for the observed history used to make predictions. As far as the exploitation of an inactive state is concerned, the prediction target may be either the occurrence probability of idle periods longer than the break-even time, or the expected length of the next idle period. Similarly, predictions may be based either on the average length of the last n idle periods, or on the length of the last activity burst, or on the first part of the current idle period.

Depending on the degree of control that the power manager has on the system, we distinguish between two main classes of DPM techniques. We call shutdown techniques those in which the power manager can only trigger shutdown transitions, while wakeup transitions are triggered by incoming requests. We call preemptive techniques those in which the power manager may issue both shutdown and wakeup commands and tries to preemptively wake up the system in order to reduce performance penalties.

Finally, we distinguish between deterministic and stochastic DPM policies. Deterministic policies take deterministic decisions based on the observed working conditions: the same decision is taken whenever the same conditions occur. Stochastic policies take randomized decisions whose probabilities depend on the observed working conditions: different decisions may be taken under the same conditions.

Timeout-Based Shutdown. The most widely used DPM techniques make use of timeouts to issue shutdown commands. Whenever a new idle period begins, a timer of duration T_{to} is started. If the workload is still idle after T_{to}, a shutdown command is issued.

According to the classification criteria introduced in Sect. 2.4, timeout-based shutdown policies observe the elapsed idle time (o) to predict the duration of the remaining part of the idle period. They are classified as shutdown techniques since wakeup transitions are usually triggered by incoming requests, and they are deterministic in nature.

Using the elapsed idle time to estimate the length of the current idle period has two disadvantages. First, the system is kept active while waiting for the timeout to elapse, thus missing the opportunity of saving energy during the first part of each idle period. Second, since the shutdown is issued when the timeout has elapsed, idle periods are exploitable only if $T_{idle} > T_{be} + T_{to}$.

On the other hand, the key advantage of timeout-based techniques is that they infer the exploitability of an idle period based on the observation of the first part of the same idle period. Hence, there is usually a good correlation between the target event $e = \{T_{idle} > T_{be} + T_{to}\}$ and the observed event $o = \{T_{idle} > T_{to}\}$. This is however not always the case. If the idle times are exponentially distributed, the elapsed time provides no information about the duration of the remaining part of the idle period.

Preemptive Wakeup. Preemptive wakeup techniques aim at reducing the performance penalty caused by the wakeup time. To this purpose, they estimate the duration of the incoming idle period (T_{idle}) both to evaluate its exploitability and to decide when to issue preemptive wakeup commands.

Denoted by $\tilde{T}_{idle}$ the estimated length of an incoming idle period, if $\tilde{T}_{idle} > T_{be}$ a shutdown command is issued at the beggining of the idle period and a timer is started to trigger a wakeup transition after $\tilde{T}_{idle} - T_{wakeup}$.

The most critical issue of preemptive techniques is the accuracy of the prediction. Although several estimators have been proposed [17, 20], their accuracy is very low and strongly dependent on workload statistics. The efficiency (resp. safety) of the estimator can be manually adjusted by adding (resp. subtracting) proper margins to the estimated value of $\tilde{T}_{idle}$.

Stochastic Control. Stochastic control techniques implement randomized policies that associate nondeterministic decisions with each observed condition.

Although the added value of nondeterminism is not intuitive, it has been shown that randomized policies provide best solutions to constrained optimization problems [4]. This can be shown with a simple example of a two-state power-manageable system with shutdown transitions triggered by external commands issued by the power manager and wakeup transitions triggered by incoming requests. Assume that the power manager has to take decisions at the beginning of each idle period and that the only information available is a good prediction of exploitability. A deterministic policy would issue shutdown commands at the beginning of each exploitable idle period. Suppose that 50% of the idle periods are exploitable, and that each service request is followed by an idle period. Also, assume that the system takes one time unit to wake up. All service requests issued by the client after an exploitable period will experience a service delay of one time unit due to wakeup. The performance penalty caused by the DPM is an average delay of 0.5 time unit per request.

Now assume that only an average delay of 0.1 time unit per request is tolerated by the workload. The deterministic policy described so far cannot be applied since it does not meet performance constraints. On the other hand, the only deterministic policy that meets the constraints is a trivial policy that keeps the system always on, providing no power savings.

The best solution to the constrained optimization problem is provided by a randomized policy that issues shutdown commands with probability 0.2 at the beginning of each exploitable idle period. In this way only 10% of service requests experience a delay of one time unit (causing an average delay of 0.1 time unit per request) and 20% of exploitable idle periods are effectively exploited to save power.

If the system and the workload can be modeled as Markov chains, close solutions to constrained policy optimization problems can be found in polynomial time [4].

2.5   An Example of Power-Manageable System

We conclude this section by introducing a simple example of power-manageable system, which will be used in the rest of the paper as a case study to illustrate the predictive methodology. The example is concerned with a battery-powered server for remote procedure calls. The overall system is depicted in Fig. 3.

The client (C) synchronously interacts with the server (S) through a full-duplex radio channel implemented by two half-duplex radio channels: RCS, from C to S, and RSC, from S to C. RCS is used by the client to send remote procedure calls to the server, while RSC is used by the server to send the results back to the client. The server also interacts with the DPM, which issues shutdown commands

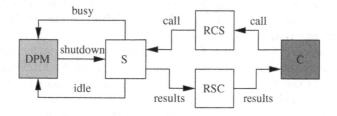

Fig. 3. Power-manageable server for remote procedure calls

in order to put the server in a low power inactive state whenever appropriate. Two more signals, idle and busy, are used by the server to notify the DPM about every change of its service state.

In its easiest implementation, the blocking client issues a call, waits for the results, then takes some time to process the results before issuing the next call. A simple timeout mechanism can be employed by the client to resend a call whenever the waiting time exceeds a given threshold. This can happen because the half-duplex radio channels are not ideal, hence they may introduce both a long propagation delay and a packet loss probability.

The behavior of the server is characterized through the following four states:

- Idle: the server is waiting for a call to arrive.
- Busy: the server is processing a call.
- Sleeping: the server has been shut down by the DPM.
- Awaking: the server has been woken up by the arrival of a call.

The server is sensitive to shutdown commands in the idle state. However, the server may also be sensitive to shutdown commands when busy, in which case a shutdown can interrupt the call processing. In the sleeping state the server consumes no power. The awaking state is a power consuming state in which the server temporarily resides while going from sleeping to busy.

Finally, the DPM sends shutdown commands to the server at certain time instants, possibly based on the knowledge of the current state of the server. There are two different policies:

- Trivial policy: the DPM issues shutdown commands with a given frequency, independently of the current state of the server.
- Timeout policy: shutdown commands are issued by the DPM upon the expiration of a fixed or random timeout after the server has entered the idle state.

3   Predicting the Impact of DPM

The DPM activities can be divided into two classes. The activities of the first class are the ones that modify the state of the power-manageable device, while the activities of the second class are the ones that collect information about the state of the power-manageable device. When the DPM is capable of modifying the state of the power-manageable device, we say that the DPM is enabled. On the contrary, when the state-modifying activities of the DPM cannot be performed, we say that the DPM is disabled.

Whenever the DPM is enabled within a battery-powered device, the behavior and the efficiency of the overall system may be altered. It is therefore important to assess in the early stage of the system design the impact of the DPM. The objective is to check that the DPM does not significantly change the system functionality and does not cause an intolerable degradation of the system performance.

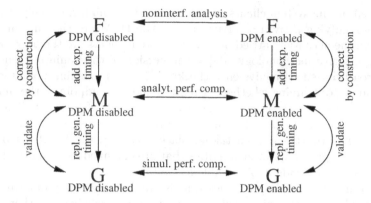

Fig. 4. Models and phases of the predictive methodology

In this section we present a methodology to predict the effect of the DPM on the functionality and the performance of a mobile battery-powered computing device. The methodology is shown in Fig. 4. As can be seen, the methodology requires to build three pairs of models of the system – functional, Markovian and general – each of which is incrementally obtained from the previous one by adding further details. Within each pair, one model refers to the system with the DPM disabled, while the other one refers to the system with the DPM enabled. The functional, Markovian and general models are then compared two by two in three different phases, in order to investigate the DPM impact on the system functionality and performance.

The three phases of the methodology are described below and will be illustrated in more detail in Sect. 5, 6, and 7, respectively, through the case study introduced in Sect. 2.5.

3.1   Noninterference Analysis of the Functional Models

The two models considered in the first phase of the methodology address only the behavior of the system. These models are used to check whether the introduction of the DPM alters the system functionality or not.

In order to assess the functional transparency of the DPM, the methodology resorts to the noninterference analysis approach [14]. The general idea behind this approach is to view a system execution as an information flow and to consider that a group of system users (high users), employing a certain set of commands, is not interfering with another group of system users (low users) if what the first group of users can do with those commands has no effect on what the second group of users can see. This approach has traditionally been applied for security purposes, as noninterference analysis can reveal direct and indirect information flows that violate the access policies based on assigning different access clearances to different user groups.

In the framework of the DPM-related methodology, the noninterference analysis is used to check whether the DPM interferes with the behavior of the system as observed by the system clients. In fact, from the noninterference perspective, the state-modifying activities carried out by the DPM are the only high ones, whereas all the activities carried out by the system clients are the only low ones.

The predictive methodology adopts the version of the noninterference analysis approach based on equivalence checking [13]. Establishing noninterference thus amounts to verifying whether – from the client standpoint – the functional model of the system with the state-modifying activities of the DPM being made unobservable is equivalent to the functional model of the system with the same activities being prevented from taking place (i.e. with the DPM disabled). In the verification process, all the activities that are classified as being neither high nor low have to be made unobservable as well.

The formal notion of equivalence that is employed to carry out this task is weak bisimulation [18], which relates two system models whenever they are able to mimic each other's behavior while abstracting from unobservable activities. Should the two functional models above turn out not to be weakly bisimilar, a Hennessy-Milner logic formula can be automatically obtained that distinguishes the two models, thereby explaining why they are not equivalent [12]. This formula can then be used as a diagnostic piece of information to guide the modification of the behavior of the DPM and/or the system in order to achieve noninterference.

It is worth pointing out that establishing noninterference prior to the introduction of a specific timing of the system activities, which may rule out some behaviors, ensures that the DPM is functionally transparent in itself, not because of the adoption of particular assumptions.

3.2   Analytical Performance Comparison of the Markovian Models

Once functional transparency has been achieved, it has to be investigated whether the DPM affects the system performance. While in general the impact of the DPM on the system behavior can be avoided by means of suitable modifications, it is practically impossible that the introduction of the DPM does not alter the quality of the service delivered by the system. Therefore, the purpose of this further investigation is to find a balance between the power consumption and the overall system efficiency.

In the second phase of the methodology the two functional models are made more complete by specifying the timing of each system activity, thus allowing for performance evaluation. Since the activity durations are expressed in this phase through exponentially distributed random variables, the derived models are Markovian models yielding continuous-time Markov chains.

These models do not need to be validated against the corresponding functional models, since they are directly obtained from the latter by attaching exponential delays to the state transitions. In other words, the two Markovian models are consistent by construction with the corresponding functional models, in the sense that the state space of each of the two Markovian models is isomorphic (up to the transition delays) to the state space of the corresponding functional model. As a consequence, whenever the two functional models meet noninterference, then so do their corresponding Markovian models.

When applying the methodology in practice, the correctness by construction and the resulting preservation of noninterference depend on the precise way in which the functional models are extended as well as on the expressive power of the formalism adopted to develop the models. As an example, in order to measure the percentage of time that the system spends in states characterized by different power consumption levels, it may be necessary to introduce self-looping transitions (with arbitrary exponential delays) in the considered states. Since they are neither high nor low, hence they can be made unobservable, such additional transitions do not affect noninterference.

More troublesome can be the specification of the fact that the duration of certain activities is negligible from the performance viewpoint, which is accomplished through the so called immediate transitions provided by some formalisms (see, e.g., [2, 7]). Since the immediate transitions take precedence over the exponentially timed ones, their use may alter the state space of the Markovian models with respect to the state space of the corresponding functional models. As a consequence, noninterference may not be preserved. Assuming that the immediate transitions are consistently used in the two Markovian models, the noninterference analysis should be repeated in the second phase only if some of the state-modifying activities of the DPM are characterized through immediate transitions. The reason is that, since these activities are the only ones to be enabled in one model and disabled in the other model, they are the only source of potential violation of weak bisimulation when they take precedence over other activities.

The two Markovian models can be solved analytically through standard techniques [21]. This opens the way to the comparison of the system with the DPM disabled and with the DPM enabled on the basis of certain performance measures – like power consumption, system throughput, radio channel utilization, and quality of service – obtained when varying the DPM operation rates. Such performance indices can easily be expressed through a combined use of cumulative and instantaneous rewards [16]. This investigation of the impact of the DPM from the performance viewpoint can then be exploited to tune the frequency of the DPM operations, in such a way that a reasonable tradeoff between the power consumption and the overall system efficiency is achieved.

3.3   Simulative Performance Comparison of the General Models

In the third phase of the methodology the two Markovian models are made more realistic by replacing the exponential distributions with general distributions wherever necessary to better characterize the actual delays.

Since substituting general distributions for exponential distributions may not be a smooth process, the general models may need to be validated against the corresponding Markovian models. For instance, in those formalisms that do not directly support general distributions (see, e.g., [7]), major modifications of the Markovian models are needed in addition to the distribution replacement. In such a case it is necessary to assess the consistency of each of the two general models with respect to the corresponding Markovian model. This is accomplished by verifying that both models result in comparable values for the considered performance measures, when substituting exponential distributions back for general distributions in the general model in a way that preserves their expected values.

As another example, noninterference may not be preserved. In fact, the replacement of exponential distributions with general distributions no longer having infinite support may alter the state space of the general models with respect to the state space of the corresponding Markovian models. This is similar to what happens in the Markovian models when using immediate transitions. Therefore, assuming that the distributions with finite support are consistently used in the two general models, the noninterference analysis should be repeated in the third phase only if some of the state-modifying activities of the DPM are characterized through distributions with finite support.

Once the validation succeeds, the two general models can be simulated via standard techniques [22] in order to estimate at a certain confidence level the same performance measures considered in the second phase with the DPM disabled and with the DPM enabled. The comparison of the resulting figures should then guide the decision about whether it is worth introducing the DPM in certain realistic scenarios. If so, the figures should also help tuning the DPM operation rates without compromising the achievement of the desired level of quality of service.

We conclude by observing that the second and the third phase both refer to a performance comparison of the system with the DPM disabled and with the DPM enabled. Since the third phase addresses more realistic scenarios, one may want to skip the second phase, thus going directly from the first one to the third one. Although possible, this is not recommended. In fact, even though the Markovian models may not be realistic, the performance figures obtained from their analytically derived solution constitute the only means to validate the simulation results of the general models in the early stages of the system design. Moreover, skipping the second phase would introduce a gap in the incremental modeling process enforced by the methodology, which may likely cause inconsistencies between the general models and the corresponding functional models.

4   Supporting the Application of the Methodology

The application of the predictive methodology requires a sufficiently expressive specification language, in order to build the functional, Markovian and general models with the DPM disabled and with the DPM enabled. In addition to that, it requires a software tool equipped with the necessary analysis routines, so that the effect of the DPM on the system functionality and performance can be assessed by comparing the properties of the models written in the language mentioned before.

Although the predictive methodology does not depend on a specific notation, in order to illustrate it we need to choose one. Here we use the architectural description language Æmilia [7], together with its companion tool TwoTowers [5], as they provide all the ingredients that are necessary to support the application of the methodology.

Table 1. Structure of an Æmilia description

```
ARCHI_TYPE                      ⊲name and formal parameters⊳

  ARCHI_ELEM_TYPES
    ELEM_TYPE                   ⊲definition of the first architectural element type⊳

      ⋮                           ⋮

    ELEM_TYPE                   ⊲definition of the last architectural element type⊳

  ARCHI_TOPOLOGY
    ARCHI_ELEM_INSTANCES ⊲declaration of the architectural element instances⊳
    ARCHI_INTERACTIONS    ⊲declaration of the architectural interactions⊳
    ARCHI_ATTACHMENTS     ⊲declaration of the architectural attachments⊳

  [BEHAV_VARIATIONS
    [BEHAV_HIDINGS            ⊲declaration of the behavioral hidings⊳]
    [BEHAV_RESTRICTIONS  ⊲declaration of the behavioral restrictions⊳]
    [BEHAV_RENAMINGS      ⊲declaration of the behavioral renamings⊳]]

END
```

We now give a brief overview of Æmilia and TwoTowers, followed by an example in which the Æmilia functional models are built for the case study introduced in Sect. 2.5.

4.1   Æmilia and TwoTowers

An Æmilia description represents an architectural type. This is an intermediate abstraction between a single system and an architectural style. It consists of a family of systems sharing certain constraints on the observable behavior of the system components as well as on the system topology. As shown in Table 1, the description of an architectural type in Æmilia starts with the name and the formal parameters of the architectural type and is composed of three sections.

The first section defines the types of components that characterize the system family. In order to include both the computational components and the connectors among them, these types are called architectural element types (AETs). The definition of an AET starts with its name and formal parameters and consists of the specification of its behavior and its interactions. The behavior has to be provided in the form of a list of sequential defining equations written in a verbose variant of the stochastic process algebra EMPA$_{gr}$ [6]. The interactions are those EMPA$_{gr}$ action types occurring in the behavior that act as interfaces for the AET. Each of them has to be equipped with two qualifiers, which establish whether it is an input or output interaction and the multiplicity of the communications in which it can be involved, respectively. All the other action types occurring in the behavior are assumed to represent internal activities.

The second section defines the architectural topology. This is specified in three steps. First we have the declaration of the instances of the AETs (called AEIs) with their actual parameters, which represent the real system components and connectors. Then we have the declaration of the architectural (as opposed to local) interactions, which are some of the interactions of the AEIs that act as interfaces for the whole system family. Finally we have the declaration of the directed architectural attachments among the local interactions of the AEIs, which make the AEIs communicate with each other.

The third section, which is optional, defines some variations of the observable behavior of the system family. This is accomplished by declaring some action types occurring in the behavior of certain AEIs to be unobservable, prevented from occurring, or renamed into other action types. Such a section is quite useful e.g. when defining a model of the system with the DPM disabled, as it can be obtained from the model of the system with the DPM enabled by simply restricting the state-modifying activities of the DPM.

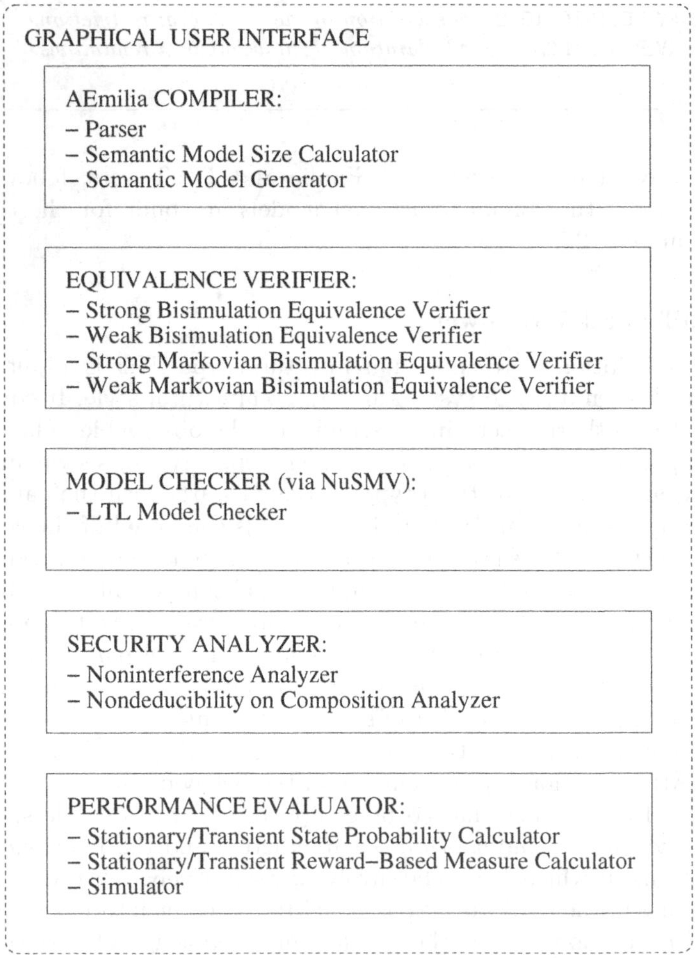

GRAPHICAL USER INTERFACE

AEmilia COMPILER:
– Parser
– Semantic Model Size Calculator
– Semantic Model Generator

EQUIVALENCE VERIFIER:
– Strong Bisimulation Equivalence Verifier
– Weak Bisimulation Equivalence Verifier
– Strong Markovian Bisimulation Equivalence Verifier
– Weak Markovian Bisimulation Equivalence Verifier

MODEL CHECKER (via NuSMV):
– LTL Model Checker

SECURITY ANALYZER:
– Noninterference Analyzer
– Nondeducibility on Composition Analyzer

PERFORMANCE EVALUATOR:
– Stationary/Transient State Probability Calculator
– Stationary/Transient Reward–Based Measure Calculator
– Simulator

Fig. 5. Architecture of TwoTowers

Æmilia is the input language of TwoTowers, a software tool for the functional verification, security analysis, and performance evaluation of computer, communication and software systems. The architecture of TwoTowers is depicted in Fig. 5. As can be seen, the study of the properties of the Æmilia specifications is conducted in TwoTowers through a mix of techniques. Among them we mention equivalence verification with diagnostics, symbolic model checking with diagnostics via NuSMV [9], information flow analysis with diagnostics, reward Markov chain solution, and discrete event simulation.

4.2   Æmilia Functional Models of the Case Study

Since a thorough description of Æmilia is beyond the scope of this chapter, we use the remote procedure call case study to exemplify the key elements of the language. In particular, we consider a simplified version of the system in which the radio channels are perfect (so that the blocking client does not need to use any timeout mechanism), the DPM sends shutdown commands independently of the current state of the server (hence the server does not need to notify the DPM about its state changes), and the server is sensitive to shutdown commands both in the idle state and in the busy state.

The Æmilia specification of the functional model of the remote procedure call case study with the DPM enabled starts with its name and the indication that there are no formal parameters:

```
ARCHI_TYPE RPC_DPM_F(void)
```

The first AET that we define is the blocking client, which synchronously communicates with the power-manageable server through the radio channel. It repeatedly issues a call, waits for the results, and processes them. While the result processing is an internal activity, the issue of a call is an output interaction and the reception of the results is an input interaction:

```
ELEM_TYPE Client_Type(void)

  BEHAVIOR

    Client(void; void) =
      <send_rpc_packet, _> . <receive_result_packet, _> .
        <process_result_packet, _> . Client()

  INPUT_INTERACTIONS
    UNI receive_result_packet

  OUTPUT_INTERACTIONS
    UNI send_rpc_packet
```

The second AET that we define is the half-duplex radio channel. Since it is perfect, it does not lose any packet, so it repeatedly waits for a packet, propagates it, and delivers it. While the packet propagation is an internal activity, the packet reception is an input interaction and the packet delivery is an output interaction:

```
ELEM_TYPE Radio_Channel_Type(void)

   BEHAVIOR

      Radio_Channel(void; void) =
         <get_packet, _> . <propagate_packet, _> .
            <deliver_packet, _> . Radio_Channel()

   INPUT_INTERACTIONS
     UNI get_packet

   OUTPUT_INTERACTIONS
     UNI deliver_packet
```

The third AET that we define in the AET section of the Æmilia specification describes the server. Its behavior is given by five defining equations. The first equation is associated with the idle state, while the second and the third equation represent the busy state. Two equations are necessary for this state because two activities are carried out – processing the call and sending the results back to the client – each of which can be interrupted by the reception of a shutdown command from the DPM. The fourth and the fifth equation are concerned with the sleeping and the awaking state, respectively. While the processing of a call and the awaking represent internal activities, the reception of a call or of a shutdown command are input interactions and the sending of the results is an output interaction:

```
   ARCHI_ELEM_TYPES

     ELEM_TYPE Server_Type(void)

       BEHAVIOR

          Idle_Server(void; void) =
            choice {
              <receive_rpc_packet, _> . Busy_Server(),
              <receive_shutdown, _> . Sleeping_Server()
            };

          Busy_Server(void; void) =
            choice {
              <prepare_result_packet, _> . Responding_Server(),
              <receive_shutdown, _> . Sleeping_Server()
            };

          Responding_Server(void; void) =
            choice {
              <send_result_packet, _> . Idle_Server(),
              <receive_shutdown, _> . Sleeping_Server()
            };
```

```
    Sleeping_Server(void; void) =
      <receive_rpc_packet, _> . Awaking_Server();

    Awaking_Server(void; void) =
      <awake, _> . Busy_Server()

  INPUT_INTERACTIONS
    UNI receive_rpc_packet; receive_shutdown

  OUTPUT_INTERACTIONS
    UNI send_result_packet
```

The last AET that we define is the DPM. It simply issues shutdown commands that are periodically sent to the server even when this is busy. The only activity carried out by the DPM is an output interaction:

```
ELEM_TYPE DPM_Type(void)

  BEHAVIOR

    DPM_Beh(void; void) =
      <send_shutdown, _> . DPM_Beh()

  INPUT_INTERACTIONS
    void

  OUTPUT_INTERACTIONS
    UNI send_shutdown
```

In the architectural topology section of the Æmilia specification we declare one instance for the server, client and DPM types together with two instances of the half-duplex radio channel type, followed by the declaration of the attachments between their interactions as prescribed by Fig. 3 up to the busy and idle triggers:

```
ARCHI_TOPOLOGY

  ARCHI_ELEM_INSTANCES
    C   : Client_Type();
    RCS : Radio_Channel_Type();
    RSC : Radio_Channel_Type();
    S   : Server_Type();
    DPM : DPM_Type()

  ARCHI_INTERACTIONS
    void

  ARCHI_ATTACHMENTS
    FROM C.send_rpc_packet    TO RCS.get_packet;
```

```
FROM RCS.deliver_packet     TO S.receive_rpc_packet;
FROM S.send_result_packet   TO RSC.get_packet;
FROM RSC.deliver_packet     TO C.receive_result_packet;
FROM DPM.send_shutdown      TO S.receive_shutdown

END
```

We conclude by observing that the Æmilia specification of the functional model of the system with the DPM disabled can easily be obtained from the previous Æmilia specification by adding what follows after the architectural topology section:

```
BEHAV_VARIATIONS

   BEHAV_RESTRICTIONS
      RESTRICT DPM.send_shutdown
```

5   Comparing the Functional Models

In the first phase of the predictive methodology we need two functional models of the system – one with the DPM disabled and the other one with the DPM enabled – in order to assess the functional transparency of the DPM through noninterference analysis. We now show how to proceed by means of the remote procedure call case study.

When using Æmilia, there are two possibilities. The first one is to add suitable behavioral variations to both functional models presented in Sect. 4.2. We recall that a behavioral variation declared for an action type affect all the action types to which the first action type is attached. The functional model in which the DPM is considered to be disabled must prevent the shutdown commands from being issued and hide all the action types that are not concerned with the client:

```
BEHAV_VARIATIONS

   BEHAV_HIDINGS
      HIDE RCS.INTERNALS;
      HIDE RSC.INTERNALS;
      HIDE S.receive_rpc_packet;
      HIDE S.send_result_packet;
      HIDE S.INTERNALS

   BEHAV_RESTRICTIONS
      RESTRICT DPM.send_shutdown
```

while the functional model in which the DPM is considered to be enabled must hide the shutdown commands as well:

```
BEHAV_VARIATIONS

  BEHAV_HIDINGS
    HIDE RCS.INTERNALS;
    HIDE RSC.INTERNALS;
    HIDE S.ALL
```

After modifying the two functional models in this way, the weak bisimulation equivalence verifier of TwoTowers can be applied to them.

A more direct way to assess with TwoTowers the functional transparency of the DPM is to use the noninterference analyzer. In this case the first functional model of Sect. 4.2 is enough, provided that in an auxiliary specification we declare which action types are high and which are low. Based on the discussion of Sect. 3.1, reflected in Fig. 3 by the different colors of the various system components, the only action type of the DPM is the only high one while those of the client are the only low ones, with all the other action types being unimportant:

```
HIGH DPM.send_shutdown

LOW  C.send_rpc_packet;
     C.receive_result_packet;
     C.process_result_packet
```

Given this additional specification, the noninterference analyzer of TwoTowers automatically produces the two functional models with behavioral variations described above and check them for weak bisimulation equivalence.

The simplified version of the remote procedure call case study of Sect. 4.2 fails the noninterference check. More precisely, when submitting the Æmilia specification of the first functional model together with the additional specification above to the noninterference analyzer of TwoTowers, the outcome is negative and the following Hennessy-Milner logic formula is returned, where "#" denotes the synchronization of two attached interactions:

```
EXISTS_WEAK_TRANS(
  LABEL(C.send_rpc_packet#RCS.get_packet);
  REACHED_STATE_SAT(
    NOT(EXISTS_WEAK_TRANS(
        LABEL(RSC.deliver_packet#C.receive_result_packet);
        REACHED_STATE_SAT(TRUE)
      )
    )
  )
)
```

This formula means that the functional model with the high action types being hidden admits a computation path along which no results are returned to the client (synchronization of RSC.deliver_packet with C.receive_result_packet) after that the client has issued a call (synchronization of C.send_rpc_packet with RCS.get_packet), whereas this path does not exist in the functional model with the high action types being prevented.

Recalled that the high actions coincides with the state-modifying activities performed by the DPM, the reason why the modal logic formula above distinguishes the two functional models is that in the latter model the DPM is disabled, while in the former model the DPM is enabled and can shut down the server while it is processing a call. Since the client is blocking and does not use any timeout mechanism after sending a call, it may happen that it will be forever waiting for a response that will never arrive. In fact, only a call can wake up the server after it received a shutdown command in the busy state, but this call cannot be issued by the client as long as the client does not receive the response to its previous call that the server was processing.

Based on the considerations derived above from the distinguishing formula, in order to make the DPM transparent to the client, we first recognize that the client should implement a timeout mechanism, so that it no longer deadlocks. This may complicate not only the client but also the server, as they now must be able to discard old packets due to useless retransmissions. On the other hand, the timeout mechanism allows the client to cope with a more realistic radio channel that can lose packets. Second, we recognize that the DPM should not shut down the server while it is busy, which is achieved by making the server inform the DPM about its state changes via the busy and idle triggers as shown in Fig. 3.

As a consequence, in order to consider a more accurate version of the remote procedure call case study, we have to modify the first Æmilia specification of Sect. 4.2 as shown in Tables 2, 3, and 4. In the DPM description, send_shutdown refers to a state-modifying activity, while receive_busy_notice and receive_idle_notice refer to information-collecting activities. We have verified with TwoTowers that this revised version of the Æmilia specification of the functional model of the remote procedure call case study meets noninterference when giving the following specification of the action type levels:

```
HIGH DPM.send_shutdown

LOW  C.send_rpc_packet;
     C.receive_result_packet;
     C.process_result_packet;
     C.expire_timeout;
     C.ignore_result_packet
```

This means that the introduction of the DPM in the realistic scenario is transparent from the functional viewpoint, in the sense that it does not alter the behavior of the system as perceived by the client.

Table 2. Æmilia functional model of the case study (part I)

```
ARCHI_TYPE              RPC_DPM_F(void)

 ARCHI_ELEM_TYPES

  ELEM_TYPE             Client_Type(void)
   BEHAVIOR             Requesting_Client(void; void) =
                          choice {
                            <send_rpc_packet, _>.Waiting_Client(),
                            <receive_result_packet, _>.
                             <ignore_result_packet, _>.
                              Requesting_Client()
                          };
                        Waiting_Client(void; void) =
                          choice {
                            <receive_result_packet, _>.
                             Processing_Client(),
                            <expire_timeout, _>.Resending_Client()
                          };
                        Processing_Client(void; void) =
                          choice {
                            <process_result_packet, _>.
                             Requesting_Client(),
                            <receive_result_packet, _>.
                             <ignore_result_packet, _>.
                              Processing_Client()
                          };
                        Resending_Client(void; void) =
                          choice {
                            <send_rpc_packet, _>.Waiting_Client(),
                            <receive_result_packet, _>.Processing_Client()
                          }
   INPUT_INTERACTIONS   UNI receive_result_packet
   OUTPUT_INTERACTIONS  UNI send_rpc_packet
  ELEM_TYPE             Radio_Channel_Type(void)
   BEHAVIOR             Radio_Channel(void; void) =
                          <get_packet, _>.<propagate_packet, _>.
                          choice {
                            <keep_packet, _>.
                             <deliver_packet, _>.Radio_Channel(),
                            <lose_packet, _>.Radio_Channel()
                          }
   INPUT_INTERACTIONS   UNI get_packet
   OUTPUT_INTERACTIONS  UNI deliver_packet
```

Table 3. Æmilia functional model of the case study (part II)

ELEM_TYPE	Server_Type(void)

BEHAVIOR	Idle_Server(void; void) =
	 choice {
	    <receive_rpc_packet, _>.
	     <notify_busy, _>.Busy_Server(),
	    <receive_shutdown, _>.Sleeping_Server()
	    };
	 Busy_Server(void; void) =
	 choice {
	    <prepare_result_packet, _>.
	     Responding_Server(),
	    <receive_rpc_packet, _>.
	     <ignore_rpc_packet, _>.Busy_Server()
	    };
	 Responding_Server(void; void) =
	 choice {
	    <send_result_packet, _>.
	     <notify_idle, _>.Idle_Server(),
	    <receive_rpc_packet, _>.
	     <ignore_rpc_packet, _>.Responding_Server()
	    };
	 Sleeping_Server(void; void) =
	    <receive_rpc_packet, _>.Awaking_Server();
	 Awaking_Server(void; void) =
	 choice {
	    <awake, _>.Busy_Server(),
	    <receive_rpc_packet, _>.
	     <ignore_rpc_packet, _>.Awaking_Server()
	    }

INPUT_INTERACTIONS	UNI receive_rpc_packet; receive_shutdown
OUTPUT_INTERACTIONS	UNI send_result_packet; notify_busy; notify_idle
ELEM_TYPE	DPM_Type(void)

BEHAVIOR	Enabled_DPM(void; void) =
	 choice {
	    <send_shutdown, _>.Disabled_DPM(),
	    <receive_busy_notice, _>.Disabled_DPM()
	    };
	 Disabled_DPM(void; void) =
	    <receive_idle_notice, _>.Enabled_DPM()

INPUT_INTERACTIONS	UNI receive_busy_notice; receive_idle_notice
OUTPUT_INTERACTIONS	UNI send_shutdown

Table 4. Æmilia functional model of the case study (part III)

```
ARCHI_TOPOLOGY

  ARCHI_ELEM_INSTANCES  C    : Client_Type();
                        RCS  : Radio_Channel_Type();
                        RSC  : Radio_Channel_Type();
                        S    : Server_Type();
                        DPM  : DPM_Type()

  ARCHI_INTERACTIONS    void

  ARCHI_ATTACHMENTS     FROM C.send_rpc_packet
                          TO RCS.get_packet;
                        FROM RCS.deliver_packet
                          TO S.receive_rpc_packet;
                        FROM S.send_result_packet
                          TO RSC.get_packet;
                        FROM RSC.deliver_packet
                          TO C.receive_result_packet;
                        FROM S.notify_busy
                          TO DPM.receive_busy_notice;
                        FROM S.notify_idle
                          TO DPM.receive_idle_notice;
                        FROM DPM.send_shutdown
                          TO S.receive_shutdown
END
```

6   Comparing the Markovian Models

In the second phase of the predictive methodology two Markovian models of
the system – one with the DPM disabled and the other one with the DPM
enabled – are built from the two functional models considered in the first phase.
The Æmilia specification of the Markovian model for the remote procedure call
case study with the DPM enabled is shown in Tables 5, 6, and 7. The Æmilia
specification of the Markovian model with the DPM disabled can be as usual
obtained from the previous one by adding what follows after the architectural
topology section:

```
BEHAV_VARIATIONS

  BEHAV_RESTRICTIONS
    RESTRICT DPM.send_shutdown
```

As can be noted, there are three main differences with respect to the Æmilia
specification of the functional model provided in Sect. 5. First, the description of
the architectural type is parameterized with respect to a set of rates (expressed
in 0.1 ms^{-1}) and probabilities concerned with the system activities, which are

Table 5. Æmilia Markovian model of the case study (part I)

```
ARCHI_TYPE              RPC_DPM_M(const rate server_proc_rate := 0.5,
                                  const rate server_awaking_rate := 0.0333,
                                  const rate packet_prop_rate := 0.125,
                                  const rate client_proc_rate := 0.0103,
                                  const rate client_timeout_rate := 0.05,
                                  const rate dpm_shutdown_rate := 0.01,
                                  const weight packet_loss_prob := 0.02)

ARCHI_ELEM_TYPES

  ELEM_TYPE             Client_Type(const rate client_proc_rate,
                                    const rate client_timeout_rate)

    BEHAVIOR           Requesting_Client(void; void) =
                         choice {
                           <send_rpc_packet, inf>.Waiting_Client(),
                           <receive_result_packet, _>.
                            <ignore_result_packet, inf>.
                             Requesting_Client()
                         };
                       Waiting_Client(void; void) =
                         choice {
                           <receive_result_packet, _>.
                            Processing_Client(),
                           <expire_timeout, exp(client_timeout_rate)>.
                            Resending_Client(),
                           <monitor_waiting_client, exp(1)>.
                            Waiting_Client()
                         };
                       Processing_Client(void; void) =
                         choice {
                           <process_result_packet, exp(client_proc_rate)>.
                            Requesting_Client(),
                           <receive_result_packet, _>.
                            <ignore_result_packet, inf>.
                             Processing_Client()
                         };
                       Resending_Client(void; void) =
                         choice {
                           <send_rpc_packet, inf>.Waiting_Client(),
                           <receive_result_packet, _>.Processing_Client()
                         }
    INPUT_INTERACTIONS  UNI receive_result_packet
    OUTPUT_INTERACTIONS UNI send_rpc_packet
```

passed as actual parameters to the AEIs in the architectural topology section.
We assume that the average server processing time is 0.2 ms, the average server

Table 6. Æmilia Markovian model of the case study (part II)

ELEM_TYPE	Radio_Channel_Type(const rate packet_prop_rate,
	const weight packet_loss_prob)
BEHAVIOR	Radio_Channel(void; void) =
	<get_packet, _>.
	<propagate_packet, exp(packet_prop_rate)>.
	choice {
	<keep_packet, inf(1, 1 - packet_loss_prob)>.
	<deliver_packet, inf>.Radio_Channel(),
	<lose_packet, inf(1, packet_loss_prob)>.
	Radio_Channel()
	}
INPUT_INTERACTIONS	UNI get_packet
OUTPUT_INTERACTIONS	UNI deliver_packet
ELEM_TYPE	Server_Type(const rate server_proc_rate,
	const rate server_awaking_rate)
BEHAVIOR	Idle_Server(void; void) =
	choice {
	<receive_rpc_packet, _>.
	<notify_busy, inf>.Busy_Server(),
	<receive_shutdown, _>.Sleeping_Server(),
	<monitor_idle_server, exp(1)>.Idle_Server()
	};
	Busy_Server(void; void) =
	choice {
	<prepare_result_packet, exp(server_proc_rate)>.
	Responding_Server(),
	<receive_rpc_packet, _>.
	<ignore_rpc_packet, inf>.Busy_Server(),
	<monitor_busy_server, exp(1)>.Busy_Server()
	};
	Responding_Server(void; void) =
	choice {
	<send_result_packet, inf>.
	<notify_idle, inf>.Idle_Server(),
	<receive_rpc_packet, _>.
	<ignore_rpc_packet, inf>.Responding_Server(),
	<monitor_busy_server, exp(1)>.
	Responding_Server()
	};
	Sleeping_Server(void; void) =
	choice {
	<receive_rpc_packet, _>.Awaking_Server(),
	<monitor_sleeping_server, exp(1)>.
	Sleeping_Server()
	};

Table 7. Æmilia Markovian model of the case study (part III)

```
                        Awaking_Server(void; void) =
                        choice {
                          <awake, exp(server_awaking_rate)>.
                          Busy_Server(),
                          <receive_rpc_packet, _>.
                            <ignore_rpc_packet, inf>.Awaking_Server(),
                          <monitor_awaking_server, exp(1)>.
                            Awaking_Server()
                        }
      INPUT_INTERACTIONS UNI receive_rpc_packet; receive_shutdown
      OUTPUT_INTERACTIONS UNI send_result_packet; notify_busy; notify_idle

   ELEM_TYPE            DPM_Type(const rate dpm_shutdown_rate)

   BEHAVIOR            Enabled_DPM(void; void) =
                        choice {
                          <send_shutdown, exp(dpm_shutdown_rate)>.
                          Disabled_DPM(),
                          <receive_busy_notice, _>.Disabled_DPM()
                        };
                        Disabled_DPM(void; void) =
                          <receive_idle_notice, _>.Enabled_DPM()
      INPUT_INTERACTIONS UNI receive_busy_notice; receive_idle_notice
      OUTPUT_INTERACTIONS UNI send_shutdown

ARCHI_TOPOLOGY

  ARCHI_ELEM_INSTANCES S   : Server_Type(server_proc_rate,
                                          server_awaking_rate);
                       RCS : Radio_Channel_Type(packet_prop_rate,
                                          packet_loss_prob);
                       RSC : Radio_Channel_Type(packet_prop_rate,
                                          packet_loss_prob);
                       C   : Client_Type(client_proc_rate,
                                          client_timeout_rate);
                       DPM : DPM_Type(dpm_shutdown_rate)

  ARCHI_INTERACTIONS    void

  ARCHI_ATTACHMENTS    ⊲same as functional model⊳

END
```

awaking time is 3 ms, the average packet propagation time is 0.8 ms, the packet loss probability is 0.02, the average client processing time is 9.7 ms, the average client timeout is 2 ms, and the average DPM shutdown timeout is 10 ms.

Second, every action can now contain the specification of its duration. This is given by exp(_) in the case of an exponentially timed action, while it is represented by inf(_, _) in the case of an immediate action. The two parameters of an immediate action are its priority level and its weight, whose default value is 1. All the other actions are called passive and get a duration only if they are attached to an exponentially timed or immediate action. Actions that are not passive cannot be attached to each other.

Third, all the defining equations of the server have been augmented with a self-looping, exponentially timed action (whose type starts with `monitor_`) that will be exploited to measure the time spent by the server in each of its states. A similar action has been added to one of the defining equations of the client, which will be used to measure the quality of service perceived by the client.

Since the Æmilia specification of the Markovian model with the DPM disabled is obtained from the one with the DPM enabled by restricting the only state-modifying activity of the DPM, the immediate actions are certainly used in a consistent way in both Markovian models. From the fact that the only state-modifying activity of the DPM is described through an exponentially timed action, it follows that noninterference is preserved when going from the functional models to the Markovian models.

In order to assess the impact of the DPM from the performance viewpoint, we concentrate on the following three measures: the system throughput, the percentage of time spent by the client waiting for the results, and the energy that is consumed by the server. Such measures are evaluated for several typical values of the DPM shutdown rate, in order to get insight in the trend of both the power consumption and the overall system efficiency.

When using the performance evaluator of TwoTowers, the following additional specification is needed in which the measures of interest are formalized via reward structures in a way inspired by [6]:

```
MEASURE throughput IS
  ENABLED(C.process_result_packet) -> TRANS_REWARD(1);

MEASURE waiting_time IS
  ENABLED(C.monitor_waiting_client) -> STATE_REWARD(1);

MEASURE energy IS
  ENABLED(S.monitor_idle_server)    -> STATE_REWARD(2)
  ENABLED(S.monitor_busy_server)    -> STATE_REWARD(3)
  ENABLED(S.monitor_awaking_server) -> STATE_REWARD(2)
```

The value of each performance measure for any of the two Markovian models is given by the weighted sum of the state probabilities and transition frequencies of the continuous-time Markov chain underlying the model, with the weights being given by the rewards occurring in the definition of the measure. It is worth recalling that every state is a vector of local states, one for each AEI. To measure the throughput, intended as the mean number of calls served per unit of time, we have to give a unitary instantaneous reward to all the transitions representing the result processing. To measure the waiting time, we have to single out those states in which the client is waiting for the results, which is accomplished by giving a unitary cumulative reward to all the states with an outgoing transition that represents the fact that the client is waiting. Finally, to measure the energy we have to give a suitable cumulative reward to every state, whose value depends on the local state of the server. We assume that the energy consumed ~~~~~~ and awak ~~~~

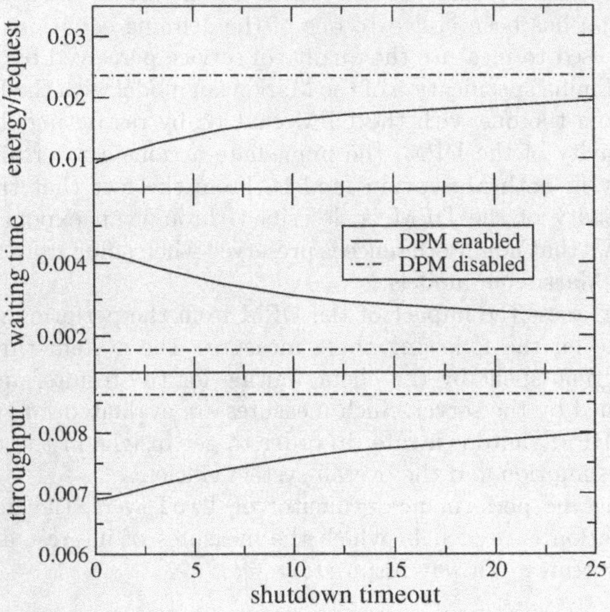

Fig. 6. Performance comparison of the Markovian models of the case study

The results of the performance analysis conducted with TwoTowers on the two Markovian models of the remote procedure call case study are reported in Fig. 6, for values of the DPM shutdown timeout between 0 and 25 ms. Dot-dashed lines refer to the system with the DPM disabled, while solid lines refer to the system with the DPM enabled. Throughput, average waiting time, and energy per request are plotted as a function of the timeout used by the DPM to issue shutdown commands. The energy per request is obtained as the ratio of the energy to the throughput.

As expected, the shorter the DPM timeout, the larger the impact of the DPM. The limiting situations are represented by a DPM that issues a shutdown command as soon as the server goes idle (timeout = 0) and by a DPM that never issues shutdown commands (timeout = ∞). In the first case the impact of the DPM is maximum, while in the last case the DPM has no effect.

From the figure we derive that the DPM is never counterproductive in terms of energy, meaning that the additional energy required to wake up the server from the sleeping state is compensated, on average, by the energy saved while sleeping. On the other hand, energy savings are always paid in terms of performance penalties – reduced throughput and increased waiting time – so that the DPM is not transparent in terms of quality of service perceived by the client.

7   Comparing the General Models

In the third phase of the predictive methodology the two Markovian models of the system have to be made more realistic through a more accurate description of the activity delays. For the remote procedure call case study this is accomplished by replacing all the exponentially distributed durations with deterministic durations, except for the packet propagation delay, which is characterized through a normal distribution.

Since Æmilia does not directly support general distributions, such a distribution replacement requires to switch from a continuous-time description to a discrete-time one regulated by a clock, in which the event occurrences are scheduled by sampling the corresponding action durations from the related distributions. The resulting general models are not shown here due to lack of space, but can be found at www.sti.uniurb.it/bernardo/twotowers/.

In order to guarantee some form of performance consistency between the general models and the corresponding Markovian models, we have verified with the performance evaluator of TwoTowers that each of the two general models, in which average-preserving exponential distributions have been substituted back for the general distributions, result in values for the considered performance measures that are comparable to those of the corresponding Markovian model. The results of the validation are reported in Fig. 7. The good agreement between

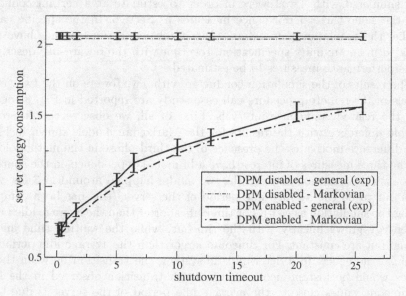

Fig. 7. Validation of the general models against the Markovian ones

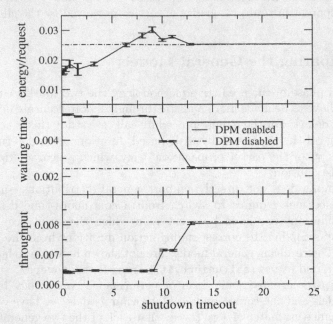

Fig. 8. Performance comparison of the general models of the case study

models is apparent. On the other hand, the values cannot be identical because of the discretization applied when introducing the general distributions.

The general model with the DPM enabled and with the DPM disabled have been simulated with TwoTowers in order to estimate at a certain confidence level the same three performance measures as Sect. 6. In the specific case of Æmilia, the simulation parameters – run number and run length – have to be provided in an auxiliary specification, together with the reward-like description of the performance measures to be estimated.

The results of the simulation conducted with TwoTowers on the two general models of the remote procedure call case study are reported in Fig. 8 together with the related confidence intervals. First of all, we observe that there is a sizeable difference with the results for the Markovian models shown in Fig. 6. This difference motivates the presence of the third phase in the methodology.

The three measures of interest have a bi-modal dependence on the shutdown timeout. The transition between the two modes happens around 11.3 ms, which turns out to be the average idle period of the server (this has been computed during the simulation as well). For timeouts shorter than the average idle period, the energy grows linearly with the timeout, while the waiting time and the throughput are constant. For timeouts larger than the average idle period, the DPM has no effect. In a deterministic system, the transition between the two modes would be instantaneous. The smooth transition observed in the figure for timeout values close to the average idle period of the server is due to the normal probability distribution associated with the packet propagation along the radio channel.

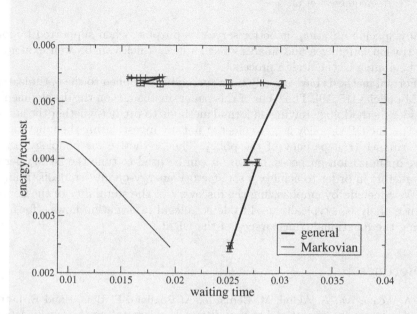

Fig. 9. Tradeoff between energy consumption and waiting time for the case study

From the figure we derive what follows in a realistic scenario. First, the DPM is counterproductive if the value of the shutdown timeout is close to the average idle period. In this case, in fact, the server needs to wake up right after a shutdown. Second, energy savings provided for short timeouts are paid both in terms of increased waiting time and in terms of reduced throughput. Third, the DPM is transparent to the client in terms of quality of service only when it does not provide any energy saving.

The results of the two performance comparisons – analytical and simulative – are summarized by the two Pareto curves of Fig. 9, which show the energy-quality tradeoff provided by the DPM when varying its shutdown timeout. The thin curve refers to the Markovian model with the DPM enabled, while the thick curve refers to the general model with the DPM enabled. The difference between the results of the Markovian analysis and of the simulation is remarkable. While in the Markovian case an optimal tradeoff is achieved, many points of the curve of the general model are beyond the Pareto curve, since they are overcome by other points both in terms of energy saving and performance. These suboptimal points correspond to the DPM timeout values close to the average idle time of the server, which make the DPM counterproductive in a realistic scenario.

8 Conclusion

In this paper we have presented and exemplified an incremental methodology to assist the design of mobile computing devices, which can be used to predict in the early design stages the impact of the introduction of a DPM on the system functionality and performance. Although the methodology is not tied to any specific notation, it better serves its purpose when supported by formal description languages and analysis techniques, which can be well exploited at the beginning of the design process.

Formal methods have already been successfully applied to the optimization of DPM policies [15, 19]. The focus of this paper, instead, is on the development of a broader methodology relying on formal methods to predict whether the adoption of a specific DPM policy is convenient or not, by investigating the functional and performance transparency of the policy. The predictive methodology can also serve optimization purposes, because it can be used to tune the DPM operation parameters in order to achieve a satisfactory energy-quality tradeoff (if any).

We conclude by emphasizing the discovery of the suitability of the noninterference analysis – typically used to detect illegal information flows – for investigating the functional transparency of the DPM.

References

1. A. Acquaviva, A. Aldini, M. Bernardo, A. Bogliolo, E. Bontà, and E. Lattanzi, *"Assessing the Impact of Dynamic Power Management on the Functionality and the Performance of Battery-Powered Appliances"*, in Proc. of the *5th IEEE/IFIP Int. Conf. on Dependable Systems and Networks (DSN 2004)*, IEEE-CS Press, pp. 731-740, Firenze (Italy), 2004.
2. M. Ajmone Marsan, G. Balbo, G. Conte, S. Donatelli, and G. Franceschinis, *"Modelling with Generalized Stochastic Petri Nets"*, John Wiley & Sons, 1995.
3. L. Benini, A. Bogliolo, and G. De Micheli, *"A Survey of Design Techniques for System-Level Dynamic Power Management"*, in IEEE Trans. on VLSI Systems 8:299-316, 2000.
4. L. Benini, A. Bogliolo, G.A. Paleologo, and G. De Micheli, *"Policy Optimization for Dynamic Power Management"*, in IEEE Trans. on Computer Aided Design of Integrated Circuits and Systems 18:813-833, 1999.
5. M. Bernardo, *"TwoTowers 5.0 User Manual"*, http://www.sti.uniurb.it/bernardo/twotowers/, 2004.
6. M. Bernardo and M. Bravetti, *"Performance Measure Sensitive Congruences for Markovian Process Algebras"*, in Theoretical Computer Science 290:117-160, 2003.
7. M. Bernardo, L. Donatiello, and P. Ciancarini, *"Stochastic Process Algebra: From an Algebraic Formalism to an Architectural Description Language"*, in *Performance Evaluation of Complex Systems: Techniques and Tools*, LNCS 2459:236-260, 2002.
8. A. Bogliolo, L. Benini, E. Lattanzi, and G. De Micheli, *"Specification and Analysis of Power-Managed Systems"*, in Proc. of the IEEE 92:1308-1346, 2004.
9. R. Cavada, A. Cimatti, E. Olivetti, M. Pistore, and M. Roveri, *"NuSMV 2.1 User Manual"*, http://nusmv.irst.itc.it/, 2002.
10. E.M. Clarke, O. Grumberg, and D.A. Peled, *"Model Checking"*, MIT Press, 1999.
11. W.R. Cleaveland and O. Sokolsky, *"Equivalence and Preorder Checking for Finite-State Systems"*, in *Handbook of Process Algebra*, Elsevier, pp. 391-424, 2001.
12. W.R. Cleaveland, *"On Automatically Explaining Bisimulation Inequivalence"*, in Proc. of the *2nd Int. Conf. on Computer Aided Verification (CAV 1990)*, LNCS 531:364-372, New Brunswick (NJ), 1990.
13. R. Focardi and R. Gorrieri, *"A Classification of Security Properties"*, in Journal of Computer Security 3:5-33, 1995.

14. J.A. Goguen and J. Meseguer, *"Security Policy and Security Models"*, in Proc. of the *3rd IEEE Symp. on Security and Privacy (SSP 1982)*, IEEE-CS Press, pp. 11-20, Oakland (CA), 1982.

15. R.K. Gupta, S. Irani, and S.K. Shukla, *"Formal Methods for Dynamic Power Management"*, in Proc. of the *IEEE/ACM Int. Conf. on Computer Aided Design (IC-CAD 2003)*, ACM Press, pp. 874-882, San Jose (CA), 2003.

16. R.A. Howard, *"Dynamic Probabilistic Systems"*, John Wiley & Sons, 1971.

17. C.-H. Hwang and A. Wu, *"A Predictive System Shutdown Method for Energy Saving of Event-Driven Computation"*, in Proc. of the *IEEE/ACM Int. Conf. on Computer Aided Design (ICCAD 1997)*, ACM Press, pp. 28-32, San Jose (CA), 1997.

18. R. Milner, *"Communication and Concurrency"*, Prentice Hall, 1989.

19. G. Norman, D. Parker, M. Kwiatkowska, S.K. Shukla, and R.K. Gupta, *"Formal Analysis and Validation of Continuous-Time Markov Chain Based System Level Power Management Strategies"*, in Proc. of the *7th IEEE Int. High-Level Design Validation and Test Workshop (HLDVT 2002)*, IEEE-CS Press, pp. 45-50, Cannes (France), 2002.

20. M. Srivastava, A. Chandrakasan, and R. Brodersen, *"Predictive System Shutdown and Other Architectural Techniques for Energy Efficient Programmable Computation"*, in IEEE Trans. on VLSI Systems 4:42.55, 1996.

21. W.J. Stewart, *"Introduction to the Numerical Solution of Markov Chains"*, Princeton University Press, 1994.

22. P.D. Welch, *"The Statistical Analysis of Simulation Results"*, in *Computer Performance Modeling Handbook*, Academic Press, pp. 267-329, 1983.

Dynamic Power Management Strategies Within the IEEE 802.11 Standard*

Andrea Acquaviva, Edoardo Bontà, and Emanuele Lattanzi

Università di Urbino "Carlo Bo",
Istituto di Scienze e Tecnologie dell'Informazione,
Piazza della Repubblica 13, 61029 Urbino, Italy
{acquaviva, bonta, lattanzi}@sti.uniurb.it

Abstract. Mobile terminals such as cellular phones, smart phones and PDAs require wireless connection to exchange information with the external world. In this tutorial we focus on wireless packet networks based on the IEEE 802.11b protocol, commonly used to build local area networks of palmtop and notebook computers. Due to limited battery lifetime of mobile terminals, energy consumption of wireless interfaces becomes a critical design constraint. Within the IEEE 802.11 standard, power conservation protocols have been implemented that trade power for performance. In this tutorial, we present a power-accurate model of wireless network interface card that allows the power/performance trade-off to be studied as a function of traffic patterns imposed by the applications. The model has been validated against measurements on real hardware devices.

1 Introduction

Wireless networks are a key enabling technology for the development of mobile and ubiquitous computing. However, several challenges characterize the design and implementation of an efficient wireless link, ranging from channel unreliability to limited bandwidth (w.r.t. wired networks), and power consumption. Recently, the latter has gained a primary role because of the limited battery autonomy of mobile terminals. In fact, a considerable amount of power is spent in a portable system in the radio frequency (RF) section. This is especially true for palmtop computers and personal digital assistants (PDA), where there are no power-hungry mechanical components (such as hard disks).

The institute of electrical and electronic engeneers (IEEE) has standardized a class of Medium Access Control (MAC) protocols that coordinate the access of mobile terminals to the radio channel and allow wireless local area networks (WLANs) to be built. Distinguishing features of protocols in this class are carrier frequency and bandwidth.

---

* Co-financed by Regione Marche within the CIPE 36/2002 framework.

M. Bernardo and A. Bogliolo (Eds.): SFM-Moby 2005, LNCS 3465, pp. 190–214, 2005.
© Springer-Verlag Berlin Heidelberg 2005

Currently, the most widespread protocol is IEEE 802.11b[1], mainly because it matches bandwidth requirements of most popular network services with limited cost of hardware interfaces. It supports also a power conservation strategy called Power Save Protocol (PSP) that allows stations to sleep when they are not transmitting or receiving data. This allows ower spent by network interfaces to sense the medium during idle periods to be saved. Since exiting from sleep state imposes a non-negligible delay, packets sent to a station are buffered by the transmitter while the receiver station is sleeping. Sleeping stations (STAs) wake-up at synchronized time instants to retrieve backlogged traffic. Sleeping intervals have a programmable duration (sleep time) that for commercial wireless interfaces are on the order of hundreds of milliseconds. During sleep periods, the card cannot receive packets, but it can wake-up to transmit. Clearly, this strategy affects system responsiveness. As a consequence, there could be a consistent impact on the quality of delay-sensitive real-time applications such has video streaming and video conferencing tools.

It is clear from the previous discussion that it is of critical importance the study of the efficiency of 802.11b power conservation strategy and the assessment of its impact on Quality of Service (QoS). In this tutorial, we describe a performance/power model of wireless network interface cards that we exploit to characterize PSP efficiency. We report also results of the validation of this model against measurements on real hardware devices. We used a client-server application as case study, where the wireless network interface on the client receives data from an application server.

All commercial wireless cards implement PSP protocol. However, only a limited sleep time duration can be set, depending on the particular implementation and firmware version. The model we describe in this paper overcomes this limitation allowing to tune sleeping period on all possible values. Validation of the model against real hardware has been made on those configuration points that match parameter values available on hardware devices. To stress the validation process, we also compare simulated and real measurements by varying the server data rate.

The rest of the paper is organized as follows. In Section 2 we give a detailed overview of IEEE 802.11b standard with particular emphasis on the power conservation protocol. In Section 3 we describe the model of a IEEE 802.11b compliant wireless network interface. In Section 4 we report the results of analisys and simulations on the model as well as the validation against real hardware measurements.

2   IEEE 802.11

In this Section we give a detailed overview of IEEE 802.11b protocol. We first describe its general specifications, than we go in to details describing the power conservation strategy. Finally, we resume some of the most important non-standard solutions proposed to save power in IEEE 802.11b wireless networks.

2.1   WLAN Architecture

Wireless networks based on IEEE 802.11b protocol can be infrastructured or ad-hoc. In the first case, there is a central coordination and synchronization element called access point (AP) which routes all the packets transmitted by mobile stations in its coverage area and provide bridging functionalities to wired networks. In the second case, stations directly communicate with each other. The first type of organization is suitable for buildings and urban areas where APs can be connected to wired backbones. On the contrary, ad-hoc networks are suitable for less accessible environments and may be used for environment monitoring and battlefields. IEEE 802.11b networks consist of four major physical components [9]:

– **Distribution System.** When several access points are connected to form a large coverage area, they must communicate with each other to follow the movements of mobile stations. The distribution system is the logical component that forwards frames to destination. 802.11 does not specify any particular technology for the distribution system. In most commercial products, the distribution system is implemented as a combination of a bridging elements and a distribution system medium, which in almost all practical cases is the Ethernet.
– **Access Points.** Frames on an 802.11 network must be converted to another type of frame for delivery to the rest of the world. Devices called access points perform the wireless-to-wired bridging function.
– **Wireless Medium.** The medium carries frames from station to station. Physical layer defines the transmission technology on the medium. Several different physical layers are defined. Initially, two radio frequency (RF) physical layers and one infrared physical layer were standardized, though the RF layers have proven far more popular.
– **Stations.** Networks are built to transfer data between stations. Stations are computing devices with wireless network interfaces. Typically, stations are battery-operated laptop or handheld computers.

2.2   Types of Networks

The basic building block of an 802.11 network is the basic service set (BSS), which is simply a group of stations that communicate with each other. Communications take place within a somewhat fuzzy area, called the basic service area, defined by the propagation characteristics of the wireless medium [9]. When a station is in the basic service area, it can communicate with the other members of the BSS. BSSs come in two flavors, both of which are illustrated in Fig. 1.

Independent Networks. On the left is an independent BSS (IBSS). Stations in an IBSS communicate directly with each other and thus must be within direct communication range. The smallest possible 802.11 network is an IBSS with two stations. Typically, IBSSs are composed of a small number of stations set up for a specific purpose and for a short period of time. One common use is to create

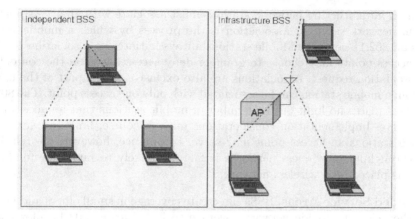

Fig. 1. Independent and infrastructure BSSs

a short-lived network to support a single meeting in a conference room. As the meeting begins, the participants create an IBSS to share data. When the meeting ends, the IBSS is dissolved. Due to their short duration, small size, and focused purpose, IBSSs are sometimes referred to as ad hoc BSSs or ad hoc networks.

Infrastructure Networks. On the right side of Fig. 1 is an infrastructure BSS (never called an IBSS). Infrastructure networks are distinguished by the use of an access point. Access points are used for all communications in infrastructure networks, including communication between mobile nodes in the same service area. If one mobile station in an infrastructure BSS needs to communicate with a second mobile station, the communication must take two hops. First, the originating mobile station transfers the frame to the access point. Second, the access point transfers the frame to the destination station. With all communications relayed through an access point, the basic service area corresponding to an infrastructure BSS is defined by the points in which transmissions from the access point can be received. Although the multihop transmission takes more transmission capacity than a directed frame from the sender to the receiver, it has two major advantages:

- An infrastructure BSS is defined by the distance from the access point. All mobile stations are required to be within reach of the access point, but no restriction is placed on the distance between mobile stations themselves. Allowing direct communication between mobile stations would save transmission capacity but at the cost of increased physical layer complexity because mobile stations would need to maintain neighbor relationships with all other mobile stations within the service area.
- Access points in infrastructure networks are in a position to assist with stations attempting to save power. Access points can note when a station enters a powersaving mode and buffer frames for it. Battery-operated stations can turn the wireless transceiver off and power it up only to transmit and retrieve buffered frames from the access point.

In an infrastructure network, stations must associate with an access point to obtain network services. Association is the process by which a mobile station joins an 802.11 network. Mobile stations always initiate the association process, and access points may choose to grant or deny access based on the contents of an association request. Associations are also exclusive on the part of the mobile station: a mobile station can be associated with only one access point. The 802.11 standard places no limit on the number of mobile stations that an access point may serve. Implementation considerations may, of course, limit the number of mobile stations an access point may serve. In practice, however, the relatively low throughput of wireless networks is far more likely to limit the number of stations placed on a wireless network.

Extended Service Areas. BSSs can create coverage in small offices and homes, but they cannot provide network coverage to larger areas. 802.11 allows wireless networks of arbitrarily large size to be created by linking BSSs into an extended service set (ESS). An ESS is created by chaining BSSs together with a backbone network. 802.11 does not specify a particular backbone technology; it requires only that the backbone provide a specified set of services. In Fig. 2, the ESS is the union of the four BSSs (provided that all the access points are configured to be part of the same ESS). In real-world deployments, the degree of overlap between the BSSs would probably be much greater than the overlap in Fig. 2.

Stations within the same ESS may communicate with each other, even though these stations may be in different basic service areas and may even be moving between basic service areas. For stations in an ESS to communicate with each other, the wireless medium must act like a single MAC-level connection. Access points act as bridges, so direct communication between stations in an ESS re-

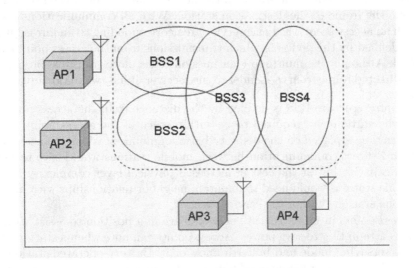

Fig. 2. Extended service set

quires that the backbone network also be a MAC-level connection. Any link-layer connection will suffice. Several access points in a single area may be connected to a single hub or switch, or they can use virtual LANs if the link-layer connection must span a large area. 802.11 supplies link-layer mobility within an ESS but only if the backbone network is a single link-layer domain, such as a shared Ethernet or a VLAN. This important constraint on mobility is often a major factor in 802.11 network design. Extended service areas are the highest-level abstraction supported by 802.11 networks. Access points in an ESS operate in concert to allow the outside world to use a single MAC address to talk to a station somewhere within the ESS. In Fig. 2, the router uses a single MAC address to deliver frames to a mobile station; the access point with which that mobile station is associated delivers the frame. The router remains ignorant of the location of the mobile station and relies on the access points to deliver the frame.

2.3   802.11 MAC Layer

The key to the 802.11 specification is the MAC. It rides on every physical layer and controls the transmission of user data into the air. It provides the core framing operations and the interaction with a wired network backbone. Different physical layers may provide different transmission speeds, all of which are supposed to interoperate. 802.11 does not depart from the previous IEEE 802 standards in any radical way. The standard successfully adapts Ethernet-style networking to radio links. Like Ethernet, 802.11 uses a carrier sense multiple access (CSMA) scheme to control access to the transmission medium. However, collisions waste valuable transmission capacity, so rather than the collision detection (CSMA/CD) employed by Ethernet, 802.11 uses collision avoidance (CSMA/CA). Also like Ethernet, 802.11 uses a distributed access scheme with no centralized controller. Each 802.11 station uses the same method to gain access to the medium. The major differences between 802.11 and Ethernet stem from the differences in the underlying medium.

On a wired Ethernet, it is reasonable to transmit a frame and assume that the destination receives it correctly. Radio links are different, especially when the frequencies used are unlicensed ISM (Industrial, Science and Medicine) bands. Even narrowband transmissions are subject to noise and interference, but unlicensed devices must assume that interference will exist and work around it. The designers of 802.11 considered ways to work around the radiation from microwave ovens and other RF sources. In addition to the noise, multipath fading may also lead to situations in which frames cannot be transmitted because a node moves into a dead spot. Unlike many other link layer protocols, 802.11 incorporates positive acknowledgments. All transmitted frames must be acknowledged, as shown in Fig. 3. If any part of the transfer fails, the frame is considered lost.

Wireless networks boundaries are represented by the point where each node may not be able to communicate with every other node in the wireless network, as in Fig. 4.

In the figure, node 2 can communicate with both nodes 1 and 3, but something prevents nodes 1 and 3 from communicating directly. From the perspective of

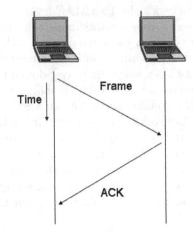

Fig. 3. Positive acknowledgment of data transmissions

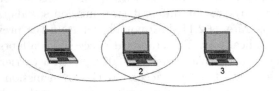

Fig. 4. Nodes 1 and 3 are hidden

node 1, node 3 is a "hidden" node. If a simple transmission protocol were used, it could happen that node 1 and node 3 transmit simultaneously, thus causing node 2 unable to receive a correct information. Furthermore, nodes 1 and 3 would not have any indication of the error because the collision was local to node 2.

Collisions resulting from hidden nodes may be hard to detect in wireless networks because wireless transceivers are generally half-duplex; they don't transmit and receive at the same time. To prevent collisions, 802.11 allows stations to use Request to Send (RTS) and Clear to Send (CTS) signals to clear out an area. Fig. 5 illustrates the procedure.

In Fig. 5, node 1 has a frame to send; it initiates the process by sending an RTS frame. The RTS frame serves several purposes: in addition to reserving the radio link for transmission, it silences any stations that hear it. If the target station receives an RTS, it responds with a CTS. Like the RTS frame, the CTS frame silences stations in the immediate vicinity. Once the RTS/CTS exchange is complete, node 1 can transmit its frames without worry of interference from any hidden nodes. Hidden nodes beyond the range of the sending station are silenced by the CTS from the receiver. When the RTS/CTS clearing procedure is used, any frames must be positively acknowledged. The multiframe RTS/CTS

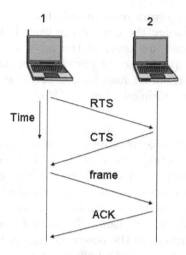

Fig. 5. RTS/CTS clearing

transmission procedure consumes a fair amount of capacity, especially because of the additional latency incurred before transmission can commence. As a result, it is used only in high-capacity environments and environments with significant contention on transmission. For lower-capacity environments, it is not necessary. User can set a RTS threshold if the device driver in most commercial cards. The RTS/CTS exchange is performed for those frames whose size is larger than the threshold.

2.4   Power Conservation Strategy

The major advantage of wireless networks is that network access does not require nodes to be in any particular location. To take full advantage of mobility, nothing can constrain the location of a node, including the availability of electrical power. Mobility therefore implies that most mobile devices can run on batteries. But battery power is a scarce resource; batteries can run only so long before they need to be recharged. Requiring mobile users to return frequently to commercial power is inconvenient, to say the least. Many wireless applications require long battery life without sacrificing network connectivity. As with any other network interface, powering down the transceiver can lead to great power savings in wireless networks. When the transceiver is off, it is said to be sleeping, dozing, or in power-saving mode (PS). When the transceiver is on, it is said to be awake, active, or simply on. Power conservation in 802.11 is achieved by minimizing the time spent in the latter stage and maximizing the time in the former. However, 802.11 accomplishes this without sacrificing connectivity.

Power Conservation in Infrastructure Networks. Power management can achieve the greatest savings in infrastructure networks. All traffic for mobile stations must go through access points, so they are an ideal location to buffer traffic. There is no need to work on a distributed buffer system that must be implemented on every station; the bulk of the work is left to the access point. By definition, access points are aware of the location of mobile stations, and a mobile station can communicate its power management state to its access point. Furthermore, access points must remain active at all times; it is assumed that they have access to continuous power. Combining these two facts allows access points to play a key role in power management on infrastructure networks. Access points have two power management-related tasks. First, because an access point knows the power management state of every station that has associated with it, it can determine whether a frame should be delivered to the wireless network because the station is active or buffered because the station is asleep. But buffering frames alone does not enable mobile stations to pick up the data waiting for them. An access point's second task is to announce periodically which stations have frames waiting for them. The periodic announcement of buffer status also helps to contribute to the power savings in infrastructure networks. Powering up a receiver to listen to the buffer status requires far less power than periodically transmitting polling frames. Stations only need to power up the transmitter to transmit polling frames after being informed that there is a reason to expend the energy. Power management is designed around the needs of the battery-powered mobile stations. Mobile stations can sleep for extended periods to avoid using the wireless network interface. Part of the association request is the *listen interval* parameter, which is the number of beacon periods for which the mobile station may choose to sleep. Longer listen intervals require more buffer space on the access point; therefore, the listen Interval is one of the key parameters used in estimating the resources required to support an association. The listen interval is a contract with the access point. In agreeing to buffer any frames while the mobile station is sleeping, the access point agrees to wait for at least the listen interval before discarding frames. If a mobile station fails to check for waiting frames after each listen interval, such frames may be discarded without notification.

TIM - Traffic Indication Message. When frames are buffered, a destination node's AID (association ID) provides the logical link between the frame and its destination. The AID indicated to which BSS a node belongs to, and is assigned by the base station. Each AID is logically connected to frames buffered for the mobile station that is assigned that AID. Multicast and broadcast frames are buffered and linked to an AID of zero. To inform stations that frames are buffered, access points periodically assemble a traffic indication map (TIM) and transmit it in beacon frames. The TIM is a virtual bitmap composed of 2,008 bits; offsets are used so that the access point needs to transmit only a small portion of the virtual bitmap. This conserves network capacity when only a few stations have buffered data. Each bit in the TIM corresponds to a particular AID; setting the bit indicates that the access point has buffered unicast frames for the station with the AID corresponding to the bit position. Mobile stations must wake up and enter the active mode to listen for Beacon frames to receive the TIM. By examining the TIM, a station can determine if the access point has

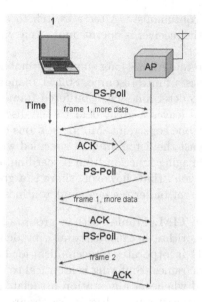

Fig. 6. PS-Poll frame retrieval

buffered traffic on its behalf. To retrieve buffered frames, mobile stations use PS-Poll (Power Save Poll) Control frames. Each PS-Poll frame is used to retrieve one buffered frame. That frame must be positively acknowledged before it is removed from the buffer. Positive acknowledgment is required to keep a second, retried PS-Poll from acting as an implicit acknowledgment. Fig. 6 illustrates the process.

If multiple frames are buffered for a mobile station, then the More Data bit in the Frame Control field is set to 1. Mobile stations can then issue additional PS-Poll requests to the access point until the More Data bit is set to 0, though no time constraint is imposed by the standard. After transmitting the PS-Poll, a mobile station must remain awake until either the polling transaction has concluded or the bit corresponding to its AID is no longer set in the TIM. The reason for the first case is obvious: the mobile station has successfully polled the access point; part of that transaction was a notification that the mobile station will be returning to a sleeping mode. The second case allows the mobile station to return to a power conservation mode if the access point discards the buffered frame. Once all the traffic buffered for a station is delivered or discarded, the station can resume sleeping.

Stations may switch from a power conservation mode to active mode at any time. It is common for laptop computers to operate with full power to all peripherals when connected to AC power and conserve power only when using the battery. If a mobile station switches to the active mode from a sleeping mode, frames can be transmitted without waiting for a PS-Poll. PS-Poll frames indicate that a power-saving mobile station has temporarily switched to an active mode and is ready to receive a buffered frame. By definition, active stations have transceivers operating continuously. After a switch to active mode, the access point can assume that the receiver is operational, even without receiving explicit notification to that effect.

Access points must retain frames long enough for mobile stations to pick them up, but buffer memory is a finite resource. 802.11 mandates that access points use an aging function to determine when buffered frames are old enough to be discarded. The standard leaves a great deal to the discretion of the developer because it specifies only one constraint. Mobile stations depend on access points to buffer traffic for at least the listen interval specified with the association, and the standard forbids the aging function from discarding frames before the listen interval has elapsed. Beyond that, however, there is a great deal of latitude for vendors to develop different buffer management routines.

DTIM - Deliverying TIM. Frames with a group address cannot be delivered using a polling algorithm because they are, by definition, addressed to a group. Therefore, 802.11 incorporates a mechanism for buffering and delivering broadcast and multicast frames. Buffering is identical to the unicast case, except that frames are buffered whenever any station associated with the access point is sleeping. Buffered broadcast and multicast frames are saved using AID 0. Access points indicate whether any broadcast or multicast frames are buffered by setting the first bit in the TIM to 0; this bit corresponds to AID 0. Each BSS has a parameter called the DTIM Period. TIMs are transmitted with every Beacon. At a fixed number of Beacon intervals, a special type of TIM, a Delivery Traffic Indication Map (DTIM), is sent. The TIM element in Beacon frames contains a counter that counts down to the next DTIM; this counter is zero in a DTIM frame. Buffered broadcast and multicast traffic is transmitted after a DTIM Beacon. Multiple buffered frames are transmitted in sequence; the More Data bit in the Frame Control field indicates that more frames must be transmitted. Normal channel acquisition rules apply to the transmission of buffered frames. The access point may choose to defer the processing of incoming PS-Poll frames until the frames in the broadcast and multicast transmission buffers have been transmitted.

To receive broadcast and multicast frames, a mobile station must be awake for DTIM transmissions. Nothing in the specification, however, keeps power-saving stations in infrastructure networks from waking up to listen to DTIM frames. Some products that implement power-saving modes will attempt to align their awakenings with DTIM transmissions. If the system administrator determines that battery life is more important than receiving broadcast and multicast frames, a station can be configured to sleep for its listen period without regard to DTIM transmissions. Some documentation may refer to this as extremely low power, ultra power-saving mode, deep sleep, or something similar. Several products allow configuration of the DTIM interval. Lengthening the DTIM interval allows mobile stations to sleep for longer periods and maximizes battery life at the expense of timely delivery. Shorter DTIM intervals emphasize quick delivery at the expense of more frequent power-up and power-down cycles. A longer DTIM can be used when battery life is critical.

Power Conservation in Ad-Hoc Networks. Power management in an IBSS is not as efficient as power management in an infrastructure network. In an IBSS, far more of the burden is placed on the sender to ensure that the receiver is active. Receivers must also be more available and cannot sleep for the same lengths of time as in infrastructure networks. As in infrastructure networks, power management in independent networks is based on traffic indication messages. Independent networks must use a distributed system because there is no logical central coordinator. Stations in an independent network use announcement traffic indication messages (ATIMs), which are sometimes called ad hoc traffic indication messages, to preempt other stations from sleeping. All stations in an IBSS listen to ATIM frames during specified periods after Beacon transmissions. If a station has buffered data for another station, it can send an ATIM frame as notification. In effect, the ATIM frame is a message to keep the transceiver on because there are pending data. Stations that do not receive ATIM frames are free to conserve power. In Fig. 7 on the left, station A has buffered a frame for station C, so it sends a unicast ATIM frame to station C during the ATIM transmission window, which has the effect of notifying station C that it should not enter power-saving mode. Station B, however, is free to power down its wireless interface. Fig. 7 on the right shows a multicast ATIM frame in use. This frame can be used to notify an entire group of stations to avoid entering low-power modes.

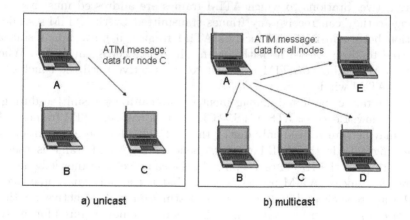

a) unicast   b) multicast

Fig. 7. ATIM usage

A time window called the ATIM window follows the Beacon transmission. This window is the period during which nodes must remain active. No stations are permitted to power down their wireless interfaces during the ATIM window. It starts at the time when the beacon is expected and ends after a period specified when the IBSS is created. If the beacon is delayed due to a traffic overrun, the usable portion of the ATIM window shrinks by the same amount. The ATIM window is the only IBSS-specific parameter required to create an IBSS. Setting it to 0 avoids using any power management. Fig. 8 illustrates the ATIM window

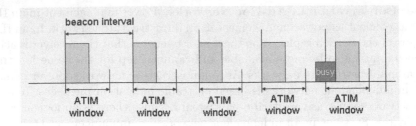

Fig. 8. ATIM window

and its relation to the beacon interval. In the figure, the fourth beacon is delayed due to a busy medium. The ATIM window remains constant, starting at the target beacon interval and extending the length of the ATIM window. Of course, the usable period of the ATIM window shrinks by the length of the delay in beacon transmission.

To monitor the entire ATIM window, stations must wake up before the target beacon transmission. Four situations are possible: the station has transmitted an ATIM, received an ATIM, neither transmitted nor received, or both transmitted and received. Stations that transmit ATIM frames must not sleep. Transmitting an ATIM indicates an intent to transmit buffered traffic and thus an intent to stay active. Stations to which ATIM frames are addressed must also avoid sleeping so they can receive any frames transmitted by the ATIM's sender. If a station both transmits and receives ATIM frames, it stays up. A station is permitted to sleep only if it neither transmits nor receives an ATIM. When a station stays up due to ATIM traffic, it remains active until the conclusion of the next ATIM window.

Only certain control and management frames can be transmitted during the ATIM window: Beacons, RTS, CTS, ACK, and, of course, ATIM frames. ATIM frames may be transmitted only during the ATIM window because stations may be sleeping outside the ATIM window. Sending an ATIM frame is useless if other stations in the IBSS are sleeping. In the same vein, acknowledgments are required for unicast ATIM frames because that is the only guarantee that the ATIM was received and that the frame destination will be active for the remainder of the beacon interval. Acknowledgments are not required for multicast ATIM frames because multicast frames cannot be efficiently acknowledged by a large group of stations. If all potential recipients of an ATIM frame were required to acknowledge it, the mass of acknowledgments could potentially interrupt network service.

Buffered broadcast and multicast frames are transmitted after the conclusion of the ATIM window, subject to DCF constraints. Following the transmission of broadcast and multicast frames, a station may attempt to transmit unicast frames that were announced with an ATIM and for which an acknowledgment was received. Following all transmissions announced with an ATIM, stations may transmit unbuffered frames to other stations that are known to be active. Stations are active if they have transmitted the Beacon, an ATIM, or are not

capable of sleeping. If contention is severe enough to prevent a station from sending the buffered frame it announced with an ATIM, the station must reannounce
the transmission with an ATIM at the start of the next ATIM window.

Stations are responsible for maintaining sufficient memory to buffer frames,
but the buffer size must be traded off against the use of that memory for other
purposes. The standard allows a station in an independent network to discard
frames that have been buffered for an "excessive" amount of time, but the algorithm used to make that determination is beyond the scope of the standard. The
only requirement placed on any buffer management function is that it retains
frames for at least one beacon period.

Alternative Approaches to Power Conservation. Different techniques have
been proposed to reduce wireless network card (WNIC) power consumption, including transmission power control [16] and MAC-level power management (PM)
[13, 18], that can be activated by the card driver when power is critical.

It has been shown [7] that an effective way to further reduce energy consumption is to create opportunities for card shutdown by network traffic reshaping at
a higher level than MAC. The basic rationale of this approach is to create long
idle periods for the NIC, so that the high shut-down transition cost (in terms of
latency and energy) can be fully amortized and power can be saved during long
shut-down times.

In many WLANs, such as home networks, a few servers connect multiple
WLAN clients to a wired network via access points (APs). In a multiclient
environment, traffic reshaping becomes a scheduling problem. While clients run
on power constrained devices, servers are typically not as power constrained.
In addition, servers can have access to the information about both wired and
wireless network conditions. For these reasons, servers are the best candidates
for efficiently scheduling data transmission to clients.

Traditionally, scheduling for multimedia traffic has been studied from two
main perspectives. In the context of multimedia data delivery across large network topologies, several QoS sensitive schemes have been proposed. These schemes
are designed to work in network elements (switches and routers) responsible to
allocate a share of the link bandwidth to multimedia streams. They are basically aimed at overcoming limitations of fair queuing schemes such as Weighted
Fair Queuing (WFQ) and Virtual Clock (VC) in providing QoS guarantees to
soft real-time applications. In this context, the Dual Queue discipline has been
proposed that tries to maximize the number of customers receiving a good service in case of congestion [10]. Real-time traffic scheduling schemes suitable to
be used in QoS oriented network architectures, such as IntServ, have been also
proposed [17].

When multimedia data must be delivered across a local area network, scheduling strategies can be implemented at the traffic source level. Several schemes
have been proposed in this context, mostly for video-on-demand (VOD) systems. These schedulers have been traditionally targeted to minimize waiting time
of clients. To ensure service robustness with respect to packet delivery latency
variations and time-varying re-transmission rates, the streaming video clients

and the server decouple frame transmission and playback through client frame buffers, which are controlled by the server via packet transmission scheduling. A traditional scheduling policy is *join-the-shortest-queue* (JSQ) (i.e., earliest-deadline first), which guarantees optimal results in terms of buffer emptiness avoidance [14].

More recent work in this area leads to the development of schedulers aimed at matching real-time constraints for scalable VOD systems [22] and QoS requirements for simultaneous video transmission [21].

Recently, the problem of traffic scheduling for multimedia applications has been addressed using the client-side communication energy as objective function for optimization under real-time constraints [3]. Authors propose energy-aware scheduling and buffer management policies exploiting the WNIC radio-off state to aggressively reduce power. Two strategies have been presented: *open-loop* and *closed-loop*. The open-loop strategy is completely controlled by the server that exploits the knowledge of the consumption rate of all clients in order to provide bursts of new frames followed by timed shut-down command that turns off the WNIC of the client for a given amount of time. The closed-loop strategy is based on a low-water-mark notification sent by each client to the server whenever the number of packets in the local application buffer falls below a given threshold. In both cases, the best energy efficiency is provided by a *join-the-longest-queue* (JLQ) scheduling policy, since it maximizes the burstiness of the traffic directed to each client.

Another alternative strategy to perform power control in wireless network comes from the observation that PSP is not effective in some traffic conditions. First, the energy efficiency of the 802.11b PM decreases and receiver wait times increase with more mobile hosts, since multiple concurrent attempts at synchronization with the beacon cause media access contention. Second, the response time of the wireless link with 802.11b PM grows because of the delay imposed by sleep periods [20]. These two issues can be resolved by careful scheduling of communication between the server and the client WLAN. Lastly, in a typical wireless network, broadcast traffic can significantly reduce the chances to enter the doze mode. Fig. 9 shows the power consumption of a WLAN card with 802.11b PM

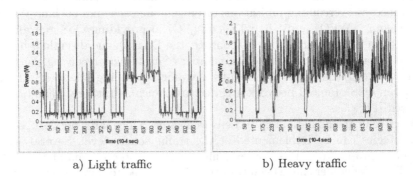

a) Light traffic   b) Heavy traffic

Fig. 9. 802.11 PM under different broadcast traffic conditions

enabled under light and heavy network broadcast traffic conditions. Clearly, as the amount of broadcast traffic increases, the WLAN spends a large amount of energy listening to it, even if no other application is running on the device. As a result, very little or no energy savings are obtained. One way to solve this problem is to turn off the card. It is important to schedule data transmission carefully, since the overhead of waking up the WLAN from the off state is large.

Many current WLANs are organized in a client-server fashion. Multiple WLAN clients connect to wired servers via APs. Servers are great candidates for efficient scheduling of data transmission to clients as they are not power constrained, and know both wired and wireless network conditions.

To overcome these limitations, a server-controlled power management strategy has been presented [5]. Authors propose a technique that exploits server knowledge of the workload, traffic conditions and feedback information from the client in order to minimize WLAN power consumption. The methodology can be employed for a wide variety of applications, ranging from video and audio streaming, to web browsing and e-mail. Two new entities are defined: a server power manager (server PM) and a client power manager (client PM). Server PM uses the information obtained from the client and the network to control the parameters of 802.11b PM and to perform energy efficient traffic reshaping so that WLAN can be turned off. Client PM communicates through a dedicated low-bandwidth link with the server PM and implements power controls by interfacing with device drivers. It also provides a set of APIs that client programs can use to provide extra information to the server.

In order to illustrate the effectiveness of the proposed approach, authors used a streaming video application as a testbed. In this case study, server knowledge of stream characteristics is exploited. Power savings obtained are of around 67% with respect to leaving the card always on, and of around 50% relative to using PSP.

3   Modeling the WNIC

In this section we describe a model that will be used to study the energy/QoS trade-off of a WNIC. We employed separate state diagrams for the operating modes of a WNIC implementing the IEEE 802.11b protocol. The state diagrams are based both on the protocol specification and on the observation of experimental current profiles. Focusing only on the reception of UDP traffic, we describe two main operating modes: always on (ON) and power-save protocol (PSP). The two operating modes can be viewed as macro-states of a top-level state diagram where state transitions are triggered by user commands.

We used this model within an functional verification and performance evaluation tool [7], that allows to study energy/QoS trade-off of the WNIC. Exploiting the capabilities of such a tool we can also study the properties of the wireless card that cannot be studied using real hardware and common simulation environments, such as the well known Network Simulator (NS) [15], that do not provide a detailed model of the wireless interface. Compared to NS, our mod-

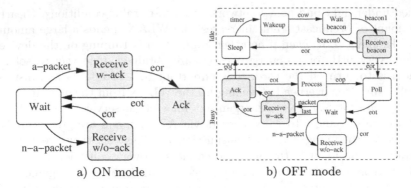

a) ON mode   b) OFF mode

Fig. 10. State diagram of the WNIC working either in ON mode (left) or in PSP mode (right)

eling and simulation environment has a completely different target. First, we model in details power consumption of the WNIC, while NS has much more approssimate power models. Second, we are not targeting a network simulation. In fact, our model does not implement collision management algorithms nor a propagation model. However, the latter can be easily added without changing the model structure.

3.1   ON Mode

The state diagram of the ON mode is shown in Fig. 10. The card waits for incoming packets that trigger transitions from wait to receive. Depending on the nature and on the correctness of the packet, the card may or may not send a MAC-level acknowledge to the base station. In particular, a positive acknowledgement is required whenever a unicast packet is properly received, while no negative acknowledgement is sent for corrupted packets, and no acknowledge is required for multi-cast or broad-cast packets. We call a-packet any packet that requires a positive acknowledge, n-a-packet any packet that will not be acknowledged.

Although the power state of the card during reception is independent of the nature of the received packet, in our state diagram we use two different receive states: receive w ack, that leads to the Ack state, and receive w/o ack, that leads back to the Wait state. State duplication is used only to represent the dependence of the acknowledge on the nature of the received packet.

3.2   PSP Mode

According to the 802.11b MAC-level protocol, the AP can perform traffic reshaping by buffering incoming packets to allow the WNIC to enter a low-power state. If the MAC-level power management is enabled, the WNIC goes to sleep for a fixed period of time as soon as no traffic is detected. While the NIC is sleeping, incoming packets are buffered by the AP. After expiration of the sleeping period,

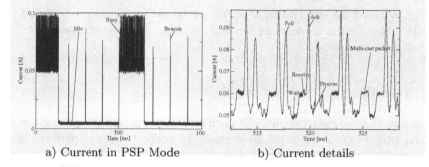

a) Current in PSP Mode   b) Current details

Fig. 11. Current waveforms of a Compaq WNIC receiving UDP traffic in PSP mode

the card wakes up and listens to the beacons periodically sent by the AP. Beacons contain a TIM that provides information about buffered packets, and are used to re-synchronize the WNIC to the AP. If there are buffered packets to be received by the client, the WNIC replies to the beacon by sending polling frames to get the back-log from the AP packet by packet. A positive acknowledgement is sent for each properly received uni-cast packet.

The state diagram that represents the behavior described above is shown in Fig. 10. For readability, states are clustered into two subsets labeled Idle and Busy. The Idle part of the graph describes the behavior of the card when no traffic is received. The card stays in a low-power sleep state until a given timeout expires. Then it wakes up and waits for the beacon. We call beacon1 (beacon0) a beacon if its TIM indicates that there is (there is no) buffered traffic for the card. If a beacon0 is received, the card goes back to sleep as soon as the beacon has been completely received, otherwise it stays awake and enters the Busy sub-graph to get the buffered backlog from the base station.

To get the buffered packets the card enters a 5-state loop that entails: sending a polling frame (Poll), waiting for a packet (Wait), receiving a packet (Receive w ack), sending a positive acknowledgement (Ack) and preparing a new polling frame (Process). Each packet contains a more bit telling the card whether there are additional buffered frames (more=1) or not (more=0). The card exits the loop as soon as the last packet (i.e., a packet with more=0) is received. Notice that, when in the wait state, the card is also sensitive to broad-cast and multi-cast packets that do not require any acknowledgement. We use the same modeling strategy employed for the ON-mode to model the reaction of the card to packets that do not require a positive acknowledgement.

3.3   Æ Milia and TwoTowers

The previous model has been described using Æmilia, an architectural description language. Æmilia is the input language of TwoTowers [6], a software tool for the functional verification, security analysis, and performance evaluation of computer, communication and software systems. The reason for resorting to the Æmilia/TwoTowers technology is that we wish to apply the methodology of [2], which is based on such technology, to study the energy/QoS trade-off of the WNIC. The Æmilia models can be found at $http : //www.sti.uniurb.it/ bernardo/twotowers/$.

4   Results

In this section we report results obtained by analyzing and simulating the WNIC model presented in the previous section. In order to assess performance and energy efficiency of a wireless link through our model, we inserted the model in a larger system model where an application server sends UDP packets to a wireless client. The server is connected through a wired link to an access point to which the card is associated. In our assessment, we tune service time (i.e. time interval among packets sent to the client) and card sleeping period (i.e. time interval among card wake-up events). To simulate channel unreliability, we considered also a probability of receiving corrupted packets at the client of 0.2%. It must be recalled that, referring to 802.11 standard, when a corrupted packet is received by the client, a retransmission is performed by the server after a timeout set to 10ms.

The modelling and simulation methodology follows the same approach explained in [2]. We obtained three classes of results, one by means of Markovian analysis and the others through simulations.

Results are organized in four parts: i) Markovian analysis, ii) simulation with exponential rates; iii) simulation with deterministic rates; iv) model validation. For each of the first three parts, we show two kinds of results: a) a Pareto curve representing optimal reliability/energy trade-off (where reliability is intended as packet loss probability); b) a packet loss probability as a function of card sleep time (i.e. aggressiveness of power management policy). Packets are lost at the access point buffer.

In the last part we show results obtained by comparing deterministic simulation energy consumption with measures obtained on the real hardware.

4.1   Markovian Model

In Fig. 12 we show Pareto optimal configurations. For a given packet loss probability, the curve allows to find card sleep times that provide minimum energy per packet. We reported results for different server service times. It can be observed that, for a given packet loss probability, energy per packet is lower if service time is lower. This can be explained because the additional power cost spent by the card in waiting state when the server service time is large. It can be also observed that this cost is higher when the card sleep time increases. This result is a consequence of the power spent by the card while in sleep state, which is not negligible and whose per-packet contribution on the energy consumption increases as sleeping time increases.

In Fig. 13 we reported the packet loss probability as a function of card sleep time. It can be observed that, as expected, for a given server service time, packet

I

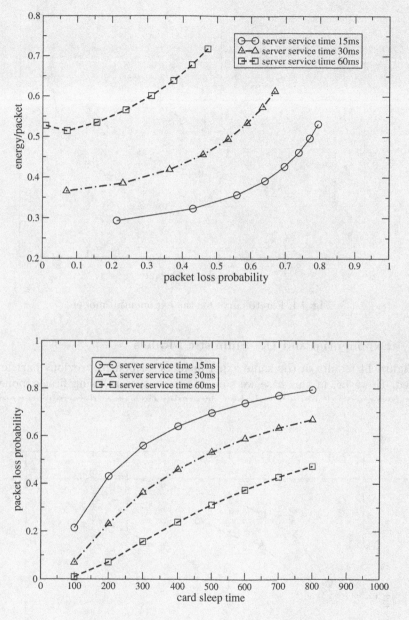

Fig. 13. Packet loss for the Markovian model

loss probability increases as a function of sleep time because of the AP buffer saturation. Clearly, the AP buffer saturates earlier for lower server service times (higher server rate). This explains the relative positions of the three curves shown in the figure. In our case study AP buffer was set to 10 packets.

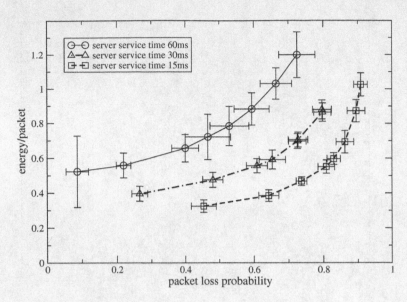

Fig. 14. Pareto curve for the exponential model

4.2 Exponential and Deterministic Models

In Figure 14 results of the same experiment described in previous part are reported. However, in this case we simulated our system using first exponential
rates (exponential model) and then deterministic rates (deterministic model).
The   1

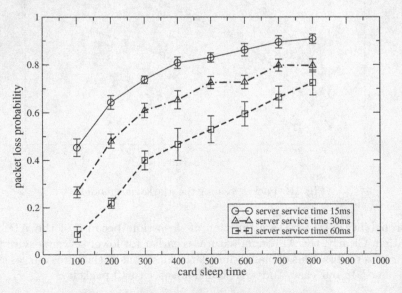

Fig. 15. Packet loss for the exponential model

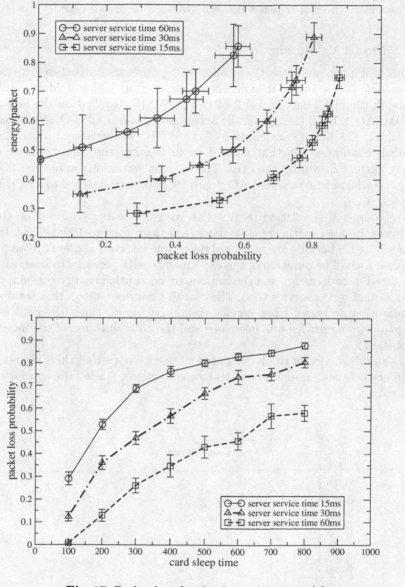

Fig. 17. Packet loss for the deterministic model

be observed that both pareto and packet loss probability curves (Fig. 12 and 13, respectively) show the same shape of corresponding Markovian curves, the only difference being an offset in absolute values. Results are averaged on 30 runs. Variances as vertical lines across simulated points.

The third part of results regards simulations with deterministic rates. The only event which is not deterministic in this simulation is the probability of packet corruption at the client.

In Fig. 16 and 17 Pareto and packet loss curves are reported. As for the previous case, the model behaviour reflects the Markovian case.

4.3   Model Validation

In this last part, we show the results of experiments carried out to validate our model. To perform our experiments we used a Athlon 4 Mobile 1.2 GHz notebook running Linux kernel 2.4.21. The WNIC installed on the laptop was a COMPAQ WL110 [11], while the access point was a CISCO 350 Series base station [8]. The power consumption of the WNIC was measured using a Sycard CardBus Ex-tender [19] that allowed us to monitor the time behavior of the supply current drawn by the card. The current waveforms were then digitized using a National Instruments DAQ Board PCI 6024E connected to a PC running Labview 6.1.

We compared simulation results with measurements performed on the real hardware. In our experiments, we fixed card sleep time to 100ms (Fig. 18) and 200ms (Fig. 19) because they are card sleep time intervals allowed by commercial cards we used. The duration of the experiments is 10 seconds. In both cases, we performed measurements and simulations by computing energy consumption as a function of server service time. The overall behaviour shows that total energy consumption decreases when service time increases, because the card receives less packets (the service rate decreases and the total duration of the benchmark is constant).

The more important result evidenced by these plots is that there is a negligible difference between simulation and real measurements, stating the accuracy of the card model.

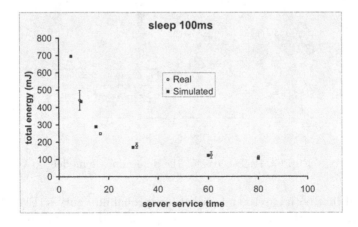

Fig. 18. Comparison among simulations and hardware measurements: sleep time 100ms

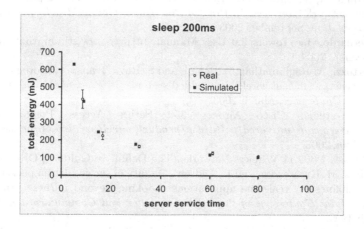

Fig. 19. Comparison among simulations and hardware measurements: sleep time 200ms

5 Conclusion

In this paper we presented a tutorial on standard power management in wireless IEEE 802.11b networks. We described in details the power save protocol (PSP) standard implemented by all commercial cards. We summarized also alternative approaches to power management proposed in the literature. Then we introduced a power-accurate model of a wireless network card targeted to the analitycal study and simulations of power/performance trade-off in a wireless link. We validated our model against power measurements carried out on real hardware commercial devices.

References

1. LAN/MAN Standards Committee of the IEEE Computer Society: Part 11: Wireless LAN MAC and PHY Specifications: Higher-Speed Physical Layer Extension in the 2.4 GHz Band. IEEE, 1999.
2. A. Acquaviva, A. Aldini, M. Bernardo, A. Bogliolo, E. Bonta, E. Lattanzi, "A Methodology Based on Formal Methods for Predicting the Impact of Dynamic Power Management", In *Formal Methods for Mobile Computing*, LNCS 3465, 2005.
3. A. Acquaviva, E. Lattanzi, A. Bogliolo, Designa and Simulation of Power-Aware Scheduling Strategies of Streaming Data in Wireless LANs, In *Proc. of ACM MSWIM*, October 2004.
4. A. Acquaviva, E. Lattanzi, A. Bogliolo, L. Benini, A Simulation Model for Streaming Applications over a Power-Manageable Wireless Link, In *Proc. of European Simulation and Modeling Conference*, October 2003.

5. A. Acquaviva, T. Simunic, V. Deolalikar, and S. Roy. Remote power control of wireless network interfaces. In *Proc. of Power and Timing Modeling, Optimization and Simulation*, September 2003.
6. M. Bernardo, TwoTowers 5.0 User Manual, http://www.sti.uniurb.it/bernardo/twotowers/, 2004.
7. D. Bertozzi, A. Raghunathan, L. Benini, and S. Ravi. Transport protocol optimization for energy efficient wireless embedded systems. In *Proc. of Design, Automation and Test Conference*, March 2003.
8. Cisco Systems, Cisco Aironet 350 Series Access Points, *http : //www.cisco.com/univercd/cc/td/doc/product/wireless/airo₃50/accsspts/index.htm*, 2003.
9. M. S. Gast, "'802.11 Wireless Networks, The Definitive Guide."', OŘeally.
10. D. Hayes, M. Rumsewicz, and L. Andrew. Quality of service driven packet scheduling disciplines for real-time applications: Looking beyond fairness. In *Proc. of Annual Joint Conference of the IEEE Computer and Communications Societies*, March 1999.
11. Hewlett Packard, WL110 Client Card Manual, *http : //h20015.www2.hp.com/content/common/manuals/bpe60027/bpe60027.pdf*, 2004.
12. C. Jones, K. Sivalingam, P. Agrawal, J. Chen, "A Survey of Energy Efficient Network Protocols for Wireless Networks", *Proc. of DATE*, March 1999.
13. R. Krashinsky, H. Balakrishnan, "Minimizing Energy for Wireless Web Access with Bounded Slowdown", *Proc. of MOBICOM*, October 2002.
14. X. Liu, Y. Xiang, and T. J. Li. Counter based routing policies. In *Proc. of High Performance Computing Conference*, pages 389–393, December 1999.
15. Network Simulator, *http : //www.isi.edu/nsnam/ns/*
16. V. Raghunathan, S. Ganeriwal, C. Schurgers, M. Srivastava, "E^2WFQ: An Energy Efficient Fair Scheduling Policy for Wireless Systems", *Proc. of ISLPED*, August 2002.
17. H. Shi and H. Sethu. Scheduling real-time traffic under controlled load service in an integrated service internet. In *Proc. of Workshop on High Performance Switching and Routing*, May 2001.
18. K. Sivalingam, J. Chen, P. Agrawal, M. Srivastava, "Design and Analysis of low-power access protocols for wireless and mobile ATM networks", *Wireless Networks*, no.6, 2000.
19. Sycard Technology, PCCextend 140 CardBus Extender User's Manual, *http : //www.sycard.com/docs/cextman.pdf*, 1996.
20. E. Takahashi, "Application Aware Scheduling for Power Management on IEEE 802.11" *Proc. of Intl. Performance, Computers, and Communications Conf.*, February 2000.
21. H. Wan and X. Lin. Multiple priorities qos scheduling for simultaneous videos transmissions. In *Proc. of International Symposium on Multimedia Software Engineering*, December 2000.
22. M. Y. Wu, S. Ma, and W. Shu. Scheduled video delivery for scalable on-demand service. In *in Proc. of the 12th international workshop on Network and operating systems support for digital audio and video*, May 2002.

Network Swapping*

Emanuele Lattanzi, Andrea Acquaviva, and Alessandro Bogliolo

Università di Urbino "Carlo Bo",
Istituto di Scienze e Tecnologie dell'Informazione,
Piazza della Repubblica 13, 61029 Urbino, Italy
{lattanzi, acquaviva, bogliolo}@sti.uniurb.it

Abstract. Wireless mobile terminals have limited storage memory due to weight, size and power constraints. Potentially unlimited virtual memory could be found on remote servers made accessible through a wireless link, but power hungry wireless network interface cards (WNIC) may reduce the battery lifetime if not efficiently exploited, actually limiting the practical interest of network virtual memory (NVM). On the other hand, when network memory is used for swapping, service performance can be an issue. In this tutorial we discuss the feasibility of network swapping for wireless mobile terminals. First, we perform extensive experiments to compare performance and energy of network swapping with those of local swapping on microdrives and flash memories. Our results show that remote swap devices made accessible through a power-manageable WNIC can be even more efficient than local microdrives. Second, we address the issue of mobility management by presenting an infrastructure providing efficient remote memory access to mobile terminals. We report experimental results obtained on a working prototype of the proposed infrastructure.

1 Introduction

Virtual memory mapped on mass storage devices can be viewed as an unlimited resource to be used to extend the main memory of desktop and laptop computers. However, in wireless mobile devices like personal digital assistants (PDAs) and cellular phones, storage memory is limited or absent due to weight, size and power constraints, thus limiting the application of virtual memory. On the other hand, if wireless connectivity is available, unlimited swapping space could be found on remote devices made available by a server and managed by the operating system. Remote memory service is implemented by means of a client-server mechanism similar to that supporting file sharing, where the server allocates a memory region to be used as a swapping space for a remote client. However, swapping over a power hungry wireless network interface card (WNIC) may limit the battery lifetime and application performance if not efficiently exploited.

---

* Co-financed by Regione Marche within the CIPE 36/2002 framework.

M. Bernardo and A. Bogliolo (Eds.): SFM-Moby 2005, LNCS 3465, pp. 215–233, 2005.

The implementation of NVM services for mobile terminals (MTs), imposes new challenges related to: i) the performance and energy efficiency of the WNIC, ii) the performance of the network and iii) the mobility of the terminal.

Network swapping has been object of research in the past decade because of its application in wired networked clusters of computers. In this context, remote swapping has been found to be more efficient than local swapping [24, 17] when high-bandwidth network links are available. In fact, accessing the physical memory of a remote server can be more efficient than accessing a local disk. These results are not directly applicable to wireless palmtop PCs, because of bandwidth limitations and energy constraints.

In general, however, the bandwidth provided by the network can be a critical bottleneck requiring location-aware proximity services.

First of all, in this tutorial we report some results of extensive experiments conducted to evaluate the performance and power efficiency of different local and remote swap devices for wireless PDAs (namely, a compact flash (CF), a micro drive (HD) and two different WNICs). Experimental results show that WNICs are less efficient than local devices both in terms of energy and time per page. However, the DPM support provided by WNICs is much more efficient than that of local micro drives, making network swapping less expensive than local swapping for real-world applications with non-uniform page requests.

In a second time we address the issue of mobility management by presenting a wireless NVM infrastructure based on a location-aware caching strategy that keeps recently-used virtual memory pages local to the base station. The infrastructure grants wireless connectivity to the MT and improves service performance. Mobility management is based on a write-back mechanism that supports service migration during handoff. Experimental results obtained on a working prototype demonstrate the feasibility of the proposed approach.

The rest of the tutorial is organized as follow. In Section 2 we briefly introduce the remote storage space concept. In section 3 we describe the key features of both local and remote storage devices that can be used for swapping, and we briefly describe the software support for remote swapping. In section 3.3 we report wireless NVM infrastructure issues. In Section 4 we describe the benchmarks and the experimental setup used to characterize each swap device in terms of power and performance and to test NVM infrastructure. In Section 5 we report devices characterization results in terms of power and performance. Finally in section 6 we propose our NVM infrastructure implementation and in section 7 we draw conclusions.

2   Remote Storage Space

The concept of remote storage has been exploited by deeply networked systems for mainly two reasons. First, remote memories or magnetic disks are used to store application and data by systems with limited or absent local mass storage space. Even if the memory is not a constraint, remote storage spaces are used as repository of data shared among different users, as in the case of file servers. Diskless workstations and mobile terminals are both computer systems characterized by limited or absent disk capacity. Access to remote data can be controlled by a network file systems. However, mobile networks require suitable protocols to handle disconnected and weakly connected operations. To this purpose, dedicated file systems and file hoarding methods have been designed [18, 11, 12]. File hoarding is the technique of preparing disconnections by caching critical data. Differently from traditional caching, the cost of miss (or failure) can be catastrophic if it occurs when the system is disconnected from the network. To identify critical data, LRU policies augmented with user-specified hoard-priority have been proposed as part of the CODA file system [18]. Here, priorities are used to offset the LRU age of an object. In addition, the user is given the possibility to interactively control the hoarding strategy (so called translucent caching concept). Automated hoarding methods have been also recently presented [12, 11].

From another aspect, remote memories can be used as swap areas to temporarily park run-time data and code when the total amount of available system memory is not enough to contain user processes. In computer clusters remote swap areas are designed to replace local swap partitions for performance reasons. In fact, high speed links may provide faster access than local magnetic disks especially under certain workload conditions, due to their high rotational latency [24, 17]. While in the former aspect the main issue is reliability and user-friendly access of remote data, here the key point is the performance. For this reason, simpler and efficient supports have been proposed [19].

Remote swap areas can be exploited also by mobile devices, where local storage space is limited and costly. Moreover, this is mainly used for storing applications or personal data. Nevertheless, the availability of a swap area increases the total amount of virtual memory. As we will explain in more detail later, need for swapping in mobile embedded devices is mainly required after a context switch to bring in data the first time they are accessed. Network swapping in mobile devices does not come for free. In fact, compared to computer clusters, they are more bandwidth and energy constrained.

Remote swapping for handheld computing systems is a recent research topic that has not been extensively studied so far. The problem of energy consumption of network swapping in mobile devices has been faced by Hom and Kremer [15]. They propose a compilation framework aimed at reducing the energy by switching the communication device on and off by means of specific instructions inserted at compile time based on a partial knowledge of the memory footprint of the application.

3   Swap Devices

We refer to the page-based swapping support provided by the Linux OS. Linux performs a page swap in two situations: *i*) when a kernel daemon, activated once per second, finds that the number of free pages has fallen below a given threshold; *ii*) when a memory request cannot be satisfied. The page to be swapped-out is selected in a global way, independently from the process that made the request.

The page replacement algorithm is based on an approximation of least recently used (LRU) policy [9].

Modern operating systems equipping palmtops and PDAs make possible to define heterogeneous support for swapping. Swapping can be performed both locally to the PDA and remotely, by exploiting server storage capabilities and network connections. More than one swap units can be enabled at the same time, with assigned priority. The unit with the highest priority is selected by default until it becomes insufficient.

3.1   Local Devices

On-board non-volatile memory is usually available in palmtop PCs to store the bootloader and the filesystem. Magnetic disks can be added to extend file storage capabilities. Swap can be made locally in palmtops as in desktop PCs. A dedicated partition can be defined in hard drives or flash memories, where the filesystem resides. Alternatively, some OS's allow the user to define a swap file that does not need a dedicated partition. Either way, the swap area comes at the price of decreasing the space available for actual storage purposes.

Compact Flash

Palmtop PCs are equipped with on-board flash memories, but additional memory chips can be installed as an expansion if an external slot is present. Memory Technology Device (MTD) drivers allow to define swap partitions or swap files on flash memories. However, being read-most devices, flash memories are not the ideal support for swapping. Nevertheless, we evaluate their swapping performance since they are always present in palmtop PCs, being sometimes the only alternative to network swapping.

Hard Disk

Today's technology made available hand-sized magnetic disks (called *mini* of *micro drives*) suitable to be installed in palmtop computers. Currently they provide a storage capability up to 5GBytes. Like traditional hard disks (HD), micro drives provide a seek time much longer than the access time to sequential blocks. For this reason, access to these kind of devices is usually performed in bursts whenever possible by exploiting on-board hardware buffers in order to compensate for the initial transfer delay. The OS tries to limit the delays by filtering disk accesses using software caches, whose size is limited by the available space in main memory. When a micro drive used as a swap device, this trade-off is even more critical, since increasing the memory space allocated for caching decreases available main memory space that results in increasing the number of swap requests.

3.2   Network Devices

In order to provide the performance required to fully exploit the channel bandwidth, remote swap files can be mapped in the main memory of a remote server. This is the choice we made for our experiments.

Network File System

NFS (*Network File System*) is used in a network to enable file sharing among different machines on a local area. The communication protocol is based on a UDP stack, while data transfers between NFS server and clients are based on Remote Procedure Calls (RPCs). The idea of using NFS to support network swapping is relatively recent [22]. To this purpose, a remote file must be configured as a swap area. This is made possible by modern operating systems that allow the user to specify either a device or a file as a swap unit.

Network Block Device

A *Network Block Device* (NBD) offers to the OS and to the applications running on top of it the illusion of using a local block device, while data are not stored locally but sent to a remote server [19]. As in case of NFS, the virtual local device is mapped in a remote file, but the swap unit is viewed as a device, rather than as a file.

This is made possible by a kernel level driver (or module) that communicates to a remote user-level server. The first time the network connection is set-up, a NDB user-level client negotiates with the NBD server the size and the access granularity of the exported file. After initialization, the user-level NBD client does not take part to remaining transactions, that directly involve the kernel NBD driver and the NBD server. No RPCs are required in this case, thus reducing the software overhead. Latest releases of NBD driver use an user level network communication, which affects the performance of the protocol, since data must be copied from the kernel to the user space address, but increases flexibility. Differently from NFS, the underlying network stack is TCP instead of UDP. This increases the reliability of network transfers, at the cost of increasing the protocol overhead.

3.3   Wireless Network Virtual Memory Infrastructure

Remote virtual memory service is implemented by means of a client-server mechanism similar to that supporting file sharing, where the server allocates a memory region to be used as a swapping space for a remote client.

The implementation of a wireless NVM services for MTs, however, imposes new challenges related to: i) the performance and energy efficiency of the WNIC, ii) the performance of the network and iii) the mobility of the terminal. In general the bandwidth provided by the wireless network can be a critical bottleneck requiring location-aware proximity services.

Using proxies in the wired network to support mobile devices is a well known technique especially for web browsers [21, 20]. To enhance adaptability to client movements and location awareness, the concept of proxy migration has been proposed [23] for different applications such as audio streaming and WWW browsing. More recently, caching mechanisms for web data on base stations have been studied [21].

To support location-aware services in cellular networks, the *personal proxy* concept has been introduced [5]. It collaborates with the underlying location management system to decide when and how often it should move following the MT. Finally, as for mobility management, a context caching approach has been presented to reduce handoff delays in 802.11 wireless networks [16, 4].

4   Experimental Setup

We performed our experiments on a HP's IPAQ 3600 handheld PC, equipped with a Strong-ARM-1110 processor, 32MB SDRAM and 16MB of FLASH. Our benchmarks were executed on the palmtop on top of the Linux operating system, Familiar release 6.0. The WNICs used to provide network connectivity were a LUCENT (hereafter denoted by NIC_{LUCENT}) and a CISCO AIRONET 350(NIC_{CISCO}), while the AP connected to the remote swapping server was a CISCO 350 Series base station [3, 7, 6]. The remote server was installed on a Athlon 4 Mobile 1.2 GHz notebook. For local swap experiments we used a 340 MB IBM Microdrive (HD) and a 64 MB Compaq-Sundisk Compact Flash Memory (CF) [14, 8]. Power consumption of both WNICs and local devices was measured using a *Sycard Card Extender* that allowed us to monitor the time behavior of the supply current drawn by the card. The current waveforms were then digitized using a *National Instruments Data Acquisition Board* connected to a PC. A *Labview* software running on the PC was used to coordinate the acquisition and bufferize current samples to compute power and energy consumption.

The remote swap NBD server was instrumented in order to collect time-stamped traces of swapping activity during benchmarks execution.

The wireless NVM service infrastructure was obtained using two CISCO 350 Series base stations. NBD servers were installed on 2.8 GHz Intel Pentium 4 machines, equipped with 2 Gbytes of SRAM running 2.6.1 Linux OS.

4.1   Benchmarks

We developed synthetic benchmarks to characterize the inherent performance of swap devices and to assess the feasibility of NVM.

For measuring the inherent cost of a page swap we developed a *characterization benchmark* accessing a data structure much larger than the available main memory without performing any computation on it. The pseudo-code of the benchmark is shown in Fig. 1. A large matrix is allocated by row and initialized and then read by column in order to maximize the number of page faults.

```
/*************** Benchmark 1 ***************/
double A[ROW][COL];
initialize(A,ROW,COL);
t0 = time();
read_by_column(A,ROW,COL);
t1 = time();
/****************************************/
```

Fig. 1. Pseudo-code of the benchmark used to characterize swap devices

```
/************** Case study ***************/ double
dummy[2048][2048], C[128][128]; double A[128][128], B[128][128];
initialize(A,128,128); initialize(B,128,128);
initialize(C,128,128); initialize(dummy,2048,2048); //swap out t0
= time(); compute_product(A,B,C); t1 = time();
/****************************************/
```

Fig. 2. Pseudo-code of the case study

The same benchmark was used to characterize swapping cost with and without write-back, invoking either `write_by_column` or `read_by_column` procedures.

Validation was based on a benchmark (hereafter called *case study*) performing matrix multiplication. The pseudo-code of the case study is reported in Fig. 2: it simply computes the product of two square matrices A and B and puts the result in a third matrix C.

Matrices A, B and C are first allocated and initialized, then a dummy matrix exceeding the size of the physical memory is initialized in order to swap A, B and C out from main memory. The initialization of the dummy matrix creates boundary conditions similar to those possibly caused by the concurrent execution of other processes. We monitor the execution time and the swapping energy caused by the execution of the `compute_product` procedure.

The distribution of swap requests for 128x128 matrices is shown in Fig. 4. The expected distribution is also plotted for comparison. The large number of pages requested at the beginning corresponds to the upload of the entire matrix B. In fact, the first column of B has to be read in order to compute the first entry of C. Since matrices are stored in memory by rows, reading the first column entails swapping in the entire matrix, as shown in Fig. 3. Subsequent page requests are

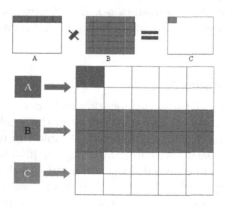

Fig. 3. Memory access during matrix product computation

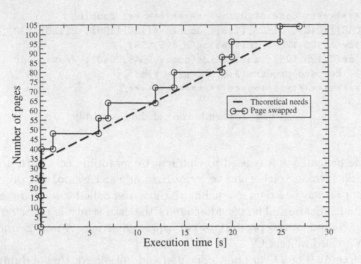

Fig. 4. Distribution of page requests

spaced in time according to the time required to compute 512×128 floating point products.

Comparing the actual requests with the theoretical needs we observe that the OS swaps 8 pages at a time, thus increasing the opportunity for DPM. However, the total number of pages request by the OS is 104, while the three matrices fit into 96 pages.

5   Characterization of Swapping Devices

In this section we present characterization results of swapping devices. In particular, in a first experiment we characterize the inherent swapping cost of each device by running the *characterization benchmark* described in section 4.1. In a second time, by using the *case study* benchmark we characterize the DPM support of each device.

5.1   Inherent Swapping Cost

We measured the system time and energy spent to execute characterization benchmarks and we divided the measured values for the number of pages swapped in/out. Characterization results are reported in Table 1 in terms of time, energy and power required by each device to swap a page of 4096 bytes. Both *read-only* and *write-back* results are reported. In general, write-back doubles the cost (in energy and time) of read-only swap, since it involves two data transfers. As expected, local devices are more efficient than WNICs. In particular, CF has an energy-per-page more than 10 times lower than all other devices.

Experimental results are reported in Table 1 in terms of time, energy and power required by each local and remote device to swap a page of 4096 bytes. Both *read-only* and *write-back* results are reported.

Table 1. Power consumption and performance of local and remote swap devices

| Swap device | | Read-only | | | Write-back | | |
Type	Mode	Time [ms]	Energy [mJ]	Power [mW]	Time [ms]	Energy [mJ]	Power [mW]
CF	local	4.1	0.201	49	8.2	0.402	49
HD	local	3.0	1.911	637	6.4	4.061	637
NIC_{CISCO}	NBD	7.0	5.934	848	14.0	10.319	735
NIC_{CISCO}	NFS	8.5	6.123	720	14.6	10.516	720
NIC_{LUCENT}	NBD	8.0	5.626	578	15.0	8.599	573
NIC_{LUCENT}	NFS	10.0	5.243	524	22.0	10.672	485

In general, write-back doubles the cost (in energy and time) of a read-only swap, since it involves two data transfers. As expected, local devices are more efficient than WNICs and CF has an energy-per-page more than 10 times lower than all other devices.

It is also worth noting that, for a given WNIC, NBD provides greater performance than NFS, at the cost of a slightly higher power consumption. Since the time reduction overcomes the additional power consumption, the energy per page required by NBD is lower than that required by NFS.

5.2   Characterization of DPM Support

In the previous section we have characterized swap devices in terms of time and energy requirements per swap page. To this purpose we designed a set of benchmarks that simply accessed data structures much larger than the main memory without performing any computation on them.

Although useful for characterization purposes, the *characterization benchmarks* are unrealistic for two main reasons. First, computation time is usually non-negligible, so that page requests are spaced in time according to a distribution that depends on the workload and on the state of the main memory. Second, the total size of the data structures accessed by each application usually does not exceed the size of the main memory, or otherwise the performance degradation would not be acceptable.

In most cases of practical interest, swapping is mainly needed after a context switch to bring in main memory data structures the first time they are used by the active process. Moreover, in handheld devices there are often only a few processes running concurrently, so that both main memory and peripherals are mainly used by a single process at the time. In this situation, the usage pattern of swapping devices are significantly different from those used for characterizing swapping costs because of the presence of long idle periods between page swaps.

Since swapping devices spend power while waiting for page requests, the effective energy per page is larger than that reported in Table 1. On the other hand, idleness can be dynamically exploited to save power by putting the devices in low-power operating modes, or by turning them off. Dynamic power

Table 2. Power states of local and remote devices

Device	State	Power [mW]	Timeout [ms]	WU-time [ms]	WU-power [mW]
CF	Read	107			
	Write	156			
	Wait	4.5			
HD	Read	946			
	Write	991			
	Wait	600			
	Sleep	24	2000	4500 ± 1980	1067
NIC	Receive	755			
(*cisco*)	Transmit	1136			
	Wait	525			
	(PSP/PSPCAM)	113	0/850	14/14	400
	Power-Off	0	any	370	451
NIC	Receive	548			
(*lucent*)	Transmit	798			
	Wait	407			
	(PSP)	38	100	1	800
	Power-Off	0	any	270	357

management (DPM) significantly impacts the performance and energy trade-off offered by each device under bursty workloads.

The DPM support provided by each swap device is schematically represented in Table 2. For each device, the key features of active and inactive operating modes are reported. Active modes are characterized only in terms of power consumption, while inactive modes are also characterized in terms of *timeout* to be waited before entering the inactive state, *wake-up time* and *wake-up power*. The data reported in the Table have been obtained by analyzing the current profiles provided by the measurement setup described in Section 4.

First of all we remark that the average power consumptions measured during page swaps (reported in Table 1) are not equal to the power consumptions measured for the devices during read/receive or write/transmit. In fact, for instance, a page swap across a wireless link entails the transmission of the page request, a waiting time corresponding to the latency of the remote device, the reception of the page and, possibly, the write-back of a swapped-out page. The average swapping power comes from the weighted average of all these contributions.

The CF has no inactive states. This is because its power consumption in wait mode is negligible, making inactive low-power states useless. On the contrary, NICs and HDs consume a large amount of power while waiting for service requests, so that it is worth switching them to low-power inactive states during long idle periods.

The Sleep state of the HD has the lowest power consumption, but the highest wakeup cost in terms of power (higher than 1W) and time (in the order of several seconds). Moreover, the wakeup time is highly unpredictable, its measured standard deviation being almost 2 seconds.

According to the IEEE802.11b standard, WNICs provide MAC-level DPM support that can be enabled via software [16].

DPM support for WNICs is fully explained in tutorial [1]. The power save protocol (PSP) provided by MAC-level DPM consists in placing the card in a low-power state called *doze mode*, in which it sleeps but wakes-up periodically to keep synchronized with the network and to check the access point (AP) for outstanding data. A polling frame must be transmitted by the card for each packet to be retrieved. PSP mode provides power savings at a cost of a noticeable performance hit. To increase performance, a variation of this policy is implemented by CISCO cards. They automatically switch from PSP to CAM (*Constant Awake Mode*) when a large amount of traffic is detected. In this case no polling frame is needed between packets since the reception and transmission happen in active mode.

Even if the power consumption in sleep state is low, it is not negligible. Moreover, the card is sensitive to broadcast traffic. A more aggressive policy would require to completely shut-off the card when no needed by any active application in the system. Thus, more power can be saved, at the price of a larger wake-up delay needed by network re-association. OS-level policies can be implemented to this purpose based on a power management infrastructure recently developed for Linux OS [2]. This infrastructure is composed by a power manager module that handles requests from applications and keeps track of their resource needs. On the other side, upon a request, the power manager can directly switch off a peripheral (WNIC in our case) if no other applications are using it. Switch off request may come from user applications through dedicated APIs or directly by a another kernel module. We exploited this feature to let the NBD driver module switch on and off the card between swapping requests.

The features of doze and power-off modes are reported for both WNICs in Table 2. We observe that the MAC-level DPM support of NIC_{LUCENT} is more

Table 3. Execution time and swapping energy required to run the *case study* benchmark

Device	Exec. time [s]		Energy [mJ]	
	Avg	Std	Avg	Std
RAM	25	0	-	-
CF	25.5	0.57	0.14	0.003
HD	25.31	-	15.20	-
(PM ON)	37.75	5.91	19.43	5.31
NIC_{CISCO}	26	-	16.51	0.01
(PSPCAM)	30.67	2.16	10.59	0.23
(PSP)	43.33	0.58	8.05	0.23
(OFF)	28.75	0.5	bf 2.47	0.09
NIC_{LUCENT}	30.25	0.5	13.60	0.56
(PSP)	30.0	0	2.54	0.096
(OFF)	30.0	0	1.76	0.08

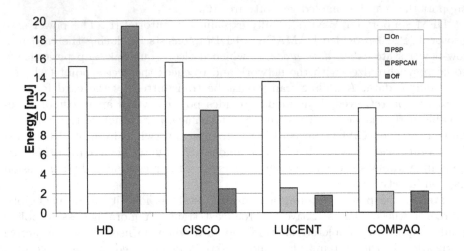

Fig. 5. Comparison of energy consumptions reported in Table 3

efficient then that of NIC$_{CISCO}$, but the DPM policy if more conservative (the timeout being 100ms).

We use *case study* benchmark to evaluate the effectiveness of the DPM strategies implemented by the swap devices.

Experimental results are reported in Table 3. Based on the results reported in Table 1 we decided to use NBD for remote swapping. In Fig. 5 we detailed the comparison among different devices.

Each device was tested with and without DPM. The two WNICs were tested with both MAC-level DPM (doze) and OS-level PDM (power-off). The DPM mode and the corresponding timeouts are reported in the first column. The performance of the CF and the CPU time obtained by running the application with data available in main memory are also reported in the first two rows for reference. The DPM of the HD was enabled by default, so that data reported on row HD are computed from previous characterization. All other data were obtained from real measurements, by repeating each experiment 4 times.

Interestingly, even without DPM, the HD consumes more energy than WNICs. This is because of its higher power consumption when idle. When DPM is enabled, WNICs become much more convenient than HD. In particular, the DPM of the HD is counterproductive both in terms of time and energy under this traffic conditions because of the large wakeup cost. On the contrary, MAC-level DPM of NIC$_{Cisco}$ and NIC$_{Compaq}$ saves respectively more than 50% and more than 80% of the swapping energy. If the power-off state is exploited, power savings become of 85% and 94%, respectively, with negligible performance loss.

Current profiles obtained by running the benchmark are shown in Fig. 6 for the Compact Flash, Cisco card without power management and microdrive. The figure evidences the strong variance of microdrive's power profile, due to

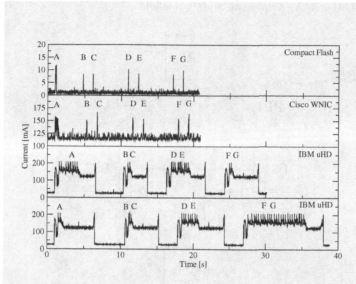

Fig. 6. Power profiles of the different swap devices during the execution of the *case study* benchmark

the variability of the head position and speed at the shutdown instants. In fact, the two bottom traces in figure are obtained running the same benchmark. As a reference, we marked swapping activity intervals with uppercase latin letters.

6 Mobility Management for Network Swapping

Although the feasibility and efficiency of remote swapping across a wireless link is demonstrated by the results provided in previous sections, providing NVM services to a MT raises additional mobility management issues. In this section we propose location-aware proximity mechanisms that can be used to support service mobility.

We discuss mobility management referring to Fig. 7. Two base stations (BS1 and BS2) are available to provide wireless network connectivity to a MT. Base stations are connected to two local servers (LS1 and LS2, respectively) connected together by means of a wide-band local link (LL). A remote server (RS) is also available, connected to LS1 and LS2 by means of multi-hop remote links denoted by RL1 and RL2, respectively. We assume the MT to be initially associated to BS1 moving toward the service area covered by BS2. We want the NVM service to survive the de-association from BS1 and the re-association to BS2.

Several solutions can be explored. However, an exhaustive exploration of NVM architectures is beyond the scope of this tutorial. In this section we are only interested in outlining a possible solution to demonstrate the feasibility of wireless NVM infrastructure. To this purpose we envision a scenario where the swap area of the MT is made available by the RS, while LS1 and LS2 provide caching/proximity services to enhance performance.

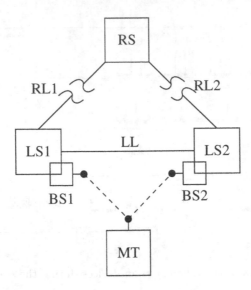

Fig. 7. System architecture

Caching is a very common solution for many types of web services [13]. For remote swapping, cache performance is even more critical due to the high access frequency and to the blocking nature of swap requests. We assume that each MT has a limited space (possibly much smaller than the total swap area) available on a given LS to cache swap requests. In the limiting situation where the cache contains all pages needed by a given application, the cache becomes a mirror and the RS is used only to guarantee coherency among different caches. In the typical case of caches smaller than swap space requirements, replacement algorithms need to be implemented.

To guarantee cache coherence across handoffs, cache contents must be either written back to the remote swap area, or migrated to the new location. In the rest of this section we outline a simple *write-back* mechanism used to support service migration.

When the MT de-associates from a BS1, all dirty pages in the cache on LS1 are written back to the remote swap area. When the MT re-associates to BS2, a new empty cache is instantiated on LS2. The new cache is initially empty and its efficiency is initially lower than that of the previous cache.

Service suspension time depends on the amount of dirty pages, which in turns depends on the cache efficiency and size. Ideally, we would like the write-back time to be completely hidden by the re-association time. To this purpose, a *location-aware write back trimming* policy can be preemptively triggered by the MT when it approaches BS2 in order to keep the number of dirty pages below a given threshold (MAX). The value of MAX represents the amount of data that can be written back during the handoff time.

6.1   Implementation

We implemented the location aware NVM infrastructure based on the NBD provided by Linux OS. The networked nature of NBD is completely transparent to other kernel components (including the bdflush daemon and the page fault handler that manage virtual memory) that may use the remote memory space as any other block device.

The implementation of the mobility management policy described so far gives rise to several issues. First, we need to be able to predict and control the 802.11b handoff mechanism in order to exploit its inherent black-out time to perform swap service migration. Second, we need to implement proximity caches. Third, we need to switch at run time from a NDB server to another. All these issues are addressed in the following.

802.11b Handoff Management

MTs use automatic active scanning to find a new BS when the signal of the current one falls under a given threshold. If a valid BS is found in range, the re-authentication phase automatically starts. Re-authentication involves the transfer of credentials and other information from the old BS (say, BS1) to the new one (BS2). If authentication is successfully completed the MT de-associates from BS1 and re-associates to BS2. The handoff protocol is completely transparent to the user. However, we need to take control of the handoff in order to exploit de-association and re-association time for swap-service migration. To this purpose we created a daemon process, running on the MT, that disables automatic active scanning and periodically scans for new BS' in range. In order to implement a user-level scanning routine we used the mwvlan driver for Wavelan IEEE/Orinoco that enables scanning control. For each BS in range we take SNR values in order to decide when to trigger handoff and towards which BS. We use a simple two-threshold roaming algorithm to trigger handoff as in the Sabino System [10]. When the SNR of current BS falls under the first threshold we scan for a new BS in range. When it falls under the second threshold we force re-association to the new BS.

Proximity Caches

Caches local to the BS are implemented as C++ objects containing a STL C++ map object. The map object is an associative container for (key, value) couples, where value can be any C++ object. To implement a cache of swap requests, we use memory pages as values and page identifiers as keys. A memory page is an instance of a simple C++ class, called Page, that contains page data and two flags, r_flag and w_flag, to store information about read and write activity to be used to implement replacement and migration policies.

Since caches need to be accessed from different servers during swap service migration they have been implemented as CORBA objects by specifying their remote interface using OMG IDL (*Object Management Group Interface Definition Language*). We used the *omniORB 3.0* CORBA Linux implementation and its SDK to generate the C++ stub and skeleton interface.

NBD Server Switching

Swap service migration entails switching between two different machines providing NBD services. In principle, this can be done by changing the socket pointer into the block device. However, the Linux NBD doesn't allow the user to do so without loosing the content of the virtual memory, thus causing a kernel panic. The key issue is making server re-association atomic in order to prevent the virtual memory management to issue swap requests during service black out. To this purpose we implemented a specific system call (NBD_CHANGE_SOCKET) locking the block device while changing the socket pointer and reestablishing the swap service. The system call can be invoked to perform swap service migration even during swap activity.

6.2   Handoff Characterization

In order to characterize service migration overhead we run the *characterization benchmark* described in Section 4.1 generating a constant pattern of swap requests at the maximum sustainable rate.

We first run the benchmark with the swap area local to the BS, without performing any handoff during execution, to obtain a baseline performance. Then we run the benchmark again while performing the handoff operations under characterization, in order to estimate their overhead by means of differential performance measurements. Two kinds of handoff operations were characterized: *BS-only handoff*, consisting of de-association from BS1 and re-association to BS2 while using the same swap server, local to both base stations; *Server-only handoff*, consisting of disconnection from a local swap server and re-connection to a new server sharing the same swap file. The joint effect of BS and Server handoffs was also measured by performing both operations during the same run of the benchmark. Each experiment was repeated 10 times.

Results are reported in Fig. 8. Notice that using local swap servers accessing a shared swap file allowed us characterize inherent handoff times, independent of the mobility management policies.

6.3   Testing the NVM Infrastructure

We tested the NVM infrastructure using the *case study* benchmark of Section 4.1. Large matrices, of 1024x1024 elements each, where used in this case to make the experiments long enough to be affected by mobility issues.

To evaluate the performance overhead caused by the NVM infrastructure, the benchmark was first executed without handoff with three different configurations of the swap server: A) using a 100Mbytes swap area installed on a local server, B) using a 100Mbytes swap area installed on a remote server, C) using a 100Mbyets remote swap area with a 12Mbytes proxy cache local to the BS. For these experiments the bandwidth of the remote link was artificially limited to 2Mb/s. The same benchmark was then executed with a synchronous handoff triggered right after computation of the first 200 rows (D).

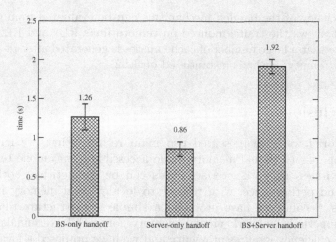

Fig. 8. Experimental hand-off time

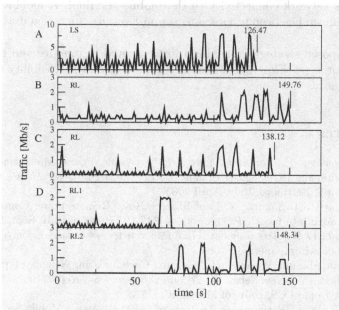

Fig. 9. Link Bandwidth Occupation of Swap Area Management Policies

Experimental traces showing the traffic generated by swap requests are reported in Fig. 9 for each experiment. The computation time of the first 400 rows is also annotated on each graph. The first three traces, referring to local, remote and cached NVM without handoff, show the impact of proximity on performance: accessing a remote swap server increases the execution time from 126.47 to 149.76 seconds, while caching provides a trade-off at 138.12 seconds. The filtering effect of the cache can be appreciated by comparing graphs B and C: graph B shows a baseline traffic of about 0.4Mb/s on the RL that doesn't appear on graph C.

The efficiency of the handoff mechanisms can be evaluated from graph D of Fig. 9, that shows the traffic induced on remote links RL1 and RL2 by write-back. Notice that a large number of cache misses is generated after re-association since a new (empty) cache is instantiated on LS2.

7   Conclusions

In this tutorial we have presented two main results. First, we have demonstrated that remote virtual memory made accessible from mobile terminals by means of wireless network interface cards can be competitive, both in terms of power and performance, with respect to local virtual memory mapped on microdrives. Second, we have proposed a simple infrastructure that provides efficient support to network virtual memory for mobile terminals. We have shown that efficiency requires proximity and we have proposed a location-aware caching strategy to keep virtual memory pages local to the base station granting wireless network connectivity to the mobile terminal. A mobility management mechanism has been proposed to support service migration during handoff events.

The proposed strategies have been implemented in practice and tested on a working prototype. Experimental results demonstrate the feasibility of network virtual memory.

References

1. A. Acquaviva, E. Bontà, E. Lattanzi, "Dynamic Power Management Strategies Within the IEEE 802.11 Standard", *Formal Methods for Mobile Computing*, LNCS 3465, Bertinoro, Italy, April 2005.
2. A. Acquaviva, T. Simunic, V. Deolalikar, S. Roy, "Remote Power Control of Wireless Network Interfaces", *Proceedings of PATMOS*, Turin, Italy, Sept. 2003.
3. Agere, *802.11 Wireless Chip Set White Paper*, http://www.agere.com/client/docs/ multimode_white_paper.pdf, 2003.
4. A. Mishra, M. Shin, W. Arbaugh, "Context Caching Using Neighbor Graph for Fast Handoffs in a Wireless Network", *Technical Report CS-TR-4477 and UMIACS-TR-2003-46*, Dep. of CS, Univ. of Maryland, USA.
5. B. Gu, I. Chen, "Performance Analysis of Location-Aware Mobile Service Proxies for Reducing Network Cost in Personal Communication Systems", *ACM/Kluwer J. on Mob. Net. and Appl.s*, 2004.
6. Cisco System, *Cisco Aironet 350 Series Access Points*, http://www.cisco.com/ univercd/cc/td/doc/product/wireless/airo_350/accsspts/index.htm, 2003.
7. Cisco System, *Cisco Aironet 350 Series Wireless LAN Adapters*, http://www.cisco.com/univercd/cc/td/doc/product/wireless/airo_350/ 350cards/index.htm, 2003.
8. Compaq, *compact flash cards*, http://www.hp.com/products1/storage/ products/storagemedia/flash_cards/index.html, 2003.
9. D. Bovet, M. Cesati, "Understanding the Linux Kernel", *OReally & Associates*, Sebastopol, CA, Jan. 2001.

10. F. K. Al-Bia-Ali, P. Boddupalli, N. Davies, "An Inter-Access Point Handoff Mechanism for Wireless Network Management: The Sabino System", *Proc. of ICWN*, 2003.

11. G. Kuenning, G. J. Popek, "Automated Hoarding for Mobile Computing", *Proc. of Symposium on Operating System Principles*, pp. 264–275, Oct. 1997.

12. G. Kuenning, W. Ma, P. Reiher, G. J. Popek, "Simplifying Automated Hoarding Methods", *Proc. of MSWiM*, pp. 15–21, Sept. 2002.

13. H. Chang, C. Tait, N. Cohen, M. Shapiro, S. Mastrianni, R. Floyd, B. Housel, D. Lindquist, "Web Browsing in a Wireless Environment: Disconnected and Asynchronous Operation in ARTour Web Express", *Proc. of MCN*, 1997.

14. IBM,   *340MB   Microdrive   Hard   Drive*,   http://www.storage.ibm.com/hddredirect.html?/micro/index.html, 2003.

15. J. Hom, U. Kremer, "Energy Management of Virtual Memory on Diskless Devices", *Proceedings of COLP*, Barcelona, Spain, Sept. 2001.

16. LAN/MAN Standards Committee of the IEEE Computer Society. *Part 11: Wireless LAN MAC and PHY Specifications: Higher-Speed Physical Layer Extension in the 2.4 GHz Band*, IEEE, 1999.

17. M. D. Flouris, E. P. Markatos, "The Network RamDisk: Using Remote Memory on Heterogeneous NOWs", *Cluster Computing*, pp. 281-293, 1999, Baltzer Science Publishers.

18. M. Satyanarayanan, "The Evolution of Coda", *ACM TOCS*, Vol. 20, Issue 2, Pages: 85–124, May 2002.

19. P. T. Breuer, A. Marin Lopez, A. Garcia Ares, "The Network Block Device", *Linux Journal*, Issue 73, May 2000.

20. R. Ruggaber, J. Seitz, M. Knapp, "π^2 - a Generic Proxy Platform for Wireless Access and Mobility in CORBA", *Proc. of ACM PODC*, 2000.

21. S. Hadjiefthymiades, V. Matthaiou, L. Merakos, "Supporting the WWW in Wireless Communications Through Mobile Agents", *Kluwer J. on Mob. Net. and Appl.s*, 2002.

22. "Swapping via NFS for Linux," http://www.nfs-swap.dot-heine.de

23. T. Kunz, J. P. Black, "An Architecture for Adaptive Mobile Applications", *Proc. of ICWC*, 1999.

24. T. Newhall, S. Finney, K. Ganchev, M. Spiegel, "Nswap: A Network Swapping Module for Linux Clusters", *Proceedings of Euro-Par*, Klagenfurt, Austria, August 2003.

Hermes: Agent-Based Middleware for Mobile Computing*

Flavio Corradini and Emanuela Merelli

Università di Camerino, Dipartimento di Matematica e Informatica,
Camerino, 62032, Italy
{flavio.corradini, emanuela.merelli}@unicam.it

Abstract. Hermes is a middleware system for design and execution of
activity-based applications in distributed environments. It supports mobile computation as an application implementation strategy. While middleware for mobile computing has typically been developed to support
physical and logical mobility, Hermes provides an integrated environment where application domain experts can focus on designing activity
workflow and ignore the topological structure of the distributed environment. Generating mobile agents from a workflow specification is the
responsibility of a context-aware compiler.

Hermes is structured as a component-based, agent-oriented system
with a 3-layer software architecture. It can be configured for specific application domains by adding domain-specific component libraries. The
Hermes middleware layer, compilers, libraries, services and other developed tools together result in a very general programming environment,
which has been validated in two quite disparate application domains, one
in industrial control and the other in bioinformatics. In the industrial
control domain, embedded systems with scarce computational resources
control product lines. Mobile agents are used to trace products and support self-healing. In the bionformatics domain, mobile agents are used to
support data collection and service discovery, and to simulate biological
system through autonomous components interactions.

1 Introduction

Industrial production processes, the in-silico daily work of bio-scientists, and
many other jobs are usually performed by executing a set of distinct, sometimes repetitive, activities [54]. Automating such an application process in a
distributed environment requires coordination of these activities, but also lower
level implementation support in sharing of data, localization of reliable resources,
retrieval of suitable information, integration of heterogeneous tools, discovery

---

* This work was supported by the Fulbright grants, by the Center of Excellence for Re-
search "DEWS: Architectures and Design Methodologies for Embedded Controllers,
Wireless Interconnect and System-on-chip" and by Italian CIPE project "Sistemi
Cooperativi Multiagente".

M. Bernardo and A. Bogliolo (Eds.): SFM-Moby 2005, LNCS 3465, pp. 234–270, 2005.

and selection of the best available services, and mobility of computational units. The application designer, whose primary expertise is in the application domain, should be free to focus on coordinating domain activities rather than being concerned with the distributed computational environment.

In the domain of production processes control, for example, supply chain management [33] has been developed mainly with workflow-oriented technology for networks of fixed distributed systems. The present need to trace products[1] and to extend the chain with customers (e.g. domestic appliances, items of clothing, food), requires flexible workflow management systems encompassing embedded systems and mobile devices (e.g. PDAs for technical assistance), and supporting code mobility (e.g. for traceability and self-healing) [41, 52].

In the bioinformatics domain, a flexible workflow management system could be used to carry out many activities whose execution environment is the Web, which is distributed and dynamic in nature, with large amounts of highly dynamic data and proliferation of (often redundant) tools. In fact, many bio-scientists aspire to automate some of the time-consuming activities to the base of wet-lab procedures, as browsing, searching and selecting resources [37, 50] so as to use flexible and expandable computational analysis and simulation tools during their in-vitro exeperiments. Advantages of moving computational "bio-instruments" over data, by delegating a mobile agent, include decentralizing execution of local activities, avoiding the warehousing of highly dynamic data, reducing network traffic, and freeing researchers from network faults and from the need to be continuously connected to a laptop. Mobile devices could also support a bio-scientist moving among different laboratories during his experiment.

Experience with these two, quite different domains suggests that applicability of Hermes-like systems is quite wide, and that many other application domains could take advantage of flexible, modular, expandable, easily configurable and scalable middleware which supports workflow management and uses mobile computation as activity implementation strategy.

Middleware technology is an emerging and promising technology that provides application designers with a high level of abstraction, hiding the complexity introduced by distribution (Figure 1)[57]. Middleware for mobile computing, in particular, is becoming a widespread technology [51, 38]. Mobile computing systems, in the sense of computing systems that can be easily moved physically and whose computing capability may be used while they are being moved, have been empowered by the diffusion of satellites and cellular technology[3].

The wide range of different developers of mobile devices has led to development of many different middleware systems, which differ in the type of computational loading (heavyweight, lightweight) of the mobile unit, the type of communication paradigm (synchronous, asynchronous) used among distributed units, and the type of context representation (transparency, awareness) provided to the mobile application. In general, a mobile system can be characterized by mobile

---

[1] European Community Directive 2001/18/EC.

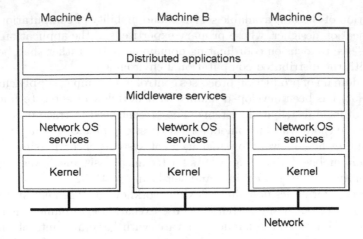

Fig. 1. A Distributed System organized as middleware [57]

device executing on a light computational load, by a intermittent connection with asynchronous communication, and by a dynamic context with awareness of resource distribution. Mascolo et al [38] provide a comprehensive survey of mobile computing middleware; B'Far [3] gives an overview of principles of mobile computing. Further distinction can be found between middleware systems developed only to support physical mobility (which are traditionally application-centred [51]) and more general middleware systems [43, 45, 31, 32] developed especially to support the coordination of mobile components, most of which are based on *tuple spaces* of the Linda model [28] to support decoupled communication.

In this work, we exploit mobile agents as computational units that logically move to support execution of a distributed application. Consistent with B'Far [3] we see mobile agent particularly suitable for the following reasons:

1. *mobile agents are inherently active because of their autonomous nature,*
2. *mobile agents use less network bandwidth in comparison to RPC or RMI,*
3. *mobile agents can display better response times owing to reduced effect of network latency on the application,*
4. *mobile agents are inherently heterogeneous,*
5. *mobile agents are autonomous and asynchronous and so can deal with intermittent network connectivity gracefully,*
6. *mobile agents can adapt extremely well.*

Providing an application designer with a transparent global view of the distributed environment, with a user-friendly programming environment and executing distributed applications exploiting mobile computation, through a light and flexible mobile middleware, is the aim of Hermes[2]. Hermes is a component-

---

[2] In Greek mythology, Hermes is the son of Zeus and Maia. He is also known as Mercury to the Romans. Hermes is Zeus's messenger, the fastest of the gods, recognizable by his winged sandals.

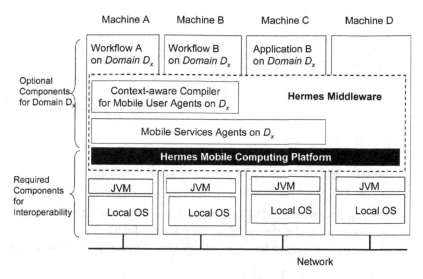

Fig. 2. A Distributed System over Hermes Middleware in heterogeneous environment. Only the Hermes mobile platform (dark layer) is required for interoperability, but additional components can be added to support workflow

based, agent-oriented system with a 3-layer software architecture [9, 15]: *user layer, system layer* and *run-time layer*. At the user layer, it allows designers to specify their applications as a workflow of activities using the graphical notation provided by JaWE editor [21]. At the system layer, it provides a context-aware compiler to generate a pool of user mobile agents from the workflow specification. At the run-time layer, it supports the activation of a set of specialized *service* agents, and it provides all necessary to support agent mobility.

One of the main features of Hermes middleware is its scalability. The present version, HermesV2 [29], is a pure Java application whose kernel requires about 80KB of memory and interoperates across a systems ranging from microprocessors to very power workstations (Figure 2). The lightness of its core is based on the unique class *Agent*, which assigns the basic features to each agent, including mobility. *Agent* is an abstract class, with two associated extensions *UserAgent* and *ServiceAgent* (Figure 3).

The main difference between run-time layer and system layer is how agents function in each. *ServiceAgents* in the run-time layer are localized to one platform to interface with the local execution environment. *UserAgents* in the system layer are workflow executors, created for a specific goal that, in theory, can be reached in a finite time by interacting with other agents, afterwards the agent die. Furthermore, for security *UserAgents* can access a local resource only by interacting with a *ServiceAgent* that is the "guard" of the resource (Figure 4).

We can summarize that Hermes uses activity-based workflow modelling, as an high-level programming language. It uses agent-based modelling as an intermediate programming language, and it uses mobile computing as run-time

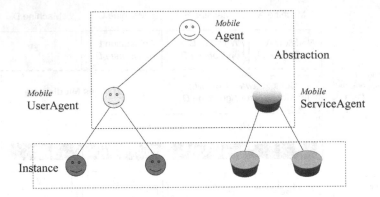

Fig. 3. Hermes agents hierarchy. The Java class "Agent" is extended with "UserAgent" which is the prototype of the the workflow executor, and with *ServiceAgent* used to interface local resources. Only *ServiceAgent* can invoke operating system functions

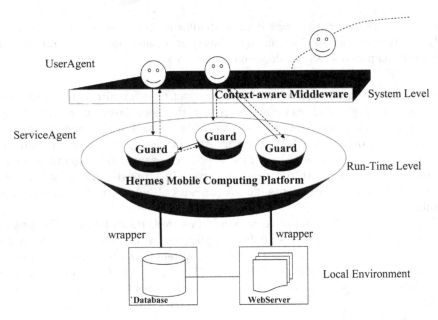

Fig. 4. Access Control in Hermes Middleware is based on different access rights given to two "Agent" extension. The instances of *ServiceAgent* act first as a barrier towards the local resources then once the a *UserAgent* has been identified as an interface

support of the execution of mobile agent systems generated with respect to the functional and non-functional requirements of the distributed application.

We have also developed a set of tools particularly meaningful for an effective implementation of Hermes middleware. Among these a generalize wrapper [4] to support the extraction and the integration of heterogeneous resources, an interface to dynamically access Web Services [60], an ontology manager which supports the mapping among different resource schemas [18] and a matchmaker to discover and select services [14]. Furthermore, we have defined a mapping from UML Activity Diagram and CSP-like process algebra to allow the analysis and verification of the behaviour of the workflow designed by the user [1].

We are also working on a graphical notation to represent the mobility and execution environment of a pool of agents, its mapping to Klaim, i.e. a process calculus for mobile computing [19]. We would like to use Klaim language and Klava, i.e. the implementation of Klaim in Java, into Hermes compiler to implement agent level workflow.

Recently, Hermes has been used as simulation programming environment in systems biology [17]. We have modelled and implemented a system to simulate carbohydrate oxidation of a biological cell. The course-grain approach allowed us to identify the autonomous computational units of the software system in those cellular elements that exhibit the behavior of a computational environment (cytoplasm, mythocondrial matrix, etc.). While all elements are agents whose activities were implemented for the case study, in future we aim to map the abstract machines for systems biology provided by Luca Cardelli [10] to Klaim within Hermes architecture. The agent mobility will characterize the real movement of cellular components within and through the cellular environments (compartments and membranes).

In the remainder of this tutorial, in Section 2 we set the context in which the Hermes middleware has been developed. In Section 3 we outline some of the formalism, techniques and systems have been chosen to bear the design of the global computing environment and we draw reader attention to Hermes software architecture. Next, in Section 4 we propose some application examples taken from our experience in designing and implementing applications within specific application domains. Finally, in Section 5 we discuss future work and conclude.

2   Setting the Context

Distributed Environment *DE*

The distributed environment (*DE*) for mobile computing we refer to consists of collection of autonomous and mobile computational units interconnected by a communication media. It can be distributed over a wide area network (as in the bioinformatics case study), over a local area network (as in the production plant) or it can be a simulation of a distributed system (the systems biology example).

The first *DE* we consider is the Web. It is characterized by dynamic execution context, intermittent connection, unpredictable congestion, faulty communication, presence of security barriers, and heterogeneous, distributed and unstable resources. The second *DE* is characterized by permanent network connection, but it still deals with the management of heterogeneous resources. The last *DE* is a virtual distribution. All the mobile computation can happen within a single machine, or among homogeneous machines or heterogeneous ones (e.g. grid computing). They vary in the way they hide and manage problems deriving from the execution environment.

In our context, there are two different logical mobile computational units: at the system level, there are flexible, autonomous, pro-active[3] units, situated in a dynamic, sometimes open, unpredictable computational environment. We call them *UserAgents*; they are created in a specific computational environment to solve problems in a certain application domain, they are coordinated by a suitable communicate model, they can move to reach a different computational environment to better fulfil the goal for which they have been created. At the run time level, there are autonomous mobile units with the special task to manage local and networks resources. We call them *ServiceAgents*, they are units created any time a new resource becomes available in the distributed environment.

Distributed Applications *DA*

A distributed application (*DA*) consists of a set of coordinated activities that use distributed resources. Workflow models are useful notations of coordination to link these activities together. If we consider a workflow as a distributed program and a workflow management (WMS) as its run-time support, the functionality provided by a WMS is similar to that offered by a middleware system in a distributed environment.

Workflow models are supported by a number of systems for business process automation and process control, but typically the model is fixed and hard-wired in the application, or configurable only through a very heavyweight customization process. In contrast, our approach makes specifying, modifying, and executing workflow a very lightweight. In the bioscience domain, for example, it is practical to develop workflow support for the varied idiosyncratic processes of individual scientists, and so free the bioscientist from from repetitive interactions with the execution environment. To the extent that workflow specifications are shared, it is also possible to incrementally support standardization of protocols and creation of a transparent analysis environment.

Workflow is specified abstractly in a graphical notation and mapped to a set of autonomous computational units (*UserAgents*) interacting through a communication medium. The mapping is achieved by a compiler that is aware not only of the contents of a library of implemented user activities but also the software and hardware environment for executing them. In our case, information available to the compiler includes available hosts and their connection topology, available services (*ServiceAgents*), the kinds of information available at different locations, and additional domain-dependent parameters. Application-independent rules for dealing with connectivity failure, service access failures, etc., are embedded in *UserAgents* and *ServiceAgents*. A user specifying workflow need not be concerned with where to search for information, in what form the information is stored, the

---

[3] For proactive, we mean controlling a situation by causing something to happen rather than waiting to respond to it after it happens.

protocols for interacting with each service, or a host of other low-level details that can be left to the context-aware compiler.

Mobile Computing

In the above described scenario, we said that user activities are mapped into system activities, by *UserAgents*. The pool of agents must coordinate to execute user level workflow, possibly by migrating from one environment to another and coping with any of the unpredictable phenomena due to distribution. The agent mobility is supported by a light platform that characterizes the middleware.

This approach to exploiting mobile computing during the development leads to the definition of a (new methodology) to guide software development, from analysis and specification, design and validation, coding and testing, deployment and maintenance. In particular, the *analysis phase* imposes the choice of application domain (e.g. bioinformatics), identification of common user activities (e.g. sequence similarity search, functional motif search, protein analysis, etc. [54]).

Next, the *design phase* concerns specification of workflow of activities and its validation by suitable tools [1]. The *coding phase* is linked to the engineering of the layer below.

At the *system layer*, the main component is the context-aware compiler, whose engineering depends on both the application domain and the execution environment requirements. The *design phase* of the compiler relies in a two steps: step 1: the *User Level Workflow* (ULW) (Figure 6) is mapped to *Agent Level Workflow* (ALW); step 2: the ALW is coded in a pool of mobile *Workflow Executors* (WEs) the *UserAgents*. The generation of a ALW also implies the choice of suitable coordination model, i.e the communication media used among agents. Also this choice is conditioned by the application domain features. The first step will generate a specification of agent level workflow whose validity must be checked. Thus, tools different from those in the upper layer will be required since the mobility is also included [42, 11, 19]. Then, the *coding phase* is linked to the engineering of the layer below as well.

Implementation of system activities is based on the services offered by the *run-time layer*, including both those belonging to the kernel and those offered by the execution environment of the application domain. In the *run-time layer* the use of mobility is tied to the physical distribution of resources. In the layered architecture, mobility can play a twofold role. At *user* agent abstract levels it fulfills a modelling function while at *service* agent level it fulfills a reliability function.

In the Section 4, we describe two applications developed for two different application domains: functional testing and self healing in domestic appliance manufacturing [8]; medical bioinformatics [2, 39, 4, 5, 40] and systems biology [17]. We outline how mobility covers different and distinct aspects of the implementation in each of these domains and finally we describe a set of services and tools we have developed for Hermes.

In the next section, first we describe the functionalities of Hermes 3-layer architecture, then we describe a methodology to develop the Hermes mobile platform for an given application domain.

3   The Hermes Software Architecture

We now describe the general software architecture of Hermes, a middleware system for the design and development of distributed applications upon a mobile computing platform. This architecture has been successfully used to design an agent-based tool integration system [16]. The architecture consists of three conceptual layers as shown in Figure 5.

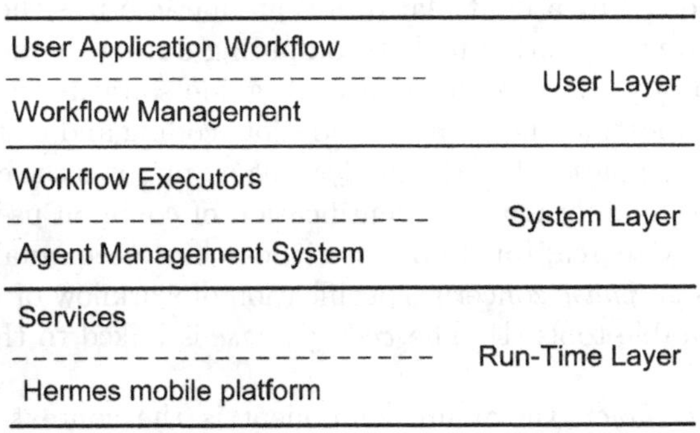

User Application Workflow	
------------------------	User Layer
Workflow Management	
Workflow Executors	
------------------------	System Layer
Agent Management System	
Services	
------------------------	Run-Time Layer
Hermes mobile platform	

Fig. 5. The 3-layer Software Architecture for Hermes Middleware. The *User Layer* provides the editing workflow environment, the *System Layer* generate a mobile agent system to support the execution of the workflow and the *Run-Time Layer* provides all necessary to interact and move along the distributed environment

A *User Layer*, on the top of the architecture, where the user specifies his application as a workflow of activities with the features described above. Since our potential users may not be computer practitioners, the specification language must be simple and intuitive to use as, in most cases, graphical notations are.

A *System Layer*, on the middle of the architecture, provides the needed environment to map a user-level workflow into a set of primitive (and already implemented) activities. The execution of these latter is coordinated by suitable model, they implement the activities at the user level and embed implementation details abstracted from the execution environment (fault tolerance, for instance). These primitive activities are implemented by autonomous software entities *UserAgent* able to react to the environment changes where they are executed. The agent-based paradigm and technology, as argued several times in the literature (see, for instance [34], and references therein), seem to be particularly suitable for designing environments populated by entities that communicate and coordinate their activities (as most of the applications of our interest are). A particular significant ingredient at this layer is the compiler that maps user level activities into system level activities. The compiler must be aware of the available a library of implemented activities but more significantly it must be aware of the environment (software/hardware resources, knowledge, services...).

A *Run-Time Layer*, at the bottom of the architecture, provides primitives and services essential for agent mobility and resources access. The kernel is the platform for mobile computing which provides primitives for discovery, mobility, communication, and security.

As the Figure 5 shows, the three layers, User Layer, System Layer and Run-time Layer, are themselves split in two conceptual levels: - the type of application running on each layer and - the infrastructure supporting the application. At the user layer, the application is the workflow and the infrastructure is the workflow management environment (editor, model checker, ...). At the system layer, the application is a pool of running agents *UserAgents* named *Workflow Executors* (WEs), and the infrastructure is given by the agent management system (compiler, model checker, query optimizer, ...). Finally, at the run-time layer, the application is given by a set of services *ServiceAgents* and the infrastructure consists of the mobile computing platform for agents mobility.

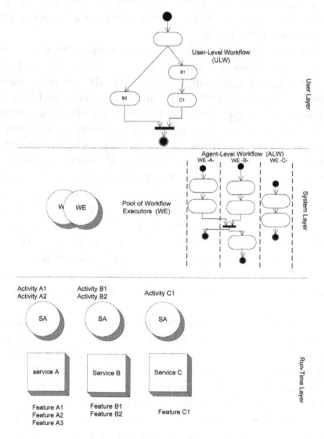

Fig. 6. Entities located at each Layer of Hermes Architecture. Any user level workflow (ULW) is mapped into an agent-level workflow (ALW) and compiled to a pool of mobile user agents, the workflow executors (WE) which interact with the service agents (SA)

The Figure 6, moreover, presents the same architecture with the entities created at each level of abstractions: the user defines a *User-Level Workflow* (ULW) specification that is mapped to an *Agent-Level Workflow* (ALW) specification; the ALW specification is then used to generate a pool of *Workflow Executors* (WEs) implementing all specified activities; WEs interact with distributed environment through through *serviceAgents*s (SA).

3.1   Hermes Layers Functionalities

It follows a detailed description of the main components and functionalities of each layer.

User Layer

The *user layer* is based on workflows and provides to users a set of programs for interacting with the wokflow management system. There are two main families of programs: programs for specifying, managing and reusing existing workflow specifications, and programs enabling administration and direct interaction with the workflow management system.

The *workflow editor* is the program that supports the workflows specification by composing activities in a graphical environment. The editor enables the specification of workflows complying with the WfMC reference model [30] and is implemented by using the JaWE [21] editor. Activities used in a workflow are configured by specifying input parameters and their effects are recognizable as modification of state variables or modification on the environment's status. The workflow editor enables the composition of both primitive and complex activities. A primitive activity is an activity that can be directly executed. A complex activity is an activity that must be specified before it can be used; the specification of a complex activity is a workflow of complex and simple activities. By using complex activities the specification of workflows is simplified because they enhance both hierarchical specification and reuse: we can use an already existing complex activity without caring of its specification. Users can use complex activities and stored workflows to increase productivity when specifying new workflows. Moreover, large libraries of both domain specific primitives and complex activities can be loaded to specialize the editor for a specific application domain.

Each activity can be configured with four parameters: the input data format, the output data format, the environment and its *description*. The *input data format* specifies which is the accepted input for a given activity. In similar way, the *output data format* specifies the accepted output data formats. The *environment* parameter is used to specify in which context an activity must be performed, since the same activity with the same parameters can be performed in different contexts. The environment is separated from the other input parameters because it can cause either the migration of a code or the selection of a specific implementation of the activity, while input parameters denote only data transferring. For example, consider an activity associated to the use of a specific tool implementation available in a given repository, it implies the deployment of tool on a remote site and the activation of the tool. In a similar way, consider an activity to search a given information on a given database, the activity is always the same, but its implementation is very different with respect to the target database, i.e., different authentication method, different querying interface and different naming, hence the information on the target database is used to select the proper implementation of the activity. Finally, the activity description is used either when it is not possible to achieve transparency or when the user prefers to decide by himself where and how to execute a certain activity.

System Layer

The system layer hosts WEs which are *UserAgents* generated from the ULW specification. WEs execute and coordinate their actions to reach the fulfilment of the ULW specification. Some of the actions executed by WEs need interaction with the services (SAs); these actions correspond to operations that must be completed by interacting with a remote service.

In the case the distributed execution environment is open, the communication between agents takes place once the negotiation of communication protocol (the ontology) is successfully accomplished. By fixing an ontology, the agreement on the semantics is guaranteed, but information that can be exchanged is constrained; in fact agents can use only concepts defined in the ontology. In the case the system has defined a shared common ontology, the ontology negotiation procedure always successes.

Now we described the two phases agent generation procedure that is performed by the compiler. In the phase 1) the ULW is mapped to an ALW, and in the phase 2) the ALW is used to generate WEs. The ALW is a specification similar to the ULW, but it takes into account the existence of the agents that will execute the actions and it contains only primitive actions (actions that can be directly executed without decomposing them in workflows). Since the compiler is under development we can not provides implementation details, but only its main functionalities.

Phase 1: Mapping the ULW to the ALW The mapping from the ULW to the ALW is performed by recursively substituting activities of the user-level specification with a workflow of primitive agent-level activities. This mapping is performed by accessing to the User-Level Activity Database (ULAD) that maintains the correspondence between user-level activities and ALW. There are other rules managing technicalities of the transformation process, for example branching of the execution is translated to an agent creation activity and a join of two branches are translated to a coordination activity between multiple agents. Moreover, in the case the compiler recognizes a set of independent activities, it can distribute them among several agents to increase parallelism. The set of activities assigned to the same agent constitutes its body, therefore the result of this mapping consists on a set of workflows: one for each agent. Activities belonging to an ALW specify actions at a low-level of abstractions that can be directly executed. Messages are sent from an agent to another by using communication activities, i.e., an activity whose execution consists on sending a message to the receiver. Actually communication consists of sending and receiving single messages, in the future we want to extend this approach to definition of protocols that must be respected during inter-agent communication.

The ALW specifies all entities involved in the execution of a workflow, thus the constraint of spatial and temporal coupling communication can be respected since the compiler knows exactly when communication takes place and which are both receivers and senders.

The compiler can optimize the ALW by applying heuristics based on parameters issued to the compiler, e.g., the compiler can try to minimize the consumed bandwidth, minimize number of generated agents, minimize number of generated messages, maximize parallel execution of activities, and check for deadlock freeness. In addition to general purpose analysis, the compiler can check specific properties on the ALW, such as verifying that the shipping procedure of a specific item begins only after the purchase is completed. Actual prototype of the compiler implements part of these features.

Phase 2: Mapping the ALW to WEs In the second step, the compiler concretely generates agents from the ALW specification. To achieve this result, the compiler uses the User-level Activity Implementation Database (ULAID) and the Database of Skeletons (DoS). The ULAID stores the implementation of the agent-level activities and the DoS stores "empty" implementation of agents (the skeletons).

A skeleton is a role-specific implementation of an agent that does not contain any behaviour, e.g., a skeleton of a traveller agent can be a lightweight implementation of an agent limiting bandwidth consumption. Particular system properties can be obtained by proper choice of skeletons, e.g., limited bandwidth consumption. The concrete WE is obtained by plugging the specified behaviour into the skeleton. In particular, the compiler behaves following these steps:

- A complex behavior CB is generated by composing as specified in the ALW the implementation of each activity contained in the ULAID.
- The compiler analyzes the CB and derives all state variables that will be necessary to complete its execution.
- A state entity SE is generated by aggregating all state variables
- A proper skeleton is selected from the DoS. The WE is created by plugging both the complex behaviour CB and state entity SE in the selected skeleton.
- The previous steps are repeated for all WEs that must be created.
- Finally, execution starts.

Actually, we are implementing the WE generation procedure by using an implementation of the skeletons that dynamically load the compiled complex behavior and the state variables at start-up by dynamic binding. Instead of generating compiled WEs, it is possible to use skeletons behaving as interpreters of ALW specifications. In such case, the WE is obtained by associating the skeleton to the ALW specification. WEs of the former type are small, i.e., WEs contain only the code for the execution of the activities, and fast, i.e., instructions can be directly executed; while WEs of the latter type are large, i.e., they implement a complete interpreter, and slower i.e., instructions must be interpreted, but they exploit the ability to dynamically modify their behavior at run-time. The organization of our system enables the use of both type of agents. Actually, we are implementing the compiler producing compiled agents, but we plan also to investigate interpretation and dynamic adaptability.

Run-Time Layer

As already described, the overall structure of the system is very complex, it supports abstract specifications that are mapped into a complex distributed and coordinated flows of activities over a large-scale distributed system. In order to master this complexity, and support the transparency of the computing distribution by using mobile computation, the run time system provides a set of active services *ServiceAgent*s to allow a secure resources access and a mobile platform to support the agent mobility. The agent mobility is performed through mobile code environment that besides mobile code, supports also security, fault-tolerance, communication, and resource management and discovery.

More in detail, *ServiceAgent*s provide access to services. When a *UserAgent* migrates and arrives in a different platform, it can query the *YellowPageService* to gain information about services offered in the platform and then it communicates with *ServiceAgent*s to gain the information it needs. This paradigm simplifies the interactions enabling the use of an agent communication language, e.g. KQML [23] or Fipa ACL [25], as a unified way to communicate with other agents, services or resources.

A detail description of the Run-Time Layer components is given in the next section.

3.2   Hermes Mobile Middleware and Its Engineering

We now describe a practical approach in developing of a modular and reusable agent-based middleware, in particular the Run-Time support of Hermes software architecture. We show the flexibility of Hermes middleware and how the followed component-based approach supports the reusability of existing artefact during the development of a middleware system for a specific application domain. As we already highlighted in the previous sections, agent-based systems are complexes [34], the development involving distribution, mobility, communication and security problems. The adoption of layered software architecture allows to master this complexity and enhances security because the interactions occurring among different layers can be monitored and filtered. In order to give flexibility to the Hermes middleware, we decided to adopt a layers plus components strategy, in fact each layer is designed as an aggregation of components.

We think that this point of view is a natural and effective approach to middleware construction and, more generally, to the development of complex systems. In the following paragraphs we give some hints of design of the Hermes kernel the detailed description can be found in [9]. We have chosen UML as architec-

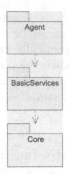

Fig. 7. 3-Layered Architecture of Hermes Mobile Computing Platform. The core supports identification, communication, loading and security; BasicServices supports discovery, mobility, creation, communication and security; Agent supports *User* agents and *Service* agents

ture description language because is widely accepted in both the academic and industrial worlds as a reference language for system design.

The Hermes kernel can be described by three components, placed in a 3-layered software architecture as shown in Figure 7. Notice that this software architecture is different from that shown in Figure 5 because this last one highlights the hierarchical dependencies among system software components, for example the *agent* component in Figure 5 is unique while in Figure 6 has two distinct functional roles of *UserAgent* and *ServiceAgent*.

The *Core layer* role is similar to the kernel of an operating system, it implements the basic features of a mobile code platform, such as communication protocols, code traceability and security. The *Core layer* is essentially free of any system strategy.

The *BasicServices layer* extends the *core* features by providing services that directly support the agents activities, e.g., agent mobility and agent communication implemented on top of inter-platform communication. The *BasicServices layer* contains system strategies, but does not implement any feature of the application domain.

The *Agent layer* is the container of all service agent and user agents of the application domain. The *BasicServices layer* is always present in any place, so that minimum support to agent execution is guaranteed.

Core Layer. The *Core* layer is the lowest layer of the architecture (Figure 8) and contains base functions of the system, such as the implementation of the inter-platform communication protocols and agent management functions. This layer is composed of four components: *ID*, *SendReceive*, *Starter* and *Security*.

To give an idea of how the design phase has been made we describe the components belonging to the Core Layer.

The ID component implements general identity management functions by managing a repository containing information about locally generated agents

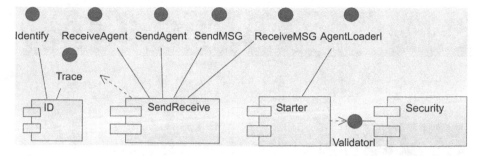

Fig. 8. The Core Layer. It supports identification, communication, loading and security

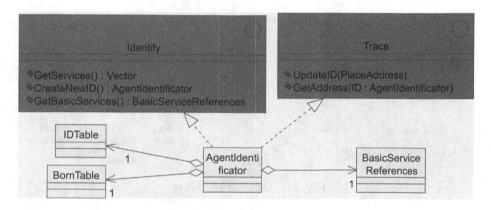

Fig. 9. ID Component

(Figure 9). This repository is accessed whenever we want to know the current position of an agent.

The *ID* component is also responsible for the creation of the identifiers to be associated to new agents. These identifiers contain information about the birthplace, date and time of the agent's creation. Agent localization is simplified by information contained directly in the "ID", such as the birth place. In fact, the birth place of an agent hosts information about the agent's current location.

A second important feature of the *Core* is the *SendReceive* component (Figure 10). This component implements low level inter-platform communication by sending and receiving messages and agents. By using the traceability services offered by the *ID* component, *SendReceive* can easily update or retrieve the exact position of a specific *user agent*.

It is important to note that every change in the communication protocol is concealed within the *BasicService layer*. The *SendReceive* component can also send and receive agent instances. This feature is reused by the upper layer to implement agent migration.

The *Starter* component processes any request for agent creation. This particular component, in fact, takes an inactive agent (just created or migrated), and checks it for the absence of malicious or manipulated code. These agents, before

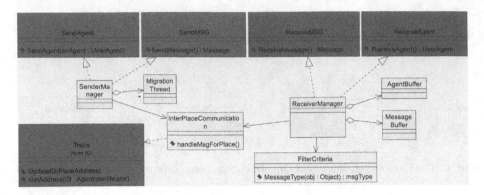

Fig. 10. SendReceive Component

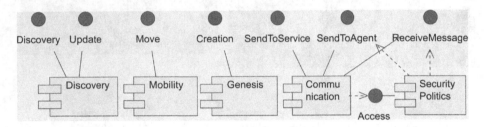

Fig. 11. BasicServices Layer

activation, are dynamically linked to all basic services of the platform. During execution the agent is isolated from the *Core layer* by the *Basic Service layer*.

The *Security* component, as mentioned above, checks for the presence of malicious code or manipulations within the agent code.

Note that at this abstraction level permissions are not an issue. The code inspection concerns only dangerous agents that attempt to perform illegal operations, such as viruses.

The BasicService Layer. *BasicServices layer* (Figure 11) has five main components: *Discovery, Mobility, Genesis, Communication* and *Security Politics*.

The *Discovery* component searches and detects service agents. When a user agent wants to communicate with a service, it will ask the *Discovery* for the right identifier to use as the message's receiver. The service detection strategy can be implemented in different ways; for example by a fixed taxonomy or by an UDDI [6], commonly used in the Web Services application domain.

The *Mobility* component enables the movement of code across platforms [27], it implements the interface used by the *UserAgent* and it accesses to components of the *Core layer* to send, receive and load agents. It is important to note that real communication between different locations can be achieved only through *Core*'s *SendReceive* component, and then migration is independent of the type of used transport. *Mobility* consists on copy the agent i.e. its code and its current state and send it to the destination platform where it will be re-started in a specific point (weak mobility). The local agent is destroyed.

The *Communication* component makes possible to send and receive agent-directed messages both in an intra- and inter-platform context. Intra-platform messages are messages sent between agents and services residing in the same platform. Inter-platform messages are messages sent to agents residing in different platforms (our system does not allow for remote communication between user agents and service agents).

The agent requesting the dispatch of a message does not need to know, effectively, where the target agent is; in fact, the ID is sufficient to post correctly a message. The *Communication* component uses one of the *Security Policy*'s interfaces to ascertain whether the specific *UserAgent* or *ServiceAgent* has the right privileges for communication, if an *Agent* is not authorized to use a service, the message is destroyed.

Before accessing resources and services, an agent must authenticate itself. The identification is performed by sending a login message to a specific *ServiceAgent*, as consequence the *SecurityPolitics* component jointly with the *Communication* component intercept the message and unlock the communication. The *SecurityPolitics* component centralizes control of permissions, protects services and resources from the user agents, and provides the administrator with an easy way to manage all permissions.

The last component of the service layer is the *Genesis* component that enables agent creation. A special case of agent creation is cloning that is performed when it is necessary to create a copy of an existing agent. The two copies differ only for the agent identifier.

A special case of agent creation is cloning that is performed when it is necessary to create a copy of an existing agent. The two copies differ only for the agent identifier.

The Agent Layer. The upper layer of the mobile platform, the *Agent Layer*, contains all service and user agents. This layer implements features of the agent-based workflows management system as described in Section 3.1.

This component has not any interface, but is has only several dependencies upon the *BasicService layer*. The *Agent* component contains a general abstract agent class and two inherited classes. *ServiceAgent* consists of agents enabling access to biological databases or providing algorithm. *UserAgent* represents agents created by biologists. User agents execute complex tasks and implement part of the logic of the application.

The HermesV2 Java implementation, has been completely designed and developed following this approach [29]. The middleware we have implemented is separated into several functional units (components) with mutual dependencies explicitly documented by UML diagrams.

We would like to mention that such an approach, based on layers and components, supports the generation of middleware for different domains as shown in [9].

3.3   Main Services and Tools for Hermes

In this section we describe some aspects, that have been significant for the implementation of Hermes middleware. The programming environment offered by Hermes consists of several tools both for design and execution of distributed applications. Some tools turn into *Agent* services, e.g. those that support resources access, resource localization, resource selection, schema mapping, etc. some others remain tools usable during workflows design, analysis, verification phases. Among *Service* agents we mention:

AIXO: XML Generalized Wrapper

AIXO is a tool developed to present any data source as a collection of XML documents. AIXO is flexible and modular, it allows to manage many input data sources ranging from HTML to XML, databases, flat file, CGI and command line programs. AIXO has been experimentally used on different resources in different contexts and successfully integrated as *wrapper service agent* in Hermes [4].

The AIXO architecture is not for a specific resource or data type; rather, it is general and suitable for a wide range of resources. An AIXO *Service* agent implementation offers a wrapper that provides an "XML view of the resource". The AIXO architecture, shown in Figure 12, is composed of three main packages: *ResourceAccess*, *ResourceToXML*, *XSLTProcessor*.

ResourceAccess manages access to the resource to be wrapped. Its implementation depends upon the communication protocol, permissions, and access policies. By using the *ResourceAccess*'s interface, data can be gathered from the resource in its native format; there is no transformation. For example, in

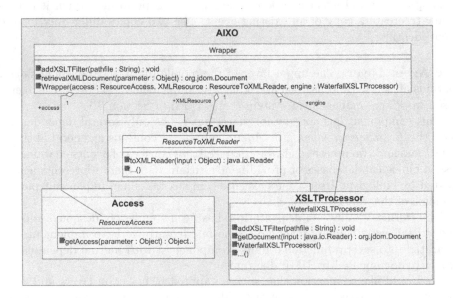

Fig. 12. AIXO architecture

the case of a Relational DataBases (RDB), the data obtained is contained in a "recordset".

ResourceToXML transforms data, provided by the *ResourceAccess* module, into XML. The transformation is *canonical* and independent of the data's semantics. Mapping from the original format to XML is performed considering only the data's structure. For example, in transforming a recordset to XML, the output conforms exactly to the schema of the table; in the case of a flat file, the transformation will derive its structure taking into account special characters such as tabular and white spaces. For an HTML text, the transformation extracts the document schema from the tags.

Finally, the *XSLTProcessor* applies a set of XSLT filters to the raw XML, provided by the *ResourceToXML*, to obtain the effective XML view of the resource. In this phase, the semantics of data plays an important role.

To create a concrete wrapper the *ResourceAccess* and *ResourceToXML* Java classes must be implemented and the *XSLTProcessor* must be configured using the appropriate set of XSL Transformations. Each wrapper is defined by an XML configuration file. The system automatically loads classes and initializes attributes. AIXO has been experimentally proven on different resources in different contexts [4].

AIXO *Service* agent can interact with OMSE (ontology management *Service* agent), below described, to dynamically find the mapping among resources schemas. An example of AIXO at work is given in Section 4.

WS²A: A Web Service *Service* Agent

WS²A is a Web Service *Service* Agent, a tool developed to access Web Services and to derive at run-time the resources access methods [60]. Briefly a Web Service is an interface which describes a set of service access methods usable through the network via XML messages. The interface hide any service implementation details.

This tool is successfully used during the research and selection process of a service that a MAS (matchmaker *Service* agent) supports. WS²A is characterized by a peculiar communication among agents which allow to manipulate unknown objects at run-time. In particular, data exchanged among agents do not use messages but objects and by using JAVA reflection technique we support the manipulation of unknown data.

MSA: Matchmaker Service Agent

Service discovery is the process of localizing resources and services available in large scale open and distributed systems. In a distributed and redundant system as the Web, it is necessary, beside localizing services, to filter them in order to obtain those which are best for the activities for which they have been requested. By the term *matchmaker* we mean a software entity, a *service* agent, which monitors services availability, maintains an updated file of all useful information for using services and possibly ensures a quality choice of them. We have developed a matchmaker and defined a *quality model* based on parameters that

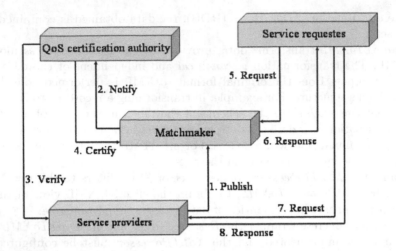

Fig. 13. Matchmaker Service Agent. Any gray box represent an agent active in the distributed environment

ensure the best choice of a service for a specific application domain. The communication protocol among matchmaker and other agents is given in Figure 13. A full description of the tool is provided in [14]. The quality model consists of two components, the first describes general quality aspects of the distributed computational environment where the service is offered, we have considered the Web, and the other includes quality features of the application domain. Any resources must fulfil the following requirements:

- *Aim*: the purpose for which the resource has been developed;
- *User target*: the list of hypothetical users;
- *Reliability*: the probability of successfully using a resource;
- *Feasibility*: the measurement of the easiness to access the resource;
- *Usability*: the measurement of the easiness to use the resource;
- *Originality*: the degree of correctness of the resource and its information;
- *Privacy*: the legal conditions of using the resource;
- *Updating*: the attendance of the resource updating;
- *Uptiming*: the maximum length of time between two resource failures;
- *Timing*: the daily time of resource activity;
- *Speedy*: the measurement of the execution time;
- *Browsing*: the measurement of the human easiness to find a resource;
- *Popularity*: the number of active consumers;

Each quality aspect above defined is quantitative measured on the basis of several parameters whose description if given in [49, 22]. The domain-dependent quality aspects is provided in section 4.

OMSA: Ontology Management *ServiAgent* Agent

The availability of automatic tools for quickly determining semantic similarity among concepts across different ontologies is useful during the processes of data retrieval and data integration, in Hermes performed by AIXO. We have developed a tool which supports the ontology management to support the mapping between domain ontology and local schema used to defines data repositories. To that purpose we have defined a similarity algorithm to compare two ontologies. The main idea is, supposing to have, in each execution environment, a shared global ontology and a local ontology, the algorithm determines similar concepts (i.e., data types, formats and terms) by computing the number of identical relationships among two concepts of different ontologies and recursively to all their derived concepts as well. The algorithm is considered an instrument that any mobile *service* agent can use to compare two ontologies, usually the application domain ontology shared at user level and that derived from the local resources schema. The detailed description of the similarity algoritm is given in [18] while an example of how the tool can be used is provided in Section 4.

LightTS-SA: lightTS *Service* agent

lightTS-SA is a *Service* agent developed to support a coordination agents via tuple space. lightTS [48] is a Java package which provides a lightweight tuple space implementation. Light because lighTS does not support the persistence, security and remote access, features that can be provided by the run-time support. We have used this service especially to coordinate agents that move in place where they do not know how to contact local services, but they can interact with lightTS service agent which comes between the requester and the provider of a service.

WISA: Web Interface *Service* Agent

WISA is a *Service* agent realised to support the expert programmer whose want to directly interact with Hermes at system layer. This *Service* agent has been designed to support some operations which characterize a user session: manage your personal account, create an agent, send an agent, get the output of the execution. To generalize the interface, the WISA communication protocol, described in Figure 14, does not allow the "Client" to directly communicate

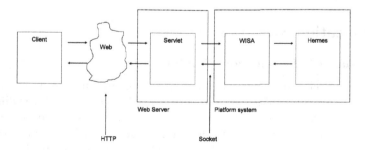

Fig. 14. WISA: Web Interface Service Agent

with WISA because the first one uses the HTTP protocol and the second one uses a protocol based on Socket and XML. To make possible the communication is needed a third component: a Web Server. The Web Server must support application server-side (Java Servlet, JSP, ASP, CGI, PHP etc.).

WfSA: Workflow Interface *Service* Agent

WfSA is a *Service* agent developed to provide an interface to end user which designs his workflow by combining the activities chosen from a give list. Note that the list of activities are those implemented at the system layer of the Hermes software architecture. The interface configured for a bioinformatics domain is give in Section 4.

Analysis and Verification Tools for Workflow

A further aspect we have dealt with is the possibility to used an automatic tool to analyse and verify the behaviour of the workflow that a user can design. Recalling that, in Hermes, a distributed applications is a workflow of activities, designed by a graphical notation usually made by JaWE editor. We have verified that there is a correspondence between the JaWE notation and UML Activity Diagram [59]. Then we have provided a process algebra view of workflows described in terms of UML activity diagrams by defining an interpretation of activity diagrams into CSP-like process algebra terms. Similar results could be obtained if we represents the workflow by a Petri Nets. To provide Hermes with a verification tool based on CSP-process algebra to apply to user workflow, we have exploit an intermediate relational language as a bridge between activity diagrams and process algebra terms as shown in the sequel and detailed discuss in [1]. The obtained results do not only show a conceptional relationship between two different notations. The advantage of our comparison is twofold. On one hand we provide different notations for "the same" system abstraction: a textual description (process algebras terms) and a graphical notation (workflows). This can be very useful during the system life cycle. On the other hand process algebras are associated with formal semantics and this has allowed the proliferation of automatic tools for system specification and verification so that our results open the possibility to exploit such tools for the verification of workflows.

4   Application Scenarios

4.1   Scenario 1: Hermes for Bioinformatics

The scenario we refer to is related to a biological domain. In the post-genomic era, the amount of available information is constantly increasing, and it is difficult to exploit available data from all sources [26]. As an example we take the context of Oncology over Internet project [44], that aims to develop a framework to support searching, retrieving and filtering information from Internet for oncology research and clinics.

Suppose the application domain involves the use of biological resources (micro-organisms, cell lines, mutations) that are essential for implementing a good, reproducible experiment. Established that high quality biological resources are available at some specialized centres (Biological Resources Centers:ATCC, DSMZ,) and their catalogues are available on-line and that many researchers assessing molecular biology databases often need find more information regarding resources to finally request materials.

Suppose to have three different domain each of one characterized by a set of activities as here described: *Cell Line domain*={A1: Find information about the cell line named x, A2: Find all cell lines derived from a specific tumour or pathology, A3: Find all Cell Lines producing a specific protein, A4: Given a specific Cell Line, find all related bibliographic references A5: Given a specific Cell Line, find all information about produced proteins}, *Mutation*={ B1: Find all mutations observed in a specific intron/exon in subjects with specific sex and life habits (i.e. smokers/ drinkers), B2: Find all mutations in subjects affected by a given pathology, B3: Find all subjects affected by a tumoural pathology and with a given protein mutation, B4: Find all mutations observed by using a given cell line, B5: Given a specific mutation, find all abstracts of the correlated bibliographic references} and *Bibliographic resources*= {C1: Select all abstracts of bibliographic references, whose text includes a given term}.

As an example consider a workflow defined to verify a *mutation* experiment by reproducing it. In particular a workflow that has a goal to retrieve abstracts from a literature databases for identifying the best *cell line* for reproducing a human TP53 mutation experiment linked to a particular tumour-habits-sex combination. Any single activity of the workflow uses bioinformatics services available on Internet in order to achieve the desired result. The user will select activities B1,B3 and B4, will provide parameters to each one: B1. Retrieve all mutations (IDs) observed in the 7th exon in men who are ex-smokers and drinkers by searching p53 mutations database SRS implementation at IST, Genova; B4. Retrieve all mutations (IDs) observed by using B9 cell line as original resource by searching p53 mutations database SRS implemerntation at IST, Genova; B5. Retrieve all abstracts of the correlated bibliographic references, of a specific mutation ID by searching Medline. And will combine them by the workflow operators as described in Figure 15.

Hermes in the context of O2I project is called Bioagent [62], it supports the design of user workflow by the interface shown in Figure 17, i.e a Workflow *Service* Agent (WfSA). The context-aware compiler will produce the set of mobile user agents whose behaviours are described in Figure 16 and implemented by a set of activities, called use cases in the Figure 17, and stored in the knowledge base. The user get the result in XHTML.

The Figure 18 shows a typical interaction between a bioscientist and *user* agents involves the following steps:

1. a bioScientist specifies the set of activities to be performed;
2. the compiler system generates a pool of *user* agents to execute the activities;
3. *user* agents migrate and clone in order to efficiently accomplish the activities;

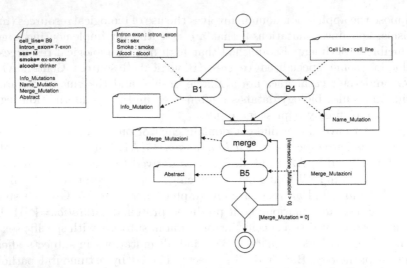

Fig. 15. Example of User Level Workflow in Bioinformatics Domain

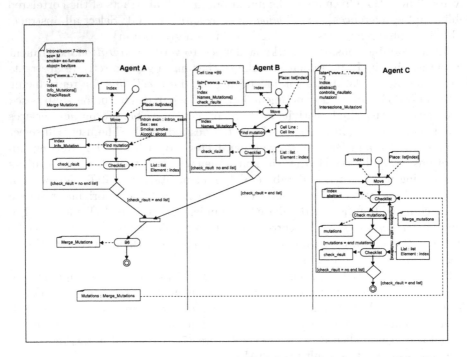

Fig. 16. An Example of Agent Level Workflow in Bioinformatics Domain

4. agents query resources by interacting with local *service* agents. *service* agent map the query to local schema by using AIXO which implements the abstraction layer so that agents interact only with XML documents. In the case in which an AIXO service agent has to manage different types of documents

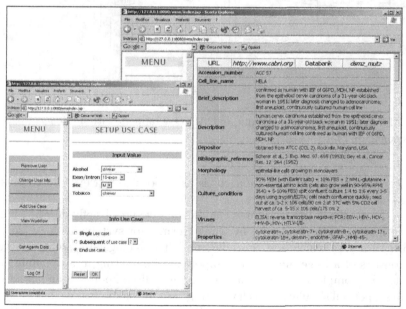

Fig. 17. User Interface for Workflow Management in Bioinformatics Domain

(ontologies mismatching) can interact with OMSE and use the ontology similarity algorithm previously mentioned.

5. *user* agents merge results and furnish data to the bioscientists.

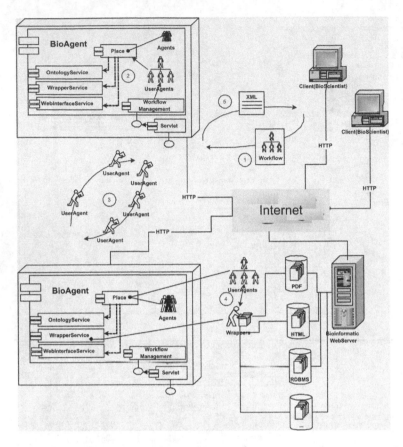

Fig. 18. Interactions Between Agents and AIXO wrappers within Bioagent[62], i.e. Hermes configured for Biologists

In this example AIXO *Service* agent is used both to retrieve and to present resources as XML documents.

To prove the flexibility of Hermes middleware we now briefly describe a case study we have recently made [17] by using Hermes for systems biology [36], i.e. bioinformatics area which aim to understand how biological systems function. A cell consists of a large number of components interacting in a dynamic environment. The complexity of interaction among cell components and functions makes design of cell simulations a challenging task for biologists. We have used an agent-oriented methodology to design a cell components as autonomous software entities (agents) situated in an environment and communicating via high-level languages and protocols (ontologies), may be a natural approach for such models. We constructed a model of cellular components involved in the metabolic pathway of *carbohydrate oxidation*. To give an idea of approach, the Figure 19 shows the set of agents identified be autonomous part of the system while Figure 20 shows the behavior of the only one component. Note that the UML Activity

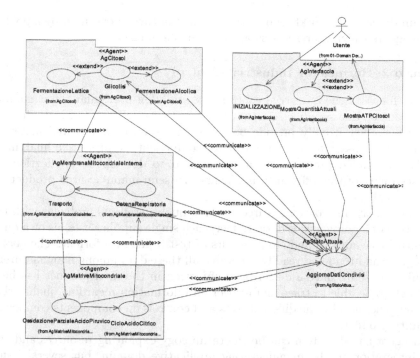

Fig. 19. The Cellular Agents Identification Diagram

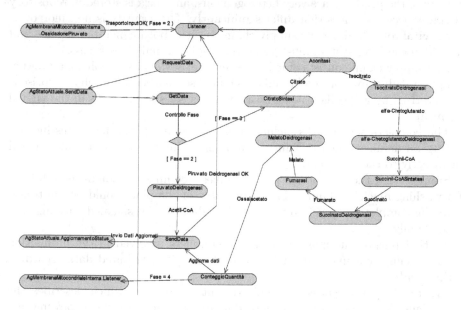

Fig. 20. An example of agent workflow, the Mitochondrial Matrix Activity Diagram

Diagram described a workflow of activity which in turn is executed by a pool of mobile agents which represents small components of the cell.

Scenario 2: Hermes for Industrial Control

Now, we focus on the industrial control case study, in particular the domain of quality control. In a supply chain, the actors are the suppliers and the production plans; the former usually provide both raw and semi-manufactured materials while the latter assemble the various input components to produce a final, more complex assembled product. We are interested to develop an application for the traceability of the different components and semi-manufactured products in terms of quality.

At first sight this context, geared towards quality, reflects problems with the integration of heterogeneous data. In fact, each single supplier uses his own quality control mechanisms and stores results of test in his own format. The goal is to integrate and rendered readily accessible all these data among manufacturers. It would be useful, once a defect or malfunction in the final product has been identified, to be able to trace and recover all information regarding quality that has been generated by the different tests and controls on components composing the faulty product.

An agent-based system can be the technology exploiting resources and services integration in the manufacturing applicative domain, but several issues must be taken into account. Embedded systems that perform the various quality tests of the products are very heterogeneous, and data is stored in repository providing access services that differ significantly. The security issues, moreover, play a vital role all along the supply chain. In fact, both generated reports and embedded checking system must be protecting from malicious access.

The supply chain consists of federated enterprises: many suppliers, a production plant, a distribution center and a technical service center. Each enterprise is characterized by a specific role and carries out a set specific tasks in the virtual organization.

The complete set of tasks includes quality testing, performance testing, reporting on damages incurred during shipment, and reports on repairs carried out directly to the customer.

Suppose that the Production plant receives a communication of the nth fault of a washing machines family. The responsible of the plant could decide to analyze the complete life-cycle testing *quality* data of the signaled washing machines family.

To that purpose he must identify any suppliers involved in the production of the washing machine and retrieve from them all distributed data regarding testing *quality* data.

Figure 21 shows a possible quality-oriented workflow which describes the human aim. The workflow consists of domain specific activities regarding any retrieval phases.

The quality-oriented workflow can be mapped into an agent-oriented workflows (Figure 22) and then compiled into a pool of agents (agent society) spe-

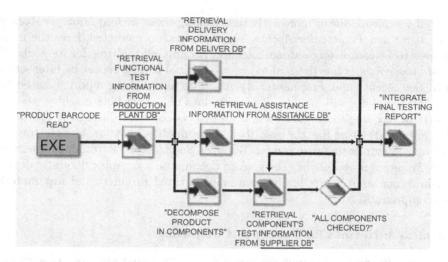

Fig. 21. Quality-oriented Workflow for the Functional Testing in the Production Control Plant

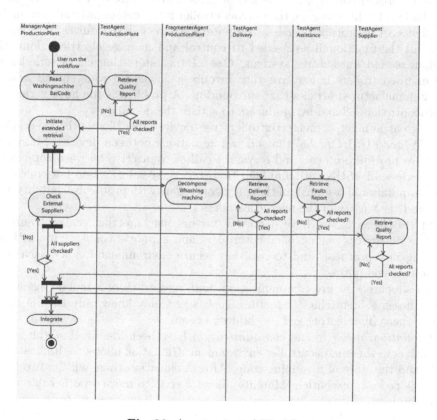

Fig. 22. Agent-oriented Workflow

cialized to execute one or more activities. Among those we find *Manager Agents*, *Test Agent* and *Fragmenter Agents*. Those agents, once created, have the main features to be completely autonomous and running all the time for its goal.

Manager Agents has the goal to create the final testing report by interacting with *Test Agents* and *Fragmenter Agents*. The final testing report, created by an XML template, will include all *quality* data of the washing machine, testing reports of any single components and all defects recorded during the product's life-cycle. *Test Agent* has the goal to retrieve *quality* data for a single component by communicating with remote *Wrapper Service Agents* (running on remote site). *Fragmenter Agents* has the goal to decompose a complex domestic device (washing machine) into a list of semi-manufactured products and raw materials (components).

Scenario 3: Hermes for Pervasive Computing

The pervasive and ubiquitous devices are computational and control systems, located in domestic environment (domotica) and in a manufactured articles. These devices are often either masked or invisible therefore they can assist us in the shadow. In this scenario, the microcontroller is the computational system for excellence. A microcontroller is a computer system that centralizes, in a single chip, all the functionalities needed to control and manage electrical domestic appliances and automotive systems. One of the interesting characteristics of the microcontrollers is low cost that favours a quick and wide spread among many manufactured articles that surround us. A problem is the huge variety of microcontrollers offered by producers to satisfy the demand.

A great number of microcontrollers use devices like bluetooth [7], echelon [20], WLan [61], IrDA [58] that allow interactions between devices. Many enterprises provide protocols and services to allow connection between computers and devices, like SUN with Jini [35]. However, these solutions do not conciliate the computational resources of the microcontrollers with protocols flexibility, the cost and the variety of the microcontrollers.

In this scenario, we have defined a virtual machine that makes transparent the differences among microcontrollers and supports connectivity without defining new protocols and to realize a secure environment for pervasive and ubiquitous computing.

To support a secure communication, and keep track of a mobile agent, we have chosen a hierarchical structure: each agent may know only the ID of its father agent (its creator) and its children agents

Clonation, *mobility* and *communication* have been identified as the kernel primitives in the microcontroller environment. Clonation allows to duplicate the code and the state of a running code. After a clonation there will be two identificable codes in execution. Mobility allows a code to move on other execution platform in proactive mode: a copy of the code and its current state is moved to the destination platform for being started from a specific point (weak mobility). Unlike the clonation, the code that performs the move primitive comes destroyed if the execution of the movement primitive succeeded. Communication directly results from the clonation primitive. After a clone operation will be created an exclusive communication channel between cloning and cloned codes. Communication (through exchange of messages) is possible only between cloning and cloned. Messages are sent-received in asynchronous-synchronous fashion.

The virtual machine relies on a calculus which describes the semantics of the minimal set of operation isolated to characterize a platform supporting mobile code [13]. The calculus for modelling mobile applications is summarized here below.

$\mathbf{A}$ is a set of basic actions, $\mathbf{A}_\tau = \mathbf{A} \cup \{\tau\}$, where τ is used to represent internal activity. $\mathcal{N}_{id}$ and $\mathcal{N}_p$ are an infinite sets of names of mobile processes and platforms,resp. $\mathcal{M}$ is an infinite set of messages.

Definition 1. (*mobile processes*)

The set $\mathbf{S}$ of sequential programs and the set $\mathbf{M}$ of mobile processes (sequential programs in execution) are generated by the following grammar:

$$S ::= \text{nil} \mid \alpha.S \mid \text{clone}(S).S \mid \text{send}(m).S \mid \text{receive}(m).S$$
$$\mid \text{go}(p, S)$$

where $\alpha \in \mathbf{A}_\tau$, $m \in \mathcal{M}$ and $p \in \mathcal{N}_p$. The set $\mathbf{M}$ of mobile processes (codes in execution) is generated by the following grammar:

$$M ::= \text{NIL} \mid \text{init}(S, \text{SP}) \mid id : \{\text{SP}, S, A\} \mid M_1, M_2$$

where $id \in \mathcal{N}_{id}$, $S \in \mathbf{S}$, $\text{SP} \in \mathcal{P}(\mathbf{M})$ and $A \in \mathcal{P}(\mathcal{N}_{id})$, nil represents a terminated sequential program.

A process whose sequential behaviour is $\alpha.S$, $\text{send}(m).S$, $\text{receive}(m).S$ and $\text{clone}(S_c).S$ can execute α, send and receive a message in $m \in \mathcal{M}$, clone itself and then behaves as S. $\text{go}(p, S)$ instructs a process to migrate to a destination platform named p and then behaves as S.

The component-based approach, used to developed Hermes and discussed in Section 3.2, allows to create new components in the Hermes core, by reusing the existing ones. We have developed a version of Hermes which adapt its components to the hardware characteristics of the microcontrollers to guarantee the function required by middleware. As an example, the communication component can be adapted for various technologies [7, 20, 35].

We have configured the Hermes platform for running with CDC of SUN [55] on PDAs. The porting of the Hermes on one particularly compact JVM for microcontrollers (like CLCD of SUN of type KVM [56, 53]), according to [53] needs libraries for sockets, serialization and reflection. Unlike many other platforms, Hermes does not use RMI [35]. The only pre-requirement on the microcontroller is the presence of a JVM. The *core* of the platform plus AIXO service is between 120KB to 160KB. Therefore the implementation of HermesV2 over a microcontroller would supports the following functionalities:

Communications peer to peer. At most two platforms are involved in every communication. Therefore it is possible to realize it without involving other partners

[12]. Every platform must only store information in order to realize communication between clonated and cloning codes currently in execution on it. This implies limited traffic of service between platforms and small tables. Substantially are draft communications to local environment.

Communications deadlock free. The communications of this model are deadlock free. According to the hierarchical structure of communication, it is impossible to establish the condition of circular wait for more that two actors. Moreover, the situation of circular wait happens only if both the actors, cloning and clonated, establish a synchronized communication. Such a situation can be easily prevented imposing that, before sending a synchronous message m, a code must control that in its own queue there is not a synchronous message sent by the receiver of the massage m. In this case the communication simply fails with exception.

Absence of timeout. Since the actor of a communication are always two codes, cloning and clonated, that may also reside on two different platforms, it is possible to determine the cause of failures in the communications. Consequently the code that sends or receives a communication can know the exact cause of the failure and always undertake appropriate operations. This is not always the case in systems where the communications is based on timeouts.

Absence of communication protocols. The communications between cloning and clonated and vice versa is not subject to protocols (ACL [24]) since the code of cloning is the same of clonated.

Security. All the requests of a code in a clonation tree (or forest of clonation trees) realize a closed system and a set of predetermined communications. The identifier produced after a clonation is only known by the cloning and it is the only handle in order to allow communication between cloning and clonated. Beyond to the communications towards the services, other shape of communication for the user code does not exist. The control of the communications allows to remove or to supply grant to the codes in execution. By removing all the communications a code becomes completely innocuous.

Correctness. Since a pool of instance relative to a code is ties at the communication network, it's possible to simulate dynamic behaviour in static background. It would be enough to eliminate from the code the primitive of mobility in order to verify the behaviour gearless of context. Moreover since the communications happen between copies of the same code is possible to verify the correctness analyzing the graph of the possible states that it can assume a code in execution [46].

5   Conclusion and Future Perspective

Mobile computing systems are computational systems that may be easily moved and whose computing capabilities may be used while they are moved. Several middleware have been proposed for mobile computing [47, 45] most of them focus on communication and coordination of distributed components. Indeed, we concentrate on a user not expert programmer, on workflow as suitable technology to hide distribution and on mobile agent as flexible implementation strategy of workflow in a distributed environment.

Our experience in developing applications in several application domains, convinces us on the necessity to create an integrated, flexible programming environment, whose user can easily configure for its domain. This leads to the developing of Hermes middleware. Hermes is structured as a component-based, agent-oriented, 3-layered software architecture. It can configured for specific application domains by adding domain-specific component libraries. The user can specify, modify and execute his workflow in a very lightweight.

Workflow is specified abstractly in a graphical notation and mapped to a set of autonomous computational units (*UserAgents*) interacting through a communication medium. The mapping is achieved by compiler that is aware not only of contents of a library of implemented user activities but also the software and hardware environment to executing them. In our case it includes also available services (*ServiceAgent*). A user specifying workflow need not to be concerned with where to search for information, in what form information is stored, the protocol for interacting with each services or the low level details that can be left to the context-aware compiler.

We are moving to the definition of a domain-specific mobile agent language to support as target language of the workflow compilation. We also plan to study the integration of Hermes with Klaim to allow the formal verification of agent-oriented workflow. Finally, we aim to experiment the use of the abstract machines for systems biology as one of the domain-specific language.

Acknowledgements

We wish to thank all the students have been involved, ver the last years, in the development of Hermes, among them we would like to mention Francesca, Davide, Lorenzo, Ezio, Leonardo, Marco, Chiara and Barbara. A special acknowledge is due to Rosario Culmone, Leonardo Mariani and Diego Bonura with who we have taken the most important development decisions.

We would like to thank Michal Young for valuable comments on a preliminary version of this paper.

References

[1] R. Amici, D. Cacciagrano, F. Corradini, and E. Merelli. A process algebra view of coordination models with a case study in computational biology. In *Proceedings of 1st International Workshop on Coordination and Petri Nets, PNC'04*, 2004.

[2] M. Angeletti, R. Culmone, and E. Merelli. An intelligent agent architecture for dna-microarray data integration. In *NETTAB Workshop on CORBA and XML: Towards a bioinformatics integrated network environment*, Genova, 2001.

[3] R. B ' Far. *Mobile Computing Principles*. Cambridge University Press, 2005.

[4] E. Bartocci, L. Mariani, and E. Merelli. An XML view of the "world". In *International Conference on Enterprise Information Systems, ICEIS*, pages 19–27, Angers, France, April 2003.

[5] E. Bartocci, S. Moeller, L. Todo, and E. Merelli. Integration of ensembl with bioagent. In *Abstract book of the Biocomp - Gruppo di Cooperazione in Bioinformatica*, 2004.

[6] T. Bellwood, L. Clément, D. Ehnebuske, A. Hately, M. Hondo, Y. L. Husband, K. Januszewski, S. Lee, B. McKee, J. Munter, and C. von Riegen. UDDI version 3.0. Published specification, Oasis, 2002.

[7] Bluetooth. http://www.bluetooth.org.

[8] D. Bonura, F. Corradini, E. Merelli, and G. Romiti. Farmas: a MAS for extended quality workflow. In *2nd IEEE International Workshop on Theory and Practice of Open Computational Systems*. IEEE Computer Society Press, 2004.

[9] D. Bonura, L. Mariani, and E. Merelli. Designing modular agent systems. In *Proceedings of NET.Object DAYS, Erfurt*, pages 245–263, September 2003.

[10] L. Cardelli. Abstract machines of systems biology. In *Transaction on Computation System Biology, special issue for NETTAB Workshop on Model and Metaphors from Biology to Bioinformatics Tools*, Lecture Notes in Computer Science. Springer-Verlag, 2005. to appear.

[11] L. Cardelli and A. D. Gordon. Mobile ambients. *Theoretical Computer Science*, 240(1):117–213, 2000.

[12] N. Carriero, D. Gelernter, and T. G. Mattson. Linda in heterogeneous computing environments. In *Proceedings of the Workshop on Heterogeneous Processing*, pages 43–46, Beverly Hills, CA, March 1992.

[13] F. Corradini, R. Culmone, and M. R. Di Berardini. Code mobility for pervasive computing. In *2nd IEEE International Workshop on Theory and Practice of Open Computational Systems*. IEEE Computer Society Press, 2004.

[14] F. Corradini, C. Ercoli, E. Merelli, and B. Re. An agent-based matchmaker. In *proceedings of WOA 2004 dagli Oggetti agli Agenti - Sistemi Complessi e Agenti Razionali*, 2004.

[15] F. Corradini, L. Mariani, and E. Merelli. A programming environment for global activity-based applications. In *proceedings of WOA 2003 dagli Oggetti agli Agenti - Sistemi Intelligenti e Computazione Pervasiva*, 2003.

[16] F. Corradini, L. Mariani, and E. Merelli. An agent-based approach to tool integration. *Journal of Software Tools Technology Transfer*, 6(3):231'244, November 2004.

[17] F. Corradini, E. Merelli, and M. Vita. A multi-agent system for modelling the oxidation of carbohydrate cellular process. In *First International Workshop On Modelling Complex Systems (MCS 2005)*, Lecture Notes in Computer Science. Springer Verlag, 2005. To appear.

[18] R. Culmone and E. Merelli. An semantic comparison of ontologies. Technical Report TR02, Dipartimento di matematica e Informatica, Universit di Camerino, 2003.

[19] R. De Nicola, G. L. Ferrari, and R. Pugliese. Klaim: A kernel language for agents interaction and mobility. *IEEE Transaction of Software Engineering*, 24(5):315–330, May 1998.

[20] Echelon. http://www.echelon.com.

[21] Enhydra. Jawe. http://jawe.enhydra.org/, 2003.

[22] C. Ercoli. Un modello di qualità per la scelta di servizi web in ambito biologico - il middleware. Master's thesis, Laurea in Informatica, Università di Camerino, a.a. 2003-2004. http://dmi.unicam.it/merelli/tesicl26/ercoli.pdf.

[23] T. Finin, R. Fritzson, D. McKay, and R. McEntire. KQML as an Agent Communication Language. In N. Adam, B. Bhargava, and Y. Yesha, editors, *Proceedings of the 3rd International Conference on Information and Knowledge Management (CIKM'94)*, pages 456–463, Gaithersburg, MD, USA, 1994. ACM Press.

[24] FIPA. The foundations for intelligent physical agent. http://www.fipa.org.

[25] FIPA-ACL. FIPA97 specification, part 2: Agent communication language. Specification, FIPA, October 1997.

[26] D. Frishman, K. Heumann, A. Lesk, and H.-W. Mewes. Comprehensive, comprehensible, distributed and intelligent databases: current status. *Bioinformatics*, 14(7):551–561, 1998.

[27] A. Fuggetta, G. Picco, and G. Vigna. Understanding code mobility. *IEEE Transaction of Software Engineering*, 24(5):352–361, May 1998.

[28] D. Gelenter. Generatve communicationin linda. *ACM Computing Survey*, 7(1):80–112, 1985.

[29] HermesV2. http://hermes.cs.unicam.it.

[30] D. Hollingsworth. The Workflow Reference Model, January 1995.

[31] IBM. TSpace web page. http://www.almaden.ibm.com/cs/TSpace.

[32] Javapace. The javaspace specification web page. http://www.sun.com/jini/spec/js-spec.html.

[33] J. Jayashankar M. Swaminathan, S. Smith, and N. Sadeh. Modeling supply chain dynamics: A multiagent approach. *Decision Sciences*, 29(3), 1998.

[34] N. R. Jennings. An agent-based approach for building complex software systems. *Communications of the ACM*, 44(4):35–41, April 2001.

[35] JINI. Jini network technology. http://wwws.sun.com/software/jini.

[36] H. Kitano. *Foundations of Systems Biology*. MIT Press, 2002.

[37] A. C. R. Martin. Can we integrate bioinformatics data on the internet? *Trends in Biotechnology*, (19):327–328, 2001. (Meeting Report).

[38] C. Mascolo, L. Capra, and W. Emmerich. Middleware for mobile computing (a survey). In E. Gregori, G. Anastasi, and S. Basagni, editors, *Neworking 2002 Tutorial Papers*, volume 2497 of *Lecture Notes in Computer Science*, pages 20–58. Springer-Verlag, 2002.

[39] E. Merelli, R. Culmone, and L. Mariani. Bioagent: a mobile agent system for bioscientists. In *NETTAB Workshop on Agents nd Bioinformtics*, Bologna, July 2002.

[40] E. Merelli, P. Romano, and L. Scortichini. A workflow service for biomedical application. In *Abstract book of the Biocomp - Gruppo di Cooperazione in Bioinformatica*, 2003.

[41] M. Merz, B. Lieberman, and W. Lamersdorf. Using mobile agent to support interorganizational workflow management. *Applied Artificial Intelligence*, 11(6):551–572, 1997.

[42] J. P. Milner, R. and D. Walker. A calculus of mobile processes, part 1-2. *Information and Computation*, 100(1):1–77, 1992.

[43] A. L. Murphy, G. P. Picco, and G.-C. Roman. Lime: A middleware for physical and logical mobility. In F. Golshani, P. Dasgupta, and W. Zhao, editors, *Proceedings of the 21st International Conference on Distributed Computing Systems*. ACM Publisher, 2001.

[44] O2I. Oncology over internet, strategic project founded by italian nationa research minestry. http://www.o2i.org.

[45] A. Omicini and F. Zambonelli. Coordination for Internet application development. *Autonomous Agents and Multi-Agent Systems*, 2(3):251–269, Sept. 1999. Special Issue: Coordination Mechanisms for Web Agents.

[46] M. Pezzé, R. N. Taylor, and M. Young. Graph models for reachability analysis of concurrent programs. *ACM Transaction on Software Engineeringn and Methodology (TOSEN)*, 4(2):171–213, 1995.

[47] G. P. Picco, A. L. Murphy, and G.-C. Roman. Lime: Linda meets mobility. In *Proceedings of the 21st International Conferece on Software Engineering (ICSE'99)*, pages 368–367, May 1999.

[48] G. P. Picco, A. L. Murphy, and G.-C. Roman. Developing mobile computing applications with lime. In *International Conference on Software Engineering archive Proceedings of the 22nd international conference on Software engineering*, pages 766–769, 2000.

[49] B. Re. Un modello di qualità per la scelta di servizi web in ambito biologico - il modello di coordinazione. Master's thesis, Laurea in Informatica, Università di Camerino, a.a. 2003-2004. http://dmi.unicam.it/merelli/tesicl26/re.pdf.

[50] R. D. Robert D. Stevens, A. J. Robinson, and C. A. Goble. mygrid: personalised bioinformatics on the information grid bioinformatics. *Bioinformatics*, (19):302 – 304, July.

[51] G.-C. Roman, G. P. Picco, and A. L.Murphy. Software engineering for mobility: A roadmap. In *The Future of Software Engineering*, pages 241–258. 2000.

[52] S. S. Mueller-Wilken, F. Wienberg, and W. Lamersdorf. On integrating mobile devices into a workflow management scenario. In I. C. Society, editor, *Proc. 11th International Workshop on Database and Expert Systems Applications (DEXA)*, pages 186–192, Hamburg, 2000.

[53] C. H. Stephan Gatzka, Th. Geithner. The kertasarie vm. In *NET.Object DAYS 2003*, pages 285–299, Erfurt, September 22-25 2003.

[54] R. Steven, C. Goble, P. Kaker, and A. Brass. A classification of tasks in bioinformatics. *Bioinformatics*, 17(2), 2001.

[55] Sun Microsystems. The CVM. http://java.sun.com/CDC.

[56] Sun Microsystems. The KVM. http://java.sun.com/clcd.

[57] A. Tanenbaum and M. van Steen. *Distributed Systems: Principles and Paradigms.* Printice Hall, 2002.

[58] TIDA. The infrared data association. http://www.irda.org.

[59] UML Revision Taskforce. *OMG UML Specification v. 1.4*. Object Magemement Group, 2001.

[60] L. Vito. Hermesv2 e web services. Master's thesis, Laurea in Informatica, Università di Camerino, Italy, a.a. 2003-2004. http://dmi.unicam.it/merelli/tesicl26/vito.pdf.

[61] WLAN. The working group for wlan standards. http://grouper.ieee.org/groups/802/11/.

[62] The BioAgent project. http://www.bioagent.net/.

Author Index

Lecture Notes in Computer Science

For information about Vols. 1–3358

please contact your bookseller or Springer

Vol. 3409: N. Guelfi, G. Reggio, A. Romanovsky (Eds.), Scientific Engineering of Distributed Java Applications. X, 127 pages. 2005.

Vol. 3408: D.E. Losada, J.M. Fernández-Luna (Eds.), Advances in Information Retrieval. XVII, 572 pages. 2005.

Vol. 3407: Z. Liu, K. Araki (Eds.), Theoretical Aspects of Computing - ICTAC 2004. XIV, 562 pages. 2005.

Vol. 3406: A. Gelbukh (Ed.), Computational Linguistics and Intelligent Text Processing. XVII, 829 pages. 2005.

Vol. 3404: V. Diekert, B. Durand (Eds.), STACS 2005. XVI, 706 pages. 2005.

Vol. 3403: B. Ganter, R. Godin (Eds.), Formal Concept Analysis. XI, 419 pages. 2005. (Subseries LNAI).

Vol. 3401: Z. Li, L.G. Vulkov, J. Waśniewski (Eds.), Numerical Analysis and Its Applications. XIII, 630 pages. 2005.

Vol. 3399: Y. Zhang, K. Tanaka, J.X. Yu, S. Wang, M. Li (Eds.), Web Technologies Research and Development - APWeb 2005. XXII, 1082 pages. 2005.

Vol. 3398: D.-K. Baik (Ed.), Systems Modeling and Simulation: Theory and Applications. XIV, 733 pages. 2005. (Subseries LNAI).

Vol. 3397: T.G. Kim (Ed.), Artificial Intelligence and Simulation. XV, 711 pages. 2005. (Subseries LNAI).

Vol. 3396: R.M. van Eijk, M.-P. Huget, F. Dignum (Eds.), Agent Communication. X, 261 pages. 2005. (Subseries LNAI).

Vol. 3395: J. Grabowski, B. Nielsen (Eds.), Formal Approaches to Software Testing. X, 225 pages. 2005.

Vol. 3394: D. Kudenko, D. Kazakov, E. Alonso (Eds.), Adaptive Agents and Multi-Agent Systems III. VIII, 313 pages. 2005. (Subseries LNAI).

Vol. 3393: H.-J. Kreowski, U. Montanari, F. Orejas, G. Rozenberg, G. Taentzer (Eds.), Formal Methods in Software and Systems Modeling. XXVII, 413 pages. 2005.

Vol. 3392: D. Seipel, M. Hanus, U. Geske, O. Bartenstein (Eds.), Applications of Declarative Programming and Knowledge Management. X, 309 pages. 2005. (Subseries LNAI).

Vol. 3391: C. Kim (Ed.), Information Networking. XVII, 936 pages. 2005.

Vol. 3390: R. Choren, A. Garcia, C. Lucena, A. Romanovsky (Eds.), Software Engineering for Multi-Agent Systems III. XII, 291 pages. 2005.

Vol. 3389: P. Van Roy (Ed.), Multiparadigm Programming in Mozart/OZ. XV, 329 pages. 2005.

Vol. 3388: J. Lagergren (Ed.), Comparative Genomics. VII, 133 pages. 2005. (Subseries LNBI).

Vol. 3387: J. Cardoso, A. Sheth (Eds.), Semantic Web Services and Web Process Composition. VIII, 147 pages. 2005.

Vol. 3386: S. Vaudenay (Ed.), Public Key Cryptography - PKC 2005. IX, 436 pages. 2005.

Vol. 3385: R. Cousot (Ed.), Verification, Model Checking, and Abstract Interpretation. XII, 483 pages. 2005.

Vol. 3383: J. Pach (Ed.), Graph Drawing. XII, 536 pages. 2005.

Vol. 3382: J. Odell, P. Giorgini, J.P. Müller (Eds.), Agent-Oriented Software Engineering V. X, 239 pages. 2005.

Vol. 3381: P. Vojtáš, M. Bieliková, B. Charron-Bost, O. Sýkora (Eds.), SOFSEM 2005: Theory and Practice of Computer Science. XV, 448 pages. 2005.

Vol. 3380: C. Priami, Transactions on Computational Systems Biology I. IX, 111 pages. 2005. (Subseries LNBI).

Vol. 3379: M. Hemmje, C. Niederee, T. Risse (Eds.), From Integrated Publication and Information Systems to Information and Knowledge Environments. XXIV, 321 pages. 2005.

Vol. 3378: J. Kilian (Ed.), Theory of Cryptography. XII, 621 pages. 2005.

Vol. 3377: B. Goethals, A. Siebes (Eds.), Knowledge Discovery in Inductive Databases. VII, 190 pages. 2005.

Vol. 3376: A. Menezes (Ed.), Topics in Cryptology – CT-RSA 2005. X, 385 pages. 2005.

Vol. 3375: M.A. Marsan, G. Bianchi, M. Listanti, M. Meo (Eds.), Quality of Service in Multiservice IP Networks. XIII, 656 pages. 2005.

Vol. 3374: D. Weyns, H.V.D. Parunak, F. Michel (Eds.), Environments for Multi-Agent Systems. X, 279 pages. 2005. (Subseries LNAI).

Vol. 3372: C. Bussler, V. Tannen, I. Fundulaki (Eds.), Semantic Web and Databases. X, 227 pages. 2005.

Vol. 3371: M.W. Barley, N. Kasabov (Eds.), Intelligent Agents and Multi-Agent Systems. X, 329 pages. 2005. (Subseries LNAI).

Vol. 3370: A. Konagaya, K. Satou (Eds.), Grid Computing in Life Science. X, 188 pages. 2005. (Subseries LNBI).

Vol. 3369: V.R. Benjamins, P. Casanovas, J. Breuker, A. Gangemi (Eds.), Law and the Semantic Web. XII, 249 pages. 2005. (Subseries LNAI).

Vol. 3368: L. Paletta, J.K. Tsotsos, E. Rome, G.W. Humphreys (Eds.), Attention and Performance in Computational Vision. VIII, 231 pages. 2005.

Vol. 3367: W.S. Ng, B.C. Ooi, A. Ouksel, C. Sartori (Eds.), Databases, Information Systems, and Peer-to-Peer Computing. X, 231 pages. 2005.

Vol. 3366: I. Rahwan, P. Moraitis, C. Reed (Eds.), Argumentation in Multi-Agent Systems. XII, 263 pages. 2005. (Subseries LNAI).

Vol. 3365: G. Mauri, G. Păun, M.J. Pérez-Jiménez, G. Rozenberg, A. Salomaa (Eds.), Membrane Computing. IX, 415 pages. 2005.

Vol. 3363: T. Eiter, L. Libkin (Eds.), Database Theory - ICDT 2005. XI, 413 pages. 2004.

Vol. 3362: G. Barthe, L. Burdy, M. Huisman, J.-L. Lanet, T. Muntean (Eds.), Construction and Analysis of Safe, Secure, and Interoperable Smart Devices. IX, 257 pages. 2005.

Vol. 3361: S. Bengio, H. Bourlard (Eds.), Machine Learning for Multimodal Interaction. XII, 362 pages. 2005.

Vol. 3360: S. Spaccapietra, E. Bertino, S. Jajodia, R. King, D. McLeod, M.E. Orlowska, L. Strous (Eds.), Journal on Data Semantics II. XI, 223 pages. 2005.

Vol. 3359: G. Grieser, Y. Tanaka (Eds.), Intuitive Human Interfaces for Organizing and Accessing Intellectual Assets. XIV, 257 pages. 2005. (Subseries LNAI).